I0146154

Marx's Critique of Politics
1842-1847

The prevailing view of Marx's early writings suggests that they comprise a set of disconnected works which share only the same author, that Marx was philosophically an idealist or Hegelian and politically a 'liberal' or 'democrat' throughout much of this period, and that he possessed no particular method of inquiry. Professor Teeple challenges these ideas in his exposition of the development of Marx's critique of politics from the earliest published writings in 1842 to the end of this period in 1847.

Eschewing the search for Marx's intellectual sources, and a narrow focus on any one of these early works, the author traces Marx's intellectual development through a careful analysis of the texts. He demonstrates an unmistakeable continuity throughout the period, arguing that Marx consciously worked out his critique of politics from a well-defined starting point in his doctoral dissertation and the *Rheinische Zeitung* articles to a logical conclusion in *The German Ideology*. Each step in this development, it is argued, not only formed an integral link but also remained in Marx's eyes valid in itself.

The basis of this continuity is seen to lie in the method Marx employed. The author contends that Marx did possess and apply a method in a conscious and consistent manner and that the method evolved concomitantly with his ever-deepening grasp of the nature of politics and its premises. Indeed, to discover the nature of this method and how it develops is to discover the implicit unity or rationality underlying Marx's early writings and to grasp fully their substance.

In a word, Dr Teeple argues that from a critique of politics at the level of politics to a critique of the premises of politics, Marx pursued in these early works what he considered to be a scientific understanding of the nature of human development. The thrust of the author's argument goes against the grain of accepted opinion, and for this reason alone the book will shed new light on Marx's widely discussed early writings and should generate considerable controversy.

GARY TEEPLE is a member of the Department of Sociology and Anthropology at Simon Fraser University.

GARY TEEPLE

Marx's Critique of Politics
1842-1847

UNIVERSITY OF TORONTO PRESS

Toronto Buffalo London

© University of Toronto Press 1984
Toronto Buffalo London
Printed in Canada
Reprinted in 2018
ISBN 0-8020-5631-8
ISBN 978-1-4875-8248-7 (paper)

Canadian Cataloguing in Publication Data

Teeple, Gary, 1945-
Marx's critique of politics: 1842-1847
Bibliography: p.
Includes index.
ISBN 0-8020-5631-8
1. Marx, Karl, 1818-1883 – Political science. I. Title.
JC233.M299T43 1983   320.5'315   C83-099102-6

TO THE MEMORY OF MY FATHER

Contents

Preface

The central purpose of this book is to expound Marx's critique of politics as that critique evolved between 1842 and 1847. Through a close and literal reading of the texts of this period, I hope to explain the development of the method and content of Marx's analysis of political relations. The contention is that these writings manifest a systematic unity which can be grasped only by examining the relation between the method and the substance of Marx's analysis.

In pursuing this argument, I have relied for source material on two principal collections of the works of Marx and Engels: namely, the recent English-language *Marx-Engels Collected Works* (MECW) (London 1975-) and the German *Marx-Engels Werke* (MEW) (Berlin 1956-68). The texts I required were not available at the time in the recent *Karl Marx – Friedrich Engels Gesamtausgabe* (1975-) edition. There are several older English translations of many of the early writings and many of these have been consulted; but the MECW is the most comprehensive and, in general, the most literal and, therefore, the most useful. To have relied solely on translations, however, would have created insurmountable problems. A mistranslation of the most minor sort – a preposition or a conjunction – can seriously distort a passage or render it obscure or even unintelligible. Stylistic liberties undertaken by the translator can also distort the original meaning, just as the translator's commitment to a doctrinal view can skew the author's intention. To overcome these and related difficulties we have referred frequently to the German, although MEW is not as comprehensive as MECW, and so on occasions this was not possible. I have checked the quotations used below, providing the German where it may aid comprehension, and I have altered the translation in many cases in order to clarify it and in other cases in order to make it more comprehensible, always providing the German as one means of justifying the alteration to the reader.

The secondary literature on the early works is, needless to say, extensive. I have attempted to consult as much of it as possible, but, as can be seen in the text, I have employed very few of the existing interpretations. Generally speaking, the thrust of the argument goes against the grain of accepted views.

Just how the argument differs from other treatments of the early works should be briefly indicated. As a whole, the argument rests on a discussion of Marx's method; that is, the fundamental approach to these early works is to discover their underlying unity by grasping the implicit methodological dynamic. That dynamic lies in what Marx perceived as the scientific method, applied consciously and with a specific purpose in mind. The whole of Marx's writings from 1842 to 1847 can be seen in this light, as the scientific pursuit or study of the essence of man.

The method I have employed is the systematic exposition in chronological order of the early writings. Followed conscientiously, this procedure has been fruitful, producing an interpretation of Marx which was not anticipated, which is more literal than interpretative, and which differs markedly from most similar attempts to review these works. Given this approach, the reader will not find the biographical and historical data so commonly employed as explanation for the development of Marx's thought. For the same reason, I eschew any *systematic* examination of the sources of Marx's ideas.

Because the search for the sources is such a prevalent method in the treatment of these texts, I submit other, substantive, reasons for refraining from such a search. First and most important, the origin of a thought has positively no bearing on the question of its value or truth. The value and truth of an idea or concept lies in its relation to the real world and in its place in a conceptual schema. Second, the partial or formal similarity of one idea to another does not account for its meaning or content. And third, the notion that a theory or method or life's work can be *explained* by discovering all the sources is patently false, because it assumes that the sum of the parts equals the whole, and because it assumes that the sources can be identified and their relation demonstrated.

If the focus is on Marx's work, to the exclusion of Engels' contribution, it is because I am treating Engels in the same way as these other sources and for the same reasons. His work on the state and on political relations, moreover, was not systematically worked out or pursued as was that of Marx. He was, of course, an important influence on Marx; but we concur with Engels' own appraisal that, whatever his contribution, Marx would have achieved on his own what was achieved more or less jointly.

If my intention is fulfilled, these following chapters will advance comprehension of the development of Marx's critique of the political and of critique itself as a method.

No endeavour such as this is possible without the assistance of many different people, whose various capacities find a modest unity in its completion. Much assistance was indirect and circumstantial, in particular that of several librarians at universities in the United Kingdom and Canada; but much was direct and my appreciation, therefore, can be specifically acknowledged. Sections of several drafts of the manuscript were typed by Elsie Trott, Lynn Kampula, Bernice Dewick, and the final draft in total by Bernice Ferrier; far from merely typing the manuscript, they were conscientious and critical readers and for their efforts I am warmly grateful. The Dean of Arts Office at Simon Fraser University was very helpful in the preparation of the final draft; the generosity shown by this office was unexpected, and much appreciated. At the University of Sussex, the members of the graduate seminar in the Department of Comparative Politics provided me with constructive and critical comments on chapters 1 and 2, and suggestions made by Bruce Graham were particularly useful. The person I worked most closely with was Theo Mars, my faculty adviser; it was my good fortune to have had the benefit of his insightful comments, and I am especially appreciative of the fact that he tolerated my speculative beginning and then encouraged me with constructive criticism through to this end.

At the University of Toronto Press, Rik Davidson provided, as always, encouragement, constructive criticism, and subtle and wise counsel, and for these I owe him many thanks.

This book has been published with the help of grants from the Social Science Federation of Canada, using funds provided by the Social Sciences and Humanities Research Council of Canada, and from the Publications Fund of the University of Toronto Press.

I am also very grateful to Madalen, who was not only responsible for my return to formal studies but also from the start of this project an astute critic of the reading of Marx which follows.

G.T.

MARX'S CRITIQUE OF POLITICS

1842-1847

Introduction
Marx's starting point:
Epicurus and the ontology of mind

In all the expositions, analyses, and debates which take as their subject matter the early writings of Karl Marx, from his doctoral dissertation to *The German Ideology* or *The Communist Manifesto*, there is one question which, while rarely confronted, has an unmistakable if often implicit presence. It concerns the nature of the transition that took place in Marx's work during the mid 1840s. And it arises, if for no other reason, because it implies the more fundamental question of how Marx arrived at the conclusions he did at the end of this period.

Opinion about the nature of his intellectual development from 1842 to 1847 seems to divide into two broad camps: one asserts an over-all continuity in his work, and the other posits discontinuity as the chief characteristic. (There are several expositions of these positions[1] so they need not be discussed here.) Underlying the former is the notion that the mature outcome of his development is a consequence which rests on premises, which in turn must be understood to make the outcome fully comprehensible. In other words, any separation of a 'young' from a 'mature,' a 'philosophic' from a 'scientific,' an 'idealist' from a 'materialist' Marx is to be seen as 'undialectical.' Implicit in the latter is the notion that there is such a separation and that it marks a qualitative break, the premises of either stage being fundamentally different and incompatible.

Regardless of the position, however, there is common contention that in these early writings Marx's thought was infused with 'philosophical' presuppositions which were Hegelian or, more broadly, idealist. It is, furthermore, commonly held that he abandoned or transformed these early assumptions in favour of those of 'science' or a form of materialism by the time he writes *The German Ideology*.

There is, to be sure, a body of evidence offered to support the claim that Marx's starting point was 'philosophical.' Notably, the frequent use of the concepts 'essence' and 'appearance'[2] and the numerous references to the 'genuine state,' the 'rational community,' or 'true democracy'[3] are taken as so many signposts pointing to his Hegelianism or idealism. The method of critique found in these writings, furthermore, is often declared 'philosophical' and not 'scientific.'[4]

Although this evidence has been frequently cited – and perhaps gained some authority through repetition – there are certain difficulties which accompany the claims. In the first place, very few commentators define what they mean by the terms 'philosophical,' 'Hegelian,' and 'idealist.' They have become so commonplace as descriptions of the early works that they are usually merely asserted, without sufficient regard for their definition or demonstration, their validity resting on the authority of accepted wisdom. Another difficulty arises in accounting for the transition from the 'young' to the 'mature' Marx. Few of the commentators ask how it is that 'idealism' changes to 'materialism,' that 'philosophy' turns into 'science,' or that fidelity to Hegel becomes devotion to history and political economy. For the argument of discontinuity, the notion of a 'break' or 'discovery' appears to suffice as explanation, but it does nothing more than beg the question; discoveries too must be explained. For the argument of continuity, there is no greater success in overcoming this difficulty. Some find the continuity in latent expressions of 'mature' concepts in the early works,[5] but how and why this potential becomes realized is not explained. Others stress external influences,[6] and here change is accounted for by positing the influence of particular authors or books, his observation of the poverty of the peasantry, or his meeting the Parisian working class, and so on. But each of these, while given as a cause of the transition, remains largely speculative; and even when Marx admits to such influences as formative ones, we cannot be sure about the nature of their effect, especially if we do not first know the content of his ideas prior to their effect.

There is a further difficulty for the latter argument, which despite the assertion of continuity only traces certain concepts *or* posits external influences as causes of Marx's changing interests. In both cases, the early writings are treated almost universally as discrete units, which although sharing the same author and certain concepts possess no internal or underlying unity. But is it not a contradiction to argue a continuity between the parts of a subject matter and yet to treat those parts as discrete elements; to see them connected only tenuously by a few shared concepts, none of which contain an explanation of their own development, or by the chance effects of external circumstances? *If there is a continuity* in the true sense of the word, there must be an internal connection between the individual works; there must be something in the works to explain their evolution as a whole.

There are, it appears, then, two related problems in the consideration of Marx's early writings. First, while it is almost universally agreed that Marx was an idealist, philosopher, or Hegelian in this period, there is very little attempt to define or demonstrate the exact nature of these characteristics. The nature of his starting point, in other words, is *not* accounted for in these widely accepted adjectives. And second, while almost all agree that Marx moved from this early position to a later 'mature' or 'scientific' one, there is little discussion of the nature of this transition. The argument for discontinuity begs the question, and the argument for continuity treats the parts of the implied whole as discrete units. The road Marx took from 1842 to 1847 is not accounted for. If there were a *development*, an unfolding of what was at first only germinal, what then was the nature of this evolution? And if there were no development, how can his intellectual movement from his purported 'idealism' to 'dialectical materialism' be explained?

This latter question, which includes the first, would require a much broader, more extensive analysis for a complete answer than is possible here. It must suffice for the present to examine this question by analysing one aspect of these early writings, which by way of example, it is hoped, will shed light on the problem as a whole.

The aspect that I have selected is Marx's critique of politics. The choice is justified in part by the current interest in the nature of the state and by the often repeated assertion that Marx had no 'theory' of the state. But more to the point, its analysis will help to answer the larger question posed above because it appears that Marx's main concern in the *Rheinische Zeitung* and in the 1843 *Critique of Hegel's Philosophy of Right* was the political. There seems no better subject to choose to examine as an example of the nature of his development than the subject matter of his first problematic.

The exposition of the development of Marx's critique of politics can begin only where his first discussion of politics begins, with his published articles of 1842. Yet there is material written by Marx prior to this date, namely, the 1837 'Letter to his Father' and his doctoral dissertation. By way of introduction, it seems fitting to consider them briefly in the possibility that they may throw light on the difficulties outlined above and thereby facilitate our comprehension of the development of his critique of politics.

6 Marx's Critique of Politics

The earliest piece of Marx's writing which can be considered to be an example or reflection of serious studies is his 1837 letter to his father. With few exceptions, commentators have interpreted it as a statement of Marx's 'conversion to Hegelianism'[7] or as evidence of his early philosophical idealism. But such a view is not without its problems.

The first lies in the failure, for the most part, of those commentators to define the meaning of idealism or Hegelianism. For our purposes here it will suffice to define idealism, leaving a description of Hegel's philosophy for later.

The fundamental characteristic of idealism is perhaps easiest to grasp in reference to one of the central problems of philosophy, namely, the relation of thought to being. Depending on how this relationship is depicted and how each side is perceived, philosophy divides into two broad tendencies – idealism and materialism. The chief difference lies in the primacy given to one side of the relation: idealism makes thought, consciousness, mind, or spirit pre-eminent, indeed, often subsuming being or reality as the idea of such, whereas materialism views thought in its many forms (the content of art, religion, philosophy, etc.) as products or functions of material existence.

Admittedly, within this definition there are many variations of idealism; but here it is sufficient to present the general concept since our object is only to discover the general camp in which Marx is to be found prior to 1842. To categorize him as idealist, then, is to suggest that the salient features of this philosophical viewpoint are to be found in his work.

To return to the letter of 1837, such a claim is difficult to maintain through an appeal to the text of the letter alone. What is of interest to us is Marx's own comments on his attempt to write a philosophy of law, which had grown to a manuscript of 'almost 300 pages' before he abandoned it. His self-criticism reveals an awareness and dissatisfaction with the approach of idealism, especially that of Fichte. He writes: 'Here, above all, the same opposition between what is and what ought to be [Gegensatz des Wirklichen und Sollenden], which is characteristic of idealism, stood out as a serious defect and was the source of the hopelessly incorrect division of the subject-matter.'[8] The 'incorrect division of the subject-matter' referred to the separation of the treatise into two parts, the first dealing with 'the metaphysics of law; i.e., basic principles, reflections, definitions of concepts,' and the second being an examination of the 'conceptual development' of 'positive Roman law.' The problem was *not* that the first, the 'ought,' was wrong in itself, any more than the abstract notion of a triangle could be wrong; the difficulty lay in the *separation* of these metaphysics from the development of real positive law, i.e., of existing law.

If the barrier to comprehending law lay in this divorced discussion of principles and definitions from all 'actual law,' or in the imposition of these metaphysics on the real subject matter, the path to 'truth,' as Marx would have it, lay in finding the former in the latter. He continues: 'in the concrete expression of a living world of ideas, as exemplified by law, the state, nature, and philosophy as a whole, the object itself must be studied in its development; arbitrary divisions must not be introduced, the rational character of the object itself must develop as something imbued with contradictions itself and find its unity in itself.'[9]

Here it can be seen that through his endeavour to write a treatise on law, Marx came to perceive what he called an 'incorrectness' in the approach of pre-Hegelian idealism and saw the resolution to the problem in the discovery of the principles, the 'ought,' of a thing *in* the real existing nature of the thing itself. As he puts it: 'From the idealism which, by the way, I had compared and nourished with the idealism of Kant and Fichte, I arrived at the point of seeking the idea in reality itself [im Wirklichen selbst die Idee zu suchen]. If previously the gods had dwelt above the earth, now they became its centre.'[10] The reference to 'gods' should be read as a metaphor or the generic name, as it were, for ideas. If for Marx they were once separated from the real world, they were now to be sought and found within it. It would be difficult to imagine a clearer expression of rejection of the chief characteristic of idealism.

Immediately following this expressed desire to 'seek the idea in reality itself,' Marx makes a reference to returning to a study of Hegel. The reason, we may speculate, lay in Hegel's claim to have reconciled thought and being, to have resolved the opposition between the two which Marx saw as the chief difficulty in his efforts to write a philosophy of law. The reconciliation consisted in thought being related to reality as its own essential creation; thought, or abstract self-consciousness, was taken as the principle which accounted for and ultimately unified *both* subject and object.[11] If Hegel succeeded in this, however, it was a resolution still within idealism, as Feuerbach was to argue later: 'a being that is not distinguished from thought and that is only a predicate or a determination of reason is only an ideated and abstract being, but in truth it is not being. The identity of thought and being expresses, therefore, only the identity of thought with itself; that means that absolute thought never extricates itself from itself to become being.'[12] If we accept Feuerbach's argument, both the subject and object in Hegel's work were aspects of thought and their unity therefore but the unity of thought with itself. Nevertheless, the reconciliation does bring the development of idealism to its culmination. And it would make sense to study this if one's concern were to effect a similar reconciliation with *being* as subject and thought as predicate.

In turning to Hegel now, Marx specifies that he has 'intentions' of going beyond this culmination of philosophy, of going beyond it in a way precisely to establish being as subject: 'I had read fragments of Hegel's philosophy, the grotesque craggy melody of which did not appeal to me. Once more I wanted to dive into the sea, but with the definite intention of establishing that the nature of mind is just as necessary, concrete and firmly based as the nature of the body [die geistige Natur ebenso notwendig, konkret und festgegründet zu finden wie die körperliche].'[13] Having rejected the idealism of Kant and Fichte, Marx is stating here his determination to discover the *ontological* basis of the mind, the products of which were ideas or concepts, through a study of Hegel.

His intention at this time, however, was not to be fulfilled; the remainder of the letter included a description of his failure, of how his efforts led to conclusions which were none other than the beginning of the Hegelian system. His studies had, to paraphrase, delivered him into the arms of the enemy – meaning, one assumes, Hegel and his idealism. It was 'a view,' he said, 'that I hated.' Convinced however that 'there could be no headway without philosophy,'[14] he made a study of Hegel from the beginning to end, together with most of his disciples. The consequence was an ambiguous attraction to this modern world philosophy.

It would be overstating the case, then, to say that he had been converted to Hegelianism; the evidence suggests a begrudging, critical acceptance of Hegel's philosophy, not the uncritical admiration of a disciple or the actual adoption of Hegelian idealism. It is true that hereafter Marx employed much of Hegel's terminology, and even as late as 1873 he admits that in *Capital* he had coquetted with the modes of expression peculiar to him;[15] but who would argue that Marx was Hegelian in 1867 or 1873? The point is that Hegel's concepts are not idealist in themselves; as Koyré argued long ago, Hegel did not attempt to use artificial, arbitrary, or abstract concepts, but a living, concrete, popular etymology.[16] It is the nature of their posited inter-relations and relation to the real world which comprises his idealism. If Marx had actually adopted Hegel's idealism he would *not* be able to say that he intended to 'seek the idea in reality itself' and that he wanted to 'establish that the nature of the mind is just as necessary, concrete and firmly based as the nature of the body.'

If these were his intentions, it would follow that his writings after the frustrated efforts he related to his father would reveal some attempt to realize them. I would contend that his doctoral studies were undertaken to fathom these very problems. But this remains to be demonstrated.

The discussion of the dissertation, entitled 'Difference between the Democritean and Epicurean Philosophy of Nature,' which follows is necessarily an abbreviated one because it is not a central concern; rather it is important to us only in order to determine the starting point of our analysis. And if we focus on the *results* of Marx's analysis of Epicurus rather than on all the steps of the argument or on the contrast with Democritus, it is again because our aim is not to fathom the whole of the dissertation but to find a beginning for the exposition of Marx's critique of politics and to dispense with certain preconceptions about his early work.

The first suggestion in the dissertation that Marx is intent on pursuing the principles of self-consciousness, of 'mind,' not as abstractions but as principles whose ground lay in material reality comes in the foreword. Here he makes a strongly asserted defence of philosophy. It is not, however, the philosophy that Hegel posits as the culmination of the development of abstract consciousness: 'abstraction comprehending itself as abstraction,' as Marx was later to remark.[17] Philosophy for him is here a function of 'human self-consciousness,' of real, existing self-consciousness and not its abstraction, its concept.

As *human* self-consciousness, philosophy must be defended against those who would make the idea into an abstraction independent of the real world. To this end, he addresses the 'theologizing intellect,' which must be understood as a reference to, *inter alia*, the work of Hegel, in which the subject confronts only itself as object and, by achieving a union of the two, achieves an infinite or absolute being.[18] Hence, it is a theology, a science of the absolute and its internal relations, in which philosophy makes peace with religion. And to this 'theologizing intellect,' writes Marx, philosophy 'never grows tired of answering ... with the cry of Epicurus: "The blasphemous is not he who scorns the gods of the masses, but he who adheres to the idea that the masses create the gods."'[19] Philosophy or secular self-consciousness, in other words, does not reject 'gods,' a metaphor for ideas, but sees them as reflections of man's own self-consciousness; that is, gods, like ideas, are products of human self-consciousness and not the absolutes of theology, and to hold such a view is the true meaning of impiety. The point is even more clearly established by Marx when he makes 'the confession of Prometheus: "In simple words, I hate the pack of gods,"' into philosophy's own declaration; that is, there will be no gods other than profane 'human self-consciousness.' The same point is made, in a footnote to the appendix of his dissertation, where he presents the ontological proof of the existence of god as being in fact a proof of the 'existence of essential human self-consciousness.'[20] If the ontological proof states that the concept of a thing begs a corresponding reality, then, 'which being,' Marx asks, 'is immediate when made the subject of thought?' The answer he asserts is 'self-consciousness' – the most immediate source of all concepts.

The foreword ends with the statement: 'Prometheus is the most eminent saint and martyr in the philosophic calendar.' In other words, philosophy finds its symbol in Prometheus, who brought the secret of fire to man from the gods so that man might develop his own arts and remove himself from subordination to the gods. And like Prometheus, philosophy must end the separation of the sacred from the secular; it must bring ideas down from the heavens and make them the content of real human consciousness.

Given the defence of philosophy found here, the foreword alone sets Marx well outside the Hegelian framework and clearly indicates the character of the argument to come.

Having completed its Promethean task, philosophy, in Marx's eyes, can no longer pursue the idea or concept[21] in abstract realms but must turn to search for it in materiality. If this is his intention we must still ask why he would take up the study of two materialist philosophers from antiquity in order to pursue it. Although the answer is to be found in the argument of the dissertation itself, we can briefly speculate here about two of the reasons. First, most commentators on Greek philosophy, including Hegel, have assumed Epicurus' atomistic theory to be but a pale or indeed borrowed version of that of Democritus.[22] Such a prejudice has precluded a grasp of Epicurean physics which in Marx's view, as we shall see, confronts the very questions from a materialist standpoint that he is pondering in the letter to his father; namely, the nature of mind, of self-consciousness, and the content of mind, ideas, or concepts. Second, on the basis of the materialist presuppositions of a science of self-consciousness in Epicurean physics, Marx develops a critical perspective on the presuppositions of empiricism which are founded on Democritean physics. The contrast between these two ancient philosophers, then, provides Marx with both a materialist interpretation of self-consciousness, a view Marx says Hegel was unable to grasp because of his 'speculative thought *par excellence*,'[23] and a critical appreciation of the materialism of empiricism.

Since the substance of his thesis begins in chapter 1, part II, this is where we begin our brief exposition. Marx makes the subject matter of this chapter the forms of motion that Epicurus and Democritus give to the atom. Both are agreed, he points out, that 'atoms in the void' are characterized by 'falling in a straight line' and by 'repulsion.' While both accept these presuppositions of materialism, there is a significant difference. The distinction between them is Epicurus' notion of the 'declination of the atom from the straight line.'

In so far as atoms exist for Democritus they do so as the negation of the void, that is, only as matter. Even though atoms are not static, given their motion as that of a straight line, their existence remains 'purely material,' the motion being determined by the void. They are ascribed 'a mode of relative being' which is their subsumption in the straight line, i.e., their relation is with something other than themselves, in the first place with the void but most immediately with the straight line; their relations are extrinsic not intrinsic.

Here the concept of the atom is strictly abstract matter; it has no form. But if the concept is to be realized, or to possess what is necessary for it to be what it is, it must possess form. And form as an atom is 'pure individuality.'[24] Pure individuality is the expression of self-sufficiency and therefore is the negation of 'any mode of being determined by another being'; and this means that the 'relative existence' of the atom in the straight line must be negated. 'The immediate negation of this motion,' writes Marx, 'is *another motion*, which ... spatially conceived, is the *declination from the straight line*.' The significance of Epicurus' notion of the declination lies here. As Marx puts it: 'If Epicurus therefore repesents the materiality of the atom in terms of its motion along a straight line, he has given reality to its form–determination in the declination from the straight line.'[25] It is through the declination, then, that the concept of the atom is 'realized,' i.e., given a *form* to complement the *materiality* established in the 'falling in a straight line,' and this form is 'the concept of abstract individuality.'

The relationship between form and matter depicted here places matter logically prior to the determination of form. And the motion underlying form is the negation of the motion which determines matter; hence, matter and form are posited as contradictory.

But there is more to this declination of the atom. Without it, according to Epicurus, the atoms would fall only in a straight line, they would not collide or meet, and therefore the material world would not have come into existence; instead, there would only be atoms falling 'like raindrops through the abyss of space.' The significance of the declination is that it explains the motion of repulsion, and, while both philosophers agree that this motion characterizes existing nature, only Epicurus presents this underlying rationale. In brief, the argument runs as follows. The declination of the atom negates the relative existence of the straight line and thereby negates 'all motion and relation wherein it is determined by another as a particular being.' But this negation of all relation, argues Marx, must find a positive expression and this can only be found in a relation to the atom itself. If each atom is related only to itself, the 'repulsion of the many atoms is a necessary realization of the declination.'[26] In a word, the emergence of the real world depends on the 'meeting' of atoms, and such a meeting can happen only if their relative existence in the straight line is negated, only if they become complete as atoms by acquiring a form as abstract individuality, through the declination.

If this is the Epicurean explanation for material existence, it is also the basis for Marx's depiction of the origin of human self-consciousness. Immediately following the above argument Marx draws just such an analogy. He begins by stating: 'man ceases to be a product of nature only when the other being to which he relates himself is not a different existence but is itself an individual human being, even if it is not yet the mind [Geist].'[27] In other words, man ceases to be wholly determined by external causes, by nature, when he begins to relate himself to other human beings and not directly and exclusively to nature. In so doing, he ceases to be a product of nature even if his established relation to fellow man is not yet a conscious one. Marx continues: 'But for man as man to become his own real object, he must have crushed within himself his relative being, the power of desire and of mere nature.' For man to become man he must objectify himself; he must have as the object of his consciousness his own universal self, that which he has in common with all. And to be his own object he must have ended his sense of dependence on, or determination by, nature. Like the atom, which becomes itself as 'abstract individuality,' 'the real soul of the atom,' only through the declination which negates its determination by the straight line, so too the human becomes human, i.e., conscious of himself as his own object, as a consequence of rupturing his direct relation to nature, his determination by nature.

Just as repulsion is the principle of the atom freed, at least in concept, from external determination, so it is the basis of man's consciousness of himself. And the first stage in self-consciousness takes the form of abstract individuality. As Marx puts it: 'Repulsion is the first form of self-consciousness, it corresponds therefore to that self-consciousness which conceives itself as immediate-being, as abstractly individual.' In separating himself from nature, in negating this relation, man must establish a positive relation, and this is done by making himself his immediate object; but since there are always many humans, never simply one, this abstract individuality is only realized in repulsion, the first form of recognition of self, the presupposition, as it were, of the development of self-consciousness.

Marx, however, does not feel that, inasmuch as abstract individuality is the first form of self-consciousness, it actually exists as such. He is careful to argue that it is only realized as a concept: 'In truth, the immediately existing individuality is only realized conceptually, since it relates to something else which actually is itself – even if the other thing confronts it in the form of immediate existence.' In other words, 'immediately existing individuality,' *independent* existence, which is individuality existing without mediation or dependence, can be realized only conceptually because its independence is established *only in relation* to 'something else which actually is itself,' i.e., a similar thing, another human. And there is still a *necessary relation* underlying abstract individuality even if the opposing thing takes the 'form of immediate existence,' of self-sufficiency, even if it purports to stand alone. Abstract individuality is only the *form* of the first consciousness of self.

Having shown how Epicurus grasped the meaning of repulsion of many atoms as a form of self-consciousness, Marx alludes to 'the more concrete forms of repulsion applied by Epicurus,' and these are 'in the political domain ... the *covenant*' and 'in the social domain *friendship*.'[28] Since repulsion is seen by Epicurus as the source of human self-consciousness, it is, therefore, the basis of the fundamental forms of human self-relation or inter-relation.

In the atomistics of Epicurus, then, Marx has answered one of the questions which arose in the 1837 letter to his father; namely, that 'the nature of the mind is just as necessary, concrete and firmly based as the nature of the body.' The nature of mind is seen to be 'concrete,' that is, as real and not abstract, and 'necessary' in the sense that it is a consequence of external causes or is determined by natural laws. Hence, by analogy to the motion of the atoms in Epicurean physics, he has accounted for the origin and nature of human self-consciousness. For Hegel, on the contrary, mind is abstract self-consciousness, that is, the *concept* of self-consciousness made into the acting subject. It is the abstraction itself which is seen to move from the stage of isolated individual consciousness to that of absolute self-consciousness, through a process of self-realization. This development is self-generated; it is not a result of external conditions. And so while Hegel begins with the concept of the isolated individual consciousness and has this consciousness as an abstraction move forward towards self-knowledge, Marx argues that abstract individual consciousness is only the first *form* of concrete human self-consciousness; that is, it has no reality *as* an abstract, solitary ego; rather it comes into existence only as a product of social life, of real, concrete, living individuals.

In the conclusion to this chapter of his thesis, Marx draws out the meaning of repulsion in the atomistics of Epicurus. Repulsion, as the consequence of the declination, the negation of the fall in a straight line, is 'the realization' of the concept of the atom. He means by this that the concept is no longer one-sidedly material but through repulsion it acquires an 'abstract form' to complement its conception as 'abstract matter.' In repulsion, the concept of the atom finds a 'synthetic unity' of abstract form and abstract matter.

Through repulsion, the concept of the atom is developed yet further. In chapter 2, Marx takes up the question of the qualities of the atom and sets out the problem in the first paragraph: 'It contradicts the concept of the atom that the atom should have properties, because, as Epicurus says, every property is variable but the atoms do not change. Nevertheless, it is a *necessary consequence* to attribute properties to atoms. Indeed, the many atoms of repulsion separated by sensuous space must necessarily be *immediately different from one another* and *from their pure essence*, i.e., they must possess *qualities*.'[29] The point is that the concept of the atom is the atom without qualities or determinateness. But in repulsion the atom distinguishes itself from other atoms and therefore from its essence, producing the necessary conclusion that it must have qualities.

But it is the consequence of possessing qualities that is the point of the chapter; and the consequence is the positing of existence, of determinate being. As Marx puts it: 'Through the qualities the atom acquires an existence which contradicts its concept; it is assumed as an externalized being different from its essence.'[30] It is this contradiction between essence and existence Marx says that is the 'main interest of Epicurus.' It is because his *concept* of the atom, realized in repulsion, is seen to contain a contradiction in which the necessary positing of properties produces an atom with a 'material nature.' If left with a material or determinate atom Epicurus would be drawn to the conclusions of Democritean materialism, of empiricism. For this reason, Epicurus 'determines all properties in such a way that they contradict themselves,' and in contradicting themselves, so too is existence contradicted, and as a consequence essence is reaffirmed, the *concept* of the atom is validated. But within it now lies the contradiction between essence and existence.

To this point Marx's main interest has been the content of the Epicurean concept of the atom. He has described how in repulsion the concept of the atom is realized as the synthesis of abstract form and abstract matter and how through repulsion the atom acquires properties which give rise to the contradiction between essence and appearance within the concept itself. We are, then, still within the world of essence.

It is in chapter 3 that Marx follows Epicurean logic in establishing a relationship between the *worlds* of essence and of appearance. His discussion rests on the distinction Epicurus is said to have made between atoms as first principles [Anfängen] and as elements [Elementen]. The distinction had given rise to speculation that Epicurus was positing two different kinds of atoms. But Marx's point is that 'they are rather different determinations [Bestimmungen] of one and the same kind.'[31] The distinction, he argues, arises out of the *realization* of the contradiction between essence and appearance and matter and form inherent in the concept of the atom. The atom as first principle and as element represent respectively the two sides of the realized contradiction.

Without expounding the argument, since it does not concern us here, Marx makes the case that the atom as concept to which Epicurus attaches the name 'first principles' *and* the atom as substratum to the world of appearance to which he gives the name 'elements' stand as the realization of the contradictions within the concept of the atom. The former is the 'absolute, essential *form* of nature,' while the latter is 'absolute matter,' the 'formless substratum,' the positive basis of nature.[32]

This point is important for Marx because the argument establishes a relation between the worlds of essence and appearance. The atoms as first principles comprise essence in the world of essence, and the atoms as elements comprise essence in the world of appearance, essence as the foundation of existence. Such a link avoids the division of the world into two incompatible worlds of principles and elements. It overcomes, moreover, the predicament faced by both idealists and empiricists who, approaching from different sides, find themselves unable to bridge the division.

The actual nature of this link is the subject matter of chapter 4, which is entitled 'Time.' For Epicurus, time does not belong to the world of essence because here the atom stands only in relationship to itself; its position is neither relative nor changeable. He posits time as 'the absolute form of appearance'; Marx goes on to explain: 'That is to say, time is determined as accidens of the accidens. The accidens is the change of substance in general. The accidens of the accidens is the change as reflecting itself, the change as change. This pure form of the world of appearance is time.'[33] By 'accidens' he is referring to that which happens or occurs without 'efficient' cause, without design – the nature of change in the world of appearance. The 'accidens of the accidens' is, as he defines it, 'the change as change'; and this as the 'pure form' of appearance is time.

It is time defined in this way that bridges the gulf between essence and appearance. Marx writes that time, which is 'the change of the finite to the extent that change is posited as change, is also the actual form which separates appearance from essence, and posits it as appearance, while it is leading it back into essence.' Time, he elaborates, is 'the abstraction, annihilation and return of all determined being into being-for-itself.' Time, then, is not only change in the objective world as change, but also the very process by which the finite is separated from itself, destroyed as the finite, and returned to its elemental form. In a word, it is time which stands between essence and appearance, which posits the finite as appearance while returning it to its essence.

Marx goes on to argue, using the Epicurean notion of time, that phenomenal nature is rightly asserted to be objective, objective being that which proceeds from the object and not the subject knowing. And from this, the argument follows that 'sensuous perception' is the 'real criterion of concrete nature,'[34] since it is through the senses that we perceive the objective world. On the other hand, the atom as foundation of phenomenal nature, i.e., essence as element, can only be perceived, Marx writes, through reason, and this is because, if we extrapolate from an earlier argument, essence manifests itself in appearance only in forms which are indifferent to it; it is not therefore apprehensible by the senses which grasp only these phenomenal forms.

We have not followed Marx's arguments in chapters 2 to 4 in detail because their length and complexity are such as to make their exposition here difficult to justify. But what Marx has done is to show that in the materialism of Epicurus, despite its limitations which are pointed out in each chapter and dealt with at length in chapter 5, the forms of appearance constitute objective existence; they comprise the sensuous world, that which is apprehended by the senses; and essence is not merely a question of first principles but of elements, the substratum of the forms of appearance, which can only be apprehended by the mind.

Marx has, then, answered here the second reason we supposed for his undertaking this subject matter as his doctoral dissertation, namely, 'to seek the idea in reality itself.' Essence or the 'idea' is no longer to be seen as one side of a world divided between essence and appearance, rather as having entered reality, albeit as substratum, thereby precluding the problem of apriority. In this Marx has provided himself with a fundamental aspect of his own materialism; as he remarked in his notebooks written in preparation for the dissertation: 'the modern rational outlook on nature must first raise itself to the point from which the ancient Ionian philosophy, in principle at least, begins – the point of seeing the divine, the Idea, embodied in nature.'[35]

It is apparent, then, that in his dissertation Marx sought to fathom, among other things, the source of human self-consciousness and the nature of the idea, the very content of this self-consciousness. In discovering both in the materiality of existence, he situates himself well outside the camps of idealism and Hegelianism. Despite appearances, the salient characteristics of his philosophy in this his earliest piece of work would appear to be directly opposite to those he is commonly assumed to hold.

CRITIQUE AND ITS DEVELOPMENT

The second problem in the consideration of Marx's early work concerns the nature of his intellectual development. As we have already seen, the argument for discontinuity begs the question and the argument for continuity points to latent concepts or external influences while treating the parts of the purported development as discrete elements. Neither argument, then, accounts for Marx's development in the genuine sense of the word, i.e., as growth engendered from within.

If the path taken in this development is determined by the means employed, then, by understanding the means, the principle determining the direction and nature of movement can be uncovered. Applied to the problem of Marx's early development, this argument points to his method of analysis as the key to unlocking it. But in so doing it raises the question of whether he employed a particular method and, if he did, what its nature was.

Because the body of this book takes up this question in its various stages between 1842 and 1847, our consideration here is confined to the work prior to 1842. If there is a method it must be found in Marx's notion of philosophy, for philosophy in the work of Hegel, perhaps Marx's chief influence at this time, and indeed generally until the mid-nineteenth century, was considered the 'science of sciences'; it was the body of principles comprising the process of acquiring knowledge, of ascertaining truths. The history of philosophy in this sense, then, is the history of the pursuit of truth.[36]

It is this point that Marx takes up in his notebooks to the dissertation. This history, he argues, proceeds as a 'rectilinear process' until it reaches 'nodal points' when it becomes an integrated consummation of existing knowledge, when 'abstract principles' are apprehended 'in a totality.' The work of Aristotle represents such a point in the history of philosophy and, more relevant to Marx's definition of philosophy, so does the work of Hegel.[37]

It is when philosophy reaches such a stage, when the principles it searches for comprise an integrated totality, writes Marx in a lengthy footnote to the dissertation,[38] that the 'theoretical mind,' the philosopher as pursuer of ideas alone, 'turns into practical energy ... and turns itself against the reality of the world existing without it.' In other words, once philosophy as existing knowledge, as the world of concepts separated from existence, is *completed* as a systematic totality at a given stage, it must direct itself to the real world which it confronts as its essential reflection. This is the turn that philosophy took after Aristotle and it is the turn, Marx implies, it takes after Hegel.

If the purely theoretical activity of philosophy turns into practical energy, then, the question of the nature of philosophy's practice is raised. Marx answers: 'The *practice* of philosophy is itself *theoretical*.' It is this theoretical practice which he calls *critique*. 'It is the *critique* that measures the individual existence by the essence, the particular reality by the Idea' [Es ist die Kritik, die einzelne Existenz am Wesen, die besondere Wirklichkeit an der Idee misst].[39] This definition of critique is what we take as the first statement by Marx of his method of analysis in the early writings.

It is, moreover, it must be stressed, a definition which concerns only the beginning point of his method; there are developments in the method between 1842 and 1847 and after, but their examination must be left to the body of this essay and its conclusions; to do otherwise here would be to make mere assertions without the possibility of demonstration. It remains, then, to examine the meaning of critique as defined by Marx in 1841-42.

It is worth noting first that there is little agreement as to what critique means, despite the now commonplace observation that almost all of Marx's works are titled or subtitled a critique. Some attempts to explain it focus on the laws of dialectical materialism as set forth by Engels; others grapple with the method of presentation as found in *Capital*;[40] some suggest a derivation from, or a similarity to, Feuerbach's 'invertive' or 'transformative' method [Umkehrungsmethode] or Kant's notion of critique;[41] and some find it in a multiplicity of methods.[42] None of these explanations, however, explains the regard in which the published early works were held in their day by friends, critics, and governments alike; they do not explain Marx's own regard for their consistency with his later work;[43] and they leave the explanation of the development of Marx's analysis, if they see a development at all, open only to external causes, i.e., they perceive no internal, methodological dynamic.[44]

If our exposition of the above definition of critique which follows overcomes these objections, it may well be asked why the method has been so illusive and so misunderstood. Some reasons can be identified here, others only later. First, the definition of method has two aspects: one is the method of analysis and the other the method of presentation. This is a distinction Marx struggled with for some time and the problem is not fully resolved until the 1860s.[45] The former must precede the latter; to focus on the latter, on presentation, then, is to miss out not only the development of the analysis of the subject matter, but also the development of the method of analysis itself. In the early works, more to the point, only the method of analysis appears. Second, the notion and use of critique in Marx's work does evolve, and this fact makes it difficult to grasp the method at any one point, unless the heart of it has been grasped at the beginning. Third, Marx makes no systematic presentation of his method of critique, thereby obliging those interested in his method to 'uncover' it.

Let us here at least set the stage for grasping his method of analysis and therefore his development in these early works, by examining the meaning of critique as defined by Marx in his doctoral dissertation and his first published articles.

If the definition of critique in 1841 is the measurement of 'individual existence by the essence,' it is the same in the *Rheinische Zeitung* in 1842-43. These two examples, in general and specific forms, will suffice to make the point: 'We must ... take the essence of the inner idea, as the measure to evaluate the existence of things.'[46] and: 'you must judge the rightfulness of state constitutions not on the basis of Christianity, but on the basis of the state's own nature and essence, not on the basis of the nature of Christian society, but on the basis of the nature of human society.'[47] In each of these quotations, the critical method is defined as the measurement, the judgement, the evaluation of individual, existing things by a comparison to the idea or nature or essence of the thing. The problem before us, then, is three-fold: what is meant by essence, existence, and judgement?

What Marx meant by essence and existence has already been expounded above. The essence as such is an abstraction, is comprised of the *conditio sine qua non* of a thing, possess no particular qualities, and constitutes the content of the concept of a thing. Essence is not however, an apriorism; as we have seen, it is found in reality as 'element,' as 'substratum,' 'as the bearer of a world of manifold relations,' as a 'foundation' which exists but only 'in forms which are indifferent and external to it.'[48] It is precisely because phenomenal forms are 'indifferent and external to it' that essence in reality must be apprehended by the mind, although on the basis of information from the senses. Existence is the empirically real and its manifestation is appearance; it is comprised of both the inessential or the contingent *and* the essential or the necessary as its substratum. Since existence is objective, sensation is the criterion for its apprehension. These are in brief, then, the definitions of essence and existence and their relationship as found in Marx's analysis of Epicurus.

Given this we can turn to the question of the meaning of judgement, measurement, or evaluation. With the abstraction of essence from existence, which is the task of philosophy, the critical philosopher is presented with two sides, as it were, to the object under consideration: on the one hand, there is the side of appearance, the phenomenon with all its particular qualities in its empirical form; and on the other hand, there is the side of essence, the object stripped of its particular qualities and grasped only in terms of its necessary characteristics, its 'species-form' to use a concept from Marx's 1844 manuscripts. The latter *as such*, essence as essence, only finds existence in the form of concepts. Thus, the critical philosopher is able to perceive *both* the concept of the thing, an abstraction in the mind, and the appearance of the thing, its empirical form. In this position, he is able to compare 'particular reality' with its 'idea.' And it is in this comparison that lies the judgement or measurement or evaluation; existence with its contingent forms is contrasted to its own internal but abstracted necessity, its own essence, and in this manner judged or measured by the degree of correspondence.

To illuminate this interpretation of Marx's critical method in 1842-43, it might be helpful to examine some real and possible objections or misconceptions. Without doubt, most of the difficulties in comprehending the meaning of critique devolve on the concept of essence. Many hold that Marx's 'essence' is like that of Hegel, an hypostatized ideal;[49] but such a notion cannot be maintained in light of the above exposition describing Marx's search for the idea in reality. Others suggest that he is moralistic,[50] i.e., his essence is a particular ideal, a particular view about the way the world should be; and it may even be suggested that such terms in the *Rheinische Zeitung* articles as the 'moral state' or the 'rational commonweal' demonstrate this point. But to see his essence of the state as a particularity does not conform to Marx's view; while it is true that all existing states possess a particular moral system, Marx is referring in these concepts to the *essence* of morality, of ethical conduct, which he argues is the 'rationality,' the unity, of the whole and the parts.[51] Proof that his essence of the state is a particular, thus making him a moralist, would require proof that this 'rationality' is a particularistic view. In the same vein, some might point to Marx's use of the concept of 'ought' [Sollen] in reference to the ideal or idea; but in response it must be said that this concept has two meanings, namely, to be right or proper according to some particular prescript *and* to be necessary. Essence, as we have seen above, is the abstraction of the necessary from the contingency of appearance. Another similar objection might assert that implicit in the critical method is a value judgement, i.e., that existence is judged in light of a value or particular ideal. But again, this requires demonstration that Marx's ideal or essence is a particular and not a universal, and such a demonstration as opposed to mere assertion remains to be carried out. A further widely accepted objection is that the critical method amounts to 'methodo-logical essentialism' and that 'essentialism' leads to idealism in one form or another.[52] The precise nature of the error in this method so labelled and of its passage to a 'doctrine of Forms or Ideas' is not cogently argued by its author; but it is worth noting that despite the absence of an argument to support the case, the charge of 'essentialism' has received a broad, albeit uncritical, acceptance as a method of science worthy only of dismissal.

In each case, except the first which rests on the notion that Marx was Hegelian or idealist, the objections concern the concept of essence. And in every case, the tendency is to dismiss the concept or to make it into some form of particular; there is no attempt to grasp it as a universal. Indeed, there is in these objections little sense that there is anything outside the limit of the particular.

But given the centrality of essence in Marx's exposition of the differences between Epicurus and Democritus, his frequent use and definition of the concept in the *Rheinische Zeitung* articles and afterwards, and the correspondence of its meaning in his writing with contemporary dictionary definitions, the difficulty is not in explaining its meaning and place in the critical method but in explaining why it is so misunderstood.

I would suggest, following the lead of Charles Taylor, that in the *empiricism* of certain contemporary trends in philosophy and the social sciences there are intellectual 'obstacles' to the acceptance of many of the principles underlying Marx's work. By 'obstacles' he means 'differences in the structure of thought ... which make one way of thinking or school of philosophy quite opaque to another, which may make one seem to the other literally meaningless or at best confused.'[53] He is referring to the British school of logical positivism and makes a convincing case, but using examples not wholly appropriate to our argument, for the incompatibility of the principles of empiricism and Marxism. Professor Meszaros makes a similar point: 'numerous concepts used by Marx – perhaps most of his key concepts – must sound extremely odd, if not altogether meaningless or self-contradictory, to all those who are used to the misleading "common-sense simplicity" of positivistic empiricism or to the neat schematic straightforwardness of philosophical formalism, or both. The difficulties of understanding, due to this condition, cannot be sufficiently stressed.'[54]

Both imply that it is the point of view of empiricism or positivism which infuses the prevailing trends in modern social science and philosophy. Indeed, since Auguste Comte, the term positivism has often been employed as a synonym for the scientific approach. But it was through the influence of the Vienna Circle[55] that positivism as the attempt to reform philosophy, to deny its 'metaphysics,' gained its wide contemporary acceptance in Britain, Europe, and the United States. This is not to say that it is without its critics;[56] and it is not to imply that in this approach there are no differences and debates; it is only to say that its assumptions are those that dominate mainstream social science and philosophy, and can be grouped loosely under the umbrella concept of logical empiricism or positivism.[57]

In searching for the obstacles in empiricism to a comprehension of Marx's method, one must be careful to distinguish the 'social positivism' of Auguste Comte, his contemporaries, and followers from 'philosophical positivism' or positivism proper. As one commentator puts it, Comte and some of his contemporaries 'gradually come to misrepresent the real positivist standpoint and combine it with theories that are alien to it. What they present is less positivism than a distortion of it.'[58] He is not arguing that the 'real positivist standpoint' cannot be found in Comte, but that there is a social and religious side to Comte's work which is 'alien' to positivism. The failure to appreciate this point can lead to conclusions which imply an acceptance of positivism by Marx.[59] It is true that some aspects of the social and political activity of positivists in France and Britain were welcomed by Marx, but these activities were not part of positivism proper.

The positivism or 'philosophical positivism' which infuses the contemporary sciences is a theory of knowledge. It is the theory which considers sense experience rather than reason as the sole source of knowledge of the world. One of the classic statements of the doctrine was made by J.S. Mill in his *Auguste Comte and Positivism*: 'We have no knowledge of anything but phaenomena; and our knowledge of phaenomena is relative, not absolute. We know not the essence, nor the real mode of production of any fact, but only its relations to other facts in the way of succession or of similitude. These relations are constant; that is, always the same in the same circumstances. The constant resemblances which link phaenomena together, and the constant sequences which unite them as antecedent and consequent, are termed their laws. Their essential nature, and their ultimate causes, either efficient or final, are unknown and inscrutable.'[60]

It is beyond the scope of this Introduction to evaluate or make a critical judgement of these presuppositions of positivism. Our task is simply to demonstrate how certain elements of this doctrine, which as a theory of knowledge underlies modern social science, throw up 'obstacles' to the comprehension of Marx's method as we have outlined above.

The very concept of science provides the first example. If science is the acquisition of knowledge, and the basis of knowledge for the logical empiricist (for Comte and Mill just as for A.J. Ayer) is the sense impressions received by the mind, then science concerns only the appearance of things, only 'phaenomena' as Mill put it; scientific theories are statements about things that are capable of 'being observed,' as Ayer would have it.[61] In his dissertation, however, Marx makes claims which suggest a different meaning for science; it was Epicurus who 'gave us the science of atomistics' because he had grasped 'the contradiction in the concept of the atom between essence and existence.'[62] In other words, before there could be the *science* of atomistics there had to be a conception of a contradictory essence and existence. Because essence and appearance did not directly correspond, science was necessary and its task was to uncover the essence hidden in the 'manifold relations' of existence. Such a concept of science was held by Marx throughout his life.[63] Democritus, to whom modern notions of science trace many of their basic principles, 'only maintained the material side,' the side of existence, according to Marx, and as a result he only 'offers hypotheses for the benefit of empirical observation.' Democritus, in Marx's view, does not proceed to the level of science because he, like modern positivists, perceives the content of knowledge as merely the empirically observable. From the point of view of positivism, then, science concerns only the empirical, and from this perspective a notion of science dependent on a difference between essence and appearance must appear as incomprehensible, confused, or idealist.

It may be taken as idealist, and this is another albeit related obstacle, because the empiricist rejects or abstains from metaphysical concepts or propositions, and essence is seen to be just such a concept. Empiricism confronts rationalism and idealism with the charge that their presuppositions are *a priori* and that no *a priori* propositions can be established through empirical observation.[64] This rejection is very much the historical springboard of contemporary positivism and remains for it an important tenet, at the same time militating against a grasp of a universal, principle, or concept as the 'thing-in-itself,' as *differentia specifica*, or as essence. As we have seen, however, Marx's concept of essence as developed in his dissertation is not transcendent or *a priori*; rather, essence has a reality in existence; there is for Marx no independent existence of essence. From the perspective of empiricism, such a position is difficult to accept when so much weight is given to the rejection of any notion of universal or concepts whose content is not the immediately empirical.

Another obstacle lies in the dismissal by empiricism of the concept of truth. If we can know only the empirical appearance of a thing, then, truth denotes only the empirical verification of its existence. In this light, truth as a 'real quality' or a 'real relation' must be seen as 'nonsense,' as indeed Ayer has argued.[65] Such a position precludes an understanding of Marx's frequent use of the concept in the dissertation, and as part of his method in the *Rheinische Zeitung* and after. It makes Marx into a writer of nonsense or, as is more commonly thought, an idealist for whom the notion of truth refers to the metaphysical or *a priori*. But truth for Marx was nothing of the sort; it was simply the essence of a thing.[66]

Similarly, the definition of a thing for Marx refers to its essence, the *conditio sine qua non* of a thing, its *differentia specifica*.[67] But from the perspective of empiricism this meaning of definition is difficult to comprehend and can be seen as another indication of Marx's idealist beginnings. Empiricism views definitions as *nominal*, as mere symbols describing the external qualities, the 'sense-content,' of things.[68] Since the appearance of individual things alone can be known, definitions are mere words, labels. In so far as this is the case, empiricism accepts the already existing symbolic conventions of a language, and the *meaning* of such conventions is determined only through the empirically verifiable correspondence of the symbol with material existence. For Marx, on the contrary, the meaning of a definition refers to its content, i.e., the essence. Definitions are not mere labels but the product of the mental activity of abstraction.

While the foregoing serves to point to some 'fundamental differences in the structure of thought' between empiricism and Marx's method, which present considerable obstacles to those who would approach Marx from the perspective of empiricism, there is another difference which is central to the exposition which follows. It has to do with ethical or moral judgements.

Morality or ethics concerns the rightness or wrongness of human conduct. The attitude of empiricism to this question has been varied, but some general statements can be made. For the most part, empiricism views the question as beyond empirical observation; moral injunctions or imperatives are seen as based on feeling or inclination; they cannot be 'true or false' and therefore are not subject to its 'scientific' mode, its 'principle of verification,'[69] and for this reason are unverifiable. Such injunctions are, moreover, seen to be founded on *particular* dispositions, for empiricism admits into existence only particularity. All moral imperatives, all 'oughts,' from this point of view are particular; but then also from this point of view there can be no criterion of judgement, except a particular. There have been attempts to circumvent this moral relativism and establish an absolute principle as the criterion, such as Kant's 'categorical imperative' and Mill's 'utilitarianism,'[70] but contemporary empiricism appears content with ethical relativism. Such a position presents a significant barrier to the comprehension of Marx's critique of politics since politics is an ethical question.

The first assertion of this political critique, already cited above, comes in the *Rheinische Zeitung*: 'you must judge the rightfulness of state constitutions not on the basis of Christianity, but on the basis of the state's own nature and essence, not on the basis of the nature of Christian society, but on the basis of the nature of human society.'[71] From the perspective of empiricism, the essence of the state or human society can only be grasped as a particular, i.e., as Marx's *particular* idealist or Hegelian concept of the 'ideal' state or society. But such was not at all his meaning.

By way of clarification, let us cite one further passage from the *Rheinische Zeitung* articles: 'The child, of course, does not go beyond *sensuous perception*, it sees a thing only in isolation, and the invisible nerve threads which link the particular with the universal, which in the state as everywhere make the material parts into soul-possessing members of the spiritual whole, are for the child non-existent.'[72] Here Marx is contrasting, in Hegelian terms, the levels of consciousness, of the 'understanding' and 'reason.' It is the latter which is able to grasp the essence and which the child is without. The essence of the state – state meaning here the body politic, the commonweal – it follows, is the organic link between the individual and 'others,' the parts and the whole. The 'whole' is to be understood as the system of relationships into which every individual is born. The link is organic because each side depends on the other for its own existence, i.e., there is no society or state without members and there are no human individuals outside of society; each part contains the whole. This is *true* for all human societies throughout time, Marx would insist; it is the *conditio sine qua non* of humanity. Where there is social life and where there are human beings, such a link must be present. For Marx the organic unity of the whole and the parts is the essence of human society.

But as we have seen the essence or nature of a thing does not necessarily coincide with its appearance.[73] While existence must contain essence, i.e., all human societies must possess a relationship between the whole and the parts, the form in which essence appears will not be absolute, unconditioned, i.e., this relationship will not be a completely organic one, a perfect identity of all individuals with the whole. Indeed, appearance may take forms which seem to be the very antithesis of its essence.

In this light, it can be seen how Marx could attempt to make ethical/political judgements within the sphere of his notion of critical philosophy, to make a judgement about morality in a manner which he considered scientific. The particular relationships of an existing society were to be measured against the essential relationships of society, and the result of this critique, this evaluation, was a measure of the 'defects'[74] of existing society. Such a notion of critical philosophy, of science, applied to the realm of morality is not at all easy for the empiricist to comprehend.

If, by way of this brief review of some of the differences between empiricism and Marx's *initial* concept of critique, some light has been thrown on the meaning of essence and critique, it remains only to summarize the differences. If all are agreed that philosophy or science is the pursuit of knowledge,[75] the same cannot be said about what constitutes knowledge or the way it is acquired. For the empiricist or positivist, only phenomena and their external relations and succession, the appearance of things, are susceptible to knowing. For Marx, the 'sense data,' as it were, are necessary as information about the real world but do not constitute knowledge. Knowledge comes with the grasping of essence through the rational processes of the mind. The object of philosophy or science, then, is to comprehend the essence of a thing,[76] for this constitutes knowledge of a thing.

This is not merely the view of science Marx held in 1841-42, but the view he asserted and employed throughout his life. Because appearance and essence do not necessarily correspond science is necessary to abstract the essence from existence. As he wrote in *Capital*: 'all science would be superfluous if the outward appearance and essence of things directly coincided.'[77]

From this perspective, empiricism is not the foundation of science but a form of ideology, a way of viewing the world which grasps only appearance, and cannot for this reason be seen as being a scientific method. To 'hold fast to appearance and take it as ultimate,' Marx critically remarks about 'vulgar economists,' is to raise the question, 'why then have any science at all?'[78] In other words, if appearance is all one can know, is the content of knowledge, there is no need of any special activity other than empirical observation to acquire knowledge. Every sensing subject becomes a scientist or every sensual experience amounts to scientific knowledge.

It is also from this perspective that Marx's comments about 'positive philosophy' in the notes and notebooks to his dissertation must be understood.[79] And when he writes later in his life that 'positivism is synonymous with ignorance of everything positive,'[80] he is referring to the fact that in his view of science knowledge is gained only through grasping essences, whereas positivism grasps only appearances and a world grasped at this level is a world uncomprehended. Marx is being ironic, of course; the positive, the real and existing, he suggests is beyond the very philosophy which makes it its sole object.

1

The State as Rational and Real: articles from the *Rheinische Zeitung*, 1842-43

The writings considered here are Marx's first published work and his first analysis of the state. They consist of one article written in early 1842, but published only in 1843 in *Anekdota*, and the articles Marx wrote for the *Rheinische Zeitung* in 1842 and early 1843. In all, Marx wrote about thirty articles for the *Rheinische Zeitung*. Several were published in successive editions of the newspaper, some were never or only partially published owing to the censorship, and some were never completed. Almost all of them dealt with political issues of the day and many of them were the subject of considerable controversy.

The *Zeitung* itself was from the beginning provocative and critical of Prussian political life. Its editors and writers were, for the most part, liberals and Young Hegelians whose views represented the political aspirations of a section of the Cologne bourgeoisie. The influence of the Young Hegelians soon came to dominate and the journal was thereafter often referred to as their organ.

It was widely talked about, yet it had a subscription of only about one thousand by the late summer of 1842, which more than doubled by early 1843. Its reputation was in part a reflection of its political notoriety; the Prussian government found its views objectionable, if not subversive, and harassed the journal with constant censorship and threats to revoke its licence to publish. The threat was invoked on 21 January 1843: it was to cease publication in April and to be heavily censored in the interim.[1]

According to his correspondence, Marx had some involvement in the founding of the journal in 1841 but he was not a participant when it began to publish in January 1842. His first contributions were published in May 1842, on the debates of the Rhenish Provincial Assembly on freedom of the press; they were well received by the editors and writers of the journal.[2] Thereafter, he wrote more and more frequently for it. In October, he became its editor-in-chief and remained so until mid-March 1843, resigning shortly before the ban came into effect.

Apparently, Marx did not consider the articles of this period as inconsistent with his later work. In 1851, long after he had worked out and formulated the main elements of his approach to history and political economy, he agreed to include his *Rheinische Zeitung* articles and the one from *Anekdota* in a proposed collection of his work, to be edited by a member of the Communist League and published in Cologne. The first issue began, with Marx's concurrence, with major sections from these articles; but the project was abandoned because of government repression.[3]

In light of the fact that Marx himself attached a certain importance to these writings, that they possess a common approach to the subject matter, and that they contain his initial critical analysis of the state, we begin our exposition here.

THE FIRST USE OF CRITIQUE

There is no exegesis of political relations in Marx's first published articles, yet politics are the central issue in almost all of them. His notion of politics is logically coherent and compelling, but it underlies the analysis and is not explicitly or systematically put forth. For this reason, our first problem is how to explicate the notion of the political which is implicit in them.

One of the most common of the various approaches to these articles is the attempt to locate them within the political or philosophical spectrum of the period. But to say that here Marx was a 'liberal' or 'liberal democrat' or 'democratic extremist' or 'revolutionary democrat' and so on, *or* to suggest that he was 'Hegelian' or 'idealist,' and then to argue that his 'theory' of the state was a concomitant, is to misconstrue the nature and content of the articles.[4]

A method which often accompanies this approach is to précis the main articles and their arguments and to place them in an historical context. Such treatment often comes close to grasping their essence, but the approach itself is cumbersome and usually leads to poorly supported generalizations.[5] Another practice is to trace the various intellectual influences to be found in these early works. The assumption, seemingly, is that the sum of the parts equals the whole; needless to say, it does not; but as a consequence of this approach, the uniqueness and the integrity of these writings are often overlooked.[6]

It is possible, however, to approach them in a way which reveals the actual nature of the analysis; it is to follow Marx's own method. By examining the articles in this manner, we can shed light not only on his criticism of political relations but also on the nature of the limitation of this method. The method in question is the critique, which we have already outlined in brief as it was defined in this period.

In the articles it is apparent that he was employing the critique, 'the practice of philosophy.' It was a method by which reason, in the person of the philosopher, would confront the real world. The ensuing struggle would result in the world becoming 'philosophical,' that is, rational, and philosophy becoming 'worldly,' that is, reason particularized. Far from being a mode of idealism, this project saw philosophy, which was in the first instance dependent on existence, now return to do battle with the 'defective' world, i.e., a world without reason, and in the process recognize its own 'defects' which were those of existence 'only with inverted factors,' i.e., reason without reality.[7]

Marx employed the method in all the articles he wrote during this period. But by early 1843, the problems and limitations of 'theoretical practice' were becoming more evident the more his work brought him into contact with the material interests of real life. Reality, in its irrational form, was not about to recognize the rationality of the critic who could perceive its essence. Philosophy may have been desirous of becoming worldly, but the world was not apparently interested in becoming philosophical. This, however, is to anticipate.

Earlier I attempted to outline the general meaning of critique as defined by Marx in 1841, but now it is necessary, before examining his critique of politics, to explain the principal elements of this *specific* critique, most important of which is the idea of the state. This concept of the universal essence of the state must be grasped for the entire critical analysis of political relations in these articles rests upon it. It is always implicit, but at times it is defined explicitly, as follows: 'recent philosophy proceeds from the idea of the whole. It looks on the state as the great organism, in which legal, moral, and political freedom must be realised, and in which the individual citizen in obeying the laws of the state only obeys the natural laws of his own reason, of human reason.'[8] 'The state itself educates its members by making them its members, by converting the aims of the individual into general aims, crude instinct into moral inclination, natural independence into spiritual freedom, by the individual finding his good in the life of the whole, and the whole in the frame of mind of the individual.'[9]

Because the central ideas here differ profoundly from contemporary liberal notions, they should be drawn out. As a concept, the state is seen as a 'whole,' an 'organism,' a community with a reality above and beyond the sum of its parts. It is only within this community that freedom can be realized; human nature being a social nature, individuals become human only in relation to others, therefore freedom can have meaning only in the reflexive relation of the particular to the whole. Law, here, is to be understood as embodying the moral essence or rational principles of human behaviour, in short, the theoretical expression of freedom. And rationality is the state of affairs in which the interests of the whole are reflected in the individual and the interests of the individual are represented by the whole.

These were the elements of Marx's concept or idea of the state, and it was against this *idea* that the *existing* state was placed in order to pose its deficiencies.

The elements comprised his premises, but they were not seen as *assumptions*, rather as *axioms*, self-evident principles or truths about the social nature of man. As Marx put it towards the end of his editorship, the *Rheinische Zeitung* 'was concerned for a moral and rational commonweal [ein sittliches und vernünftiges Gemeinwesen]; it regarded the demands of such a commonweal as demands which would have to be realized and could be realized under *every* form of state.'[10] These essential demands, and the above definitions, which are nothing but the expression of man's social essence, bear a striking resemblance to Hegel's discussion of natural law in his essay, *Natural Law, and* to Aristotle's definition of the state, which Hegel cites as his authority: 'The state comes by nature before the individual; if the individual in isolation is not anything self-sufficient, he must be related to the whole state in one unity, just as other parts are to their whole. But a man incapable of communal life, or who is so self-sufficing that he does not need it, is no part of the state and must be either a beast or a god.'[11]

The concept of the state as found in these articles remains a valid dictionary definition today, but latterly it is more common for the state to have a narrower meaning, namely, the government and its organs. This latter sense is present in these articles and it appears variously as the political state [der politische Staat], the government, administration or authority [Regierung], and an organ of the state [Staatsorgan]. This distinction is not uncommon in the political theory of this period and earlier and can be found notably in Aristotle's *Politics*[12] and Hegel's *Philosophy of Right*.

Marx's use of the terms by and large corresponded to Hegel's distinction.[13] The *state proper* comprised both the subjective, particular elements, and the objective, universal side; in short, the individual life of the community and the embodiment of its 'totality,' the constitution. The *political state* referred to the objective aspect only, the formal organization that stood at the head of society, the constitutional elements, comprising the executive, legislature, and monarchy. It was an 'organ of the state,' however, and as such stood below natural laws and owed its origins to the existence of these laws. It was perceived as the power within or of, not over, the community and reflected the essence of the state.

In these articles, Marx's use of the critique to analyse the political state revolved on this very point. The *essence* of the political state, its laws, form of representation, and so on comprised the unity of the general and particular; and against this definition the *existing* political state was measured. Hence, if the Prussian government were a *true* authority, it would as a particular embody the essence of the state proper, of the community at large. To the degree and in the ways that it did not reflect the essence, it was 'defective' or arbitrary. This was the heart of his critique of political power in 1842 and early 1843.

Because there is a continuity of approach throughout all the articles, that is, because the analysis in all of them rests on this initial definition of critique, their content can be treated thematically, rather than chronologically. This is not to say that Marx's thinking did not evolve during this period, but it is to say that it did not change fundamentally.

The order of the themes which follow is not entirely arbitrary; we begin with the most fundamental concepts. But the order is imposed because there is no evident logical order in the articles. As presented here, the themes are meant only as illustration of the early use of critique and its result. Those which have been chosen clearly derive from the texts of the articles; while they are not the only themes, they are the principal *political* subjects of Marx's critique.

RIGHT AND PRIVILEGE

The concepts of right [Recht] and privilege figured prominently in Marx's critique of the state. By rights he meant those *informal* claims, entitlements, or justifications which rested on natural law, the rational principles in social behaviour. Once formalized they constituted the content of *true* law. Privilege, on the contrary, was used to refer to special rights or, more commonly, 'positive rights' which also were informal but specific to certain groups, stratas, classes, or individuals. They were not based on natural law but depended for their existence on the sanction of positive law. Indeed, once formalized they comprised the content of *positive* law.

Marx first used these concepts in the article, 'Debates on the Freedom of the Press,' in which the question of the publication of the proceedings of the Provincial Estates Assembly [rheinischen Landtags] was one of the central issues. The Assembly had been granted permission to publish its proceedings by royal decree in the spring of 1841; but, according to its first publication, it had debated how 'to make *a wise use* of the permission granted.' This, Marx stated, implied that publication depended on an *arbitrary* decision of the Assembly; but true provincial, i.e., community, control of the Assembly assumed that the publication would be a 'legal necessity' such that the proceedings would be 'public facts.' By exercising its discretion, the Assembly was delimiting the province's discretion. As Marx put it: 'Privileges of the estates are in no way rights of the province. On the contrary, the rights of the province cease when they become privileges of the estates.'[14]

The point was expanded to show how the contradiction between privilege and right had evolved. 'The estates of the Middle Ages,' he wrote, 'appropriated for themselves all the country's constitutional rights and turned them into privileges against the country.'[15] This historical description was elaborated in another article, the 'Debates on the Law on Thefts of Wood.' Here Marx argued that whenever 'customary rights' of the poor, such as rights to use common land and to gather wood and even berries which were based on 'forms of property' of indeterminate character, were transformed into 'legal rights' which required property to be determinate, i.e., private, the customary rights were abolished and became 'rights' by virtue of legislation, making them privileges of certain classes and stratas.[16]

The historical evolution of the Provincial Assembly itself, which represented the estates and which, in turn, represented different forms of combined property and privileges, was the making of privilege into right, the abolition of customary rights and the creation of privileged rights. As Marx argued, 'the rights of the Provincial Assembly' were 'no longer *rights of the province* but *rights against the province.*' It was a 'peculiar spectacle,' he wrote with apparent irony, that the nature of the Assembly required the province 'to fight not so much through its representatives as against them.' The essential nature of the Assembly, however, was obscured by the appearance, the 'mystical significance' of its supposed embodiment of state right,[17] the rights of the community.

Inasmuch, therefore, as the political state legislated estate privileges, it denied the rights of the state proper; in other words, the rights of the state were usurped in the enactment of privileged rights by the political state. The Provincial Assembly did not represent the province, indeed, their respective interests were contradictory. If the Assembly appeared to embody provincial rights, it was illusory; its essential character was the embodiment of privilege as right.

LAW AND LAWS[18]

In an article on the Prussian censorship, written in January and February 1842, but published in 1843, Marx opened with a declaration to examine the new censorship law critically, basing his right to criticize on the nature of censorship. '*Censorship* is *official criticism*; its standards are critical standards, hence they least of all can be exempt from criticism, being on the same plane as the latter.'[19] In other words, censorship is the judgement or measurement of material for publication by the standards of officialdom, arbitrary standards. Marx, of course, is being ironic for he is about to 'judge,' to criticize, censorship itself, by measuring it against the concept or definition of law.

The issue concerned a censorship 'instruction' promulgated by the Prussian government in December 1841. According to the preamble, the new law was to renew observance of an earlier censorship edict of 1819. Although both were censorship decrees, the difference between them which Marx drew was that 'at that time [1819] *laws on the freedom of the press* were the object of expectation whereas now it is *laws on censorship*.'[20]

The distinction pointed to what Marx called 'the basic defect in the nature of censorship which no law can remedy.' Law, in Marx's eyes, was in essence the legal face of universal norms; laws by definition were *prescriptive*, they rested on the general will of the public. In this sense, a law on the freedom of the press could rightfully be called a law; but a law on censorship was different. It was not derived from the customary social order but was imposed on it; it was *proscriptive* in nature.[21]

Marx elaborated this distinction later in the article when he turned to a comparison of the old and new decrees. The former contained an element of 'rationalism,' a sense of the unity of the general and particular; whereas, the latter was infused with a spirit of orthodoxy, a viewpoint of the particular. On these grounds, the two were incompatible; the old edict 'included under the aim of censorship also suppression of "what offends against *morality* and good manners."' But the new instruction changed this, making the offence against morality and good manners the 'violation of "propriety and manners and external decorum."' Marx commented on this change: '*Morality as* such, as the *principle of a world* that obeys its own laws, *disappears*, and in place of the essence[,] external manifestations make their appearance, *police respectability, conventional decorum.*'[22]

The difference between the old and new decrees, between the rationalism of the former and the orthodoxy of the latter, was the *nature* of the law. In the former was recognized the principle of morality as the basis of social order; laws were emanations of the society itself. In the latter, the essence of community, that is, morality, disappeared and a form of external control, not 'instinctive' or 'natural' to the community, was substituted.

The new censorship instruction not only proscribed the publication of certain viewpoints but also the viewpoints of published articles. The banned tendencies, however, were left undefined. Marx characterized these 'laws against tendency' which give 'no objective standards' as 'laws of terrorism' typical of a state of emergency. Such laws, moreover, 'which make their main criterion not *actions as such*, but the *frame of mind* of the doer, are nothing but *positive sanctions for lawlessness.*'[23] In other words, a law which focuses on thought and not action, which has no objective standard, was fundamentally arbitrary; but more, because it was couched in the frame of a law, it was a 'positive sanction' for arbitrariness, i.e., for lawlessness.

Having analysed the nature of a law against tendency, Marx turned to the nature of the government that could produce such a law. 'The law against a frame of mind is *not a law of the state* promulgated for its *citizens*, but the *law of one party against another party*.' 'The *moral state* assumes its members to have the *frame of mind of the state*, even if they act in *opposition to an organ of the state*, against the *government*. But in a society in which *one* organ imagines itself the sole, exclusive possessor of state reason and state morality, in a government which opposes the people in principle and hence regards *its anti-state frame of mind* as the general, normal frame of mind, the bad conscience of a faction invents laws against tendency.'[24]

Such laws, Marx asserted, could not be the product of a rational state but were that of a partisan government. In other words, the 'moral state,' that is, the *essential* state where the general and particular were united, where the individual shared the same frame of mind as the whole, could not promulgate a law against a frame of mind without being self-contradictory. So it was that members could act against an *organ* of the state, the government, without necessarily being of a frame of mind different from the state. On the other hand, the government that could enact such laws presumed that *its* 'reason' and 'morality' were that of the state, but in so doing it stood opposed to the people and contradicted the essence of the state. Its position therefore was anti-state, which it only imagined as general in decreeing anti-state or divisive proscriptive laws.

The 'bad conscience,' in Hegelian terms, was the will which opposed reason and the universal. The (good) conscience was that which sought 'to find within its own reason the universal reason.' Therefore, in saying the 'bad conscience of a faction invents laws against tendency,' Marx meant that the government did not reflect the will of the whole in its laws; in fact, its own will ran counter to that of the whole.

This was the nature of the critique of law. In this and other articles Marx subjected existing laws on censorship, divorce, wood theft, and communal reform[25] to the same method of analysis. The real law was juxtaposed with its essence, and its deficiencies, its partisan nature, and that of the government which enacted it was thereby exposed.

PRESS FREEDOM AND CENSORSHIP

The nature of laws on freedom and censorship of the press has been broadly defined, but, because Marx dedicated two of his longest articles to the subject, it is worth examining the question in greater depth.

In his first article published in the *Rheinische Zeitung*, 'Debates on Freedom of the Press ...,' Marx made the distinction which he had put forth in the earlier but yet unpublished article on the Prussian censorship decree. If 'a contrast is drawn between the press law and the censorship law, it is, in the first place, not a question of their consequences, but of their basis, not of their individual application, but of their legitimacy in general.' 'The censorship law has only the form of a law. The press law is a *real* law.' 'The censorship measure is not a law. The press law is not a measure.'[26]

The difference lies in their legitimacy. In essence, law is the 'theoretical expression' of a natural social order, it is the conscious statement of public will, and therefore it finds its basis in the state as a whole. This is the nature of the press law. Censorship, on the other hand, Marx wrote, 'is a precautionary measure of the police against freedom,' and therefore cannot be seen as a law in its ideal sense. It is the opposite of law; it is the arbitrary action of one 'member' of society.

The distinction was expressed by Marx in a more obvious application of the critique: 'From the standpoint of the idea, it is self-evident that freedom of the press has a justification quite different from that of censorship because it is itself an embodiment of the idea, an embodiment of freedom, a positive good, whereas censorship is an embodiment of unfreedom, the polemic of a world outlook of semblance against the world outlook of essence; it has a merely negative nature.'[27]

The comparison of freedom of the press and censorship parallels the contrast between essence and existence. The free press embodies freedom, the ideal, the very essence of man; that is, the unity of the individual and the whole. Censorship is the denial of free expression and therefore it embodies unfreedom. It is the stance of the particular in opposition to the general, of appearance against essence; in this sense, it is 'the polemic of a world outlook of semblance.' Because a positive nature comes of a unity of the general and particular and because censorship is an action of the particular for itself, censorship 'has a merely negative nature.'

Marx's critique of censorship, largely confined to the articles on the Prussian censorship and the debates on freedom of the press, led to several insights into the nature of the political state and its relation to the state proper. In so far as the political state promulgated censorship decrees, laws against freedom of the press, it was acting arbitrarily, without legitimacy in the state proper. Censorship, then, Marx could say was an act of lawlessness; it was the antithesis of true law. The legitimacy of the government which produced such a measure rested on the police; it was a 'police state,' a 'coercive state,' a 'bureaucratic state,' which stood opposed to the people.[28]

THE STATE AND THE CHRISTIAN STATE

In his criticism of the Prussian censorship decree and in another article in the spring of 1842,[29] Marx took issue with the suggestion that a Christian state could be created or, indeed, was conceivable. In both cases, the question was treated similarly by means of the critique.

In the former article, Marx pointed out that one of the differences between the old and new censorship laws was their respective attitudes to religion: the former sought to 'protect' religion in general from criticism; but the latter, while purporting to do the same, also wanted to create a Christian state.[30] The problem for both, said Marx, was that religion in general was in fact the particularity of religion; what was common to each was its insistence or its belief that its specific, peculiar character was the *essence* of *true* religion. It was not possible, then, to protect religion in general; in fact, it was 'irreligious' to think so.

But the law-makers behind the Prussian censorship instruction wanted a Christian state. This was inconceivable as well, wrote Marx, because it was impossible to define a Christian state except in terms of a particular religion. Since in Prussia there were both Catholic and Protestant Christians, one or the other would have to 'reject' the state 'as heretical' because its 'innermost essence' would be 'contrary to him.'[31]

There was a more important point to be made, however, and that concerned the relation between religion and morality. 'The specifically Christian legislator,' wrote Marx, '*cannot recognize morality* as an independent sphere that is sacrosanct in itself, for he claims that its inner general essence belongs to religion.' The principles of religion were such that they sought to impose an external order, a religiously derived order, and could not recognize the order that emanated from society itself. 'Morality' and religion were not compatible; as Marx put it: 'Morality recognizes only its own universal and rational religion, and religion recognizes only its particular positive morality.' In more general terms, he argued, 'morality is based on the *autonomy* of the human mind, *religion* on its *heteronomy*.'[32]

The point can be put as follows: true morality springs from the spirit of the people, it is autonomously derived social order; the principles of religion, on the contrary, represent the subjection of society to external laws, a heteronomously derived social order. A Christian state then would impose positive laws; its reality would contradict the essence of the rational state. As Marx put it, the Christian state has as its aim, 'not a free association of moral human beings, but an association of believers, not the realization of freedom, but the realization of dogma.'[33]

THE POLITICAL STATE AND THE ESTATES[34]

By means of critique, Marx was able to perceive the existing nature of political rights, of the religious state, of law and censorship, and of the political state, i.e., its particularistic nature and its opposition to the state as a whole. But by late 1842 and early 1843, his analysis became more specific; the focus on the dichotomy of essence and appearance remained but its application became less abstract; his 'philosophy' was becoming more 'worldly.'

Among the subjects which shifted his emphasis to more specific, material issues was the Provincial Assembly debates over the law on thefts of wood.[35] One aspect of these debates concerned the desire of the forest owners to have their own gamekeepers empowered by law to apprehend and punish 'infringers' of the forest regulations. To the notion that a private employee would become a state official, Marx retorted: 'This logic, which turns a servant of the forest owner into a state authority, *turns the authority of the state into a servant of the forest owner*. The state structure, the purpose of the individual administrative authorities, everything must get out of hand so that everything is degraded into an instrument of the forest owner and his interest operates as the soul governing the entire mechanism. All the organs of the state become the ears, eyes, arms, legs, by means of which the interest of the forest owner hears, observes, appraises, protects, reaches out, and runs.'

The conclusion was no longer simply that appearance, when characterized by conflict between the general and particular, contradicted its essence; rather, the embodiment of the general was now seen as pressed into service by and for the particular. The political state was an 'instrument' employed by the interests of private property. The defective nature of society was defended by certain classes; indeed, the existence of an unfree society was in their interests.

The article concluded with a precise summary of the issue at stake in these debates. It was the conflict between private interests and the principle of law. The Assembly had voted, wrote Marx, on whether to sacrifice the latter for the former or *vice versa* and 'interest outvoted law.' In other words, the Assembly, as representative of particular interests, had sacrificed the interests of the whole to its own. In so doing, it had 'completely fulfilled its mission'; that is, 'it represented a definite *particular interest* and treated it as the final goal.' And thus, 'it trampled the law under foot ... [as] *a simple consequence of its task.*'[36]

A few months later, at the end of 1842, Marx summed up his more specific analysis of the political state, its basis in private interest. 'The provincial assemblies, owing to their specific composition, are nothing but an association of particular interests which are privileged to assert their *particular limits* against the state. They are therefore a legitimized self-constituted body of non-state elements in the state. Hence by their very *essence* they are *hostile* towards the state, for the particular in its isolated activity is always the enemy of the whole, since precisely this whole makes it feel its *insignificance* by making it feel its limitations.'[37] Marx clearly saw that the political state represented private interest and that it was antagonistic towards the state, but the basis of this contradiction was posed in terms of tension arising from the non-correspondence of the whole and one part. There was little hint in these articles of the economic basis of the antagonism that Marx would later point to; the analysis was always firmly in the context of *how* existence differed from essence, not *why*.

THE POLITICAL STATE AND REPRESENTATION

There are two questions here, the meaning of electoral representation and the problem of unrepresented classes. Marx treated both by means of the critique.

The essence of electoral representation was (and is) a process of mediation between the citizens of a state and their political embodiment, the government. The issue was first mentioned in the article on the debates on freedom of the press in which Marx pointed to the consideration by the Assembly to keep its debates secret.

Such contradictory action, a public authority keeping secrets from the 'province' it supposedly represented, was, in part, explained by the fact that, no sooner than were representatives elected, the electors 'renounced' their 'own judgement and understanding,' which was then 'solely incorporated in the chosen representatives.' As Marx described it metaphorically: 'the political reason of the province always falls on its own sword as soon as it has made its great invention of the Assembly, but of course to rise again like the phoenix for the next election.'[38] The point of course was that electoral representation as found in the Assembly was limited to selecting and voting. Once the representative had been chosen, the rights of the whole disappeared to rise again only at the next election and in the interim became the privilege of the particular.

This Assembly consisted of estates' representatives, as Marx stressed, not of representatives of the province. In so far, then, as it did represent classes and stratas they were for the most part – as aristocracy, lesser nobility, clergy, landed gentry, and bourgeoisie – not representative of the people as workers and peasants but of 'unreal,' anachronistic, 'non-state spheres of life.' Thus Marx could say that, during Assembly elections, the elections of estates' representatives, the state dissolved 'itself in carrying out the act that should be the supreme act of its internal unification.'[39] Inasmuch as the mass of the people were not represented, the Estates' Assembly did not reflect the state proper; the political state *was* the estates.

Marx went further than simply pointing to the contradictions of political representation; he challenged the very idea of representation. 'In general, to be represented is something passive,' he wrote, and the state that requires representation is 'spiritless' and 'imperilled' as a state. 'Representation must not be conceived as the representation of something that is not the people itself. It must be conceived only as the people's *self-representation* [Selbstvertretung].'[40] This notion was part of Marx's idea of the state; as a necessary relation between the whole and the parts, man could only fulfil his nature by actively partaking in political life; and as soon as the very content of the state became political, the political *form* of the state would disappear.

The question of unrepresented classes was a very topical issue of the time. And in the autumn of 1842 at a convention of French scientists in Strasbourg, there were discussed Fourier-inspired proposals for bettering the position of the 'non-propertied classes.' A conservative German newspaper seized on a speech by one delegate – in which he had compared the demands of 'the estate that owns nothing to share in the wealth of the middle classes, which are now at the helm,' with the struggle of the bourgeoisie against feudalism – and reproached it with the charge of communism, painting the *Rheinische Zeitung* with the same brush for reporting the speech.

Marx replied stating that there was nothing novel in 'the talk in Strasbourg' but, on the contrary, the point made was 'obvious to everyone in Manchester, Paris and Lyon,' cities where large strikes and demonstrations had in the recent past been staged. Marx, then, turned the charge of communism around and asserted that in Germany the ideas of the communists were in fact harmonious with the policies of the reactionaries, who had been advocating, *inter alia*, the creation of 'artisans' corporations' in the hope of mitigating some of the implications of wide unemployment in Germany. 'Who is it that talks of *artisans' corporations*? The reactionaries. The artisans' estate, they say, ought to form a state within a state. Do you find it remarkable that such ideas, expressed in modern language, therefore take the form: "The state ought to be turned into an estate of the artisans"? If for the artisan his estate ought to be the state, and if the modern artisan, like every modern person, understands, and can understand, by the state only the sphere common to all his fellow citizens, how can you combine these two ideas except in the idea of an artisans' state [Handwerkerstaat]?'[41]

It was not only the talk of communists but also that of reactionaries, wrote Marx with an ironic twist, that called for an artisans' state. It was they who advocated the creation of 'corporations,' voluntary organizations for self-help and perhaps even political representation, but which amounted to 'communities' within the state. Such an idea 'expressed in modern language,' that is, through strikes and demonstrations, said Marx, took the form of demands for a state of the artisans' estate. The implicit conclusion within these demands was then drawn out by means of a syllogism. The reactionaries and the communists shared the 'idea of an artisans' state.'

The idea, however, had been worked out in 'philosophical practice.' It did not have a real basis, according to Marx, who in the same article said that 'communist ideas in their present form [do not] possess even *theoretical reality*, and therefore [the *Zeitung*] can still less desire their *practical realization*.' In other words, communist ideas had no apparent basis in the real world and because of this there was no possible means for their realization. Nevertheless, he added, these ideas would be subjected to criticism 'after long and profound study' because ideas, unlike actions, could become 'fetters,' even 'chains,' on the mind.

Even though Marx was not prepared to admit a reality underlying the ideas of communism – little description of working-class activity entered these writings – his argument had unveiled the logic of a workers' state. It was almost a year later after intensive study that he did conclude there was a reality beneath these ideas.

THE CONTRADICTION AND ITS RESOLUTION

By contrasting the real activities of the political state with its essential nature, Marx was able to point to the contradictions within the system of government of Prussia. More than merely demonstrating the 'defects' of a political system, his method also offered a view of the solution and a means to achieve it. If the problem were the disunity of essential elements in existence, the solution was to be found in their unity and the means to this solution in critique itself.

Other writers of the period also sought to create this unity, but only in their theories. Hegel, whose *Science of Logic* was very likely the immediate inspiration of the contemporary critical writing, solved the contradiction by depicting the existing political state as essence, by making the real rational. The Young Hegelians did not follow Hegel in finding unity everywhere in existence, but in resurrecting the contradiction placed it solely in the sphere of theory; their critiques and debates rarely escaped the ethereal realms. The works of Cieszkowski, Hess, and Ruge all contained some utopian ideal or some facsimile of the Hegelian absolute.[42] But for Marx, who was neither utopian nor Hegelian, the solution was to unite the *existing* discordant whole and its parts, the political state and the members of the state, and thereby bring existence into harmony with its essence.

In an article concerning the destitute conditions of vinegrowers in the Mosel district in Germany, published in late January 1843, he set forth the solution. The problem was the inability of the government to help the destitute peasants; there was 'a contradiction between reality and administrative principles.' On the one hand, the administration because of its 'bureaucratic nature' was able to perceive 'the reasons for the distress not in the sphere *administered*, but only in the sphere of *nature* and the *private citizen*, which lies outside the sphere administered.' In other words, the cause of distress from the bureaucratic point of view lay outside the ken of the administration. Whatever the intentions of the administration, the bureaucracy could do nothing because the source of the distress was beyond its legal purview. On the other hand, despite their distress, the vinegrowers' opinion or judgement was based on 'private interest' and therefore could not be accepted as necessarily correct. Nor could the vinegrowers expect bureaucratic principles to be extended or changed to meet their distress when the whole of society was composed of 'a multitude of private interests' which also suffered. Neither the political state as bureaucracy nor the vinegrower as the particular was able to perceive the truth of the situation, to speak for the whole, and bring about a solution.

It was at this point that Marx introduced his proposal: 'In order to solve this difficulty, therefore, the rulers and the ruled alike are in need of a *third* element, which would be *political* without being official, hence not based on bureaucratic premises, an element which would be of a *civil* nature without being bound up with private interests and their pressing need. This supplementary element with the *head of a citizen of the state* and the *heart of a citizen* is the *free press*. In the realm of the press, rulers and ruled alike have an opportunity of criticising their principles and demands, and no longer in a relation of subordination, but on terms of equality as citizens of the state; no longer as *individuals*, but as *intellectual forces*, as exponents of reason.'[43]

The question of a free press was a constant theme in these articles and it was apparent that Marx did see the free press as a plausible, though perhaps not feasible, solution to the contradictions unveiled by his use of critique. It was never advocated in the manner of a campaign, but implicitly, and, explicitly as above, it appeared throughout this period as the 'third element,' the mediator between the divergent elements of existence and therefore the means to bring reality into accord with its essence.

A free press could perform this role because it was the 'embodiment of freedom'; through it a particular interest could be made a general one and the general the particular. The desires and needs of the people could be expressed without bureaucratic or other mitigating influences; truth could be distinguished from untruth by the exercise of criticism; the distinction between rulers and ruled would disappear; and on the foundation of a free press there would be but 'citizens of the state.'[44]

The solution was logically consistent with the analysis *and* it was concrete. But it was also defective: the article in which it was put forth was one of the last Marx wrote and published and was specifically one of the reasons the government heavily censored further articles and ultimately banned the *Rheinische Zeitung*. The political state as the defender of particular interests was not to be persuaded to relinquish its power in the interests of the whole. The critic, moreover, could easily be fettered and ultimately silenced. A free press might well be necessary to a free society, but it was not the *means* to that society.

CONCLUSIONS

Marx's critique of politics begins here in the *Rheinische Zeitung* articles of 1842-43. By employing the critical method, defined at this time as simply the judgement of existence by the essence, he is able to produce revelations which in themselves are sufficient to awaken consciousness about the nature of political institutions, and, in so doing, to make himself an intolerable critic in the eyes of the government.

By comparing the elements of the existing society to their definitions, Marx produces a cogent and insightful analysis of the Prussian state. He shows certain laws to be 'defective,' indeed beyond remedy, when contrasted to the essence of law; censorship of the press is shown to be a 'police measure,' an arbitrary act, when compared to a free press, the essence of the press; the existence of a Christian state is revealed as mass of inconsistencies in light of the rationally defined state; the privileges of wealth and power are demonstrated to be the usurpation of the rights of the people; political representation is revealed as a sham in relation to the idea of 'the people's self-representation.' The range of subject matter is much longer.

The analysis is not solely concerned with demonstrating the 'defects' of reality, that is, with showing how the elements of reality diverge from a rational unity. In some of the later articles in particular, Marx attempts to expand the analysis of these inconsistencies; for example, in his examination of the debates over the law on thefts of wood, he reveals how the political state is pressed into service as an 'instrument' of private interests. The conclusion goes beyond *simply* showing that existence is characterized by open contradiction; it is the first step towards posing the question: why the inconsistency? Nevertheless, the point of this expanded analysis does not go beyond the confines of the method, which are defined by the question how existence differs from essence, not why. Throughout these articles, this level of analysis and the method on which it rested remain fundamentally the same.

The method, as we have seen, presupposes the definition of the state, of society, as a rational whole or an organic unity.[45] It is against this definition and its components that existence is measured and, for this reason, it is the basis on which the validity of the critique of the state rests. Marx employed the definition as if it were a logical necessity, arguing that no society or state can exist outside its members and no individual can be human unless he belongs to society. This relationship he saw as the *conditio sine qua non* of all states or societies and, as such, it comprised the fundamental definition of society. As a definition, it is the starting point of the syllogistic, the content of the critical method as employed here.

The difficulty with the method as used by Marx here is that it is confined to the syllogistic, the judgement, and its starting point, in this case, as the abstract definition of the state. What this means is that the comprehension of the subject matter is limited to demonstrating the conformity or non-conformity of existence and essence and the ways in which the correspondence or lack of it is manifested. He is restricted by this method to grasping *how* reality is 'defective' and is not able to broach the question *why*. This difficulty does not affect the validity of the syllogistic conclusions; but it does prevent an explanation, the discovery of the reason or cause of the 'defectiveness' in the nature of reality itself.

It would appear that the method, as conceived at this time, is not only intended to expose the 'defects' of reality, but also supposed to solve the 'defects' and produce a unity, thereby bringing existence into conformity with its essence. This is the task Marx envisages for the free press, the presumed embodiment of critique. It is to act as the 'third element,' the middle term as it were, which is interposed between 'the rulers and the ruled,' and which mediates the division and creates a unity. This vision is one of the free press as syllogism.

From this depiction of the critical method it is possible to see the meaning of Marx's first formulation of the relation between theory and practice. As he wrote in 1841; 'the *practice* of philosophy is itself *theoretical*. It is the *critique* that measures the individual existence by the essence.' The proper activity of philosophy or science is to grasp the essence or definition, which in reference to the syllogistic is the starting point. The practice of philosophy, then, is the side of judgement, the employment of essence to measure reality, which is to complete the syllogistic. This is critique, a practice which itself is theoretical. Such is the critical method as Marx employs it in the *Rheinische Zeitung* articles.

There are two related problems in this formulation of critique as theoretical practice. The first concerns the relation of essence to existence. Marx appears to assume that, inasmuch as existence contains its essential elements, albeit not in a rational form, it is *capable* of realizing its unity *if* its 'defects' are revealed. The nature of this capacity is never made clear. The second concerns the free press, critique as practice, in the relation between essence and existence. By means of providing a forum for rational discussion, the free press would move the disunited elements of existence towards unity, thereby bringing reality into correspondence with its essence. In a word, divided reality is assumed to be responsive to reason and the free press to be the means for the realization of its unity.

These are difficulties, it should be stressed, which pertain to the side of practice, the idea that critique can realize the unity of the divergent elements it uncovers. If this idea is removed from the definition of critique, critique remains as a method of judgement, of deduction, although this in itself is a limitation inasmuch as critique as defined here does not encompass the process of induction.

Contrary to the expectations of the method as practice, reality in the shape of the Prussian state proved not to be responsive and whatever hopes there were for a free press died with the censorship and enforced closure of the *Rheinische Zeitung*. In the spring of 1843, then, in light of the failure of philosophy to realize itself by means of theoretical practice, both the adequacy of the method and of the comprehension of the nature of the state must have come into question.

By way of a brief digression, it should be added that this notion of critique, the intermediation of the critic as syllogistic, is Hegelian in form alone. If the often repeated characterizations of Marx as Hegelian in this period suggest more than this, they misinterpret the nature of the method. Other than the formal similarity, the differences are fundamental: Hegel is not seeking to change reality, Marx is; Hegel's essence is an active force, an hypostasized concept, Marx's essence is but a definition, an axiomatic definition; Hegel sees in the modern state reason realized, whereas Marx perceives the state and its institutions as defective. The mistakes in his notion of critique in 1842, furthermore, are *not* a question of idealism, properly defined. Similarly, the charge that Marx is here a Young Hegelian misunderstands the nature of his critique of politics in the *Rheinische Zeitung*. Throughout this period, Marx is openly critical of many Young Hegelians, the thrust of his criticism being that their notion of essence, while different from Hegel's, is nevertheless hypostasized, religious.[46]

If the method as an analytical procedure reveals a defective state, it raises questions about these defects which it cannot explain; as a means of change, moreover, the method proves a failure. When the *Rheinische Zeitung* was closed, Marx returned to his studies and to what he called 'a critical re-examination' of Hegel's *Philosophy of Right*, in order 'to dispel the doubts' which had arisen from his critical writing in the journal. The doubts, we surmise, were the two questions posed above, namely, the relation between essence and existence, and the role of critique in the analysis of and attempt to change political relations.

2

State and Civil Society, or the Question of Sovereignty: the 1843 critique of Hegel

In the *Rheinische Zeitung* articles of 1842 and early 1843, Marx viewed the world as a critic. His analysis of diverse political questions comprised almost invariably a demonstration of how the essential elements of existence failed to correspond to their conceptual unity, how the existing political state deviated from the definition of the rational state. Although the method proved insightful, revealing the defects of reality, it was itself defective as a means of resolving the dichotomy.

Use of the critique had revealed to Marx that the political state represented not universal but particular interests. Private interests, in fact, actively employed the 'organs of the state' for their own ends; and political representation was a mere formality which did not change the fact that the provincial assemblies represented private not public interests. In short, behind the defective existence lay entrenched 'material interests' whose hold on political power was not to be dislodged by the words of a critic.

The disclosure that such interests were the foundation of the existing forms of political life could easily lead to doubts about the capacities of critique as defined here for analysis and for political change, about the role of the philosopher as critic. The mere portrayal of the defects of political forms in light of an 'ideal' had shown neither *why* the defects existed nor the path by which to realize social change, although it had revealed that which thwarted the designs of the critic by resisting such change. Thus, to dispel the doubts about the nature of his method and his analysis of the state, it would seem necessary that Marx grasp the actual relation between these political forms and their material content. Such is our surmise about the rationale for the following step in the formation of Marx's analysis of the state.

On resigning as editor from the *Rheinische Zeitung*, Marx 'eagerly seized the opportunity to withdraw' to his study. 'The first work' he undertook 'to dispel the doubts' which assailed him 'was a critical re-examination of the Hegelian philosophy of law' [Hegelische Rechtsphilosophie].[1] The result of this work was a manuscript produced between March and August 1843 containing a detailed analysis of the section concerning the constitutional relations of the state [das innere Staatsrecht] of Hegel's *Philosophy of Right*.[2]

Marx's manuscript, which on its eventual publication in 1927 was entitled *A Contribution to the Critique of Hegel's Philosophy of Right* (hereafter *Critique*), has been treated by almost all commentators by and large in one of two ways. One has been to analyse the text as an application of Feuerbach's method of criticizing Hegel, and the other to present the text as Marx's 'break with Hegel and idealism,' as his 'passage to materialism and communism.' These positions, however, appear to have gained their credibility more through repetition than critical analysis.

On the question of Feuerbach's influence, most writers make much of Marx's supposed adoption of the 'transformative' or 'invertive' method [Umkehrungsmethode]. Some have argued that the *Critique* is simply an exercise in the Feuerbachian method; but leaving aside such extremes, very few venture an analysis of the text without a few paragraphs dedicated to Feuerbach.[3] The main difficulty with this position is the lack of firm evidence to *demonstrate* the alleged influence; it is only asserted.

What is offered as evidence time and again is Marx's not infrequent inversion of the subject and predicate as a way of criticizing Hegel's philosophy. Feuerbach, it is contended, first advanced this method in April 1841 in *The Essence of Christianity* and then more explicitly in 1843 in his *Provisional Theses for the Reform of Philosophy*. The argument was that Hegel had hypostasized his concepts, had made them independent *things* which acted as subjects while the finite world became the predicate. In reality, said Feuerbach, the relation was the inverse: concepts were mere predicates of real, material things. Thus, to 'reform' speculative philosophy, to arrive at the true relation between concepts and reality, it was necessary to invert Hegel's subject and predicate.[4] Commentators juxtapose this method with Marx's analysis of Hegel, but the 'influence of Feuerbach' is never established beyond the argument by analogy.

All this is not to say that Marx was not influenced by Feuerbach; indeed Marx read his work with keen interest and by his own admission was influenced by it; but it is to say that commentators on the *Critique* have stressed the influence beyond any defensible limit. Besides the weakness of argument by analogy, it is not difficult to suggest other shortcomings of the position. The relation of subject and predicate, for instance, is a question as old as philosophy itself, and since antiquity the materialist critique of idealism has pointed to these inverted factors. It cannot be said, then, as many writers imply, that Feuerbach's method was original. Moreover, it is not plausible, as Avineri insists,[5] that Marx had to wait until Feuerbach revealed his method because he lacked 'a methodological device' with which 'to tackle' Hegel's philosophy. Not only was the inversion of subject and predicate an ancient theme, but also it was known to Marx who employed it well before April 1841 in the preparatory work to his dissertation in defence of the materialism of Epicurus. 'All philosophers,' he wrote, 'have made the predicates themselves into subjects.'[6] A further point on Feuerbach's influence, usually overlooked,[7] concerns the limits of his use of the method. Essentially, Feuerbach's critique of Hegel begins and ends with the charge of formalism and its demonstration. With Marx, as we shall see below, criticism of Hegel goes far beyond this charge.

One of the assumptions underlying the stress on Feuerbach is the common notion that Marx was an idealist or Hegelian prior to writing the *Critique*; in other words, it is suggested that Feuerbach provided Marx with the key to a materialist critique of Hegel. This argument is similarly only asserted; and though much has been written about the alleged passage from idealism to materialism, the arguments are made in a near vacuum of evidence.[8] They overlook, moreover, at least two points. First, Marx's doctoral dissertation, which was submitted two years prior to the *Critique* and which contrasted two theories of materialism, can be read as an implied criticism of Hegel and certainly of idealism. As pointed out, Marx wanted to defend his notion of philosophy against 'theologizing philosophy' which may be seen as a reference to Hegel. And his attempt in the dissertation to establish a material foundation for the existence of mind, self-consciousness, and for ideas, the content of self-consciousness, can only be read as the inverse of the idealist relation between thought and being.[9] If this interpretation is correct it is evident that the argument that Marx was idealist or Hegelian in 1843 is problematic.

Second, philosophical idealism understands the mind, spirit, idea, god, etc., *as primary* in the relation of thought to being. It would be better called 'idea-ism' to avoid the ambiguity entailed in Marx's discussion of the ideal *as essence*, particularly in the *Zeitung* articles. Essence, as Marx uses it, is *dependent* on being and has no existence 'as such' outside the real minds of existing people. It can be said that Marx does not employ the concept of essence or ideal as the determining or primary factor in any of his published work, that he is clearly a materialist in 1841, and, therefore, that it makes no sense to speak of a transition from idealism to materialism in the 1843 *Critique*.

Much is made of Marx's alleged liberalism in this period; commentators who hold this view appear to be unaware that political theory in Germany had made many criticisms of the logic of liberalism by 1800 and that Hegel's *Philosophy of Right*, first published in 1821, contains a trenchant critique of the rudiments of liberalism.[10] A great deal is also made by commentators of Marx's supposed change from a position of radical democracy to his first positive discussion of communism in the *Critique*. This question, however, is somewhat more involved than the above issues and will be treated as it arises in the text below.

If, then, the 1843 *Critique* is arguably neither an exercise in Feuerbachian method nor 'a break with idealism and Hegel,' it must be asked what its significance is in Marx's development. Part of the answer has already been alluded to; to wit, Marx's desire to understand the nature and implications of the relation between private interests and the political state, and to comprehend the shortcomings of his method. But this in turn raises a question about the choice of Hegel's *Philosophy of Right*: why this political treatise and not another? We shall attempt an answer to this question and then return to a fuller discussion of Marx's intention in writing the *Critique*.

In *The Philosophy of History*, Hegel defines history as the progressive realization of the Idea, of Reason, of the unity of the universal and particular. This unity as actuality, he argues, is to be found only in the modern constitutional monarchy.[11] All other historical forms of state are imperfect realizations, manifestations one-sidedly emphasizing either the universal or the particular.

In Plato's *Republic*, for instance, social position is determined by the 'government,'[12] through a system of examinations; individuals are assigned occupational classes according to their 'nature.' Here there is no room for subjective, individual freedom; the *formal* embodiment or representation of the body politic stands as absolute. Thus, the 'principle of particularity' in so far as it may arise must do so in *opposition* to the principle of universality.[13] The universal as the political state, as form, seeks to deny the particular as individual freedom, as its very content.

It is with the coming of Christianity, writes Hegel, that the principle of subjective freedom is first established.[14] The principle *by itself* knows no limits; it is 'measureless excess' if unrestricted by the universal. In terms of political theory, it is embodied in liberalism, which says Hegel amounts to 'the atomistic principle, that which insists upon the sway of individual wills.'[15] By positing the particular as absolute, liberalism is not compatible with the notion of a rational state; it degrades the concept of government as the unity of the general and particular, making it a mere mechanism for the protection of property and the regulation of contractual relations. Here subjective freedom of the particular stands opposed to the restraint of the universal. The particular as content seeks to deny a unity, a universal, as form.

Now, in the *Philosophy of Right*, Hegel attempts to overcome the opposition of the universal and particular as found in the *Republic* and in liberalism, to demonstrate their unity in what he calls the rational state. Rationality in the state comprises, according to Hegel, (*a*) 'so far as its content is concerned,' a unity of subjective and objective freedom; i.e., the will of the particular is identical with the will of the universal, and, (*b*) 'so far as its form is concerned,' legislation and principles, objective order, which reflect the unity of wills of subjective freedom.[16] Thus, the form and content of the rational state are interdependent; they demand each other, unlike their relation in Plato's *Republic* or in liberal constitutions.

But Hegel does not postulate the rational state merely as the resolution of past theoretical failures. Just as these theories reflect the essential characteristics of states of the past and present, the rational state is seen by Hegel as the *essence* of the modern state as constitutional monarchy. The *Philosophy of Right* is an attempt to depict the stage (Hegel implied the final one) at which the historical realization of reason had arrived in the constitutional monarchy. Here, he feels, is the first historical manifestation of rationality in the state.

Hegel, in fact, portrays the state of his own time, Marx argues, and not the essential, rational state. His depiction therefore contains all the contradictions and contrarieties found in that state (and indeed many found in the modern constitutional monarchy of today). Hence, his political philosophy, first, claims to have resolved the historical dilemma over the relation between the universal and particular and, second, paints in considerable detail an archetype of the existing state of his day. No other political theorist prior to or contemporaneous with Hegel surpasses his work in this latter aspect.

It was quite logical, then, that Marx should choose to re-examine the *Philosophy of Right* in order to dispel at least one of his 'doubts,' which we surmised concerned the relation of private property to the political state. Hegel's work asserted the unity of private and public elements and constituted the most advanced and complete analysis of the modern state. If there were contradictions in the existing modern state, therefore, they could be revealed and their nature analysed by measuring Hegel's depiction of this existing state against the rationality he purported to find in it.

But how was Marx to approach this 'critical re-examination' of Hegel's political philosophy? The answer, usually given in terms of Feuerbach's so-called transformative method, is more plausibly to be found in a letter written by Marx to Arnold Ruge in March 1842, a full year before the presumed actual date of writing the *Critique*.[17] In it he says he intends 'a criticism of Hegelian natural law, in so far as it concerns the *internal political system*. The central point is the struggle against *constitutional monarchy* as a hybrid which from beginning to end contradicts and abolishes itself.' To this he adds a somewhat cryptic phrase: '*Res publica* is quite untranslatable into German.' It is suggested that in these sentences, and not in Feuerbach, is to be found Marx's fundamental approach to Hegel's *Philosophy of Right* in the *Critique*.

The first point in the letter is that the constitutional monarchy is a self-contradictory, self-abolishing *hybrid*. Anything comprised of heterogeneous or incongruous elements is a hybrid. In a political context, as in a parliamentary 'hybrid-bill,' the concept refers to a combination of incompatibles, of public and private elements. Given this, it is reasonable to assume that Marx intended to criticize Hegel's claim to have resolved the opposition of the universal and particular in the constitutional monarchy, that the 'resolution' was in truth a hybrid, a heterogeneous mixture and not a rational unity. And furthermore, that he intended to show that the persisting contradiction could only be resolved by the abolition of the constitutional monarchy itself.

This raises the second point; namely, the meaning of *res publica* and its 'untranslatable' nature. In the work of Cicero, with whom Marx was most certainly familiar, the phrase refers to that state which is 'a moral community,' an association in which law reflects common agreement, which is truly, as one writer translated it, 'the affair of the people.'[18] If this were the meaning Marx intended, then, it would appear that he was planning to counterpoise *res publica* to the constitutional monarchy as the solution to the hitherto contradictory relation of the universal and particular. In this sense, *res publica* represents the 'ideal,' essential, social nature of man, in which the political is subsumed, and against which the 'defects' of constitutional monarchy can be measured. It is untranslatable in 1842 because he knows no concept which adequately expresses the synthesis it contains. In 1843, in the *Critique*, it becomes democracy or 'true' democracy and in 1844, communism; yet throughout this period, its content remains fundamentally the same.

Bearing these notions in mind, the self-contradictory hybrid and *res publica*, we can approach the *Critique* more or less as Marx approached it. In so doing, we can uncover the very nature of his critique of the modern state. Our interest is not, however, the complete work in *all* its aspects, rather it is two-fold: first, to draw out Marx's critique of Hegel's political philosophy in so far as it is a critique of the modern state, but not as the logic of deduction of the categories of the state; and second, to expound Marx's evolving position on the nature of critique as a method.

The questions that concern Marx are dealt with by Hegel in the first part of a subsection of the *Philosophy of Right* entitled 'The State [Der Staat].' This part contains his discussion of 'Constitutional Law' or internal policy [Das innere Staatsrecht] which is itself subdivided, the first division being 'The Internal Constitution as Such [Innere Verfassung für sich].' Included under this title are: 'The Crown [Die fürstliche Gewalt],' 'The Executive [Die Regierungs-Gewalt],' and 'The Legislature [Die gesetzgebende Gewalt].' In these sections is to be found Hegel's analysis of the relation between the whole and its parts, of 'ethical life [Sittlichkeit],' as epitomized in the constitutional monarchy. Their content concerns, in a word, the question of sovereignty, the structure of power and authority in the body politic.[19]

The first three paragraphs of the section on 'The State' (257-59) constitute a preamble to the discussion of the internal policy. They define the state in terms which move from the abstract to the concrete, but each stage contains the question of the relation between the universal and the particular. It culminates with the stage where the Idea of the state is 'immediate actuality,' where it is 'the individual state as a self-dependent organism.'[20]

It is precisely the analysis of this concept of the state as *organism* which comprises the content of Hegel's section entitled 'Das innere Staatsrecht' and the subject matter of Marx's *Critique*. For this reason, it is worth citing here at length a definition given by W.T. Stace, which contains the principal elements of this concept: the state is:

an organism which is self-differentiating in such a manner that the life of the whole appears in all the parts. This means that the true life of the parts, i.e., the individuals, is found in and is identical with the life of the whole, the state. The state is thus only the individual himself objectified and eternalized by the elimination of his merely accidental and ephemeral features and the retention of what is universal in him. The individual is *implicitly* universal. Universality is his essence. The state is the *actual* universal, and is thus simply the individual actualized and objectified. Thus the state is no alien authority which imposes itself externally upon the individual and suppresses his individuality. On the contrary the state is the individual himself. And it is only in the state that his individuality is realised. For this reason the state is the supreme embodiment of freedom, for in being determined by it the individual is now wholly determined by his essential self, by that which is true and universal in him.[21]

The contradiction in this depiction, as in Hegel's concept, it should be noted, is the assumed existence of the whole, separate from the individual, despite the assertion that the state is the individual himself and that the state is an organic unity. We shall see below how this contradiction figures in Marx's critique.

Having arrived at the stage of the actual, immediate state, Hegel now, in the following twelve paragraphs, proceeds to examine the *general* relations between the whole and the parts. The specific institutions which embody these relations, namely, the monarch, the executive, and the legislature, are treated afterwards. Thus, in paragraph 260, where Hegel begins his exposition of the internal polity, he begins by defining the concrete relations of the universal and particular, 'the state,' he writes, 'is the actuality of concrete freedom.'

By 'concrete freedom' Hegel is referring to the relations of organic unity as the level of actuality. The particular interests of individuals are fulfilled or truly free only in so far as they reflect the interests of the universal, and the latter embody freedom only in so far as they reflect the interests of the former. This, moreover, says Hegel, is the very 'principle of modern states' and characterizes it as having 'prodigious strength and depth' because of this interdependent nature of the whole and its parts.[22]

This is the point at which the extant portion of Marx's manuscript implicitly begins, and the first issue to be touched upon is the nature of Hegel's 'concrete freedom.' Juxtaposed to this concept as the 'identity' of the spheres of particular and general interests, Marx places in parenthesis the words '*sein sollenden, zweischlächtigen.*'[23]

With the former, Marx is pointing to the fact that this 'identity' is an 'ought,' an 'essence,' which, as in paragraphs 257 to 259, is an hypostasized concept. The *assertion* that it finds actuality in the state does not suffice as demonstration of its reality; 'concrete freedom' remains an 'essence' unconnected with the real world. In the second word, it is apparent Marx does not see a 'dual identity' (as one translation would have it) in 'concrete freedom' but rather a thing of two embattled sides or, as it were, an 'identity' consisting of an internal *duel*. These two points, in a general sense, set the stage for the entire *Critique*. In other words, implied in these two concepts are most of the fundamental criticisms that Marx will make of Hegel in this text. That is to say, Hegel's 'organic unity' is not a reality but only an 'essence' without relation to the real world, and the reality of what he does describe is a self-contradictory hybrid.

Hegel proceeds in paragraph 261 to qualify the organic relation. On the one hand, he describes it, as in paragraph 260, as a relation in which the 'spheres of civil law and personal welfare and the family and civil society' find their 'immanent end' in the state. They, as the 'spheres' of particularity, are related to the state, the general sphere, as means to an end. On the other hand, 'over against' [gegen] the former, the state stands as an '*external* necessity and their superior authority' and the spheres of particular interest are described as 'subordinate' and 'dependent.' Thus, at the same time, the whole is related to its parts as 'immanent end' *and* 'external necessity.'

The first substantive issue Marx takes up is the meaning of 'external necessity.' By and large, he simply delineates Hegel's qualification of the nature of organic unity (or concrete freedom) and draws out the implications. External necessity, by definition, must dominate that which is secondary or subordinate. The relation of the state as external necessity to the spheres of civil society, etc., is therefore *contrary* to the *essential* relation of the whole and the parts, to the inner nature of the organism. The very relations of subordination and dependence, writes Marx, denote 'an "external," *imposed*, illusory identity,' quite the opposite of a spontaneous and coherent unity. Besides revealing an involuntary union, 'subordination' and 'dependence' also point to 'the aspect of estrangement [der Entfremdung] within the unity.' Though this comment is not developed, Marx obviously sees the state in Hegel's exposition as objectified universality which assumes an *external* existence and stands opposed to the spheres of the particular as an 'autonomous' entity. The whole of the above argument is summed up in a phrase: Hegel, writes Marx, sets up 'an unresolved *antinomy*. *On the one hand*, external necessity, *on the other hand* immanent end.'[24]

In the following section of the *Critique*, which examines paragraphs 262 to 274 of the *Philosophy of Right* up to Hegel's consideration of the monarch, Marx, in effect, elaborates his analysis of the two sides of this antinomy. Commentators usually treat this section, it should be added, primarily as a critique of Hegel's method.[25] Here, it is true, Marx appears to focus on Hegel's idealism, i.e., the inversion of subject and object, but to see this as a critique primarily of method or logic is to miss the specific issue in question, which is Hegel's depiction of the relation of the whole and its parts, of the nature of sovereignty. It is because this relation in the *Philosophy of Right* is unfolded in terms of Hegel's idealist logic that Marx's criticism appears to be primarily one of method. For our purposes, the criticism of method must be viewed primarily as a means for criticizing Hegel's depiction of the relations of the body politic.

The reason Hegel introduces the state as 'external necessity' in paragraph 261 comes clear in paragraph 262. 'Over against' the spheres of particularity, the idea of the state is an 'external necessity' because it is through the spontaneous activity of this *idea*, the 'ethical Idea,' realizing itself that the family and civil society are produced, first as ideal spheres and then as the 'finite phase' whose material content is 'assigned' by the 'actual Idea.'[26] The idea of the state is the active subject which 'separates off from itself' its 'finite phase' as predicate.

Marx begins his commentary on this paragraph by revealing the logical inconsistencies of Hegel's argument. But his main criticism deals with the relation of the state to the family and civil society. 'The idea is made the subject,' he writes, 'and the *actual* [wirkliche] relation of family and civil society to the state is conceived as its *internal imaginary* activity.' In truth, however, 'family and civil society are the premises of the state; they are the genuinely active elements, but in speculative philosophy things are inverted.' This contrast is made several times by Marx: on the one hand, 'Family and civil society constitute *themselves* as the state. They are the driving force,' and on the other hand, 'According to Hegel, they are on the contrary *produced* by the actual idea.'[27]

This is no mere contrast. In the former case, the particular (family and civil society) is related to the general (the state) as subject and object. Since the general can *only* exist as determined by the particular, the relation of subject and object here presents no inconsistency. In the latter case, however, there are difficulties. With Hegel, the starting point is the idea of the state. But it can only find actuality by dividing into family and civil society, which form its 'finite phase,' a necessary step before returning to itself as 'infinite actual mind.' As Marx points out, however, family and civil society are a *conditio sine qua non* for the actual idea of the state. There is, therefore, a problem here: 'the condition is postulated as the conditioned, the determinant as the determined, the producing factor as the product of its product.'[28] By starting with an abstract logical category, Hegel falls upon an unsolvable inconsistency; his subject becomes the predicate of its own predicate. Phrased another way: the necessity behind his 'external necessity' can no longer be seen as the spontaneous activity of the idea but is in fact the family and civil society. Thus, Marx is able to show that the state as 'external necessity' is inconsistent with the notion of organic unity.

In his commentary on the next several paragraphs Marx makes similar points; namely, Hegel inverts the subject and predicate and therefore the nature of the transition between the two. The actual transition of the particular into the general is not treated as it actually evolves, but is treated as a transition which begins in abstract realms and descends to the real world. The same argument is made against Hegel's definition of the state as organism.

By presenting the state as an organism, Hegel asserts the unity of the whole and its parts. And to see the 'political constitution [die politische Verfassung]' as embodying the organic unity, 'to look upon the variety of authorities no longer as something (in)organic, but as a living and rational differentiation' is, writes Marx, 'a great advance.'[29] It is because, in promulgating this view, political theory comes very close to grasping the essence of the state. Prior to this, it had generally sought to deny the state's organic nature and instead stressed, as does liberalism, a mechanical unity which depicts the whole as the mere sum of its parts, or, as does Plato's *Republic*, an absolute unity which makes little or no allowance for particular freedom. With Hegel, however, the state as organism combined both the universal and particular in a mutually interdependent, rational unity.

Despite the importance of 'this discovery,' as Marx put it, Hegel's presentation of it is not without its problems, which by and large derive from his idealism. The actual relation, says Marx, is established in the 'aspects' or 'facets' of the constitution moving as subject towards organic unity, as predicate. But Hegel's design is just the opposite: 'the idea is made the subject, and the distinct aspects and their actuality are conceived as the idea's development and product.'[30] There are two difficulties that arise from proceeding in this manner; i.e., beginning with an abstract idea of organism, and out of it developing the political constitution.

First, the abstract idea of organism is as applicable to an animal as to a political organism. There is nothing in the idea itself to differentiate one from the other. It is no more justifiable to deduce a political constitution from the idea of organism than to deduce the interrelation of the head, legs, and body of an animal. Hegel has not provided the *differentia specifica* of the political and therefore his 'deduction' of the constitution is a deduction of 'mere names.' In short, says Marx, this approach gives us the 'appearance' of understanding, but because the 'specific character' of the constitution is simply an abstract predicate, we are left uncomprehending.

The second problem is perceived in a stylistic device of Hegel's; namely, the insertion of the word 'thus' at the point of transition between the abstract idea of organism and its specific content. For Hegel the word serves as a bridge allowing his concepts to descend from the ideal world into the real. But Marx points to the emptiness of such a 'transition,' saying that Hegel has 'not advanced one step beyond the general concept of ... the organism.'[31] He adds, 'no bridge has ever been built *whereby one could pass from the general idea of organism to the specific idea of the organism of the state or the political constitution*, and no such bridge can ever be built.'[32]

What Hegel does, Marx continues, is to 'dissolve the "political constitution" into the general abstract idea of "organism," ' and to begin his formal analysis at this point making it appear that he derives real content from his abstractions. But these abstractions are hypostasized, cut from their real roots in materiality, and given a form from the sphere of pure logic. Hegel employs them as logical concepts, moving them according to precepts and rules drawn from this sphere. The result, according to Marx, is not a philosophy of the state but of logic. The real subject of interest is 'not the logic of the matter, but the matter of the logic.' 'The logic does not serve to prove the state, but the state to prove the logic.' 'In place of the concept of the constitution,' Hegel gives us 'the constitution of the concept.'[33]

In this section of the *Philosophy of Right*, it is Hegel's intention to describe the general relations of the universal and the particular in the modern state, to elaborate his notion of the state 'as the actuality of concrete freedom.' Marx's criticism up to this point, which is far more penetrating than we have been able to show, exposes Hegel's tenuous fabrication of the actuality of 'concrete freedom.' His purpose, however, is not to dismiss the idea of organic unity *per se*, it is only to dismantle Hegel's idealistic construction of organic unity in the modern state, the constitutional monarchy.

In this light, there are at least two conclusions which can be drawn from Marx's treatment of Hegel so far. First, by making his starting point, his subject, the abstract state, Hegel incurs an irresolvable inconsistency for his theory. His abstraction demands a basis in the 'finite' world, but in this requirement it negates itself as subject and becomes the predicate of its own alleged predicate. No such inconsistency arises when the subject is the concrete specific parts with the concrete whole as predicate. Here the whole has no more significance than the embodiment of the universal which arises from the particular. Marx's demonstration of this inconsistency, moreover, reveals the problem with conceiving the state as an external necessity over against the family and civil society. By deriving the state from outside the relation of the general and particular, Hegel introduces something external to the essential duality, the mediated unity of subject and predicate. Here is the source of Hegel's unresolved antinomy between the state as external necessity and immanent end.

Second, and again because he begins with an abstraction, this time the general idea of organism, Hegel cannot effect a transition, except through stylistic means, from this general idea to the specific idea of organic political relations. Without *political differentia specifica*, which do not inhabit the general idea of organism any more than the parts of an animal's body, there is no possibility of deducing the political organism. The import of this criticism is that Hegel's organism, his concrete freedom, or immanent end remains an essence, an idea, which has no means for becoming either specifically political or concrete.

SOVEREIGNTY: THE ONE OR THE MANY?

From these general relations which constitute the internal polity, Hegel turns to an examination of the constitution proper 'for itself' [Innere Verfassung für sich], and analyses the interrelations of the crown, the executive, and the legislature, in that order.

In the first paragraph on the 'monarch's authority,' Hegel says that in this authority is contained three elements. The first two[34] are part of the internal polity and so, with respect to these elements, says Marx, the authority of the monarch is consonant with the organic nature of the state. But the third element, 'the element of final decision,' makes monarchical authority a 'self-determining' subject, and this is inconsistent with the first two. As Marx puts it: 'Insofar as this element of "final decision" or "absolute self-determination" is separated from the [first two: the constitutional elements], we have *actual will* as *arbitrariness*.'[35] In other words, the power of final decision is incompatible with, indeed the very opposite of, rational authority; the former is external necessity and the latter is immanent end.

This inconsistency is found only *within* the sphere of monarchical authority. This is so because Hegel makes the organic nature of the state into an 'ideality [Idealität]'; that is, the constitutional elements, that which comprises the political state [der politische Staat] and embody the state's unity, are made into an abstraction, 'the substantial unity.' It is all very well to have an idea of organic unity, but, as Marx argues, a rational state calls for a 'conscious' relation of the whole and the parts, whereas a 'substantial unity' is an *immediacy* with 'purely internal' or 'purely external' relations.[36]

The idea of organism, this ideality, then, stands apart from the particular; it is 'linked with' the latter only 'formally and accidentally.' Hegel's 'state functions and activities' stand in 'abstract isolation' and 'the particular individual in antithesis to them.' But, writes Marx, Hegel forgets that in reality the two are linked by a bond of substance: the *essence* of the particular person is his 'social quality [soziale Qualität]' and state activities and functions 'are nothing but modes of being and modes of action of the social qualities of men.'[37]

This ideality, in effect the idea of sovereignty, of self-determination, is therefore 'not developed into a conscious rational system,' but appears either as 'an external constraint imposed by the prevailing power' or 'as a blind, unconscious result of self-seeking.'[38] It becomes a rational actuality only in times of war or emergency. Sovereignty, the 'essential feature of the state,' thus, becomes a 'mystical substance' cut off from its actual source, its true subjects, its real dependence on the particular, and stands opposed to the latter.

Having 'deduced,' or at least defined, his idea of sovereignty, Hegel is now ready to 'deduce' the monarch. The deduction is straightforward; it is merely asserted; he says that sovereignty, which is so far only an idea of universality, can come into existence as only self-determining subjectivity, embodying the power of 'final decision.' This subjectivity, 'the decisive element of the whole,' is *therefore* 'but *one* individual, the monarch.'

Since the criticism of this 'deduction' by Marx and others[39] is somewhat involved and not pertinent to our task we shall pass over the details. Suffice to say, in Marx's words, 'Hegel is concerned to present the monarch as the true "God-man," as the *actual incarnation* of the Idea.'

By defining the monarch as 'the personality of the state' and 'sovereignty incarnate,' however, Hegel creates some difficulties for his theory. If at first sovereignty is but an idea in the possession of no one, and enters the realm of existence only as the sovereign person, the monarch, then, it is clear that 'all other people are excluded from this sovereignty ... and from political consciousness.'[40] If, moreover, the distinguishing characteristic of the monarch and the reason he embodies sovereignty is the element of 'the final decision' ('actual will' as arbitrariness, as Marx put it), then, sovereignty as 'personified reason' reduces to the maxim of Louis XIV: 'L'état, c'est moi.'

Hegel's alleged deduction of the monarch as the embodiment of sovereignty – as the 'One,' as a unit – amounts to mere assertion and as such it rests on suspect logical grounds. After criticizing the logic,[41] Marx turns to the political issues entailed. 'If the king is the "actual sovereignty of the state,"' he writes ironically, 'it ought to be possible for "the king" to count as an "independent state" also in external relations, even without the people.' By incarnating sovereignty in the monarch, Hegel makes the people extraneous to the actuality of national sovereignty – an absurd proposition. 'But if he is sovereign,' continues Marx, 'inasmuch as he represents the unity of the nation, then he himself is only the representative, the symbol, of national sovereignty.' This is the only *logically* plausible interpretation of sovereignty, on the basis of which Marx concludes: 'National sovereignty does not exist by virtue of him, but he on the contrary exists by virtue of it.'[42]

But this Hegel will not admit; 'sovereignty belongs to the *state*,' that is, it is a question pertaining to the *whole* and *not* the parts, the people. Thus, continues Hegel, to speak of *the sovereignty of the people* 'in opposition to the sovereignty existing in the monarch' is a 'wild idea,' a 'confused notion.' The confusion, however, is Hegel's, writes Marx. But in the confusion are two central issues about sovereignty. The first is posited as a query by Marx: 'Is not that sovereignty which is claimed by the monarch an illusion? Sovereignty of the monarch or sovereignty of the people – that is the question.' Second, although the *same* sovereignty cannot exist in the monarch and the people at the same time, it is possible to speak of two *different* 'entirely contradictory concepts of sovereignty, the one a sovereignty such as can come to exist in a monarch, the other as can come to exist only in a *people* ... One of the two is an untruth, even if an existing untruth.'[43] The two issues are different but the question at the heart of each is the same: can sovereignty whatever its appearance be anything in essence but sovereignty of the people?

This is the point in the *Critique* at which Marx introduces the notion of democracy. It is juxtaposed to Hegel's constitutional monarchy in which sovereignty is severed from its base and stands embodied in the monarch in opposition to the people. Democracy, on the contrary, is sovereignty of the people; it is actual organic unity in which the whole is related to the parts as a reflection of the latter and as such is dependent on them and changes as they change. In this sense, democracy is the essence of sovereignty and as such is the 'solved riddle of all constitutions.'[44]

Marx means by this that, although all constitutions attempt to define the relations of the general and the particular, they inevitably emphasize one side to the detriment of the other side. Out of this distortion arise political inconsistencies and logical contradictions and profoundly intricate attempts to overcome them. But these riddles can be identified and examined for what they are *in light of* the notion of democracy, of the essential relations of the whole and parts, of the social organism.

It is not our intention to pursue Marx's meaning of democracy at this point because it will be dealt with in the conclusions. But it is important to note that Marx's use of the method of critique in 1841-42, to expose the defects of the Prussian government, is now being employed to analyse the incongruities of Hegel's depiction of the modern state. Democracy, as organic unity, is the essence of all constitutions, which includes, of course, the constitutional monarchy.

The main point in comparing the constitutional monarchy to 'true' democracy is to show the deficiencies of the former. In democracy, the authority

of the monarch, as a 'state function,' would be established in a 'fluid' movement of the elements of the state. In the monarchy, it is established by
heredity, a fact which means the monarch is made 'of different stuff.' But,
says Marx, 'in a rational organism the head cannot be of iron and the body of
flesh.' The whole organism must be 'fluid' and no one element or member
can stand outside the mutual interdependence.[45]

The contrast also allows Marx to argue that 'the constitution of the constitutional monarchy is *irresponsible*'; that is, there is no moral accountability;
the constitution is embodied in one person whose distinguishing characteristic is arbitrariness. By contrast, the democratic constitution is by definition
responsible; it is the essence of accountability, being the reflection of the
rational interaction of the members of the state.

In the final analysis, Hegel does not have an organism in the constitutional
monarchy; 'all he has is merely a mass of particular spheres connected by an
external necessity.'[46] It is only in the monarch, the external necessity, that
the relation of one private person to the whole is realized. The one as sovereignty incarnate stands over and opposed to the many.

BUREAUCRACY: UNIVERSALITY AS MERE FORM

In Hegel's constitutional monarchy, as in the modern state, the 'spheres of
particularity' are delimited by an 'external necessity.' How this delimitation
is accomplished, how the constitution is administered, is the question Hegel
now takes up. It is the role of the executive which is to be expounded.

Hegel's treatment, however, is 'the usual explanation,' says Marx;[47] in
fact, it 'does not deserve to be called a philosophical exposition' because
'most of the paragraphs could stand word for word in the Prussian Common
Law [preussischen Landrecht].' There is, moreover, no logical deduction
that executive functions must be the prerogative of a 'particular, separate
power' in the state, rather than 'one function, one attribute of state citizens
as such' as would be the case in democracy. Furthermore, the only philosophical point Hegel makes about executive power is that it is the 'subsumption' of the 'particular under the universal [Besonderen unter das
Allgemeine].' And even the use of this concept is inverted: Hegel does not
ask if this 'subsumption' is an 'adequate' or 'rational' relation but posits the
concept and 'contents himself with finding a corresponding existent for it.'
He gives, says Marx, '*a political body to his logic*: he does not give *the logic of
the body politic*.'[48]

The 'subsumption' of the particular in the universal is not a singular task
but one that is two-fold. It involves, on the one hand, the relation of corpora-

tions and local bodies to the government and, on the other hand, the relation of the executive to civil society. They constitute in Hegel's opinion two forms of 'identity' of the state and civil society. But, as Marx attempts to show, they merely hide the fundamental duality of the modern state as Hegel depicts it.

The one side, then, concerns corporations, which deserve a brief explication. According to Hegel, they comprise, after the family, the 'ethical basis' of the state.[49] He means by this that in *limited* particular spheres within civil society, corporations unite the general and particular. They may be understood to refer to 'trade guilds' or even non-economic organizations such as 'religious bodies, learned societies and sometimes town councils.'[50] In question here is how the particular is subordinated to the general in corporations and local bodies.

The answer Hegel gives is straightforward: the subordination or subsumption is 'effected by a mixture of popular election by those interested [,] with appointment and ratification by higher authority.' In other words, the elected representatives of particular interests and appointed officials who comprise the 'mixed selection' of administrators in corporations and local bodies constitute, in Marx's words, 'the *first relationship* between civil society and state or executive, their *first identity*.'[51] But how superficial, comments Marx: it is only a 'mixture' which is a *mechanical* blend, as mixed as the components are compatible. It is a mixture, continues Marx, in which 'private property and the interest of the particular spheres' stand 'against the higher interest of the state.' The 'antithesis between private property and state' remains; the mixed selection of officials does not *resolve* the duality, it merely constitutes a 'compromise, a treaty, a *confession* of unresolved dualism.'[52] Hegel has not demonstrated the subsumption of the particular in the universal but has described a concessionary agreement which *mitigates* but does not resolve the antithesis.

The second side of this subsumption involves the 'state proper,' the executive civil servants [die exekutiven Staatsbeamten] and their relation to civil society. Hegel poses the relation in the following way: the spheres of particularity in civil society are 'seen to' or 'superintended by' the 'representatives of executive power' and 'higher advisory officials.'

The latter, comments Marx, are 'not "of," but "against" civil society.' 'The state does not reside in, but outside civil society.' Therefore, one cannot speak of a unity for the antithesis persists. Not only is the antithesis 'not transcended [nicht aufgehoben]' but it 'has become a "legal," "fixed," antithesis.' As Marx elaborates: 'By means of deputies the "state" – an entity alien and ulterior to the *essence* of civil society – asserts itself over against civil society. The "police," the "judiciary" and the "administration" are not deputies of civil society itself, in and through whom it administers [verwaltet] its *own* general interest, but representatives of the state for the administration of the state over against civil society.'[53]

Hegel's attempt to get around this persistent antithesis is found in his discussion of the method of recruitment of civil servants. Since there is 'no immediate natural link' between the official and his office – that is, unlike the monarch, civil servants are not 'born' to office – there must be 'objective' means for their appointment; and these are 'knowledge and proof of ability.' 'Such proof,' argues Hegel, 'guarantees that the state will get what it requires' and 'guarantees to every citizen the opportunity to devote himself to the general estate.'

It is this 'opportunity,' writes Marx, that constitutes Hegel's 'second affirmative relationship between civil society and the state, the *second identity*.' But like the first, it is 'very superficial' and 'dualistic.' It is analogous to the chance 'every Catholic' has 'to become a priest; i.e., to separate himself from the laity as from the world.' Pursuing the analogy, Marx asks rhetorically: 'Does the clergy confront the Catholic as an other-worldly power any less on that account? The fact that anyone has the opportunity to acquire the right of *another* sphere merely proves that in his *own* sphere this right has no reality.'[54]

Far from demonstrating Hegel's case, that the particular is 'subsumed' in the universal, this 'opportunity' proves the opposite, that the particular and universal are mutually exclusive and antagonistic. This 'defect' is brought into focus when Marx contrasts this division in the modern state with the unity of the 'true' state: 'In the genuine state ['Im wahren Staat'] it is not a question of the opportunity of every citizen to devote himself to the general estate as one particular estate, but the capacity of the general estate to be really general – that is, to be the estate of every citizen.'[55]

According to Hegel, the realization of the opportunity comes through knowledge and proof of ability – i.e., examinations – but, in the final analysis, 'the selection of a particular individual ... is the prerogative of the monarch.' In other words, the opportunity itself is delimited by the arbitrariness of the last word of sovereignty incarnate.

The actual separation of civil society and the state is revealed not only in this arbitrariness but also in the examinations. Here 'political knowledge' is made the criterion for positions in the civil service. But political knowledge, protests Marx, 'is a requirement without which a person in the state lives outside the state, cut off from himself, from the air.' 'In a rational state [In einem vernünftigen Staat],' continues Marx, this could not be so because in such a state everyone would need to be 'political,' that is, conscious of the relation of the general to the particular. There would be here, suggests Marx, examinations for shoemakers but not for citizenship because that would be to examine the very essence of man, his social being itself. In Hegel's modern state, the examination is 'nothing but a Masonic rite, the legal recognition of a knowledge of citizenship as a privilege.'[56]

Once appointed to an official position, writes Hegel, the civil servant must be 'freed' from 'subjective dependence and influence' in order to pursue the higher aims of the state. This is accomplished by guaranteeing his livelihood, his salary. And this, says Marx, is where 'the *real identity* of civil society and the state is established.' Re-phrasing with evident sarcasm, he writes: 'The civil servants' *pay* [der Sold] is the highest identity which Hegel constructs.'

It is not an identity at all; the fact that 'state activities' are transformed into 'official posts' actually 'presupposes the separation of the state from society [Gesellschaft].' The truth of the matter is that the pay of civil servants 'constitutes the inner stability' of the modern monarchy. In this form of state, then, it is only the livelihood of the civil servant which is guaranteed; everyone else is left to the vagaries of the market place in civil society.[57]

The difficulty at this point for Hegel is that his identity has the distinct appearance of 'a dominant pole.' His executive appears as 'an antithesis to civil society.' He must, therefore, search for means to demonstrate that civil society will not suffer 'the abuse of power by government departments and their officials.' The protection of civil society against 'the abuse of power' by the bureaucracy derives from several sources.[58]

The most significant, for our purposes, is the 'hierarchical organization and answerability' of the bureaucracy. The point is that the responsibility of all levels of bureaucracy to higher levels and ultimately to the crown amounts to a form of control. Marx retorts that hierarchical control constitutes the *internal* constraints of the bureaucracy and therefore *leaves open* the question of 'protection against the "hierarchy."' The problem is the way Hegel poses the question, writes Marx, which is: 'As if the hierarchy were not the *chief abuse*, and the few personal sins of the officials not at all to be compared with their *inevitable* hierarchical sins. The hierarchy punishes the official if he sins against the hierarchy or commits a sin unnecessary from the viewpoint of the hierarchy. But it takes him into its protection whenever the hierarchy sins in him; moreover, the hierarchy is not easily convinced of the sins of its members.'[59]

In sum, in so far as Hegel sets forth the executive of the modern state, it is as 'state officialdom.' But this sphere, 'dedicated to the maintenance of the state's universal interest,' contains 'nothing but unresolved conflicts' – conflicts, moreover, whose only synthesis, as it were, 'are the civil servant's *examinations* and their *livelihood*.'[60]

The executive as bureaucracy, as Hegel expounds it, cannot resolve these contrarieties because it is, in fact, *based on* the fundamental antinomy of the modern state, the separation of the state from civil society. That is to say, if there were no separation, there would be no need for an executive as bureaucracy to attempt the 'subsumption' of the particular in the universal.

Bureaucracy, then, presupposes the separation and, moreover, presupposes the organization of civil society in corporations, i.e., groupings of particular interests or, to use a contemporary term, interest groups. In other words, if in civil society there were one single (common or co-operative) interest for all individuals, that interest would be *ipso facto* general and the separation of the general and particular would be no more. But competing individuals and interest groups which comprise civil society deny common particular interests and give rise to the need for an executive bureaucracy 'to maintain the general state interest.'

The general state interest, however, is an abstraction and has no content other than the particular interests of civil society. Thus, the bureaucracy that Hegel outlines has no content of its own and, indeed, says Marx, it is 'only the "formalism" of a content which lies outside itself.'[61] The content is the corporations, the interest groups that characterize civil society. Because of the separation of the *state*'s form and content, the corporations, to paraphrase Marx, become the materiality of the bureaucracy and the bureaucracy the spirituality of the corporations.

The relation of the state's separated form and content has according to Marx both a historical and contemporary dimension. In that period of history when common social interests first begin to become a thing apart from society itself, to become objectified universality, the bureaucracy 'fights against' the old social structure in which universality is dispersed among local authorities and interest groups. But once the state achieves its separation and once civil society as the people begins to free 'itself from the corporations' through its drive for an organic unity 'by its own rational impulse,' the bureaucracy works to restore a social structure based on interest groups. This it must do because the bureaucracy *presupposes* the corporations and their 'fall' presupposes the fall of bureaucracy. As Marx puts it: 'The consequence [i.e., bureaucracy] fights for the existence of its premises [i.e., corporations] as soon as a new principle [i.e., the rational impulse of civil society] challenges not their *existence* [i.e., of corporations], but the *principle* of their existence [i.e., the universal as a particular].'[62] Whereas earlier, concludes Marx, the bureaucracy fought against 'the existence of the corporations in order to make room for its own existence,' now it fights to preserve their existence, because their principle is the basis of the principle of bureaucracy.[63]

The principle of bureaucracy is 'the "state consciousness," the "state will," the "state power," as *one corporation* [i.e., the bureaucracy] – and thus a *particular*, *closed* society within the state.' Having so defined the nature of bureaucracy, Marx examines more fully the contradictory relation between the bureaucracy and corporations. One of his central points is put as follows: 'The "general interest" [i.e., the bureaucracy] can maintain itself against the particular [i.e., the corporations] as "something particular" [i.e., as bureaucracy] only so long as the particular maintains itself against the general [i.e., individuals in civil society] as "something general" [i.e., as corporations embodying groups of private interest].' In other words, the bureaucracy can *monopolize* the general interest only so long as that general interest is kept divided by the organization of particular interests in corporations. To maintain its position, the bureaucracy must 'protect the *imaginary* generality of the particular interest,' i.e., the notion that *all* interests are particular and self-seeking. And this illusion in turn is necessary 'to protect the *imaginary* particularity of the general interest,' i.e., the notion that bureaucracy as a corporation can embody the universal.[64]

There is much more that Marx says about the bureaucracy, but our main concern – his critique of Hegel and the main elements of his view of the bureaucracy – has been set forth. What remains, however, and what must not be overlooked is his summation.

Since the bureaucracy presupposes the separation of the state and civil society, the re-uniting of these two would spell the end of the bureaucracy. 'The abolition of the bureaucracy is *only* possible by the general interest *actually* – and not, as with Hegel, merely in thought, in *abstraction* – becoming the particular interest, which in turn is only possible as a result of the *particular* actually becoming the *general* interest.'[65]

The resolution is not left at this level of generality, however. Marx points out that Hegel finds the identity of the universal and particular in one class, in the 'civil servants and members of the executive [who] constitute the greater part of the *middle class*.' In an 'organic structure,' it is true, says Marx, that the 'nation' can 'appear as *one* estate, the *middle estate*.' Hegel's constitutional monarchy, however, is hardly such a structure, divided as it is. Yet, with the disappearance of this division of the state and civil society, one estate actually would comprise the nation. In this sense, 'the executive power,' concludes Marx, 'belongs to the entire nation to an even much higher degree than the legislative power.'[66]

In his discussion of the third and last structure of the internal polity of the state, Hegel wants to synthesize the terms of civil society and state. It is here, in the legislature, that the mediation of the bifurcated state purportedly takes place.

Hegel begins his analysis with the assertion that the task of the legislature is to develop and extend the laws as embodied in the constitution. He adds, however, that the legislature *presupposes* the constitution and that the constitution 'lies wholly beyond direct determination by the legislature.' It is with this antinomy, which is not merely a theoretical but also an historical and existing contrariety, that Marx begins his critique of the legislature.

This antinomy consists in the following. On the one hand, the *power* to organize the universal (the laws) is given by the constitution to the legislature and this power, *ipso facto*, 'reaches beyond the constitution,' i.e., it can change the constitution. On the other hand, the *authority* behind this power is only that as given in the constitution, which derives its content (the laws) from an authority *'prior to'* and *'outside'* itself, namely, the people. Thus, the legislative *power* contradicts legislative *authority*. The legislature stands opposed to the constitution in so far as it seeks to change the constitution. The latter is a system of laws whose determination is 'beyond' the legislature, while the former embodies the power to 'extend' and 'determine' this system of laws.[67]

Hegel seeks to evade the contrariety by suggesting that the constitution is not initially 'completed' and must therefore 'become.' This gradual 'alteration' is supposed to explain the apparent inconsistency. But it is the same as saying, writes Marx, that 'the constitution is unalterable, but actually it is altered.' 'The *appearance* contradicts the *essence*.' The antinomy remains.

The question of gradualness is subjected to further analysis by Marx. 'The category of *gradual* transition is,' he says, 'in the first place, historically false; and in the second place it explains nothing.' By this, he means first that the constitutional changes of the profound sort that Hegel is discussing do not happen gradually but suddenly. To be sure, there are 'particular changes ... but for a *new* constitution a real revolution has always been required [förmlichen Revolution bedurft].' Second, he dismisses the notion of gradualness as saying anything about the actual transition, i.e., how it takes place, why any change at all, and so forth. Gradualness is only a *descriptive* quality, which is historically inaccurate.[68]

Are there, then, only two alternatives for constitutional change: legislative gradualness which contradicts the constitution *or* revolution which establishes a new constitution? To this Marx answers, 'If the constitution is not merely to suffer change,' and its fixed 'illusory appearance is not finally to be violently shattered; if man is to do consciously what otherwise' is done surreptitiously through legislative gradualness, 'it becomes necessary that the movement of the constitution, that *advance*, be made the *principle of the constitution* and that therefore the real bearer of the constitution, the people, be made the principle of the constitution. Advance itself is then the constitution.'[69]

By making his starting point and subject the constitution and his predicate the legislature, Hegel constructs an incongruous relationship in which the predicate is empowered to change the subject. The only way around this inconsistency is to make actual change a surreptitious, gradual, 'unconscious' process; but herein Hegel makes the actual *irrational*, for rational change must be conscious change. The only way to dissolve this contrariety is to make the subject what it must logically be, namely, the people, the 'legislative authority' outside and prior to the constitution which is the predicate. In this way, as the people's internal polity changes, so too the constitution.

If the *only* way to resolve the conflict between the constitution and legislature is to make the subject the legislative authority outside the constitution, then, should constitutional change be a prerogative of the legislature? Or, as Marx poses and answers the question: 'Does the "constitution" itself ... properly belong to the domain of the "legislative authority"? This question can only be raised (1) when the political state exists as the mere formalism of the real state, when the political state is a distinct domain, when the political state exists as "constitution"; (2) when the legislative authority has a different source from that of the executive authority, etc.'

The reply is significant because it signals the difference between a truly human state, an integrated state, and a political state, a divided state. In the first place, it is only in the latter that the constitution is a question for legislation; in the former it is *rational* and under constant revision. In the second place, the question could not arise if the *source* of authority were the same for both the legislature and the executive, the illusory embodiment of the universal, namely, the people. In Hegel's modern state, the authority of the legislature lies in the people and the authority of the executive in the crown or god.

With the constitution as predicate and the people as subject, the antinomy between constitution and legislature dissolves and the question of change is reformulated. 'Posed correctly, the question is simply this: Has the people the right to give itself a new constitution? The answer must be an unqualified "Yes," because once it has ceased to be an actual expression of the will of the people the constitution has become a practical illusion.'[70] If the constitution is *not* of and for the people then it is an illusion, albeit a 'practical [praktische' one, that is, one that has real political import. To be practical and not an illusion, to be actual, it must be capable of being changed by the people whose expression it is.

The constitution *as* a constitution, as a political entity whose legitimacy derives from the monarch, however, 'collides' with the legislature. This collision, according to Marx, is in fact an expression of 'a contradiction in the concept of the constitution,' in the notion of a constitution *separated* from the people. In the rational state, on the other hand, the constitution comprises 'the fundamental attributes of rational will [die Fundamentalbestimmungen des vernünftigen Willens].' It is *not* a political entity but a 'political credo,' the expression of a people's consciously determined internal polity. In this sense, the legislature does not decide on how the 'whole' will be organized, how the law will be extended and developed, but it will 'only discover and formulate' the law which arises from conscious, rational interaction of the people.[71]

After expounding the general function of the legislature, Hegel turns to examine the mediating function. What requires mediation are the two 'extremes' of his modern state: the monarch and civil society which stand in opposition as the one and the many. We have already seen how Hegel attempts to mediate the monarch through the activities of the executive, the bureaucracy. Now, he puts forward the means by which civil society is mediated; namely, the estates element. It is in the legislature that these mediating elements (the estates and executive) unite to form the synthesis, the organic unity, of the one and the many.

The demonstration of this unity, insists Marx, is nothing more than assertion. The elements of the purported synthesis are based on different principles and cannot be anything but an 'imaginary' unity covering a real conflict. It is here, within the legislature, Marx points out, that the second 'unresolved collision' in Hegel's modern state is found. It is between the estates element as legislative authority and the executive as monarchical authority. In effect, they are two conflicting claims to representation of the universal.

Hegel's solution is not his, properly speaking, but the solution as found in the existing political system. It involves the *nature* of the universal represented by the estates. In the legislature, 'the estates element is a deputation of civil society to the state'; it confronts the state 'as the "many."'[72] This is to say, in so far as the estates element deals with 'matters of general concern' or 'public affairs [allgemeine Angelegenheit]' it does so as 'the *empirical generality* of the opinions and thoughts of the *many*.' In short, the estates do not become a coherent unity but remain a divided plurality in the legislature as in civil society. The contrariety is thus hidden, for 'state consciousness,' consciousness of the universal, is restricted to 'the inadequate form of the bureaucracy,' while the 'real, *empirical* state spirit, public consciousness' as found in the estates element is seen as 'a mere pot-pourri of "thoughts and opinions of the many."'' As Marx summarizes it: 'Hegel idealizes the bureaucracy and empiricizes public consciousness.' As long as the estates element remains an 'empirical generality,' the 'many,' it can make no real claim to embodying the universal.

The explanation of this situation is made by Hegel in a mystical fashion. He begins not with human subjects objectifying themselves in 'public affairs' but by positing 'matters of general concern' or 'public affairs' as subject, as existing "*in themselves*," as the business of the government.' Public affairs, then, have an '*essential*, actual existence' without any relation to the people. 'The actual business of the people,' observes Marx, 'has come into being without action by the people.' But the ideal entity 'public affairs' requires a *form* and this it finds in the 'empirical generality' of the estates element. However, because public affairs already have an *actuality* as the business of government, they require the estates element as *mere form*. Public affairs as such, 'in themselves,' are the abstract content of government activity, but this governmental *form* does not correspond to the essence of this abstract content. On the other hand, public affairs '*for themselves*' exist as a pure *formality* as the estates element; but this form (the form of the universal) does not correspond with the content (as the 'many,' 'empirical generality') of the estates element.[73]

In other words, in Hegel's *Philosophy of Right* and in the modern state, the actual bearer, the true source of public affairs or the universal, has a political significance which is purely formal. This is the estates element, the representatives of civil society in the legislature. It has the form of the general but a content which is merely the plurality of private interests. It represents the people but not in terms of their general concerns, rather in terms of competing private concerns.

Marx summarizes this part of his analysis of the legislature of the modern state in the following passage (the numbers are added):

The constitutional state is the state in which the state interest as the actual interest of the nation [des Volkes] exists *only* formally[1] but, at the same time, as a *determinate form* [bestimmte Form] alongside the actual state. Here the state interest has again acquired actuality *formally* as the interest of the nation, but it is only this *formal actuality* which it is to have. It has become a *formality*, the *haut goût* of national life, a *ceremonial*.[2] The *estates* element [das *ständische* Element] is the *sanctioned*, *legal lie* [gesetzliche Lüge] of constitutional states, the lie that the *state* is the *nation's interest* [das Interesse des Volkes], or that the *nation* is the *interest of the state*. This lie reveals itself in its *content*.[3] It has established itself as the *legislative* power, precisely because the legislative power has the general for its content, and, being an affair of knowledge rather than of will, is the *metaphysical* state *power* [die metaphysische Staatsgewalt];[4] whereas in the form of the executive power, etc., this same lie would inevitably have to dissolve at once, or be transformed into a truth.[5] The metaphysical state power was the most fitting seat [der geeignetste Sitz] for the metaphysical, general illusion of the state [allgemein Staatsillusion].[6][74]

The passage is well worth explicating.

[1] In the constitutional state, the actual *national* interest has only a *formal* existence in the estates element in the legislature; what parades as 'national interest' is in truth *private* interest.

[2] These national interests do have a 'definite' form, a 'formal actuality,' which consists in the ceremonial aspects of state life: the rites, the symbols, the pageantry, etc.

[3] The estates element is a *lie* because, while it represents civil society, the people, it does so not as the general but as particulars; the lie is revealed in the fact that it is private interest that characterizes the estates and civil society. It is 'sanctioned' and 'legal' because it is established 'in law,' as part of the constitution of the state's internal polity.

[4] Because the estates element is the illusion of 'general concerns' it assumes legislative power which in fact deals with the abstract general. But because the content of *legislative* power has to do with abstractions ('an affair of knowledge') and not with execution ('will'), the estates element or the legislature is a 'metaphysical' power, i.e., an abstract power, a power existing in thought but not in reality.

[5] When in 'the form of executive power' (a singular), this lie, the particular parading as the universal, would on the one hand 'dissolve' because here the particular could parade only as the singular *or* 'be transformed into a truth,' on the other hand, if the particular *actually* became the universal as in an organic state.

[6] The 'metaphysical state power,' i.e., the estates in the legislature (a fictional, purely formal representation of the general) constitutes the logical 'repository' for the state which exists only as an abstraction, *as* a metaphysical entity, as an illusion of the general.

The notion that the estates element mediates the 'extreme' of civil society through representation of the people's interests in the legislature is, then, pure illusion. The myth of the 'matters of general concern' being represented by the many hides the truth of that representation, its particularity, and complements a second myth, i.e., that the interests of the whole are embodied in the executive or monarch.

Besides mediating the state and civil society by representing the latter in the legislature, the estates along with the executive mitigate, according to Hegel, the appearance of the monarch and civil society as isolated extremes. With respect to civil society, the estates do this through their position in society, which has the effect of preventing 'individuals from coming to form a *multitude* or a *crowd*' without the 'organic views and intentions' of members of estates. The estates effectively prevent, then, the formation of 'views and intentions against the state.' If such views and intentions were allowed to develop, they would comprise, as Marx points out, 'a *definite orientation*' and would themselves become 'organic,' outside the so-called organic state. As long as individuals are kept isolated or partially united in estates, the ability to see their intrinsic unity lies outside themselves, 'outside the masses and hence they cannot set themselves in motion, but can only be moved, and exploited as a massed force, by the monopolists of the "organic state."'[75]

This is the role of the estates in 'mediating' the extreme of particular interests in civil society vis-à-vis the state. But if these individuals do happen to form a multitude or a crowd and constitute 'a mere massed force against the state,' then 'it becomes clear,' writes Marx, 'that it is no "particular interest" which contradicts the state' but that it is 'an actual organic view' of the mass, which is not that of the state and which cannot be realized in the state. In this situation, where the mass as organic confronts the state, the estates play a role of dissipation. The multitude is fractionalized in their continued, persistent use of estates and in the creation of estates; they become 'occupied' with the 'illusion of their own objectification.' In this sense, 'the "estates" preserve the state from the non-organic crowd only as a result of the disorganization of this crowd.'[76]

We have explored in part Marx's criticism of Hegel's attempt to show how the mediating functions of the estates contribute to the organic unity of the state. This mediation, however, does not bring the universal and particular together. As Marx puts it: 'The antithesis of government and nation is mediated by the antithesis between *estates* and *nation*.' The opposition is merely displaced not overcome. Yet Hegel is intent to demonstrate an organic unity.

His resolution of this antithesis, the 'true link' between the particular and the universal, is established in 'the estates element in the legislature' where 'the civil estate [the agricultural and business estates] acquires political significance and effectiveness.' But the civil estate, protests Marx, is 'the unpolitical estate'; it belongs to civil society which is the antithesis of the political state. How can it be both civil and political when Hegel's state, like the existing modern state, is bifurcated along these lines?

On the one hand, Hegel *asserts* that civil and political life are identical and that this can be seen in the Middle Ages when the estates had political as well as social significance. Marx at great length exposes the confusion of Hegel: the separation of civil and political society is an *actual* division of the modern state which cannot be welded by recalling the past significance of a long since altered socio-political relation. On the other hand, Hegel locates the political significance of the civil estate in the legislature. This location, Marx notes, speaks for itself; as we have seen, the legislature embodies the separation of civil and political life and therefore the activity of the civil estates here 'is itself proof of the separation.'[77] Hegel, according to Marx, sees the estates element as an expression of the separation and yet wants to posit it as containing 'an identity which is not there.'

If Hegel's attempted solution to the antithesis of civil society and the state is not plausible, what then does happen when the civil estate becomes political, i.e., appears in the legislature? The very nature of civil society, says Marx, is its lack of political significance; indeed, civil society stands in opposition to and separate from the political state. Consequently, in the legislature the civil estate cannot be what it is but must 'give itself up as civil society, as civil estate.' The 'political significance and effectiveness' of the civil estates, then, cannot find expression in the form of civil estates but only in the form of the *individuals* who comprise the civil estates.[78]

Thus, the division of society into the political state and civil society effects a division in the individual. On the one hand, he has a social existence but only as a member of civil society and as such he is not part of the state; the state stands against him as an external necessity. On the other hand, as a citizen of the state, he can only act as an individual; his social existence is of no consequence. Yet, it is here in his political activity that the individual 'acquires importance as a *human being*, or that his quality as a member of the state, as a social being, appears as a *human* quality.'[79] In civil society his social existence can be expressed only as a private individual; in the political state, it is only as an individual that he can express his social essence.

This dualism within the individual, and the dualism of the political state and civil society, is resolved by Hegel by giving a dual significance to the concept of estate. In civil society, Hegel gives estate a purely civil or social significance, whereas, in the legislature, he gives it a double sense, both civil and political. In the medieval world, argues Marx, 'when the structure of civil society was still political and the political state was civil society,' this double sense of estate was non-existent; it was one and the same thing. In modern society, this identity of civil and political position ('estate in the medieval sense') can only be found in the bureaucracy. Otherwise, the separation holds true. The estate of civil society has no political essence attached to it. 'It consists of separate masses which form fleetingly and whose very formation is fortuitous and does *not* amount to an organization.'[80] What is singularly characteristic about civil society, writes Marx expanding on Hegel, is that a 'lack of property' and a '*class* of *direct* labour' appear to form the 'ground upon which' the constituent groups of civil society 'rest and move.' Hegel's supposed solution to the dualism of modern society not only does not resolve the contradiction but also does not account for the 'ground' on which civil society rests.

If, then, this dualism is not resolved in the legislature of Hegel's *Philosophy of Right*, anymore than it is resolved in the parliament of the modern state, why does it remain unresolved? What is it about the antithesis that keeps it from being resolved? In the *Critique*, Marx's explanation ranges over several pages, but the following is an attempt to summarize the argument.

Reflecting the division in modern society, Hegel conceives the state as divided between the 'monarchical principle and the people, between the will of the state as *one* empirical will and as *many* empirical wills.' The reconciliation of these two extremes, according to Hegel, takes place in the legislature where delegates of both sides meet. While Hegel takes this to be the mediating ground, Marx argues that, far from uniting two extremes, the legislature is a mere *mixtum compositum* and *not* the heart of an organism. The delegates of the monarchical authority, the executive, mediate (or, perhaps better, mitigate) one extreme and likewise the estates mediate the other extreme. But there is nothing to mediate these two mediating elements. Though they were 'supposed to mediate between civil society and the monarch,' the antithesis merely takes on another form within the legislature; the '*opposition* seems to have become an opposition set for battle and also an *irreconcilable contradiction* [unversöhnlichen Widerspruch].' As Marx continues, 'This "mediation," therefore, has indeed a very great need, as Hegel rightly shows, for "its *mediation* to be *actually* effected." It is itself rather the existence of contradiction than of mediation [Vermittelung].'[81]

How is it that Hegel thinks the antithesis can be mediated and Marx insists that it is an irreconcilable contradiction? It is because Hegel 'arbitrarily and inconsistently places the monarch and estates in polar opposition.' That is to say, though he may see them as two extremes of the same essence and therefore as the identity of opposites, as able to be mediated, his definition of them in fact makes them *real extremes* with no inherent unity or 'identity' or relation and so not susceptible to mediation. As Marx expresses it: 'Real extremes cannot be mediated precisely because they are real extremes. Nor do they require mediation, for they are opposed in essence. They have nothing in common, they do not need each other, they do not supplement each other. The one does not have in its own bosom the longing for, the need for, the anticipation of the other.'[82]

It is the impossibility of mediating real extremes that lies at the root of the dualism in Hegel's state. As Hegel portrays them, the empirical one and the empirical many have no intrinsic unity which desires realization. They are 'actual opposites' which can only confront each other not as lovers but as fighters. There is here no dialectical opposition, only real opposition.

Hegel tries 'arbitrarily and inconsistently' to portray the antithesis of monarch and civil society as a 'polar opposite' because as such the extremes could be truly mediated to bring about their unity and not merely mitigated. Polar opposition is reflexive opposition, summed up in the phrase, 'les extrêmes se touchent.' This is a relation in which the two extremes have a single essence; for example, 'north pole and south pole are both *pole*; their *essence* is identical; similarly, *female and male* sex are both *species*, one *essence*, human essence.' These extremes are '*differentiated* essence'; they are what they are (i.e., their existence is) *only* as one side of a bifurcated essence. Real opposition, on the other hand, is the difference between 'pole and non-pole, human and *non*-human species.' This is a 'difference of *essences* – between two essences.'[83]

If Hegel had derived executive authority from legislative authority so that the former rationally reflected the latter, then the executive and the legislature would have constituted reflexive, and not real, mutually exclusive, extremes. Their common essence would have been the rational will. Instead, Hegel derives executive authority and the legislative authority from two entirely different sources; their respective authority rests on entirely different bases and so they do not share on essence; they are mutually exclusive essences and as such cannot be mediated.

THE UPPER HOUSE

Hegel does not admit to the impossibility of mediation but he does admit that the 'possibility of harmony' is as likely as the 'possibility of hostile confrontation' (*PR*, paragraph 304) between the two extremes. The latter possibility arises from the fact that the estates do not mediate in the same way as does the executive as bureaucracy, which, as we have seen, takes the monarchical principle into civil society through the corporations. The estates merely mediate the extreme of civil society but do not reach over to the other side; i.e., they do not contain any aspect of the monarchical principle. In the legislature, this lack of mediation on the estates' side gives the lie to the actuality of harmony and points to the antithesis of the monarchical principle and civil society. Hence, Marx writes exposing Hegel's reasoning, 'the *appearance* of an *actual identity* between the monarchical will and the will of the estates must be established.' 'As the monarch is democratised in the executive, so this "estates" element must be *monarchised* in its delegation.'[84] The unity which is not actually there must be made to appear to be there.

The '*unity* of the *non-united*,' says Marx ironically, is established in the Upper House, the House of Lords. And because it is comprised of a component of the estates element (the agricultural class) which has similarities to the monarch, this house is 'the highest *synthesis* of the political state in the organization under consideration.' Marx is quick to point out, however, that no genuine unity is established. 'This component of the estates element is the *romanticism* of the political state, the *dreams* of its ... harmony with itself.' In the absence of true unity, 'so long as estates and monarchical power are in *actual* harmony, get on with each other, the *illusion* of their *essential* unity is an *actual*, hence *effective*, illusion.'[85] But it is only an illusion.

What is it about this agricultural or peasant class [Bauernstand] that enables it to play this important mediating role? It is the fact that it is based on 'family life' and 'landed property' and shares its 'natural' basis in the family and its 'will' based on the land with the monarch. Marx plays upon the superficiality of this rationalization and then sums up Hegel's position by exclaiming: 'What an anomaly altogether, that the highest *synthesis* of the political state should be nothing but the synthesis of landed property and family life!'[86]

In placing the political synthesis of the modern state in the peasantry, Hegel is attempting to unite two antithetical systems, claims Marx. 'Hegel wants the medieval-estates system, but in the modern sense of the legislature, and he wants the modern legislature, but in the body of the medieval-estates system! This is the worst kind of syncretism.' The criticism is clear: Hegel makes the mediating role in the modern legislature a task for an estate in the medieval sense. In making his solution syncretic, however, he exposes the truth of the mediation of the civil estates in the legislature; i.e., they must become that which they are not in order to mediate between what they are and the monarch.

There is something more about the peasant class which makes it 'particularly fitted for political position and significance,' says Hegel. And this is the nature of its capital: it is 'independent alike of the state's capital, the uncertainty of business, the quest for profit, and any sort of fluctuation in possessions ... [and] likewise independent of favour, whether from the executive or the mob' (306). In a word, its capital is landed property become independent by being 'an *inalienable heritage*, burdened with *primogeniture*.' In an addition to this paragraph, Hegel insinuates that primogeniture, the right of inheritance by the eldest son, is a 'demand of politics,' is promoted and encouraged, even established, by the state in order to avoid the political effects of unstable private property in the 'business class' and to find a source of political stability.

Nevertheless, the operative element here is landed property. If the principle of the peasant class is landed property as independent or sovereign private property and if this class comprises the legislative Upper House which is the 'highest *synthesis* of the political state' in Hegel's system, then Marx can deduce that: 'The political constitution at its highest point is therefore the *constitution of private property*. The supreme *political conviction* is the *conviction of private property*.'[87]

Primogeniture is a right that emanates from private property in its independent sovereign form as landed property. It is an expression of 'landed property as sovereign private property.' And this is private property whose base is outside the 'wealth of the state' and which does not participate in this general wealth and therefore is not subject to the vagaries, dependence, and fluctuation of socially related wealth. It is the quintessence of *private* property.

Hegel wants to justify primogeniture by treating it as a 'demand of politics,' as 'determined by something else.' In fact, says Marx, 'primogeniture is a consequence of *perfect* landed property, it is fossilised private property, private property (*quand même*) at the peak of its independence and intensity of its development, and that which Hegel represents as the purpose, the determining factor and prime cause of primogeniture, is rather its effect, its consequence, the power of *abstract private property* over the *political state*; whereas Hegel represents primogeniture as the *power of the political state over private property*. He makes the cause the effect and the effect the cause, the determining the determined and the determined the determining.'[88]

In other words, though Hegel wants to make primogeniture appear to be a result of the 'demand of politics,' it is in fact an expression of the independent form of private property. Thus, while Hegel thinks that primogeniture on which the state rests is imposed by the state on private property in order to ensure the stability of one sector of private property, the actual relation is the reverse: private property in its quintessential form as primogeniture establishes itself at the centre of the political state.

Even if we begin from Hegel's perspective, however, and see the political state protecting and encouraging primogeniture, the end result is the same. 'What power does the political state exercise over private property in primogeniture? This, that it *isolates* private property from family and society, that it turns into *something abstractly* independent. What then is the power of the political state over private property? the *power of private property itself*, its essence brought into existence. What remains for the political state in contrast with this essence? The *illusion* that the state determines when it is being determined.'[89]

In drawing out the implications of the house of peers as the final synthesis of the state and of its principle as primogeniture, Marx turns the logic of Hegel's 'state' completely around. The state is not the embodiment of 'ethical life;' it is the expression of the will of private property which in fact breaks the ethical bonds of family and society. That the political state embodies rational freedom is mere illusion; freedom becomes independence and 'political "independence" is construed as "independent private property."' Moreover, writes Marx, 'when "independent private property" has in the political state, in the legislature, the *significance of political* independence, then it *is* the *political independence* of the state.'[90] National independence is not the independence of a people but the independence of a nation's private property.

THE LOWER HOUSE

Hegel now turns his attention to the 'second section of the estates' which he calls the 'mobile part of civil society' but defines earlier as the 'business class.' Its political involvement in the legislature comes through election and delegates: a form of participation quite the opposite of the agricultural class which is directly political inasmuch as its social being is at the same time political being. He does not want these representatives delegated by civil society 'as atomistically dispersed into individuals,' rather 'as articulated in its already instituted associations,' communities and corporations.' It is in this way that civil society in the form of 'corporations,' etc., 'acquires a connection with politics.' Individuals as members of corporations are to be political but not *as* individuals (*PR*, 308).

What this means, according to Marx, is that the political representation of civil society 'becomes the *privilege* of the corporations, etc.' The political significance of the civil estates is bound up in the political privilege of one of its elements. Such a position has two important implications for Hegel's theory. The first is that by adopting it Hegel 'entirely abandons' the notion of the political state as the 'highest actuality of social being, existing in and for itself' and gives it 'a precarious reality' which 'is dependent on something else.'[91] In short, if the state requires the corporations to mediate for it, then, the state cannot be seen as an organic unity 'in and for itself'; it is dependent on 'outside' 'supports.' The second is that 'political right as the right of corporations, etc., wholly contradicts political right as *political* right, i.e., as the law of the state – the law of the citizens.' In other words, political right is the law pertaining to a citizen's relation to the state and, if that relation is broken or mediated, so too is political right.

Hegel wants the civil estates, the 'democratic element,' to be represented in the political state by 'associations, communities and corporations' because of the way he envisages civil society – as 'empirical generality.' Given this, the question of representation becomes a dilemma in which the choice is between civil society as the many participating in the 'general affairs of the state through *delegates*,' or *all* doing this as *individuals*. The answer is obvious because the dilemma is a superficial one, as Hegel admits and Marx stresses; it is merely a question of numbers, not of the *meaning* of representation. The question can be posed in this way because the state and civil society are separated and thus representation can have no real political content or meaning. Representation is strictly formal representation; and therefore it is reducible to a question of numbers.

Representation in the 'abstract-political state' does not go beyond a question of numbers because here political life is abstract, not real. Political life is the estrangement of the universal from the particular; and in a political society their unity occurs principally as form. Hence, universality remains an abstraction, a formality; and particularity remains abstract individuality. Whether the many through its delegates participates in 'political life' or whether all do as *individuals* is a dilemma which has no bearing on the actuality of political participation; it is, as Marx puts it, 'an *abstract*-political question.'[92]

To formulate the question properly, the universal must not be separated from the particular or understood as the mere sum of individuals, i.e., as the 'full *count* of *individuality*.' It has to be an 'essential, spiritual, actual quality of the individual.' In the rational state, the dilemma does not arise: 'In a really rational state,' writes Marx, the relation is as follows: '"*All should* not *individually* participate in deliberating and deciding on the general affairs of the state," for the "individuals" participate in deliberating and deciding on the *general affairs* as "all," i.e., within the society and as members of society. Not all individually, but the individuals as all.'[93]

The rational state presupposes that the 'all' has a meaning beyond the mere sum. The 'all' represents a social integrity which is embodied, because of the rationality of the state, in each individual. In this sense, the individual is not an individual *pur et simple*, but a social being whose essence is inextricably tied to his community, his 'all.' The individual can act *as* an individual only by denying his social being, which is to deny himself.

This is the position in which Hegel finds himself when he asserts that, in Marx's words, '"all" are to participate "individually" in "deliberating and deciding on the general affairs of the state."' The rational state aside, this perception of political participation is self-contradictory, claims Marx: 'Already the concept *members of the state* implies that they are *members* of the state, a *part* of it, that it takes them as *part of it*. But if they are a *part* of the state, then, of course, their social *being* is already *their real participation* in it. They *are* not only part of the state, but the state is *their* portion. To be a conscious part of something means consciously to acquire a part of it, to take a conscious interest in it. Without this consciousness, the member of the state would be an *animal*.'[94]

To be but a member of the state, then, is by definition to be a participant in it. It is not a question of whether members ought to participate, as Hegel suggests, because that would presume some subjects not participating and therefore not really being members of the state. The 'idea that all should participate in the affairs of the state' is only the wish to be real members of the state. Hegel's problem of all participating individually arises from the fact that political life is separated from civil life. The legislature embodies the 'totality of the political state' and therefore it is only there that one can become a complete member of the state. Hegel can be scathing about the idea of all participating in the general affairs because he understands the general affairs only in terms of the legislature. But in so far as all of civil society wants to participate, says Marx, it 'is merely the striving of civil society to give itself *political* being or to make *political being* its actual being. The striving of *civil society* to turn itself into *political* society, or to turn *political* society [i.e., the legislature] into *actual* society, appears as the striving for as *general* as possible a participation in the *legislative power*.'[95]

This striving for legislative power is not, Marx cautions, 'because of its *content*,' which as we have seen above is the plurality of private interests. It is 'because of its *formal* political significance,' that is, because of the legislature's purported, illusory concern with the 'affairs of all.' Given this, the logical 'goal of popular desire' should be 'executive power' because here lies the ability to *act* in the name of the whole. But this ability to act is not to be *arbitrary* as constituted in the modern state but to be the power to 'discover and formulate' the *actual* law – that which reflects the organism and not the particular *per se*.

At this point, the critique of Hegel is not Marx's central concern. The subject matter, the 'striving' referred to, is in fact a discussion of the implications of electoral reform being demanded in France and England prior to 1843. There are two parts to this discussion of electoral reform in the *Critique*: the *essence* of the question *and* the form in which electoral reform *actually* manifests itself, i.e., the question 'from the point of view of *interests*.' The latter part may not have been written or at least is not to be found in the extant portion of the manuscript of the *Critique*. We are left, therefore, only with the former, the *essential* meaning [eigentumlichen Wesen] of electoral reform. This, however, must not be understood as Marx's idealism, as a hope for revolution wedged into the process of electoral reform.[96] It must be read as the *intrinsic meaning* of such reform, i.e., the significance of it, in itself, without reference to specific, real movements for reform.

The question of electoral reform as it appears historically is defined as 'the *extension* and greatest possible *generalisation* of *election*, both of the right to *vote* and the right to *be elected*.' Our subject matter, in a word, is the demand for universal enfranchisement. An understanding of the essence of this demand begins with the essence of *election* [die Wahl], which Marx defines as 'the *actual relation* of *actual civil society* ... to the *representative element*.' It is 'the *immediate*, *direct*, not *merely representative but actually existing* relation of civil society to the political state.' To paraphrase Marx, elections express [bildet] the foremost political interest of civil society.

In achieving universal enfranchisement, civil society completes its political existence but only as an abstraction from itself, as a political existence in an abstract-political state. The '*consummation* [die Vollendung] of this abstraction is at the same time its transcendence [Aufhebung].' Here lies the essential meaning of electoral reform; the striving for reform is intrinsically the striving for a unity of political and civil life. As Marx elaborates on the meaning of this transcendence: 'In actually positing its *political existence* as its *true* existence, civil society has simultaneously posited its civil existence, in distinction from its political existence, as *inessential*; and the fall of one side of the division carries with it the fall of the other side, its opposite. *Electoral reform* within the *abstract political state* is therefore the demand for its *dissolution*, but also for the *dissolution of civil society*.'[97]

That the achievement of universal enfranchisement does not necessarily lead to the dissolution of the separation of political life from civil life is obvious. At the same time, it is not a completely implausible route to this unity.

The point at issue here, however, is what the demand for electoral reform *in essence* means. How the demand is *actually* expressed, how it is mitigated, distorted, and employed by real 'interests' is another question.

TRUE DEMOCRACY: THE SOLVED RIDDLE

The demand for universal suffrage is in essence a demand for self-determination, for the end of the opposition of the political state and civil society. It is at heart, then, a demand for *true* democracy. And the nature of this democracy is the essence, the 'ideal,' in Marx's critique of Hegel's modern state.

Marx writes that 'democracy is the solved riddle of all constitutions.' What is this riddle that all constitutions apparently share? It is the separation of the general and particular in one form or another. How is democracy the solved riddle? Its constitution, says Marx, 'is constantly brought back to its actual basis, the *actual human being*, the *actual people*, and established as the people's *own* work.' If the riddle is a form of separation, its solution is an actual unity of the general (the constitution) and the particular (the people).[98]

As this unity, 'democracy is the *essence of all* state constitutions – socialized man [sozialisierte Mensch], as a distinct state constitution.' In other words, in democracy the relation of the general and particular forms an organic unity, whereas in other systems this relation may purport to be so but is in reality an imperfect variation. This distinction may be made another way: in democracy, 'man does not exist for the law [the general] but the law for man – it is a *human manifestation*; whereas, in other forms of state man is a *legal manifestation*' – i.e., man is defined by a constitution alien and opposed to him.[99]

In non-democratic states, 'the *law*, the *constitution* is what rules, without really ruling,' or prevailing; that is, it rules but does not infuse 'the content of the remaining, non-political spheres'; it remains a separate force. In democracy, the political and non-political spheres are fused: 'the law, the state itself, insofar as it is a political constitution, is only the self-determination of the people, and a particular content of the people.'[100]

In this sense, 'democracy is content and form.' The content, the people, do not act 'politically' as 'abstract individuals' but as members of the state, as social beings whose very essence is defined by the state, the form. The modern state, on the contrary, is characterized by the dualism of form and content. The real *content* of the constitution here is private property, but it lies outside the *formal* political relations of the general and the particular. Political life is purely formal. The modern state is merely a state form and political activity a formal activity.

Marx's critique is, in part, carried out by comparing the Hegelian depiction of the modern state with a concept of the essential state, the concept Hegel sought to impose on the modern state. At every step in Hegel's analysis, Marx attempts to demonstrate, *inter alia*, the inherent dualism, the separation of the political state as the embodiment of the whole from civil society as particularity. For Marx, as for Hegel in theory, the whole and the parts form two sides of a single relation in which one side cannot exist without the other. What Marx tries to show is that this relation, in Hegel's depiction of the modern state, is contrived, assumed, merely asserted, and never in fact demonstrated. The whole and the parts remain separate and distinct, and, moreover, find themselves in opposition to each other.

They stand as a contrariety, in real opposition, because Hegel has defined each in abstraction from the other; he has depicted them as unconnected and 'immediate.' As such, their relation requires mediation or better, mitigation, for they never can be truly mediated or unified. It is in the final analysis a mechanical relation Hegel has described and not an organic one; for in an organic or rational state, the whole and the parts mediate each other and do not require mediation by any third party.

If Marx's intention were to show that Hegel had failed to find in the modern state an organic unity, it was fulfilled. He demonstrated the inherent contradictions in the relations of the existing modern state and, in the process, clarified the notion of the organic state, relieving Hegel's definition of its inconsistencies.

CONCLUSIONS

This criticial analysis of Hegel's *Philosophy of Right* is undoubtedly one of Marx's most fruitful pieces of work. Almost everything he writes hereafter bears the imprint of the discoveries concerning politics and method arrived at here.[101] He kept the manuscript with him throughout his life and clearly referred to it in writing, among other things, such essays as 'The Eighteenth Brumaire of Louis Bonaparte,' in which the wording of some passages is very close to that of the *Critique*. But the question before us is: what does Marx accomplish in this analysis?

The doubts which assailed him as editor of the *Rheinische Zeitung*, we surmised, concerned the nature of the state which resisted the critical voice of reason and the nature of the method of critique which confined itself to the syllogistic judgement and held expectations about the means of realizing philosophy. In the introduction to this *Critique*, published as an article months after the manuscript was written, Marx suggests that what could be accomplished in such a critique was precisely the answer to these questions.

'The criticism of the *German philosophy of state and law*,' he writes, 'is both a critical analysis of the modern state and of the reality connected with it, and the resolute negation of the whole *German political and legal consciousness* as practised hitherto.'[102] It remains to describe and summarize the results of his critical analysis of the modern state *and* of the method of speculative philosophy.

First, Marx identifies the chief characteristic of the modern state, its fundamental duality. He demonstrates that, despite the apparent unity of government and the people, there is an inherent separation of the whole and its parts; the state is revealed as an alien force which stands over and opposed to the people. This conclusion was already perceived, by and large, in the *Rheinische Zeitung* articles.

Second, he shows how this separation is based on the internal divisions of civil society. That is, as long as individuals remain divided amongst themselves in civil society, the state can appear to be embodied as the whole in the form of the bureaucracy or the legislature. It is, then, the atomistic principle of civil society which is the premise on which rests the state as alien and opposed to the people.

Third, although the political state purportedly embodies the whole, it does so only in a *formal* sense; the real content of the political state is private property. The whole is only reflected in the ceremonial side of the political state, while the real purpose of the political state is the affairs of private interests. The constitution is not the determining element, it is rather the determined; and private property is its foundation, its determinant.

Fourth, the legislature contains a contradiction in its relation to the constitution: the *power* of the former to change the latter transcends its *authority*. This contradiction exists in all constitutional governments and cannot be overcome unless the 'real' bearer of the constitution, the people, be made 'the principle of the constitution.' As long as the principle of the existing constitution is private property, the contradiction remains.

Fifth, in so far as the individual has a relation to the whole, i.e., to the political state, it is a purely *formal* relation. There is and can be *no* real direct involvement in public affairs. Elections of representatives are an illusory involvement; indeed, public affairs are themselves an illusion for they exist only in a formal sense; the real affairs of the political system are the affairs of private property.

Sixth, the individual who lives in such a bifurcated state is himself divided. On the one hand, he exists as an atomistic individual in civil society pursuing purely selfish interests. On the other hand, in so far as the individual partakes of communal life he must do so in the political sphere, distinct and separate from his personal life. This communal existence is, moreover, fleeting and formal; yet it is only here, when man engages in political life, that he can be seen as truly human, because to be human is to be part of a rational unity, to be related in an active and direct way to the social whole.

There are other significant conclusions about the nature of the modern state that Marx draws, but these are the principal ones. He demonstrates, in a word, that political relations in the modern state are an open contradiction, and the source of this contradiction is to be found in the nature of private property.

To arrive at such fecund results requires a firm possession of the way to proceed. Although Marx may not have had this firm grasp at the outset, he certainly developed it within the *Critique*; indeed, part of his intention, we surmise, was to discover the problems with his method as employed in the *Zeitung* articles. It is the question of method to which we must now turn.

About two-thirds of the way through the *Critique*, there is a lengthy parenthetical remark. It is here that Marx sets forth his first reformulation of the meaning of critique. Because of its length we should examine it in stages; the first paragraph reads:

Hegel's chief error is to conceive the *contradiction of appearances* as *unity in essence*, *in the idea*, while in fact it has something more profound for its essence, namely, an *essential contradiction*, just as here this contradiction of the legislative authority within itself, for example, is merely the contradiction of the political state, and therefore also of civil society with itself.[103]

On the basis of his analysis thus far, Marx asserts that Hegel's 'chief error' is to imagine or to formulate a real, existing contradiction *as* a 'unity in essence.' The real contradiction in the legislature, in other words, is conceived as an essential unity, as the realization of rationality; whereas, in actuality, the nature of the legislature is *not* an integral whole, but rather an 'essential contradiction'; that is, its very essence is contradictory. To rephrase the argument, Hegel supposes existence, despite apparent disunity, to be in essence an organic unity, as if all existence in essence were organic. In fact, many aspects of existence, as in the case of the legislature, may be by nature contradictory.

It might be added that while Marx saw it as an error to conceive of the legislature as a unity in light of its essential, definitional inconsistencies, he did not see it as an error to conceive of the state or society as an organic unity, though in reality its integrity may not be manifest. The reason was as follows: the legislature, he argued, exists because of a contradiction in society; it is the product and embodiment of that contradiction and will disappear when the contradiction is transcended. In reality, society too appears to be composed of disparate, antagonistic elements, but what characterizes all societies despite the existing disunities, he asserted, is a necessary relation between the individual and others, between the parts and the whole. In this intrinsic characteristic lies for Marx the validity of the *concept* of society as an organic unity, despite the existing disparities.

Marx continues his reformulation:

Vulgar criticism falls into an opposite, *dogmatic* error. Thus it criticises the constitution, for example. It draws attention to the antagonism of the powers, etc. It finds contradictions everywhere. This is still dogmatic criticism which *fights* with its subject-matter in the same way in which the dogma of the Holy Trinity, say, was demolished by the contradiction of one and three.

Here, Marx may be chiding the Young Hegelians, and perhaps even himself. 'Vulgar criticism,' he asserts, is a '*dogmatic* error.' By dogmatic he means, following Hegel, the assertion of two opposing propositions, only one of which can be correct.[104] We are thinking of the early formulation of critique as the measurement of existence against an essence, which for the Young Hegelians was closer to a supposititious ideal than to Marx's definition. As pointed out, this method cannot go beyond the assertion of the truth or falsity of existence. 'Vulgar criticism,' moreover, is the 'opposite' of Hegel's error because it finds reality out of step with its concept; 'it finds contradictions everywhere,' whereas Hegel finds unity everywhere. It is still dogmatic even though it '*fights* with its subject matter,' for it fights on the premise that the demonstration of the defectiveness of existence alone will transform existence, that the defect solved in thought is the defect resolved.

Marx completes the parenthetical comment with a statement of his revised position:

True criticism, by contrast, shows the inner genesis of the Holy Trinity in the human brain. It describes the act of its birth. So the truly philosophical criticism of the present state constitution not only shows up contradictions as existing; it *explains* them, it comprehends their genesis, their necessity. It considers them in their *specific* significance. But *comprehending* does not consist, as Hegel imagines, in recognizing the features of the logical concept everywhere, but in grasping the specific logic of the specific subject.

Unlike dogmatic criticism, which presumes to demolish its subject matter by demonstrating its non-conformity to a presupposed definition, 'true criticism' pursues the 'inner genesis' of the subject matter; i.e., it seeks to demonstrate the cause of its coming into being. It reveals 'contradictions as existing' by analysing the concrete object, but it does not stop here; it 'explains them' by grasping their inner formation, their process of coming into being, by analysing their own specific, *internal* design. The comprehension of the subject is not then, as Hegel would have it, to conceive everything real as a rational unity, but to analyse 'the specific logic of the specific subject.'

In this passage, Marx posits a critical reappraisal of his method: it is dogmatic to presume to show reality as defective by comparing it to a presupposed definition or, in the case of the Young Hegelians, an hypostasized ideal. Now, critique must not only uncover these defects or contradictions in reality, but also fathom the reason why they exist. And it must explain the contradiction by studying its existing nature, its 'specific logic.' (To help avoid some possible misunderstandings, we should point out that in the *Rheinische Zeitung* articles Marx does presuppose a definition of the state as organic unity and complementary concepts of law, freedom, etc., but none of these are hypostasized ideals.)

In this reformulation, there is a revised notion of the relationship between essence and existence. Essence is no longer the beginning point of the method, the definition against which existence is judged. Rather, the nature of existence itself must first be grasped and essence, then, comprehended as the analytically derived definition of the object in question.

This revised conception of the relationship has an implication for the concept of theory and practice as found in the *Rheinische Zeitung*. There, practice is a part of the critical method itself; it is seen as mediation by the critic or free press by virtue of knowledge of the essence. Now, in arguing that 'true criticism' must explain the contradictions and that this can be done only by analysing the specific logic of the existing contradictions, Marx removes the side of practice from critique. If the reason for the contradiction lies in reality, however, the solution must also lie there. Hereafter, the element of practice is to be sought in the existing contradiction itself.

The critique of Hegel's *Philosophy of Right* follows this revised critical approach. It may be said to be characterized by two aspects of the method. First, the critique seeks to *uncover* the inconsistencies of reality by analysing reality itself. (Hegel's description of the constitutional monarchy follows the logic of the existing state.) Second, it attempts to *explain* these 'essential contradictions,' to pursue the empirical reason for the demonstrated inconsistencies, by further analysis.

The first aspect itself has two related sides. One is the analysis of the subject, the constitutional monarchy, to discover its contradictions; this is the derivation of its principle. The other rests on this analysis: it is the derivation of the true essence. It is to set aside the inessential or the idiosyncratic, and to abstract the essential characteristics by analysis. It is the 'genus' of the subject matter. As such, it may serve as the essence against which to measure particular examples or aspects of the existing subject; it is also the means by which all subjects of the same genus may be judged, i.e., comprehended.

Such is the meaning of the concept of 'true democracy' in this critique of Hegel. Marx introduces it after he has analysed the existing contradiction of sovereignty and demonstrated that in truth sovereignty can be nothing but sovereignty of the people. 'True democracy' embodies this definition of sovereignty and, as such, is the genus of all constitutions or, as Marx puts it, 'the solved *riddle* of all constitutions.'

The appearance of this concept, under the rubrics of 'true democracy,' the 'genuine' or the 'rational' state, is understood almost universally as an example of Marx's idealism. It is difficult to find a commentator, however, who actually *argues* the point; the appearance of these concepts is taken as sufficient proof. But to understand them in this manner is to misunderstand their meaning. As definitions, they derive from analysis; they embody the essence of the subject, and therefore may be employed as explanatory devices for all objects within the compass of the definition, in this case, all constitutions, all political systems. They are employed in the same manner in which the rational state or law was employed in the *Rheinische Zeitung*, without the assumption of critique as practice, and without a suggestion that the definition or essence derives from any source other than reality itself.

With the inconsistencies of the modern state uncovered, and the underlying rationality defined, Marx is able to carry out the second aspect of his newly formulated critique. The reason why the fundamental contradiction exists must be discovered by analysis of the nature of the contradiction itself. The reason, because it gives rise to the existing contradiction, furthermore must contain both sides of it and therefore must also point to the nature of its solution. What was formerly seen as the role of the critic and free press now is to be sought in the reason for the contradiction, in the nature of existence itself.

There are two lengthy digressions in the *Critique*; and one is concerned with discovering the reason for the fundamental contradiction in the modern state, the separation of the political state from civil society. It is found in the discussion of bureaucracy. Bureaucracy, the executive, is shown to stand in an antithesis to civil society; indeed, it is this antithesis which characterizes political relations; but Marx now analyses the reason for this separation. The bureaucracy, as the embodiment of the state, he argues, stands separate from civil society because of the divisiveness of civil society itself. The separation presupposes the organization of civil society as particular and antagonistic interests. Moreover, the 'general' interest embodied in the bureaucracy is nothing more than the totality of particular interests; truly general or state affairs emerge only as the ceremonial side of political life. In this digression, Marx examines at length just how the nature of civil society as divided particular interests requires a separate executive to manage the affairs of these interests as particulars and how in turn bureaucracy must maintain these interests as particular if it is to remain as executive. The point here is that at the source of this relationship is the organization of civil society as a system of competing, particular, material interests – the very interests which comprise the content of the bureaucracy.

This conclusion is complemented by the results of the second digression. It is undertaken to fathom the nature of primogeniture which Hegel makes the principle of the class which forms 'the highest *synthesis* of the political state.' If this class embodies 'the highest synthesis,' then, its principle must also be the principle of the political state. From Hegel's description of primogeniture and his own historical research, Marx is able to deduce the following: 'Primogeniture is the political meaning of private property, private property in its political significance, i.e., in its general significance. The constitution is here therefore the *constitution of private property*.'[105] The idea that the political state determines is now perceived as an illusion; it is but a consequence of, a thing determined by, private property.

Thus, by going beyond the mere demonstration of the contradictions of the modern state, Marx uncovers the source, the reason, for the contradictions through an examination of their existing nature. The reason for the separation of the state from civil society, the content of 'executive' decisions, and the very essence of the constitution itself, all devolve upon private property. If the point of making this critique of Hegel were to answer the questions arising in the *Zeitung* articles, to fathom the nature of the modern state and the import of material interests, then, Marx has achieved his purpose.

His analysis goes further yet and explores the preconditions for the solution to the separation of state and civil society. If the separation rests on the divisiveness of civil society, then the continued fractionalization of the masses means continued separation; and conversely, the masses organized as an organic unity would spell the end of the separation. This point arises again in the concluding digression examining the intrinsic meaning of the demand for electoral reform, for universal enfranchisement. Here, it is argued that its essential meaning is the striving of the members of the state for a unity of political and civil life. Considered abstractly, the achievement of the universal franchise would mean the complete integration of civil society with the political state and the transcendence of the separation. In both of these examples, Marx is exploring the necessary preconditions which would lead to a solution to the contradiction and he is searching for them within the contradiction itself.

By way of summary, we may say that Marx has 'negated' the critical method as employed in the *Rheinische Zeitung*. Instead of presupposing the definition and discovering contradictions by comparing reality to it, he now engages in direct analysis of the subject in order to uncover its contradictions and to derive its essence. Instead of assuming, moreover, that the mere demonstration of contradictions by a critic would bring their unity, he now inquires about the empirical reason for the contradiction, and as a result of this enquiry, he is able to grasp the nature of the preconditions necessary for their solution. To paraphrase Marx, a precise formulation of the question provides the answer.

The answers in the *Critique* present new questions. The meaning of political emancipation, the nature of private property, and the preconditions for the transcendence of political society are the chief questions which arise here. And these questions imply another: namely, what is the relationship between the critic who grasps the answers and reality which provides them? The answers to these questions demand not only further development in the method, but also further analysis of political realities.

3

Political and Social Emancipation: articles from the *Deutsch-Französische Jahrbücher,* 1843-44

If the doubts that Marx had in early 1843 concerned his method and the nature of the political state and its relation to material interests, these doubts had been largely resolved in his *Critique of Hegel's Philosophy of Right.* The method was reformulated, the relation between the state and private property defined, and the nature of the modern political state systematically dissected. Indeed, the latter is analysed to such a degree that there is little more to be said at the conceptual level about political relations *per se.*[1]

Underlying the analysis in the *Critique* is the axiomatic proposition that it is man's nature to be social; that man can only become human in the context of a social organism; that it is man's relation to his social whole, his norms and mores, laws and constitution, which makes man human. A conscious, critical relationship of the individual to the collectivity, then, is the epitome of a truly rational society, a society in which the whole is a conscious reflection of the needs and aspirations of the people, but rather than standing outside them, it is embodied in each individual.

The modern political state, which purportedly embodies the general interest, is seen by Marx to stand over against civil society; it is separated from and opposed to this sphere of the particular. The political state is presided over, indeed monopolized by, a particular class, the bureaucracy. The relation of the individual to the political state, then, is a purely formal one, taking place through representatives who do not represent the general interest but rather particular interests. The general exists only in a formal sense; it constitutes the ceremonial side of political life. In short, the political state is an abstraction from its true content, the people; it is an entity estranged from and standing in opposition to them. Thus, in the modern state, the individual is cut off from a conscious, active connection with the collectivity, except in a formal way at election time. For the most part, he exists as an individual, alienated from his collectivity, and to that degree alienated from his humanity.

The actual content of the political state, Marx argues, is not the national interest but material interest. It is the totality of divided, particular interests as found in civil society, outside the political state proper. The political state, or more particularly, the bureaucracy, that monopolizes the 'general interest,' *presupposes* the organization of civil society in the form of competing interest groups. In other words, the organized particular interests of civil society constitute the content and presupposition, the necessary antecedent, of the modern political state. Hence, the origin and underlying rationale of the dualistic character of the modern state, i.e., its separation of the general and particular, is to be found in the history and nature of civil society, the sphere of private property.[2]

In so far as Marx resolves the questions about the nature of the political state and defines its relation to material interests in his *Critique* of Hegel, he throws up new questions. Now he must confront the nature of civil society for it is the 'premise' of the political state, the source of the division of modern society. The means to transform or transcend this society, moreover, will be found in civil society for every premise contains not only its antithesis but also the elements which lead to a new synthesis.

In the next group of articles to be considered, those written by and large in 1843, we find, first, a consolidation of ideas developed in the *Critique*, and second, the first tentative response to questions raised in that analysis. There are different formulations of solutions to problems worked out in the analysis of Hegel, the solution to certain political questions not included in the *Critique*, the initial search for answers to the new problems, and the first assertion about the role of the proletariat in transcending the *political* nature of modern society.

All these elements are to be found in the work Marx published in the short-lived journal, *Deutsch-Französische Jahrbücher* (D-FJ), which appeared early in 1844. To these writings – the letters by Marx to Ruge between March and September 1843, and the articles, 'On the Jewish Question' and the 'Contribution to the Critique of Hegel's Philosophy of Right, Introduction' – we shall add the rejoinder of July 1844 by Marx to Ruge on the meaning of the uprising of the Silesian workers. It is entitled, 'Critical Marginal Notes on the Article "The King of Prussia and Social Reform. By a Prussian,"' and it constitutes a complement to and extension of the position Marx advances in the 'Introduction.'

The three letters by Marx in the *Deutsch-Französische Jahrbücher* re-express and expand many themes already articulated in the *Critique*. They comprise, in a word, Marx's reflections on the political situation in Germany, on the possibility of change, and on the role of the radical critic. It is not so much his analysis of Germany that is our concern, however; it is rather the underlying unity of the political analysis.

The first letter, written in March, reveals a disillusionment with Germans (perhaps occasioned by his resignation from the *Rheinische Zeitung* early in that month) but at the same time an abiding confidence in 'the impending revolution.'[3] The theme of the letter is his 'feeling of national shame.'

At first glance, shame is an odd concept for the radical and controversial former editor of the *Zeitung* to be using. It admits of a feeling of unease or pain that accompanies recognition or awareness of degradation, humiliation, or inferiority. That Marx can feel this derives from the fact that he is travelling in Holland where liberalism affected the making of the 1830 constitution. The Dutch, therefore, possess a modicum of political liberty, which serves to heighten Marx's consciousness of the predicament of German politics. 'The most insignificant Dutchman,' he notes, 'is still a citizen compared with the greatest German.' Outside of Prussia, moreover, there is a general awareness about the lack of political freedom in Prussia. The 'pompous cover of liberalism has fallen away,' he writes, 'and the most disgusting despotism in all its nakedness is disclosed to the eyes of the world.'

In contrast to a liberal state, the despotic rule in Prussia points to the German's lack of liberty; and in itself the despotism reveals 'the emptiness of our patriotism and the abnormality of our state system.' Both revelations produce shame, the painful consciousness of subjugation, of freedom denied, and therefore of humanity denied.

But what is the relation of shame to revolution? Shame, responds Marx, 'is already revolution of a kind; shame is actually the victory of the French Revolution over the German patriotism that defeated it in 1813.' This is to say that shame is the first step out of acceptance or ignorance; it is the first glimmer of awareness of a defective state of affairs. For the Germans, it arises in the contrast of the French Revolution, the assertion of political freedom, with German patriotism, the affirmation of political unfreedom. And if shame were to be felt by a whole nation, reasons Marx, 'it would be like a lion, crouching ready to spring.' It would be like a nation gathering its strength to overturn despotic rule.

Alas, admits Marx, the wretched Germans 'are still patriots'; they revel in their ignorance, their subjugation. Yet, he suggests that the nature of the political state itself will cure them of their patriotism. The rule of William IV is a 'comedy of despotism' which eventually must bring upon itself a revolution because the state cannot forever suffer its own reduction to 'a kind of harlequinade.' How long before a buffoon is recognized for what he is? How long before the people take themselves seriously?

The concept of shame, a strange device for political analysis, provides Marx with some new insights. His use of it reveals shame as an unsystematic, mundane, non-philosophical expression of critique; it appears more specifically here as a rudimentary recognition of political defects. As such it is a form of consciousness that is at least a tentative step towards social revolution. It is itself a sort of revolution in that it is a change of consciousness, a change that is clearly necessary before political or social revolution is at all possible. Marx is not arguing that revolution comes from a change of consciousness[4] but that a change of consciousness is a necessary antecedent to revolution.

In a reply to Marx's letter, Arnold Ruge, the co-editor of the D-FJ, disagrees with optimism about the 'impending revolution.' Instead, Ruge sees the Germans as defeated, resigned to suffer under despotic rule, with no capability of carrying out a revolution.[5]

In his response written in May, Marx rejects Ruge's despair and reasserts his own optimism about the future: it will be 'our lot,' he insists, 'to be the first to enter the new life alive.' Ruge's appraisal of the German situation cannot be ignored, however, because of its apparent truth; i.e., the Germans do accept their lack of freedom and even glorify it by becoming patriots. Marx does not disagree entirely but wants to expand the analysis and furthermore define the basis of his optimism. The theme of the reply concerns 'the philistine and his state,' the materialism and narrowness of life in Germany that gives rise to Ruge's despair. Although 'it is true that the old world belongs to the philistine,' writes Marx, he is not to be shunned or feared, but rather 'it is worth while to study this lord of the world.'[6]

The philistine is 'lord of the world ... only because he fills it with his society as maggots do a corpse.' He has become a lord by feeding on the decay of feudalism; it is the crassest form of existence, mere feeding. It is not, therefore, in the nature of this society to require freedom because it is a society which merely consumes. As such, it is therefore a society of slaves and slave-owners.

Precisely because this society lacks freedom, it lacks humanity. It is therefore man's 'sense of freedom' which must be 'aroused again in the hearts of these people,' states Marx, if this society is to become 'a community of human beings united for their highest aims, into a democratic state.' Freedom comes with the conscious unity of the individual and his collectivity; the degree of this unity is the degree of humanity, the degree of fulfilment of man's generic essence.

The philistine world, however, is without this sense of unity; it is a world of masters and slaves, neither of whom by definition can be human. Thus, the principle of this world, writes Marx, 'is the *dehumanized world.*' It is '*a political world of animals*' – political, because there are rulers and ruled; and a world of animals, because this separation is complete.

'The most complete philistine world,' Marx asserts, is Germany. Here, the people's 'loftiest thoughts do not go beyond a bare existence.' They have no aspirations beyond the narrowness of material need. Those who rule take this abjectness into account, though they are little less philistine than the ruled. Their attitude reflects the baseness of existence of the people as philistines: when rulers are paid homage, they see only animals. As Marx puts it: 'Despotism's sole idea is contempt for man, the dehumanized man, and this idea has the advantage over many others of being at the same time a fact. The despot always sees degraded people.' 'The monarchical principle in general is the despised, the despicable, *the dehumanized man* [der entmenschte Mensch].' 'Where the monarchical principle has a majority behind it, human beings constitute the minority; where the monarchical principle arouses no doubts, there human beings do not exist at all.'[7]

Marx is here pointing to the relationship between the dehumanized man and the despotic ruler; they are complementary sides of a single phenomenon, the absolutist state. Despotic or monarchical rule is arbitrary rule; and where it exists it reflects the situation in which the people are completely separated from their affairs of state, in which they are without a political existence,[8] without a relation to their whole; and therefore they exist as individuals only, unfree and dehumanized.

Marx also points to the nature of this relation: 'the philistine is the material of the monarchy, and the monarch always remains only the king of the philistines.' It is, in other words, the philistine world that throws up the possibility of monarchical rule and monarchical rule can only be rule over philistines. As it stands, the relationship cannot be changed by either side: the king 'cannot turn either himself or his subjects into free, real human beings' while he remains a king; and the philistines cannot say that they want to become human beings while they remain philistines.

The desire to become truly human, to be free, can only be fulfilled if the premise of this relationship (the philistine world) is overcome and its corollary (despotism) with it. The only way out of 'the political world of animals,' argues Marx, is 'the abandonment [Verlassen] of the basis of this world and the transition to the human world of democracy [den Übergang zur Menschenwelt der Demokratie].'

He ends the letter by indicating how the 'abandonment' is already in process. 'The enemies of philistinism, in short, all people who think and who suffer,' are daily awakening to the desire for freedom. Moreover, 'the system of industry and trade, of ownership and exploitation of people,' is rapidly pushing this awakening towards 'a rupture within present-day society.' 'The existence of suffering human beings [Die Existenz der leidenden Menschheit], who think, and thinking human beings, who are oppressed, must inevitably become unpalatable and indigestible to the animal world of philistinism which passively and thoughtlessly consumes.'[9]

This is certainly among the earliest statements by Marx on the means of transforming the bourgeois or philistine society. Within the premise itself there is the term that will negate the premise and its consequence. This term comprises not only the suffering human beings as created in the system of trade and industry but also the oppressed thinking humans. Both are human beings, but only in the sense that both think and suffer and therefore are aware of their unfulfilled humanity. They are complementary in that they embody the two prerequisites of Marx's revolutionary theory: the oppressed philosopher/intellectual and the suffering masses: theory and practice.

This theme is carried over into the third letter, but here it is placed in the context of a debate over the function and direction of the new journal. If the second letter closes with a description of the growth of a new world in the womb of the old, the third letter concerns the role of the critic as midwife. The philosopher as critic and his relation to real struggles and actual political life is the theme of this last letter.

Marx begins by asserting that 'everyone will have to admit to himself that he has no exact view [Anschauung] what the future should be [was werden soll].' Not to be lamented, this situation is advantageous because the contributors 'will not dogmatically anticipate the world, but only want to find the new world through criticism [Kritik] of the old one.'[10] It is the critique that he wants to see as the guiding principle of the D-FJ.

If it is the critique of 'all that exists' that is to be the *raison d'être* of the journal, then, the journal cannot put forth 'any dogmatic banner.' The critic is the very opposite of the dogmatist; the former deduces his propositions from reality or reason, the latter presents his as if his authority were sufficient. If it is, moreover, as all the contributors of this exchange agree,[11] that a truly human society is to be its ultimate goal, then the journal must examine those theories which purport to have the solution to the human predicament. Thus, what more obvious subject to begin to criticize than the existing theories of communism – 'dogmatic abstractions,' as Marx calls them. It is not the idea of communism he is referring to but the theory and practice already in existence.

The communism in question is that 'taught by Cabet, Dézamy, Weitling, etc.' Each advocated a form of association which, although based on co-operative labour, held the individual at a premium and neglected the universal aspect, the 'community.'[12] For this reason, Marx says that *this* communism 'is itself only a special expression of the humanistic principle, an expression which is still infected by its antithesis – the private system [Privat wesen].' It is possible, in other words, to do away with private property but not thereby to create true communism. Such theories are 'only a special, one-sided realisation of the socialist principle'; i.e., they contain the principle of 'public' or 'national' or collective ownership of property, and therefore are bound to give rise to contending doctrines stressing other aspects of socialism.

The socialist principle focuses on the question of private property and advocates communal or social ownership. It is, therefore, Marx writes, 'only one aspect that concerns the *reality* of the true human being.' It is not enough for the critic who adheres to the humanistic principle merely to propound socialism; man is not simply an economic being; the critic must also pay attention 'to the theoretical existence of man;' it is necessary also to criticize 'religion, science, etc.' In a word, the journal must concern itself with man's material existence and the development of his self-consciousness.

In suggesting how the analysis is to be done, Marx presents at this point the first systematic, albeit brief, exposition of his method of critique.[13] The critic, he says, must make real phenomena, material being, or spiritual, theoretical beliefs, 'in whatever form they exist' his 'point of departure.' To proceed from some 'ready-made system,' some preconceived doctrine, is to confront the world in a one-sided or arbitrary fashion; it is, as it were, to judge the world before the case is heard. To take the world as it is, is the only undogmatic starting point.

The critic, then, can 'start out with any form of theoretical and practical consciousness and from these specific forms of existing reality unfold the true reality as its obligation and its main design [und aus den *eigenen* Formen der existierenden Wirklichkeit die wahre Wirklichkeit als ihr Sollen und ihren Endzweck entwickeln].' But what does this mean and how is it possible?

The answer is found in the somewhat enigmatic phrase that precedes this sentence. 'Reason,' writes Marx, 'has always existed, but not always in a reasonable form.' It is logical to assume, since Marx had just completed his long critique of Hegel's *Philosophy of Right*, that the meaning he gives to 'reason' derives from Hegel. And for Hegel, history is reason progressively realizing itself as the consciousness of freedom[14] – freedom being the unity of the universal and particular. Given that Marx does not adopt the idealism of Hegel, it may be assumed here that by reason he means the *potential* or essential freedom of man, which has always existed in the relation of the individual to the state but not always in a reasonable form because this relation has rarely, except in very limited ways, been realized as a true and conscious *unity*. It usually appears with an emphasis on one side or the other, as in Plato's *Republic* or in liberal theories. Nevertheless, the potential unity is *implicit* and against this the imperfect relation can be measured. The truth of 'any form of theoretical and practical consciousness' is understood by comparing it to the 'reason' implicit within it. This potential is 'its obligation and its main design.'

Why must man strive to realize his essence as the 'main design' and 'purpose' of man? At first glance the question appears to be metaphysical, but in reality it is no more metaphysical than the growth of an oak from an acorn. The acorn must, of course, develop into an oak, for the oak is the 'obligation and main design' of the acorn. Marx, however, is referring here only to the process of comprehending the essence; the problem of realizing it is still to be considered.[15]

However Hegelian this may sound, it must be stressed that the essential aspects of Hegel's philosophy are *not* present. Reason, for Marx, is not the governance of God in the world.[16] History is not the progressive realization of the Idea, of Reason. The point of departure is not the Spirit, the abstract world. And the existing world is not an aspect of the realization of the Idea. The 'reason' that Marx employs, this potential unity, this concept of freedom, is but the essence of man which may or may not find a genuine expression in existing forms of reality.

As far as present life is concerned, continues Marx, it is the political state that 'contains the demands [Forderungen] of reason' in 'its *modern* forms.' In other words, the political state purports to be a representative power, though this does not imply the realization of 'socialist demands' [sozialistischen Forderungen]. That is, its representativeness is illusory; it is not real democracy. Furthermore, the political state 'assumes that reason has been realised,' that it has achieved genuine freedom. But this assumption is at the centre of its main contradiction, i.e., 'between its ideal function and its pre-requisites.' That is, the political state professes to represent the interests of all as all but in fact presupposes the hegemony of private interests. In these assertions, it may be noted Marx appears to be presenting certain conclusions from his analysis of Hegel's *Philosophy of Right*.

The critic, then, is able to uncover the truth of the political state, its improvement over earlier forms of representation and its defectiveness, by contrasting it to the realization of genuine freedom. But the pursuit of this truth is not an end in itself: 'In analyzing the superiority of the representative system over the social-estate system, the critic will *interest* in *practice* [prak-tisch] a large party. By raising the representative system from its political form to the universal form and by demonstrating the true significance under-lying it, the critic at the same time compels this party to transcend itself [über sich hinauszugehn] for its victory is at the same time its defeat.'[17] Marx is saying that the pursuit of the truth of the estates system will coincide with the political aspirations of the unrepresented. In turn, the demon-stration of this coincidence will move the unrepresented to demand repre-sentation, and this demand fulfilled is in essence not only the victory of the unrepresented but also the abolition of itself as the unrepresented.

Finally, the role of the critic and his relation to the real world is succinctly summarized by Marx: 'nothing prevents us from making criticism of politics, participation in politics, and therefore *real* struggles, the starting point of our criticism, and from identifying our criticism with them. In that case we do not confront the world in a doctrinaire way with a new principle: Here is the truth, kneel down before it! We develop new principles for the world out of the world's own principles. We do not say to the world; Cease your struggles, they are foolish; we will give you the true slogan of struggle. We merely show the world what it is *really* fighting for, and consciousness is something it *has* to acquire, even if it does not want to.'[18] He has moved a long way from his position in the *Rheinische Zeitung* articles. No longer does he see the role of the critic as mediator between two sides; now, the critic must take up the real struggles of the world and seek to give them clarity.

The themes of the three letters bear a continuity even though their appa-rent relation seems distant. The underlying thread is consciousness of free-dom and its realization. If the Germans have only patriotism, and no shame, it is only a matter of time before despotism 'knocks the patriotism out of them' and courts a revolutionary fate. If Germany is a society of philistines, whose logical consequence is despotic rule, it will itself produce 'suffering human beings, who think, and thinking human beings, who are oppressed,' and who together will overturn philistinism. If there is to be freedom, then the critics who comprehend it and the 'large party' which desires and struggles for it must work as one.

Throughout these letters the meaning given to freedom denotes the unmediated relation of the individual to the social whole. It is human emancipation and not political freedom that Marx sees as necessary for the realization of the essence of man and as the criterion of social progress. The meaning of political and human emancipation and the means for achieving the latter are the themes that Marx explores in depth in the articles that follow.

THE MEANING OF POLITICAL EMANCIPATION
AND THE PREREQUISITE OF SOCIAL EMANCIPATION:
'ON THE JEWISH QUESTION'

Marx's essay 'On the Jewish Question' is divided into two parts which reflect and expand the conclusions he reached following his analysis of Hegel's *Philosophy of Right*. The first part examines the meaning of political emancipation, in part, by contrasting it to human emancipation, the rational unity of the individual and his society. The second concerns the social prerequisite for human emancipation, i.e., the transformation of civil society. In both, the argument is made in the form of a rebuttal of the views of Bruno Bauer. But because our subject is the development of Marx's views, the commentary on Bauer will be kept to a minimum. And because many of the points made in this essay were already made in the *Critique*, they will be noted only briefly here.

Marx's article is not about the Jewish question in itself; rather, the Jewish question is used as a vehicle to outline the nature and means of political emancipation. Nevertheless, a note about the context is in order because Bauer does deal with the Jewish question as a question of the nature of the Jews.

The Jewish question arose in Germany in the early nineteenth century because the civil rights extended to Jews under Napoleonic rule had been withdrawn in an edict in 1816. Under William IV, the role of Jews in political and civil life became increasingly restrictive because the king desired to rule a Christian state. By the early 1840s, Prussian liberals, who had kept alive the ideas of the French Revolution, made the demand for political emancipation of the Jews an important political issue.

In his pamphlet, *Die Judenfrage*, Bruno Bauer poses 'the question of Jewish emancipation,' according to Marx, as the question of 'the *nature* of the

Jew who is to be emancipated and of the Christian state that is to emancipate him.'[19] Regarding the former, Bauer writes that for the Jew to become a citizen and remain a Jew is to have 'his Jewish and restricted nature triumph always in the end over his human and political obligations.' To be emancipated, therefore, the Jew must renounce his religion. As for the latter, Bauer maintains that the abolition of a 'privileged religion' will bring the abolition of that religion and religion as such.[20] For the Christian state to emancipate the Jew, it must emancipate itself from Christianity.

To pose the question in this fashion, says Marx, aside from entangling the author in contradictions, reveals a 'one-sided formulation.' That is, Bauer makes the question of Jewish emancipation into a theological question. He gives a theological solution to what is really a political question. The question that Bauer neglects to ask, and which points to the source of his contradictions, is 'what kind of emancipation?' In not doing so, he confuses the problem of human emancipation, which would require general emancipation from religion, with political emancipation, which would require only the political state to be emancipated from religion, *inter alia*. The proper subject of criticism, suggests Marx, is the nature of political emancipation. Whereas Bauer asks whether the Jews in maintaining their religion have the 'right to want political emancipation,' Marx asks whether political freedom necessitates the abolition of religion.

Bauer's mistake is to extrapolate from the German situation where no political state as such exists, where instead a Christian state confronts the Jew on a religious basis. Here, the Jewish question *is* a theological question. But in North America, where the political state exists as a secular entity, the relation of the political state to religion is not theological but political. The one-sidedness of Bauer's formulation of the Jewish question as a theological question, then, becomes obvious: civic emancipation is quite possible without religious emancipation.

In light of the North American states where there is no state religion but a flourishing number of religious sects, Marx poses the question anew: 'What is the relation of *complete* political emancipation to religion?' Or to recast it: if political freedom is not inconsistent with the persistence of religion, what does this persistence say about political freedom? The answer begins with the assertion that 'the existence of religion is the existence of a defect'; i.e., religion is the expression of the alienation of man's essence, of the consignment of his essence to an imaginary world. The 'source of this defect' lies 'in the nature of the state itself': religion is a 'manifestation of secular narrowness'; it is evidence that man as philistine, as he is in civil society, has no real relation to his social being. Thus, Marx states, 'religious narrowness' is explained by 'secular narrowness' or 'restriction,' by which he means man's separation from his social whole. The latter must be overcome in order to abolish the former. The persistence of religion points to the nature of political emancipation and its relation to human emancipation. Political emancipation, by admitting to the persistence of religion, reveals its difference from human emancipation.[21]

The point is that, contrary to Bauer's argument, political emancipation is the 'emancipation of the state from ... *religion* in general,' but it is not general emancipation from religion. The 'limits of political emancipation,' says Marx, are clearly 'evident in that 'the state can be a *free state* [Freistaat] without man being a *free man* [ein freier Mensch].'[22]

The political emancipation of the state from religion is similar to its emancipation from private property. The abolition of the 'property qualification for suffrage,' it is pointed out, is the revocation of the *political form* of private property. But though the political privileges of private property may be annulled, private property itself remains. Marx expands this theme: 'The state abolishes, in its own way, distinctions of *birth, social rank, education, occupation*, when it declares that birth, social rank, education, occupation, are *non-political* distinctions, when it claims, without regard to these distinctions, that every member of the nation is an *equal* participant in national sovereignty, when it treats all elements of the real life, of the nation from the standpoint of the state.'[23]

These distinctions, then, are declared 'non-political,' they are banished from playing a formal role in politics by the emancipated state. But they are not abolished; in fact they comprise the presuppositions of the political state. It is only because of the existence and persistence of these distinctions, of all elements that divide man from his fellow man, that the political state can assert a universality which is separated from the individual. 'The perfect political state,' Marx claims, 'is, by its nature, man's *species-life*, as *opposed* to his material life.'

Complete political emancipation effects a division in society. Man's species-life is elevated to the political state and his life as an individual is consigned to civil society. In emancipating itself from religion, the political state relegates religion to the sphere of civil society. Religion, then, as with the other elements of civil society, stands in opposition to the political state, separated from the state, as one of the preconditions of political emancipation. It is this relation of religion in general to the political state that the Jewish question 'reduces itself' to in the final analysis, concludes Marx.[24]

Although the process of political emancipation separates man from his social whole and therefore is 'not the final form of human emancipation in general,' it is nevertheless the 'final form of human emancipation *within* the hitherto existing world order.' In other words, the strict division of society into a public sphere and a private sphere and the accompanying banishment of religion from the former to the latter, is not a 'stage of political emancipation,' asserts Marx, 'but its *completion.*'[25] That man in the modern republic should be divided into 'Jew and citizen, Protestant and citizen, religious man and citizen' is not inconsistent with 'citizenhood'; it is an aspect of political emancipation itself, 'the *political* method of emancipating oneself from religion.'

Consigned to the realm of civil society, religion may dissipate into any number of sects but it does not vanish. On the contrary, writes Marx, in the democratic republic 'religion remains the ideal, non-secular consciousness of its members, because religion is the ideal form of the *stage of human development* achieved in this state.'[26] It is the duality of the modern state, the separation of 'individual life and species-life' [Gattungsleben], the division of 'life in civil society and political life [zwischen dem Leben der bürgerlichen Gesellschaft und dem politischen Leben],' that creates the need for religion. Man in the political state is religious because his life as a member of the state is confined to a political form and severed from his essential life; he is religious because life in civil society is individualistic; man is cut off from his fellow man; and both of these separations, two sides of the same coin, find a supposed resolution in religious belief, an imaginary link to one's fellow man and one's social whole.

More than merely consistent with the persistence of religion, the democratic republic embodies the spirit of Christianity, that is, the individualization of man's relation to God, to species-life. This is the 'sovereignty of man' – as an individual. In Christianity, this relation is 'a dream,' 'a fantasy,' but in democracy it is a 'tangible reality,' a 'secular principle.' This is to say that man in the political democracy participates in political life, in his species-life, as an individual, emerging from the isolation of life in civil society to do so and returning to this isolation afterwards.

At this point Marx summarizes his position. 'Political emancipation from religion leaves religion in existence, although not a privileged religion.' Religion is here consigned to the sphere of civil society and stands with all the other aspects of civil society in contradiction to the political state. The democratic state which abolishes privileged religion is, in fact, 'the consummation of the Christian state'; that is, the relation of political democracy to the citizen is the Christian relation of the individual to God. And finally, political emancipation from religion is not 'the emancipation of the real man from religion.'[27]

This last point leads Marx to conclude, in contradistinction to Bauer, that the Jew can be emancipated in a political sense 'without renouncing Judaism completely,' but that political emancipation is not to be confused with human emancipation. The fact that the Jew can remain a Jew and be politically emancipated reveals the limitations of political freedom.

But if Marx here exposes the confusion over the nature of political and human emancipation in Bauer's argument, there still remains the question of the 'rights of man.' Is not religious partisanship incompatible with such rights? Bauer insists that particular interests, including religious differences, need to be forsaken in order 'to receive the universal rights of man.' As Marx deals with it, the question becomes: Are the 'rights of man' human rights? Implicit in Marx's critique of the rights of man is his notion of man as human, man who is consciously, critically united with the social whole.

The rights of man, properly speaking, must be distinguished from the rights of the citizen, begins Marx. The latter [droits du citoyen] concern rights pertaining to 'participation' 'in the *political* community, in the *life of the state*.'[28] The former [droits de l'homme] concerns 'the rights of a *member of civil society*, i.e., the rights of egoistic man, of man separated from other men and from the community.' These rights, then, cannot be understood to refer to man as a human, rather to man as an alienated individual.

To illustrate the point, Marx examines the definitions of the chief elements of the rights of man as given in the French constitution of 1793. Liberty is the central principle and it is defined as the right to do anything that does not overstep the rights of others. Described this way, Marx points out, it 'is based not on the association of man with man, but on the separation of man from man. It is the *right* of this separation, the right of the *restricted* individual, withdrawn into himself.' The 'practical application' of this right, he continues 'is man's right to *private property*,' w^h.ich is nothing but the right to dispose of 'one's property ... at one's discretion.' Liberty and its application, says Marx, 'form the basis of civil society. It makes every man see in other men not the *realisation* of his freedom, but the *barrier* to it.' Liberty, under the rubric of the 'rights of man,' is not only *not* freedom in a human sense but a positive hindrance to true freedom.[29]

As for 'equality' as a right of man, it is a corollary of liberty; it is the recognition of man as 'a self-sufficient monad,' a man defined as separated from his community. The right to security as 'a right of man' is the culmination of the rights of civil society. It is, says Marx sardonically, 'the concept of *police*,' the notion that the highest purpose of the state is to protect individual interests. 'The concept of security does not raise civil society above its egoism. On the contrary, security is the *insurance* of its egoism.'[30]

Marx summarizes his position by asserting that none of these rights of man, despite the use of the concept of man, embodies a notion that is broader than man the individual, 'separated from his community.' As he elaborates: man here 'is far from being conceived as a species-being; on the contrary, species-life itself, society, appears as a framework external to the individuals, as a restriction of their original independence. The sole bond holding them together is natural necessity, need and private interest, the preservation of their property and their egoistic selves.'[31]

Having demonstrated the limitations of the rights of man as promulgated in the French Revolution, Marx is faced with the question of why it is that political revolution can be made in the name of liberty and yet proclaims this liberty in so narrow a fashion, as the 'rights of egoistic man.' How is it that political emancipation finds citizenship and the political state reduced to 'a mere *means* for maintaining these so-called rights of man,' that the political community becomes the 'means' and the egoism of civil society the 'aim,' and that the essence of man is construed not as 'man as citizen' [der Mensch als citoyen] but as 'man as bourgeois' [der Mensch als bourgeois]?

The answer that Marx presents hints at the source of political revolution, but for the most part it is a description of what happens in political revolution. The 'political revolution,' he writes, 'is the revolution of civil society'; that is, political revolution is the assertion of the principle of civil society over against the principle of the old society. 'The character of the old society,' namely, feudalism, was 'directly political.' In other words, the structure of feudal society, its forms of association, comprised '*discrete* societies within society.' These forms 'determined the relation of the individual to the *state as a whole*, i.e., his *political* relation, that is, his relation of separation and exclusion from the other components of society.'[32] The consequence of this structure was the embodiment of 'the unity of the state' and its concomitant powers in a single ruler.

The overthrow of this form of sovereign power, the 'establishment of the political state,' and 'the dissolution of civil society into independent *individuals*' are 'accomplished by *one and the same act*,' namely, the political revolution.[33] It revolutionizes the political nature of feudal society by separating political life from civil life. It changes the nature of political relations but does not do away with politics. It clarifies the contradiction between the individual and society without resolving it. The abstraction of political life from civil society makes the latter, as a world of individual interests, the 'precondition' and therefore 'the natural basis' of the former.

Because political man is 'abstract' and 'artificial' and because bourgeois man is 'sensuous' [sinnlichen] and 'immediate,' it is the latter which is taken to be the real nature of man. Political emancipation divides man such that 'the real man is acknowledged only in the form of the *egoistic* individual, and the *true* man only in the form of *abstract citizen*.'

This, then, is the result of political emancipation: man is resolved into two contradictory natures: as member of civil society, he is an egoist, an isolated individual; as citizen, he is allegorically moral, that is, abstractly human (human in abstraction). Human emancipation comes with the union of man as individual and citizen. As Marx puts it: 'Only when the real, individual man re-absorbs in himself the abstract citizen, and as an individual human being has become a *species-being* in his everyday life ... will human emancipation have been accomplished.'[34]

The first part of 'On the Jewish Question' is a critique of political emancipation. Marx is concerned to demonstrate the limitations of the modern state, to reveal the meaning of persisting political relations. This is achieved by contrasting man who is politically emancipated with the concept of man who is truly human. The contrast is made, it should be noted, in the form of a historical sequence. The political nature of feudal society, Marx says, is resolved 'into its component parts,' man as individual and man as citizen, by the political revolution. But this duality which characterizes modern society represents an unresolved contradiction; it can only be resolved with the advent of human emancipation, the integration of citizenhood and the individual.

Marx does not leave the question here; he points to the source of this duality, whose abolition, by implication, must bring an end to the division in modern society. If the basis of this duality is civil society, then it is the transformation of civil society which is necessary in order to make man truly human.

This is the subject matter of the second part of the article. Here, Marx for the first time in any detail puts forward the idea that it is the annulment of civil society that will transform the defective nature of the modern state. If the significance of the Jewish question in Part I is that it points to the limitations of political emancipation, then in Part II it is that it points to the need to transform civil society in order to achieve human emancipation.

The problem to be solved, as it appears in the title of Bauer's article, is: 'The capacity of the modern Jew and Christian to become free.' Bauer deals with it, according to Marx, as if it is 'purely a religious question,' as if the theological content of a religion determines the adherent's ability to be emancipated. But Marx wants to 'break with the theological formulation of the question.' The 'Jew's capacity for emancipation' is not a question of the nature of his religion in itself, says Marx, but a question of 'the relation of Judaism to the emancipation of the modern world.' In other words, because Judaism has a 'special position' 'in the contemporary enslaved world,' it is necessary to grasp this position in order to understand the capacity of the Jew for emancipation. Thus, Marx reformulates the question. 'What particular *social* element has to be overcome in order to abolish Judaism?'

The 'special position' of the Jew is the 'secular basis' of his religion. And this basis is '*practical* need, *self-interest*.' His secular practice is 'haggling' and his secular goal is 'money.' This secular basis is nothing but the epitome of the market-place, the world of trade and commerce. It is the essence of civil society. For this reason, Marx writes that freedom from haggling and money, from commerce and its medium, from the secular basis of Judaism, would bring the emancipation of the Jew. But more, it 'would be the self-emancipation of our time.' The whole of society would be emancipated. The 'special position' of the Jew lies in the correspondence of the basis of his religion with the basis of the modern state. This congruity allows Marx to claim that '*the emancipation of the Jews*, in the final analysis, is the emancipation of mankind from *Judaism*.'[35] In other words, the *un*emancipated state of mankind is due to the reign of trade and commerce, which also happens to be the basis of Judaism and the source of the unemancipated state of Jews.

At this point in the essay, Marx examines the social implications of the dominance of money and in doing so clearly employs the concept Judaism in *both* a literal and figurative way. It is not only the Jew but also the nature of bourgeois man that is analysed here under the same rubric.[36] But because our concern is with the political, we shall not here extend our exposition to the Jewish nature of civil society. Suffice to say that his discussion here presages in a limited way many of the themes that will appear in the 1844 manuscripts.

It is still necessary to place Marx's analysis of Judaism in the perspective of the D-FJ articles. While it is political revolution that reduces the political nature of feudal society to its constituent parts, the political state and civil society, it is the developed form of Christianity, as the 'spirit of civil society' that confirms man's isolation in civil society, that 'completes' on the side of *theory* 'the estrangement of man from himself and from nature [die Selbstentfremdung des Menschen von sich und der Natur].' It is only in the wake of these changes that Judaism as the *practical* principle of civil society triumphs. Selling [Veräusserung], says Marx, 'is the practical aspect of alienation [Entäusserung].'[37] In other words, as long as man is political man, that is, an atomistic individual separated from his real social being, religion will continue to be the spirit of civil society, the objectified, alien, social essence; and money will remain the substance of civil society, the objectified, alien, social product.

Marx now returns to the original question about the capacity of the Jew to be emancipated and restates his earlier position: 'Once society has succeeded in abolishing the *empirical* essence of Judaism – huckstering and its preconditions – the Jew will have become *impossible*, because his consciousness no longer has an object, because the subjective basis of Judaism, practical need, has been humanized, and because the conflict between man's individual-sensuous existence and his species-existence [individuell-sinnlichen Existenz mit der Gattungsexistenz] has been abolished. The *social* emancipation of the Jew is the *emancipation of society from Judaism*.'[38] This conclusion is on the one hand a retort to Bauer and on the other hand the disclosed solution to the problem stated at the end of Part I of the article. The prerequisite of human emancipation is the abolition of civil society and of its precondition, money.

THE MEANS TO SOCIAL EMANCIPATION:
THE INTRODUCTION TO THE *CRITIQUE OF HEGEL*

With the main contradiction of the modern state and its source now uncovered the problem becomes the means to resolve the contradiction. This is the question that Marx takes up in the introduction to the *Contribution to the Critique of Hegel's Philosophy of Right*.

The answer is given largely in terms of the question of German emancipation, although I try to give it a wider meaning. It is presented, moreover, as the result of the development of philosophy and of industry. It is the answer that history provides for its own question[39] in that the answer is given once the question becomes real. In the criticism of religion and in the rise of industry lies the nascent answer. In the criticism of the state and in the growth of the proletariat the answer makes its first appearance. Marx's 'discovery' of the contradiction implicit in the modern state and its solution in the union of theory and practice, then, are presented as a statement of the truth of the present stage of the development of history. It is not Marx's imposed solution but his articulation of history's own solution.

Marx begins by saying that in Germany 'the *criticism of religion* is in the main complete,' a reference no doubt to the work of Ludwig Feuerbach, in particular, among others.[40] To this he adds: 'and criticism of religion is the premise of all criticism.'[41] Religion is the manifestation of man's estrangement from his social whole; its existence signifies the absence of the 'true reality' of man's 'human essence.' As long as man is in the 'grip of religion' he will seek solace from his isolation in real life in a fantasy, a belief in a world 'beyond.' The criticism of religion, however, exposes religion as an invention by man, as a reflection of man's own self. It is the criticism of religion, then, which first raises the question of man's separation from himself and therefore points to the essential need of man for some form of union with his fellow man. This need is the basis of the critique of existing man.

Such criticism, suggests Marx, 'dissilusions man' from seeking his 'true reality' in the heavens and obliges him to find it in himself. Inasmuch, then, as man rejects religion he begins to reject the world that gives rise to religion. The question of religion is answered with the question of the nature of the world that needs religion. So it is, writes Marx, that 'once the *holy form* of human self-estrangement has been unmasked,' the '*task of philosophy* ... is to unmask self-estrangement in its *unholy forms.*' 'Thus the criticism of heaven turns into the criticism of earth, the *criticism of religion* into the *criticism of law* [*Kritik des Rechts*] and the *criticism of theology* into the *criticism of politics* [*Kritik der Politik*].'[42]

The critic, who but defines or clarifies the questions that history sets itself, now must examine law and political relations, i.e., the nature of the state 'which needs illusions.' For Marx, this task is embodied in 'the criticism of *German philosophy of state and law* [Staats- und Rechts-philosophie],' especially as it culminates in the work of Hegel. The reason, continues Marx, lies in the fact that a critique of this work 'is both a critical analysis of the modern state and of the reality connected with it, and the resolute negation of the whole *German political and legal consciousness* as *practised* hitherto, the ... most universal expression of which, raised to the level of a *science*, is the *speculative philosophy of law* itself.'[43] The critique of German political theory, most scientifically formulated by Hegel, then, has a dual outcome: the defects of the modern state depicted in the theory and the deficiencies of the related process of analysis are revealed. The modern state as well as the accompanying form of consciousness is critically dissected.

The completion of this critique exposes questions which can only be resolved 'by one means,' says Marx, namely practice [die Praxis]. His *Critique* of Hegel and the result of other studies point to the conclusion that the contradictions of the modern state go beyond the mere dichotomy of the general and particular; they consist of real, material elements with their own means, motives, and interests.

As if in response to his problematic *Rheinische Zeitung* formulation of the role of critique and its relation to the real world, he now writes that critique alone cannot change the world: 'The weapon of criticism cannot ... replace criticism by weapons, material force must be overthrown by material force.' In other words, no amount of criticizing in itself will effect a resolution of the contradictions. But theory is not therefore to be dismissed: 'theory also becomes a material force as soon as it has gripped the masses. Theory is capable of gripping the masses as soon as it demonstrates *ad hominem*, and it demonstrates *ad hominem* as soon as it becomes radical. To be radical is to grasp the root of the matter. But for man the root is man himself.'[44]

Theory, as the critique of the modern state, can become 'a material force' once it becomes part of the consciousness of the people. It grips the masses by revealing its 'non-disinterest' ('*ad hominem*') and it does this by grasping the nature of man himself, his social essence. But what is it about the radicalism of German theory, the grasping of man's essence, that moves it to be 'not disinterested,' that gives it is 'practical energy'? It is that 'it proceeds from a resolute *positive* abolition [Aufhebung] of religion. The criticism of religion ends with the teaching that *man is the highest being for man*, hence with the *categorical imperative to overthrow all relations* in which man is a debased, enslaved, forsaken, despicable being.'[45]

The knowledge and disclosure that 'man is the highest being for man,' i.e., that man's essence is his social nature, his relations, his unity with the social whole, leads to 'the categorical imperative to overthrow all [debased] relations.' In other words, once the fundamental principle of man is grasped, that principle comes to determine or assess the validity of all of man's relations and obliges action – in order to be true to the principle – where the principle is not realized.[46]

Such is Marx's further addition to the concept of critique. Though it is largely foreshadowed in his third letter in the preface of the D-FJ, this formulation for the first time reveals how Marx saw the relation of theory to practice. Radicalism is the pivot of this relation.

Even so, theory can be radical and not taken up in practice. It can perceive the truth of a situation and yet not find the masses to grip. 'It is not enough for thought to strive for realisation, reality must itself strive towards thought.'[47] If, in other words, there is no social class in civil society that 'has any need or capacity for general emancipation,'[48] i.e., that has radical needs, then radical theory will not be transformed into a material force; it will remain only theory.

For radical theory to become a material force engaged in the overthrow of debased human relations, it must be grasped by a class whose striving for emancipation embodies the transformation of civil society, the source of the contradictions in the modern state. This class, claims Marx, must have 'radical chains'; i.e., its oppression must arise from the 'roots' of modern society, its foundation must be in the relations of private property. It must be a 'class of civil society' but not 'of civil society'; i.e., it must grow out of civil society but not find its interests corresponding to those of civil society. It must be 'an estate [Stande] which is the dissolution of all estates,' i.e., a class whose appearance and political significance is the demise of the other classes and their political significance in civil society. It must be a 'sphere' [Sphäre] in which exploitation is general in nature. It must be a class 'which can no longer invoke a *historical* but only a *human* title,' i.e., its appearance marks the end of history, its emancipation is the realization of reason. It must 'not stand in any one-sided antithesis to the consequences but in an all-round antithesis to the premises of the German state [des deutschen Staatswesens],' i.e., it is not *only* opposed to the political state (the consequence) but also is the complete antithesis of civil society (the premise of the German state). It is the class whose emancipation is the emancipation of 'all other spheres of society' because its emancipation makes society a society of one sphere, that of the whole man. The class that fulfils this description, says Marx, is the proletariat.

The proletariat, continues Marx, comes into being 'as a result of the rising *industrial* development.'[49] It grows with the growth of industrial wealth – wealth, of course, as private property. Private property accumulates on one side and the proletariat, without private property, grows in number on the other. Thus, when the proletariat demands 'the negation of private property,' it is merely asserting the very principle that society in a *negative* way forces on the proletariat, i.e., that the people who are everything have nothing. The negation of private property would mean that no one would have private property and that everyone would have all property.

The negation of private property would constitute the negation of the modern state; it would mean, in a word, human emancipation. For this, the proletariat with its radical chains and, moreover, the critic with his radical theory are necessary. Hence, Marx says: 'As philosophy finds its *material* weapons in the proletariat, so the proletariat finds its *spiritual* weapons in philosophy.' Only in this union is human emancipation possible. As Marx concludes: 'The head of this emancipation is philosophy, its *heart* is the *proletariat*. Philosophy cannot be made a reality without the abolition [die Aufhebung] of the proletariat, the proletariat cannot be abolished [nicht aufheben] without philosophy being made a reality.'[50] The unity of man with his fellow man cannot come about without the emancipation of the proletariat and the emancipation of the proletariat is *ipso facto* the unity of man with his fellow man.

This conclusion has given rise to considerable comment in the form of speculation about Marx's 'discovery' of the role of the proletariat. How is it that Marx is able to arrive at such a formulation? The suggested explanations include a 'reversal' of the Hegelian notion of a universal class, a usurpation of the Judeo-Christian idea of salvation, an 'ethical indignation' at the poverty of the proletariat, and Marx's involvement with French working-class movements in Paris in late 1843, among others.[51] But what these explanations fail to appreciate is that it is Marx's analysis of the contradictions of the modern state that leads him to see the objective significance of the proletariat. It is not Marx who gives this significance to the proletariat; it is history, the movement of private property; Marx provides only the explanation. Whether it likes it or not, reasons Marx, the proletariat is the only variable in society that can, and moreover, must, resolve its contradictions. This conclusion derives from empirical analysis of the social position of the proletariat and its premise, civil society.

His critique of the modern state demonstrated that political emancipation, far from being the final form of emancipation, was the liberation of society from the directly political character of feudalism. The democratic republic was an advance over feudalism in that with its creation, the fundamental contradiction of man's nature, namely, the relation of the individual to his collectivity, was set forth in the form of the contradiction of the isolated man in civil society and the abstract state. The source of this separation, the premises on which rested the political state, was civil society as the sphere of private property, of commerce and industry. All of this Marx examined in considerable detail in his *Critique of Hegel's Philosophy of Right*. He noted there that civil society was also characterized by a 'class of direct labour' and 'lack of property.' And later in the introduction he wrote that 'industrial development' was producing a class 'of civil society' but not 'of civil society,' a class which arose out of the growth of wealth as private property but which contradicted the principle of private property, the principle of civil society.

This critique led him to see that the premise of the modern state produced its own opposite in the proletariat; and that by calling for the negation of private property, the proletariat was calling for the transformation of civil society, the negation of its premises. This, in turn, as the demise of the premise of the abstraction of the political state, would reunite man with his abstracted collectivity; it would bring in its wake human emancipation.

But human emancipation, the outcome of the resolution of the contradiction of private property and the proletariat now grown to constitute the state as a whole in content though not in form, required not only 'a heart' in the proletariat but also 'a head' in philosophy, in critical theory. Hence, critique was 'no longer an end in itself,' but in so far as it was radical and expressed the needs of a radical class of the proletariat, it was aligned in opposition to the 'material force' of the interests of private property.

To indicate the development of Marx's concept of the role of critique it is worth digressing briefly to review his use of the concept a year earlier in the *Rheinische Zeitung* articles. There his stated goal was 'the free human being'[52] or 'a moral and rational community':[53] in short, the rational unity of the universal and particular. While this goal has not changed, only broadened or deepened, the means of achieving it have. In the article on the Mosel vinegrowers, Marx proposed to resolve the differences between the bureaucracy (the universal) and the vinegrowers (the particular) by means of the free press.[54]

Here, critique appeared as an end in itself in the form of the critical press, in which, said Marx, freedom was embodied because through it the conflicting interests of the universal and particular could be resolved; the free press possessed the head of the universal and the heart of the particular. The problem of 'theoretical practice' as portrayed in the free press was not that it was idealist; i.e., it did not attempt, as the Young Hegelians did, to solve the real problems only in theory. It was an attempt to put theory into practice, but it was faulty because the *nature* of the contradiction it was trying to resolve was not completely comprehended. To correct the inadequacy of 'theoretical practice' it was necessary to return to the contradiction and to grasp its premise, for here in the premise lay the antithesis and also the implied synthesis. When Marx completed his critique of Hegel's *Philosophy of Right* he was obliged, on the basis of his new awareness of the nature of the modern state, to revise his notion of the practical role of critique. It was not the free press that was to emancipate man; it was the proletariat and the task of the critic was to make the proletariat aware of its historical position. Theory was now seen as complementing the practice of the proletariat.

In the summer of 1844, Marx writes an article in which the analysis is on the same political level as the preceding articles. For this reason, it is discussed here. In it he analyses, first, the limitations of the political point of view, an analysis which complements his earlier examination of the limitations of political emancipation. And second, he discusses the implicit meaning of workers' revolts, just as he had drawn out the implicit significance of elections and the demands for extension of the franchise in the 1843 *Critique*.

In early June 1844, the weavers in several Silesian towns staged a series of riots. According to Engels, their condition, already impoverished by poor wages, was exacerbated by increased competition from machine-manufactured linen goods made in England. The military was called out to quell the riots which spanned several days and many weavers were killed or injured.[55]

Arnold Ruge, the co-editor of the D-FJ with Marx, wrote a report on the riots for a German émigré journal in Paris, *Vorwärts*. In it he claims that the King of Prussia has not made any formal proposals for reform because the 'unpolitical' nature of Germany makes it impossible to see that the limited 'distress of the factory districts is a matter of general concern.' Instead, he says that the King sees the riots as if they were simply a local problem and 'due to *deficiencies in the administration or in charitable activity.*'

Marx's reply to Ruge, entitled 'Critical Marginal Notes on the Article "The King of Prussia and Social reform,"' reiterates and expands many themes enunciated in the D-FJ articles. The response is in two parts. In the first, Marx argues that it is not the 'unpolitical' nature of Germany but, on the contrary, the *political* viewpoint that prevents an understanding of the social roots of this distress, and that the political perspective is in fact constrained in its explanation and limited in solutions by its very nature.

This section begins with a description of how pauperism is understood in England – a political country and '*the country of pauperism,*' where pauperism is 'not *partial* but *universal.*' Despite the political nature of England, Marx says, the main political parties, the Whigs and the Tories, do not see the source of this distress 'in politics in general' but in the policies of the other. Even 'English political economy' is unable to grasp the cause of poverty and, among other reasons, posits 'neglected education' as the source.[56] If political England cannot understand the cause of pauperism, then, concludes Marx, can it be the unpolitical nature of Germany that prevents understanding in Germany?

But Ruge also argues that the 'unpolitical condition' of Germany accounts for the reason the King 'finds the cause of pauperism in deficiencies in the administration and in charitable activity.' Here, as well, Marx counters by pointing out that in political England the 'increase of pauperism' is explained by just such 'deficiencies.' The 'acute state of English pauperism' is explained by reference to the 'Poor Law itself' which is tantamount to saying, as Marx puts it ironically, that 'the means prescribed by law against the social malady, is alleged to promote the social malady.'[57]

Marx reviews other explanations of pauperism and the several attempts by both political England and France to deal with the question. The conclusion he arrives at is that 'insofar as the states have occupied themselves with pauperism, they have either confined themselves to *administrative* and *charitable measures*, or they have retreated to less than administrative action and charity.'[58]

But can it be otherwise? Marx asks rhetorically. The state cannot see the 'source of social maladies' in the state and 'system of society' [Einrichtung der Gesellschaft – Ruge's phrase] because from 'the *political* point of view' the state and the 'system of society' are one and the same. That is to say, from the perspective of government, of the state as separate from the people, the state is the embodiment of the social system and outside the state there is only civil society, which is not *social* but *individual*. For this reason, writes Marx, the source of poverty is not seen in the social system itself but in 'laws of nature,' 'private life,' or 'injudicious activity of the administration' – none of which touch upon the real source, the nature of the society itself.

Inasmuch as the state sees the cause in administrative 'shortcomings,' it seeks the solution in administrative 'measures.' The state has no other way of dealing with the matter because '*administration* is the *organizing* activity of the state.'[59] But whatever the 'intention or goodwill' of the administration its measures are limited to 'a *formal* and *negative* activity'; it cannot embrace *positive* measures that go to the root of the problem because the existence of the state itself is based on the persistence of the source, the persistence of civil society. 'Where civil life and its labour begin,' says Marx, 'there the power of the administration ends.' In the face of the growth of industry and its consequences in civil society, the state is impotent for this '*slavery of civil society* is the natural foundation on which the *modern* state rests.' Therefore, to abolish [aufheben] poverty would be to abolish its roots in private property and to abolish private property would be to abolish the premises of the modern state and therefore to abolish itself. However, concludes Marx, '*suicide* is against nature.'

As a consequence, the state 'can perceive *only* formal, accidental deficiencies in its administration and try to remedy them.' It cannot admit to 'the *inherent* impotence of its administration' because that would be to admit to its own impotence, and a state that does not believe in itself cannot exist for long as a state. The argument in this section is summarized as follows: 'The mightier the state, and the *more* political therefore a country is, the less is it inclined to grasp the *general* principle of *social* maladies and to seek their basis in the *principle of the state*, hence in *the present structure of society*, the active, conscious and official expression of which is the state. The *political* mind is a *political* mind precisely because it thinks *within* the framework of politics. They keener and more lively it is, the more *incapable* is it of understanding social ills.'[60]

Here is the heart of the first part of Marx's rebuttal. The failure to grasp the true source of social distress is due not to the unpolitical nature of a state but, on the contrary, to its political nature. The political perspective cannot perceive the truth about the source of social ills because it is itself a product of this source, the principle of private property in civil society.

In the second part of his retort, Marx takes up Ruge's contention that the German poor, the weavers in this case, do not see beyond their own immediate needs, problems, and district. Marx replies that to see the German workers in a proper perspective they must be compared to the first steps of the English and French workers, for to be sure 'the *German* movement ... is *just beginning*.'

Even so, the Silesian weavers are not so limited as Ruge suggests; Marx points to the weavers' song which 'proclaims ... opposition to the society of private property'; moreover, the uprising reveals a 'consciousness of the nature of the proletariat,' a beginning which is comparable to the present consciousness of the French and English workers. As for the level of awareness of the German workers, Marx points to the works by Weitling which he states are theoretically 'often superior even to those of *Proudhon*.'[61] In a word, the German workers, given their promising beginning, and the weakness of the German bourgeoisie, have an excellent chance of moving towards socialism.

Among the arguments that Ruge makes, and that Marx criticizes, there is the prophesy of a bloody demise of 'all uprisings which break out in ... disastrous isolation of people from the community.' This allows Marx to analyse the nature of the isolation which underlies the workers' revolt. He begins by asserting that 'all uprisings, without exception, break out in the disastrous isolation of man from the community [*alle* Aufstände ohne Ausnahme *in der heillosen Isolierung des Mensch von Gemeinwesen* aus],' that '*every* uprising must presuppose isolation.'[62] The political revolution, as in 1789, springs from the isolation of the citizen from the political community; and its success abolishes this isolation. But the nature of the workers' isolation is different from previous forms of isolation. As Marx puts it: 'The community from which the worker is isolated by *his own labour* is *life* itself, physical and mental life, human morality, human activity, human enjoyment, *human* nature. *Human nature* is the *true community* of men.'

This passage bears the mark of Marx's economic and philosophical studies but is not inconsistent with earlier conclusions – and the use of critique is plainly visible. Now we can see the specific source of the workers' isolation, the nature of his own labour, and the community from which he is isolated, namely, the essential nature of man himself. For man to be whole man he must have a rational unity with the society in which he lives. The separation from this social whole, 'this essential nature,' says Marx, is 'incomparably more universal, more intolerable, more dreadful, and more contradictory, than isolation from the political community.' He continues: 'Hence, too, the abolition [die Aufhebung] of this isolation – and even a partial reaction to it, an *uprising* against it – is just as much more infinite as *man* is more infinite than the *citizen*, and *human life* more infinite than *political life*.'

The transcendence of this isolation that afflicts the workers leads to the unity of the individual with his collectivity. Even limited struggles, moreover, aimed against this isolation contain a universal demand: 'however *partial* the uprising of the *industrial workers* may be it contains within itself a *universal* soul; however universal a *political* uprising may be, it conceals even in its *most grandoise* form a *narrow-minded* spirit.'[63]

The contrast here is similar to the earlier comparison of political emancipation and human emancipation. Still, the latter is not without its political side, even after a political revolution has taken place. The socialist revolution is both political, in a certain sense, and social. As Marx concludes: '*Revolution* in general – the *overthrow* of the existing power and *dissolution* of the old relationship – is a *political* act. But *socialism* cannot be realised without *revolution*. It needs this *political* act insofar as it needs *destruction* and *dissolution*. But where its *organizing activity* begins, where its *proper object*, its *soul*, comes to the fore – there socialism throws off the *political* cloak.'[64]

The last *political* act is the proletarian revolution.

CONCLUSIONS

Many of the developments in analysis and method in the 1843 *Critique* are expanded in the articles Marx published in the *Deutsch-Französische Jahrbücher* and *Vorwärts*. In the order of their appearance, the articles betray a logical unfolding as the method of inquiry, the consequent analysis, and the preconditions for a solution. Specifically, he outlines the revised method in a prefatory letter to the journal; he employs the method in the article, 'On the Jewish Question,' to advance his analysis of politics; and then he examines the prerequisites for social change, for the solution to the contradiction of political relations, in the introduction to the *Critique*. We see here an integrally related development of the method of critique and the critique of politics. Let us examine these points briefly.

In the last of three letters by Marx which, with letters by other contributors, stand as the preface to the first issue of the *Jahrbücher*, he writes about the meaning of criticism, how the journal should approach its task. He begins by asserting that he is 'not in favour of raising any dogmatic banner,' thus juxtaposing his method, the presentation of which follows, to dogmatism, just as he did in the manuscript study on Hegel.

'Reason has always existed, but not always in a reasonable form.' Marx declares that reality is rational, but it does not always appear in a rational form. Given this underlying rationality, the critic may begin with any subject and, by analysing its existing, concrete forms, discover its contradictions and in uncovering them also uncover the implicit rationality. This is the 'true reality' of the subject matter, meaning that, despite the existing form, the elements of implicit rationality are there in existence. It is 'its obligation [Sollen]' because the 'true reality' comprises the implicit unity of the essential elements, their logically necessary relationship. As its definition, it is what the subject must be or become. It is 'its final goal' inasmuch as all existence strives to become that which it is by definition, in essence.

The second aspect of critique is also found in this letter. If reality strives towards its definition, then the discovery and articulation of its 'true reality' will coincide with the purpose of that aspect of reality striving for its realization. In fact, since real struggles are the manifestation of efforts to realize the underlying rationality, the critic may take them as the starting point of analysis. The truth of reality corresponds to the intentions of the struggle within reality itself. The truth of a critic's theoretical discoveries, therefore, coincide with the practice of 'a large party,' an aspect of reality. Such is the new, albeit tentative, formulation of Marx's notion of the unity of theory and practice. It is the consequence of a revision of the critical method as employed in the *Rheinische Zeitung*.

Both of these aspects of critique, the analysis of reality and of the nature of its contradictions and the relationship of this analysis to practice, are developed at some length in the two D-FJ articles which follow. In these articles may be found a very clear example of how the development in the method of critique is at the same time the development in the analysis of political relations. While both continue to evolve in mutual response in significant steps up to 1847, and in minor ways thereafter, nowhere again is the subject matter developed in a manner so clearly parallel to changes in the method first made in the 1843 *Critique*.

The first aspect of critique is found in the first article, 'On the Jewish Question.' The article is not simply about the Jewish question but about the nature of political emancipation, and the Jewish question, which is in part a political question, is merely an appropriate vehicle for such an analysis. In the first part of the article, we find part of the first aspect of the new method, namely, the analysis of reality to discover its nature and contradictions. Bauer formulates the Jewish question as a religious question, but wrongly, reasons Marx, arguing that it is in fact a question about the nature of political emancipation. To grasp the meaning of political emancipation, he turns to an examination of the constitution of the United States, *inter alia*, and on this basis shows that the Jew need not renounce his religion, as Bauer argues, in order to be politically free.

The analysis of the nature of political emancipation provides Marx with a grasp of its 'true reality,' that is with the concept of human emancipation, the unity of the individual and society, the implicit rationality contained in political emancipation. This concept permits Marx to grasp the sense in which political emancipation is the completion of political development, but not the completion of human emancipation.

Just as Marx examines real states in order to grasp the nature of political emancipation, he analyses the existing declarations of the rights of man in order to grasp their nature. His analysis demonstrates the rights of man to be bourgeois rights, rights whose principle is private property. Precisely for this reason, the political state, whose content is the private, material interests of civil society, makes the rights of man the foundation of its constitution.

If the duality of the modern state is due to the nature of civil society, then, the explanation of the former is to be found in analysis of the latter. This is the object of Part II of the article. While the significance of the Jewish question in Part I is to demonstrate the limitations of political emancipation, it is now to show the nature of civil society and the need to transform civil society in order to achieve human emancipation. The transformation of the secular basis of the Jewish religion, trade and commerce, runs the argument, is the emancipation of the Jew from religion and at the same time the human emancipation of society.

If Marx now understands the nature of political emancipation and the nature of the prerequisite for human emancipation, he must still uncover the means by which the latter can be achieved. In the second article, he examines the two sides to this problem. The first is the relation of theory to practice, i.e., how theory is able to 'grip the masses' once it becomes radical. In the *Rheinische Zeitung* articles, theory and practice were bound together in the critique itself; now the relationship is an external one, albeit a necessary one. The second side concerns the class whose striving and interests are synonymous with human emancipation. On the basis of his examination of the precondition for emancipation, Marx is able to outline the prerequisites which must characterize the class which is to grasp the theory, which is but its own interests abstractly formulated, and transform political society. The class which conforms to these prerequisites is the proletariat, a class whose interests are the direct opposite of those of private property, private property being the principle of civil society and the reason for the duality of the modern state.

These articles, in short, reveal a systematic development of Marx's method of critique and critique of politics. The two are mutually complementary: with his method reformulated his analysis of politics broadens and deepens, and the more comprehensive the understanding of political relations and the more adequate the method must become in response to the demands of analysis. Although both continue to evolve, the method and analysis of politics, as expressed here in the *Deutsch-Französische Jahrbücher*, may be considered valid, even in light of the entire corpus of Marx's work.

More specifically, the articles possess Marx's fundamental position on the relation between theory and practice and on the meaning of political emancipation and of the rights of man. They also contain his first examination of the role and meaning of money and of the proletariat. All of these issues are questions arising from the 1843 *Critique* of Hegel. With their presentation here, Marx by and large completes his analysis of political relations *at the level of politics*.

Because the analysis of politics is thus more or less complete, the questions which now arise concern the cause of political relations, the source of the duality of the modern state. It is to these questions that Marx now turns. His pursuit of the answers comes down to us in the form of the so-called 1844 manuscripts.

4

Private Property and Communism: the Paris manuscripts and 'Comments on James Mill,' 1844

The answers to the political questions confronted by Marx thus far have all pointed to the phenomenon of private property. In the *Rheinische Zeitung* articles, towards the end of 1842, Marx not only demonstrated the defects of political relations in Prussia but also unveiled the particularistic nature of the political state – its subservience to material interests. In the 1843 *Critique* of Hegel, he dissected the nature of politics and the relation of the political state to private property. The analysis revealed that the very existence of political relations was a defect, a separation of the political state from the people; that this separation presupposed a civil society of private, competing interests; and that the political state, the supposed (or formal) embodiment of general interest, was in fact a consequence and instrument of private property.[1] In the *Deutsch-Französische Jahrbücher* articles, published in early 1844, Marx took these conclusions further, arguing that to overcome the duality of modern society, its political nature, the presupposition of this division, the system of trade and commerce, civil society, had to be transformed. The means of this transformation arose from this same system of industry and trade: civil society was producing the instrument of its own demise – the modern proletariat.[2]

Each time, therefore, that the critique of politics was deepened or broadened, it came to rest at the question of private property. The critique, as a critique of politics *per se*, had little left to analyse. The question now raised took it beyond the sphere of purely political relations. Just as the 'criticism of theology turned into the criticism of politics,' then, the criticism of politics had to turn into the criticism of political economy, the sphere of private property.

None the less, the fact that the analysis of political relations led Marx to examine economic relations does not imply that he was abandoning the sphere of the political. The point of a critique of political economy was to go beyond the limits of mere political analysis; it was to uncover and analyse the *premise* of politics. Such a critique was necessary not only to grasp the rationale for the division of modern society but also to understand the creation of the proletariat and the nature of its servitude and opposition to capital. It was modern political economy which held the secret to the relations of modern domination and subjugation. The question now, then, is how a critique of political economy furthered the unmasking of human self-estrangement 'in its unholy forms' that Marx began in his critique of politics.

In Paris, between April and August 1844, Marx began his first examination of the concepts of political economy. It has been preserved, only in part, in the form of notes made on the principal economists of the day and in a set of four manuscripts which Marx evidently began, judging from the preface, with the intention to publish. Sections of the notes, in particular on James Mill's *Elements of Political Economy*, and all the extant portions of the manuscripts were first published only in 1932.[3]

Since this date, the Paris manuscripts (entitled on publication *Economic and Philosophic Manuscripts of 1844*, hereafter EPM) have given rise to a vast secondary literature, a fact which caused one commentator to argue that they were 'the most talked about philosophical work in this century.'[4] Despite their fragmentary, incomplete nature, their lack of an obvious internal structure, and their often aphoristic and even archaic philosophic language, the EPM have inspired considerable interest and controversy.

Because most of the controversies, particularly the 'young versus mature Marx' and the 'philosophy versus science' debates, involve a comparison of the EPM with work written after 1845, they cannot be discussed here. Yet, because the controversies and the method of expounding the Paris writings are closely related, we can begin to answer some of the problems arising in the debates by examining the method of their presentation.

One of the most successful presentations is found in Meszaros' *Marx's Theory of Alienation*. He focuses on what he considers to be the central concept in the EPM, to wit, alienation. Its manifestation in various spheres provides the organizational rationale for the book; i.e., we find the rubrics: economic, political, ontological and moral, and aesthetic, all of which constitute 'aspects' of alienation. These are imposed categories, however, and the obvious depth of Meszaros' comprehension of the material strains against such an organization. The contradiction between the form of his presentation and the content of the manuscripts reveals itself in the necessary repetition of several central ideas and in the fact that little is revealed about the questions the concept of alienation was intended to answer or the degree to which it succeeds in providing the answers.[5]

Other presentations,[6] not so successful, attempt straightforward expositions of part or all of the EPM as they stand. For the most part, they treat these writings in isolation from Marx's earlier work, thereby presenting and attempting to comprehend them in a near vacuum. The limitations of these expositions are often directly related to this contextual vacuum. To fail to see the relation of the EPM to prior questions arising from earlier work is often due to preconceived notions of these writings as Marx's 'discovery' of political economy or as his 'break' with a 'philosophical' past.[7] But 'discoveries,' and 'breaks' must be accounted for; left as mere assertions they beg the question. It is necessary, therefore, to search for a link *or* to explain the lack of such to the earlier work.

By returning to the articles Marx wrote for the *Deutsch-Französische Jahrbücher*, we can delineate the questions arising from his work immediately prior to writing the manuscripts. In the second part of 'On the Jewish Question,' Marx points to the Jewish (i.e., commercial) nature of civil society as the reason for the opposition between the individual and his collectivity. He identifies the egoism and competition that arise out of the relations of trade and commerce and in turn create this separation, but he does not outline the exact nature of the relation of commerce to this separation. That commerce creates a civil society of competing individuals and therefore creates the need for the modern state is understood, but how commerce gives rise to this separation of man from his fellow man remains an open question.

In the introduction to the *Critique of Hegel's Philosophy of Right*, Marx argues that the class which will emancipate the whole of society will arise out of civil society, it will come into being 'as a result of the rising industrial development.' How this class, the proletariat, actually does rise and why it is destined to confront capital and transform society are questions not fully answered.

Furthermore, this transformation of society, the realization of philosophy, which accompanies the victory of the proletariat and its abolition of itself as a class, is not examined except in very general terms, i.e., as the unity of the universal and the particular, as man's nature, as true democracy, as communism. The meaning of communism, of man's social nature, has yet to be analysed in depth.

If these are the fundamental questions facing Marx following his *Critique of Hegel* and the D-FJ articles, and if our procedure following Marx is valid (in the process of induction the answer to every question raises new questions), then it follows that the Paris manuscripts should reflect Marx's search for answers to the above questions. If they do not, then, indeed, we may suppose a 'break' with the previous work and go in search of the reason. The very structure of the Paris writings, however, implies that the above questions constitute the rationale of this work.[8]

What survives of the Paris manuscripts comprises four distinct sections, although most publications compress the material into three. The content of each section bears directly on the questions we have delineated. The first manuscript, for example, begins with an examination of forms of private property: wages, profit, and rent – private property being for Marx the presupposition of the separation of the state from its members. It is in this section that Marx first comprehends the nature of private property as the result of alienated labour, and thereby comprehends the source of the duality of modern society. In the second manuscript, although only a few pages remain, it is possible to see that Marx was examining how the working class arose out of the movement of private property and how labour and capital developed as an antagonistic contradiction. The resolution of this contradiction, the transcendence of the system of private property, constituted the end of alienation, in a word, communism. It is in the third manuscript that Marx explores, *inter alia*, the nature of communism, the nature of man's social essence, and its coming into being.

Underlying the exposition which follows is the hypothesis that the content of the three manuscripts comprises Marx's pursuit of the answers to the questions raised in the D-FJ articles.

THE FIRST MANUSCRIPT: WAGES, PROFIT, RENT, AND ALIENATED LABOUR[9]

Almost three-quarters of the first manuscript consists of a review of the contemporary literature in political economy. It is organized after the 'trinity formula' of economic theory, namely, wages, profit, and rent, and consists of Marx's distillation of the subject matter, interspersed with numerous quotations illustrating the source of many of his assertions. It is not a review, however, without intention.

Wages, profit, and rent are forms of private property, forms which correspond to private property as labour, as capital, and as land. It is the inter-relationship of these elements as political economy understands it that Marx delineates with the purpose of criticizing.

The first several pages on wages quite clearly derive from Adam Smith's *Wealth of Nations*. It is not so much the analysis as the implications drawn which distinguish the two. Smith begins by asserting: 'In that original state of things, which precedes both the appropriation of land and the accumulation of stock, the whole produce of labour belongs to the labourer.'[10] But as soon as land and the means of production become private property, the 'whole produce' which formerly was solely the labourer's property becomes divided into rent, profit, and wages. The wages of labour thereafter, according to Smith, 'depends everywhere upon the contract ... [between master and workman] whose interests are by no means the same.' Reasserting this point, Marx begins his analysis with the sentence: '*Wages* are determined through the antagonistic struggle between capitalist and worker.' The remainder of his first paragraph closely parallels a passage in Smith in which the advantages of the masters in this dispute are outlined,[11] but the implications of these advantages remain for Smith implicit. For Marx the conclusion is clear: since all the advantages of this separation of land, labour, and capital lie with the capitalist and landowner, the separation is disadvantageous *only* for the worker. How the separation works against the labourer is the subject of this section.

The salient points of Marx's discussion as derived largely from Smith are as follows. First, under capitalism the production of workers is subject to the laws of supply and demand and therefore reproduction takes place on the same basis as every other commodity. Labour itself becomes a commodity subordinate to the needs of capital. Second, although reduced to a commodity, the worker is 'the most wretched of commodities.' That is, no matter what the state of the wealth of society, the worker suffers. After demonstrating the case, Marx summarizes: 'Thus in a declining state of society – increasing misery of the worker; in an advancing state – misery with complications; and in a fully developed state of society – static misery.'[12] These are the consequences of the separation of land, capital, and labour implicit in Adam Smith's treatise. Third, and following from this discussion, Marx reviews several paradoxes concerning wage-labour as found in political economy. For example: 'Originally and in theory the whole product of labour belongs to the worker,' claims the political economist, 'but at the same time he tells us that in actual fact what the worker gets is the smallest and utterly indispensable part of the product.'[13] The worker produces everything but 'must sell himself and his humanity' in order to buy anything; only labour increases the value of nature's materials, but the capitalist and landowner who do not work 'are everywhere superior to the worker and lay down the law to him'; and 'while the interest of the worker, according to the political economist, never stands opposed to the interest of society, society always and necessarily stands opposed to the interest of the worker.'

These, and other paradoxes mentioned by Marx, represent the inconsistencies of political economy regarding the question of wages of labour. He is pointing to inadequacies in political economy, its failure to grasp the nature of the relation between labour and capital. How Marx will reveal the source of these inadequacies, how he will criticize political economy is here only hinted at. The problem, he intimates, lies in the conception of labour. In political economy, labour is perceived 'in the abstract as a thing; labour is a commodity.'[14] It is a thing whose purpose is 'the mere increase of wealth.' Those who labour are seen merely as workers, 'as a working animal – as a beast reduced to the strictest bodily needs.' Such a perspective dehumanizes the worker and makes labour an abstraction, with the consequence that no direct relationship between the worker and his product can be perceived. For this reason, the question why those who produce do not own and those who own do not produce does not arise. Only the owner of property and the accumulation and disposition of his wealth are at issue for the political economist.

'Profit of Capital' is the title of the next section, and it too derives largely from Adam Smith, although a number of other political economists are cited at length. Marx's first concern is to define capital and its relation to labour. Capital, he writes following Smith, is 'stored-up labour.' But it is more than this; it is the private appropriation of stored-up labour; it is 'private property in the products of other men's labour.'[15] How is it that some are proprietors of capital and others not? 'By virtue of *positive law*,' law which is arbitrary and not natural,[16] replies Marx citing J.B. Say, an epigone of Adam Smith. Say's position is only a partial explanation, of course; he does not explain the source of private property; he provides only one reason for its perpetuation, its inheritance sanctified by law.

The inheritance of capital accords certain powers to its possessor. Smith asserts that possession conveys 'the power of purchasing; a certain command over all the labour, or over all the produce of labour, which is then in the market.' To which Marx concludes: 'Capital is thus the *governing power* over labour and its products.' The point is expanded in several quotations from Smith and Say.

It is possible to see in this an element of Marx's later argument. That is, capital is stored-up labour and is a power over labour and its products; but since labour produces capital, it can be said that the worker is dominated by the products of his own labour.

It is not simply that capital governs labour; the very interests of capital stand 'in hostile opposition to society.' According to Smith and Say, the public interest is not at one with the interest of capital, rather the capitalists are 'a class of people who have generally an interest to deceive and to oppress the public.' Apparently, Marx is satisfied with the strength and clarity of Smith's argument to leave this assertion unaccompanied by any commentary. The problem this 'opposition' poses, however, is not left undiscussed.

If capital is a power over labour, if it stands opposed to society, and if all social advance works to the advantage of capital, not the public, not labour, then, what defends society against the interests of monopoly capital? The political economists answer, competition amongst capitals; through competition, wages rise and prices are lowered, all 'to the advantage of the consuming public.' But this is an ideological response, an assumed truth. Drawing on Smith and others, Marx is able to demonstrate that political economy itself reveals how competition leads to monopoly. The competitive system necessarily develops into a monopoly system. In competition, profits on capital decline but the small capitalist is 'the first to suffer.' The larger the capital, the more able to withstand diminishing profits due to competition. Big capital, moreover, can buy more cheaply in larger quantities than small capital and therefore can sell more cheaply. Big capital can afford a higher ratio of fixed to circulating capital and therefore produce commodities more cheaply than small capital[17] and thereby enhance its ability to accumulate. In these ways, among others, competition leads to the destruction of small capitalists and the growth of big capitalists, whose numbers are always diminishing. As Marx argues: 'Competition among capitalists increases the accumulation of capital. Accumulation, where private property prevails is the *concentration* of capital in the hands of a few; it is in general an inevitable consequence if capital is left to follow its natural course, and it is precisely through competition that the way is cleared for this natural disposition of capital.'[18] This 'natural disposition of capital' is also the natural disposition of landed property; i.e., in both cases competition leads to monopoly. To the question of landed property and rent of land Marx now turns.

As in his discussion of the determination of the wages of labour, Marx draws on the work of Smith and Say to discover how the rent of land is decided. It is established, he writes 'as a result of the struggle between tenant and landlord.'[19] In this struggle, as in the struggle for wages, the system of private property favours only one side. It is the landlord, through his ownership (monopoly) of the land, who benefits from all the natural advantages of the land and from all the improvements the tenant may make.

The landlord is also able to turn to his own profit all the advances made by society in general. Citing Smith and Say, Marx points to the fact that rent increases as population increases, as the means of communication improve and multiply, as new means of production and new inventions come into play, as the price of commodities declines and wages rise. Indeed, all social improvements appear to lead to an augmentation of rent.

Inasmuch as the landlord 'exploits every benefit which comes to society,' says Marx, we cannot conclude, as does Smith, that 'the interest of the land-lord is always identical with that of society.'[20] On the contrary, in a system of private property, 'the interest which an individual has in society' stands in 'inverse proportion to the interest society has in him.' To demonstrate this point with respect to landowners, Marx reviews how political economy itself views the nature of this contradiction. If rent increases with the general increase of social wealth and the latter is 'identical with the increase of poverty and slavery,' then increasing rent and increasing poverty are related movements. Similarly, the relation between the landlord and the tenant farmer, and the farm worker and his wages, and 'factory workers and capital-ists' are found to be contradictory. But political economy does not only out-line how the landlord's interest stands opposed to that of society; it also shows how each landlord's interest differs from the other. It is to this ques-tion of competition that Marx next turns.

Competition between landlords works in a similar way to that between capitalists; it leads 'to the accumulation of large property and to the absorp-tion of small capital by it.'[21] After presenting the reasons why competition moves in this direction, Marx asserts that a 'further consequence' of this competition is the intermingling of landed and industrial capital, such that the 'distinction between capitalist and landowner' disappears, resulting in the development of only two classes – 'the working class and the capitalist class.'

The competition and consequent monopoly of land, which leads to the destruction of the landowners as a separate class also 'drives the overwhelm-ing majority of the population into the arms of industry' and reduces farm labourers 'to utter wretchedness.'[22] Amongst the workers competition in-creases and wages decline, and wages are further reduced by capital's efforts to meet foreign competition. The necessary result of all these movements is, says Marx, revolution. Private property in land, as private property in indus-try, follows this course to self-destruction. Only then, only when the move-ment of capital has created the conditions and the means for the abolition of private property, will man be able to learn to believe in himself, will private property become human property.

Here, Marx's review of the movement of private property ends. He has produced a coherent description of the relations of wages, profit, and rent as found in political economy and a set of conclusions analytically drawn from this description. Marx is explicit about what he has done; he has 'proceeded from the premises of political economy' and 'on the basis of political econ-omy itself, in its own words, [he has] shown that the worker sinks to the level of a commodity and becomes indeed the most wretched of commodities; that the wretchedness of the worker is in inverse proportion to the power and magnitude of his production; that the necessary result of competition is the accumulation of capital in a few *hands*, and thus the restoration of monopoly in a more terrible form; and that finally the distinction between capitalist and land rentier, like that between the tiller of the soil and the factory worker, disappears and that the whole of society must fall into the two classes, – the *property owners* and the propertyless *workers*.'[23]

The movement of these forms of private property, then, can be grasped from the existing literature on political economy. But inasmuch as political economy 'begins with the fact of private property,' it does not raise questions about the nature of private property or how the movement of private property arises out of this nature. Its premise left unexamined, political economy can grasp only the appearance of this movement and not the underlying rationale. Greed and competition, factors taken as external to the economy proper but which are in fact its consequences, are seen as the only motive forces in the system.

To be able to explain private property, however, would be to understand the nature of the system itself – its movement and consequences. This is the task Marx sets himself in this concluding section to the first manuscript: 'to grasp the essential connection [den wesentlichen Zusammenhang] between private property,' indeed, the whole system of estrangement, and the '*money* system [*Geld*system].'[24] The essential link lies in the nature of private property itself, that is, its nature as alienated labour. Marx therefore goes on to analyse the relation between private property and alienated labour.

Contrasting his starting point with that of the liberal economist who posits a fictitious state of nature, which begs the question to be answered, Marx writes, 'We proceed from an *actual* economic fact.' The economic fact that he employs is the central paradox in political economy, noted earlier in the section on 'Wages of labour'; namely: 'The worker becomes all the poorer the more wealth he produces, the more his production increases in power and size. The worker becomes an ever cheaper commodity the more commodities he creates. The *devaluation* of the world of men is in direct proportion to the *increasing value* of the world of things. Labour produces not only commodities: it produces itself and the worker as a *commodity* – and this at the same rate at which it produces commodities in general.'[25]

This paradox, says Marx, means that 'the object which labour produces – labour's product – confronts it [labour] as *something alien*, as a *power independent* of the producer.' In other words, this economic fact points to a form of separation of the producer and his product, in which the producer finds himself opposed by his very product. Yet, in theory, the 'product of labour is labour which has been embodied in an object, which has become material: it is the *objectification* of labour. Labour's realisation is its objectification.' The point here is that there is nothing in the concept of labour or its product to suggest any intrinsic form of separation; indeed, the product is the realization, the materialization, of labour; labour is the act and its product the creation; one cannot exist without the other. In the sphere of political economy, however, writes Marx: 'this realisation [Verkwirklichung] of labour appears as *loss of realisation* [Entwirklichung] for the workers; objectification as *loss of the object and bondage to it*; appropriation as *estrangement*, as *alienation* [als *Entfremdung*, als *Entäusserung*].'[26] Hence, objectification, which is merely the realization of labour, appears for the political economist (i.e., in a system of private property) as alienation, as the estrangement of the producer and his product.

The distinction between objectification [Vergegenständlichung] and alienation of labour [Entfremdung] is explored by Marx at greater length, but the conclusion is the same: the more the worker in a system of private property objectifies his labour the more he becomes 'a servant of the object' he creates. The distinction is important because it provides Marx with the basis for criticizing the concept of labour in political economy. 'Political economy,' he writes, 'conceals the estrangement inherent in the nature of labour by not considering the *direct* relationship between the *worker* (labour) and production.'[27] The point is that political economy cannot grasp the paradox for what it is, an estrangement, because it does not take in to account objectification as the direct relation between labour and its product; instead it sees objectification as alienation. Thus, palaces for the rich and hovels for the poor appear as a normal state of affairs, in spite of the knowledge that the worker produces the palace. The argument is expanded: '*The direct relationship* [Das unmittelbare Verhältnis] *of labour to its products is the relationship of the worker to the objects of his production*. The relationship of the man of means [des Vermögenden] to the objects of production and to production itself is only a *consequence* of this first relationship – and confirms it ... When we ask, then, what is the essential relation [das wesentliche Verhältnis] of labour we are asking about the relation of the *worker* to production.'[28]

The definition of objectification as the direct relation of the producer and his products, as the essential relation of labour, as a self-evident truth, allows Marx to take this first step in the critique of political economy, to demonstrate the inadequacy of conceiving the essence of labour as alienated labour, a problem which, we shall see, lies at the heart of political economy's inability to explain private property. Failure to make the distinction denies an understanding of the nature of private property and prevents a comprehension of its transcendence.[29]

There are implications[30] of this 'actual economic fact,' this estrangement of objects of production, and to these Marx now turns. 'If the product of labour is alienation,' he writes, 'then production itself must be active alienation, the alienation of activity, the activity of alienation.' Labour itself, the very act of producing, is alienated. The worker, it follows, perceives labour as 'external to himself' as 'not voluntary,' and inasmuch as labour is the expression of himself, his 'life-activity,' its alienation is 'the loss of his self.'

From the above, Marx deduces a further implication of alienated labour. He begins with a definition of man's essence: 'man is a species-being' [Gattungswesen], by which he means man is only man in relation to his 'own' [Gattung], to his community; man as an individual *pur et simple* is nothing. Man is defined as a being whose essence is his relationship to society. But this essence is established and maintained through man's activity which must in the final analysis be productive activity. Because productive activity is always defined by society, man realizes his relation to his community under the terms and conditions of the society he is born into. In that man is a social being, deriving his meaning as an individual from society, and in that he realizes this essence or nature through his socially-defined productive activity, he is a 'species-being.'[31] The 'life of the species [das Gattungsleben]' can only be expressed through man's practical activity which requires inorganic nature as its material or instrument. Since his productive activity is always socially defined, man, in 'his work upon the objective world,' confirms his species-essence.

Inasmuch as alienated labour separates man from his relationship to nature, the objective world, and from labour as his own life activity, it estranges man from his 'species,' from his collectivity. For it is in the direct relation of his own labour and the material on which he works, both socially defined, that man confirms his social nature. Thus, alienated labour changes for man 'the life of the species into a means of individual life.' In other words, life activity, which for man is socially defined activity, activity confirming the individual's relation to his collectivity, becomes through alienated labour merely a means to physical existence as an individual.[32] The expression of one's life activity, of one's social nature, is reduced to work as a means of subsistence, a despised and resented form of labour.

There is one further aspect to alienation that Marx isolates: 'An immediate consequence of the fact that man is estranged from the product of his labour, from his life activity, from his species-being is the *estrangement of man* from *man* [die Entfremdung des Menschen von dem Menschen].'[33] Because man is a species-being, that is, defined in terms of his relation to his collectivity, to others, alienation from this social nature means also alienation from his fellow man.

Having examined these aspects of alienated labour, Marx returns to his point of departure; namely, the actual economic fact, the paradox that the product of labour confronts its producer as an alien and independent power. He has encapsulated this fact and its implications in the concept of alienated labour and now enquires as to how this concept 'expresses and reveals itself in reality.' It is here that Marx attempts to demonstrate the relation between alienated labour and private property.

Alienated labour manifests itself as follows: if the worker does not own the product of his labour or indeed his very labour activity, then, it must be that it belongs to someone else. In other words, estranged labour manifests itself as a type of relationship between men in which non-producers possess and producers do not. But it is in fact through alienated labour that this relationship is confirmed. As Marx elaborates: 'through estranged labour man not only creates his relationship to the object and to the act of production as to powers* that are alien and hostile to him; he also creates the relationship in which other men stand to his production and to his product, and the relationship in which he stands to these other men. Just as he creates his own production as the loss of his reality, as his punishment; his own product as a loss, as a product not belonging to him; so he creates the domination of the person who does not produce over production and over the product.'[34]

It is through alienated labour, through his estranged activity, then, that man creates the relationship between himself and the products and activity of labour, such that the latter stands as hostile and alien powers over him. It is also through alienated labour that man creates the relationship of producer to non-producer as one of domination. These are the relationships of private property. 'Private property,' concludes Marx, 'is thus the product, the result, the necessary consequence, of alienated labour.'

Political economy begins with private property, but it does not explain it, according to Marx. What he does, instead, is to begin with an actual economic fact, that the worker becomes poorer the more he produces, and from it he deduces the concept of alienated labour. The manifestation, the material expression, of alienated labour in real life is the fact of private property. Hence, he asserts, 'private property ... results by analysis from the concept of *alienated labour*; i.e., of *alienated man*, of estranged labour, of estranged life, of *estranged* man.'[35] That which political economy only assumed, Marx has now explained.

Initially, alienated labour produces private property, but with the development of a system of private property, the 'relationship becomes reciprocal,' and thus private property is not only the *product* of alienated labour but also 'the *means* by which labour alienates itself.'[36] This relationship is further considered in the Appendix below.

In the light of his exposition of the concept of estranged labour and its relation to private property, Marx examines two 'unresolved controversies.' The first concerns arguments put forward by socialists or social reformers who regard a rise in wages as a means of improving the lot of the working class or who think the 'equality of wages' is the 'goal of social revolution.' Wages, however, are only a form of private property, notes Marx; they are 'a necessary consequence of labour's estrangement.' Wage-labour is alienated labour. An increase of wages, then, does not affect labour's alienation; it is 'nothing but better *payment for the slave* and would not win human status and dignity for the worker or his labour.' Through alienated labour, regardless of the amount of wages, the worker produces the conditions of his own enslavement. As for Proudhon's demand for *equality* of wages, its realization would place all men in the same relationship to their labour as the wage-labourer to his labour. If all men were wage-labourers they would create a society [Gesellschaft] as owner of their labour and its products, a society 'as an abstract capitalist.'[37] Wages, writes Marx in summary, 'are a direct consequence of estranged labour and estranged labour is the direct cause of private property.' In this *relationship*, wages and private property in general stand on one side and alienated labour on the other. The demise, therefore, of the system of private property or of wage-labour is at the same time the demise of alienated labour.

The political expression of this demise is the subject of the second 'unresolved controversy' examined by Marx. The passage deserves quotation in full: 'From the relationship of estranged labour and private property it follows further that the emancipation of society from private property, etc., from servitude, is expressed in the *political* form of the *emancipation of the workers*; not that *their* emancipation alone is at stake, but because the emancipation of the workers contains universal human emancipation – and it contains this, because the whole of human servitude is involved in the relation of the worker to production, and all relations of servitude are but modifications and consequences of this relation.'[38]

If it is through alienated labour that the worker produces private property – and if private property, the essence of civil society, is the presupposition of politics, of the separation of the state from the people – then 'the emancipation of society from private property,' that is, the transcendence of modern society divided by its premise, private property, will take the form of the workers establishing their own political hegemony, displacing the hegemony of private property. This is not merely the exchange of one form of class rule for another; it is fundamentally a strike against society divided into classes, against the source of that division. Class relations, indeed, 'all relations of servitude are but modifications and consequences' of the 'relation of the worker to production.' By overturning his relation to production, by asserting his ownership of the products of his labour, the worker emancipates the whole of society from private property.

With this statement Marx by and large summarizes his answer to the question we surmised to be the rationale for the first manuscript. It is in the estranged relationship of the worker to the products of his labour and to his labour activity that lies the root of private property. Estranged labour is, initially, the cause of private property, although later, private property becomes the means by which labour is alienated. Once established as a system, private property has as its consequence the political state, which represents and defends the interests of private property. The contradiction between labour and capital, then, finds its expression ultimately as the conflict between the political state and the workers, between the instrument of the propertied and the non-propertied. The emancipation of the workers, then, is the emancipation of society from the divisions synonymous with private property.

With the first manuscript left unfinished, it is apparent that Marx had not completed the task he set himself; namely, 'to grasp the essential connection between private property,' indeed, the whole system of estrangement, *and* 'the *money* system,' i.e., the social system whose principle is money. He has examined the nature of private property, but the nature of *society* as a system of private property and the relation of private property to *money* remain, in this manuscript at least, unanswered questions. For the answers, we must turn to an extended set of notes which Marx wrote as part of a commentary on James Mill's *Elements of Political Economy*.[39]

Before the relationship of private property to the money system can be examined, the concept of money must be defined. Beginning with Mill's characterization of money as 'the *medium* of exchange,' Marx continues: 'The essence of money is not, in the first place, that property is alienated in it, but that the *mediating activity* of movement, the *human*, social act by which man's products mutually complement one another, is *estranged* from man and becomes the attribute of money, a *material thing* outside man ... the *relation* itself between things, man's operation with them, becomes the operation of an entity outside man and above man.'[40] The essence of money, in part, is that the complementarity of human production, the means of social relations based on alienated labour, is not direct but estranged and embodied in the form of a thing. Money is the alienated form of the relation between things, that is, of social relations in a system of private property.

There is more to the definition: 'Owing to this *alien mediator* – instead of man himself being the mediator for man – man regards his will, his activity and his relation to other men as a power independent of him and them. His slavery [Sklaverei], therefore, reaches its peak.' Because social relations in a system of private property become an attribute or a function of money, man's will (his faculty of decision), his activity (life activity/productive activity), and his relation to others (exchange of products) all appear as determined by money. In this, man's slavery is epitomized: his very social nature is determined by powers outside himself; it is now predicated on relations of money.

If, in the philosophy of Feuerbach, man's social nature forms the content of religion and is the essence of God and this God, in turn, dominates the lives of men, Marx here argues in a similar vein that money, as the estranged form of man's social relations, becomes a veritable God, an existing power over man. 'It is clear that this mediator now becomes a *real God*, for the mediator is the *real power* over what it mediates to me. Its cult becomes an end in itself. Objects separated from this mediator have lost their value. Hence the objects only have value insofar as they *represent* the mediator, whereas originally it seemed that the mediator had value only insofar as *it* represented *them*.' Money becomes an active God, an independent power over man, because all that man produces finds its value represented by money and money alone. Separated from this mediator, man's products become valueless; the purpose of production is lost and hence life loses meaning. Money, like a God, bestows value to the products of labour and therefore to life itself in a system of alienation.

It follows from the above quotation that: 'This *mediator* is therefore the lost, estranged *essence* of private property, private property which has become *alienated*, external to itself, just as it is the *alienated* species-activity of man, the *externalised mediation* between man's production and man's production.' The exchange of private property initially is facilitated by a mediator which 'had value only insofar as it represented' the objects of exchange. We surmise by this mediator Marx meant the earliest forms of money, such as cowrie or dentalia shells and wampum. Later, the mediator becomes an object of value in itself and private property then derives its value only in so far as it can be represented by the mediator. In this sense, money becomes the 'estranged *essence* of private property'; that is to say, private property has no value outside of its relation to money. Money is the quintessence of private property.

There are two related aspects, then, to the definition of money. First, money is alienated private property, which in turn is the material embodiment of alienated labour; and second, it is 'the *alienated* species-activity of man,' that is, it is the medium of man's social activity, of his exchange of the products of his alienated labour. Such is Marx's definition drawn out of Mill's characterization of money as the medium of exchange.

Marx summarizes this definition by returning to the analogy of God and money. He writes: 'Christ *represents* originally: 1) men before God; 2) God for men; 3) men to man. Similarly, *money* represents originally, *in accordance with the idea* [seinem Begriff nach] of money: 1) private property for property; 2) society for private property; 3) private property for society.' These are the developmental stages of the *concept* of money, Marx cautions; history is not so neat. Initially, money would have been implicit; the system of exchange would have been barter; at best, forms of money in the shape of salt or cattle might have arisen. With the appearance of money proper, money as money, social relations find their alienated expression as money and therefore money represents society in exchange for private property. With the full development of the money system, money, i.e., alienated private property, becomes the sole purpose and end of society.

Marx extends the analogy and writes: 'But Christ is *alienated* God and alienated *man*. God has value only insofar as he represents Christ, and man has value only insofar as he represents Christ. It is the same with money.' If we substitute the appropriate concepts we arrive at the following. Money is *alienated* private property and alienated *society* (man). Private property has value only in so far as it represents money, and man has value only in so far as he represents money. This is Marx's definition of money – a definition which remains remarkably consistent from the *Grundrisse* to *Das Kapital*.[41]

In this definition the answer to the question he posed in the first manuscript is clearly implied. But Marx puts forth the question and answer in explicit terms: 'Why must private property develop into the *money system*? Because man as a social being must proceed to *exchange* and because exchange – private property being presupposed – must evolve value. The mediating process between men engaged in exchange is not a social or human process, not *human relationship*; it is the *abstract relationship* of private property to private property, and the expression of this *abstract* relationship is *value*, whose actual existence as value constitutes *money*. Since men engaged in exchange do not relate to each other as men, *things* lose the significance of human, personal property. The social relationship of private property to private property is already a relationship in which private property is estranged from itself. The form of existence for itself of this relationship, money, is therefore the alienation of private property, the abstraction from its [private property] *specific*, personal nature.'[42]

Despite the lucidity of this statement it is worthwhile to trace the thread of its argument. Man is a social being and therefore must exchange; exchange, presupposing private property, requires the notion of value; and value finds its material expression in money. Even in primitive exchange, such as barter, value is implied and the development of money, therefore, latent. In a word, the evolution of exchange must need give rise to a money system.

The money system itself evolves and in the process money progressively distances itself from the 'money value of the material in which it exists.'[43] In other words, it increasingly takes on symbolic forms, such as paper money and assorted 'notes,' which are devoid of value in themselves. Such forms are 'the more perfect mode of existence of *money as money*'; that is to say, they act purely as money, a medium of exchange, without any inherent value such as is embodied in gold or silver. The appearance of these forms of money, says Marx, are 'a necessary factor' in the evolution of the money system. The culmination of this development is found in 'the *credit system* [Kreditwesen], of which banking [das Bankwesen] is the perfect expression.' By the credit system, Marx implies nothing more than the contemporary meaning; namely, a system in which goods and services may be used or possessed and paid for later. It is exchange based on temporary 'trust.'

With the increased use of credit in commerce and the decline of the use of money for immediate payment, it appears, writes Marx, 'as if the power of the alien, material force were broken, the relationship of self-estrangement abolished and man had once more human relations to man.' But such notions, which accompanied the spread of credit and underlay certain French 'socialist' theories of banking, are a matter of appearance only. In fact, the credit system extends man's alienation. As Marx puts it, with indignation: 'the self-estrangement, the de-humanization [Selbstentfremdung, Entmenschung], is all the more *infamous* and *extreme* because its element is no longer commodity, metal, paper, but man's *moral* existence, man's *social* existence, the *inmost depths* of his heart, and because under the appearance of man's *trust* in man it is the height of *distrust* and complete estrangement [die völlige Entfremdung].'[44]

The defence and elaboration of this statement comprise much of the remainder of Marx's discussion of credit. But before this, he makes two small points about the relation of credit and money. Despite appearances, the *content* of credit is, of course, money; in the final analysis, the creditor must be *paid*. The 'content of the trust' involved in credit, moreover, is nothing more than the knowledge that the recipient of the advance is 'able to pay.' These points made, perhaps directed at those who see in credit the demise of money, Marx turns to the question: 'what constitutes the essence of credit?'

He prefaces the definition with a brief examination of the only two sorts of relationship in which 'credit is conceivable.' The first is the credit extended to the poor man. Here, 'the life of the poor man and his talents and activity serve the rich man as a *guarantee* of the repayment of the money lent.'[45] In other words, money is loaned on the basis of the poor man's ability to work and his virtue and reputation. The second is credit extended to the 'man of means.' This relation is more the rule for credit than the first, and in it '*credit* becomes merely a medium facilitating exchange, that is to say, *money* itself raised to a completely *ideal* form [eine ganz *ideale* form]': that is, money as a *medium* of exchange, without any physical embodiment.

None the less, in both cases, credit is extended on the basis of an assessment of a man's ability to pay. From this conclusion, Marx sets forth his definition and its elaboration:

Credit is the *economic* judgement on the *morality* of a man. In credit, the *man* himself, instead of metal or paper, has become the *mediator* of exchange, not however as a man, but as the *mode of existence of capital* and interest. The medium of exchange, therefore, has certainly returned out of its material form and been put back in man, but only because the man himself has been put outside himself and has himself assumed a material form. Within the credit relationship, it is not the case that money is transcended in man, but that man himself is turned into *money*, or money is *incorporated* in him. *Human individuality*, human *morality* itself, has, become both an object of commerce and the *material* in which money exists. Instead of money, or paper, it is my own personal existence, my flesh and blood, my social virtue and importance, which constitutes the material, corporeal form of the *spirit of money*. Credit no longer resolves the value of money, into money but into human flesh and the human heart.

This passage requires little explication; suffice to say that this definition completes the concept of alienated labour as found in the Paris manuscripts. The development of private property culminates in the credit system.

Before Marx draws this conclusion he examines how credit, once credit as a system is established, operates 'in deceitful ways [auf doppelte Weise].' Under the guise of 'an extreme economic appreciation of man,' it works towards the further estrangement of man. First, it exacerbates the social divisions already thrown up with the advance of capital. 'The antithesis between capitalist and worker, between big and small capitalists, becomes still greater since credit is given only to him who already has, and is a new opportunity of accumulation for the rich.'[46] Second, it raises 'mutual pretence, hypocrisy and sanctimoniousness' to a peak because the man 'without credit' is not only judged to be poor but also suffers 'a pejorative moral judgement that he possesses no trust, no recognition, and therefore is a social pariah. In addition to his actual privation, the poor man endures this ignominy and the humiliation of having to *ask* the rich man for credit.' Third, because credit is the '*nominal* existence of money,' *counterfeiting* can only be done in the material of the debtor's own person. In this situation, the debtor 'makes himself into counterfeit coin,' he 'obtains credit by stealth, by lying, etc.' Moreover, the credit relationship itself, both on the part of lenders and borrowers, 'becomes an object of commerce'; that is, lenders and borrowers play one off against the other. In this, the relationship becomes 'an object of mutual deception and misuse.'

Inasmuch as a government seeks a loan, Marx suggests that 'the state occupies exactly the same place' as does the individual seeking credit described above. In other words, the power of the creditor over the debtor is the same if the debtor happens to be a government. 'In the game with government securities,' he asserts, 'it is seen how the state has become the plaything of businessmen, etc.'

There is one further point, which needs only to be cited: 'The *credit system* finally has its completion in the *banking system*. The creation of bankers, the political domination of the bank, the concentration of wealth in these hands, this economic *Areopagus* of the nation, is the worthy completion of the money system.'[47] The development of the money system, through the credit system, culminates in the banking system. The bank, as the largest possessor and manipulator of money and credit, becomes the final arbiter and highest court in the economic life of the nation.

With this, Marx completes his analysis of the evolution of the system of alienation, of private property. At its highest point, the system estranges man's moral being, his position in society, by making it the basis of credit, an object of commerce. Credit and banking spur the concentration of wealth, and therefore of power, in society, and leave no aspect of human life untouched by the attribute of dissimulation. Even the state comes under the sway of the credit system and becomes for its creditors an object of manipulation.

Marx began this analysis of alienation with the economic fact that the worker became poorer the more wealth he produced. The product of man's labour was alienated from man; and inasmuch as the product was alienated, so too was the act of production. From these two aspects, Marx deduced that man was alienated from his community and from his fellow man. But the analysis of alienation did not end here. Alienated labour was the cause of private property and the system of private property necessarily developed into the money system. Within the money system there evolved the systems of credit and banking, and with these, all aspects of estrangement were intensified and man's moral being, every aspect of *human* life, was brought within the system of alienation. The system of credit and banking was, wrote Marx, 'the height of *distrust* and complete estrangement.'

So far Marx has analysed the nature of alienated labour, its consequence, namely, private property, and the development of a system of private property. In a word, he has briefly outlined 'the relation of *alienated labour* to the course of humanity's development.'[48] But in this analysis he has focused largely on the individual and the consequences of this system of alienation for the individual who is, naturally, a member of society. Not a great deal has been said, however, about this other side of the human equation, i.e., the nature of society or community. It is to this question that Marx turned next in his 'Comments on James Mill.'

One of the first points Marx makes is that society is 'no abstract universal power [keine abstrakt-allegmeine Macht] opposed to the single individual'; rather, it is the social relations, the real, concrete activity between individuals, which is expressed as 'the essence of each individual,' as 'his own activity,' life and existence.[49] Because society is comprised of the social relations of its members, it follows that through these relations man creates his own community. But man does not create this community as he sees fit; he creates and re-creates it according to the relations in which he stands to other men, relations determined in the evolution of human production and exchange.

The nature of society, then, depends on the nature of the interrelations of its members. In so far as its members are alienated from each other, the community can appear only 'in the form of estrangement.' That is, 'to say that *man* is estranged from himself, therefore, is the same thing as saying that the *society* of this estranged man is a caricature of his true [or genuine] communal essence [die Karikatur seines wirklichen Gemeinwesens].' By true communal essence he means the conceptual unity of the universal and particular. In other words, individuals who stand in an estranged relation to others, who reproduce themselves within a system of alienation, can create a society only *as* a system of estranged relations.

The political economist, writes Marx, perceives existing society as it is and describes it appropriately as a system of 'exchange and trade,' as a 'series of mutual exchanges,' as a 'commercial society' whose members are all 'merchants.' This is *not* an inaccurate view, for what else could a society be in which the interrelationships of its members were estranged? The difficulty here is that 'political economy *defines* the *estranged* form of social intercourse as the essential [wesentliche] and *original* [ursprüngliche] form corresponding to man's nature.' It is not that political economy misapprehends the existing form of society, but that it mistakes the existing form, the estranged form, for the truth of society, its essence or its definition.

We may briefly digress here to point out Marx's use of critique. He begins in these comments with the political economists' notion of exchange as society. This notion is compared to the definition of man, at the same time the definition of community, which is man's *social* nature; i.e., man is not human except in a system of mutual and reciprocal relationships and society is not human society except as such a system. Man and his society are one and the same. It is this *comparison* which allows Marx to suggest that society as 'a series of mutual exchanges' is not the essential form of society. But let us examine his analysis of society as exchanges of private property more closely to grasp the unsocial nature of such a society.

To analyse the relations between men, he takes again as his starting point the view of political economy, which is the same starting point of the 'real process.' In other words, in reality the relations between men begin in the same way that political economy depicts them. They are the relations of 'property owner to property owner.'

Man defined as a property owner 'proves his personality and both distinguishes himself from, and enters into relations with, other men through this exclusive ownership.'[50] In a system of private property, man's self, his identity, is contained in his possessions. Relations between men, which are relations of exchange, then, constitute a '*loss* or *surrender* of private property,' which, it follows, is at the same time 'an alienation of man.' As Marx summarizes it: 'The *social* connection or *social* relationship between the two property owners is therefore that of *reciprocity* in *alienation* ... or *alienation* as the relationship of both property owners.'[51]

Within the system of private property, the meaning of society or community is but the exchange of private property. '*Exchange* or *barter* [trade] [Der Tausch oder der Tauschhandel] is therefore the social act, the species-act [Gattungsakt], the community [das Gemeinwesen], the social intercourse and integration of men within *private ownership* [Privateigentums], and therefore the external *alienated* species-act. It is just for this reason that it appears as *barter*. For this reason, likewise, it is the opposite of the *social* relationship.' Society, then, in the eyes of the political economist *and* in reality is civil society. Every individual is but a trader or merchant and relationships amount to the exchange of private property. This is not a society of social relationships, rather of unsocial relations in that every exchange involves distrust and calculation. Indeed, the basis of this relation, remarks Marx elsewhere, is 'mutual plundering.' As *existing* society it is the very opposite of the essence, the definition, of society.

Marx now examines the consequence for private property of its exchange. In this act of 'reciprocal alienation,' private property itself becomes estranged. It is freed from its nature as 'the produce of the labour of its owner' and juxtaposed to another private property. In this juxtaposition each product becomes the representative for the other; they become 'equivalent' or 'substitutes' for each other. This new mode of existence as an equivalent is its *value* and is manifested as its *exchange-value*.

The development of exchange and therefore of exchange-value necessarily gives rise to money, as we have seen Marx argue earlier. If money is the consequence of the development of a system of exchange and if the nature of existing society is exchange of private property, then money is the summation, the embodiment, the concrete expression, of existing society, the totality of man's relationships.

Money, remarks Marx in the Paris manuscripts, is the mediator in relations between men, and as this mediator it is also the incarnation of men in such a system. 'Money is the *procurer* between mans' need and the object, between his life and his means of life. But *that which* mediates *my* life for me, also *mediates* the existence of other people for me. For me it is the *other* person.'[52] It follows that: 'If *money* is the bond binding me to *human* life, binding society to me, connecting me with nature and man, is not money the bond of all *bonds*? Can it not dissolve and bind all ties? Is it not, therefore, the universal agent of separation [das allegemeine Scheidungsmittel]? It is the true *agent of separation* [Scheidemünze] and the true *cementing agent* [Bindungsmittel], it is the *galvano-chemical* power of society.'[53] In a word, money is the estranged *social* nature of man and the very means by which man's *estrangement* is reproduced. It is private property itself alienated, the product of alienated labour twice removed.

With the definition and analysis of money and the money system, Marx has completed an outline of the relation of alienated labour to the course of human history. In so doing he has grasped the reason for man's separation from fellow man, the consequent separation of man into public and private life, and the reason for the perpetuation of these forms of estrangement.

In the 1843 *Critique of Hegel's Philosophy of Right*, Marx discovered that the existence of a state separate from and opposed to the people was a consequence of the nature of civil society. The principle of civil society, moreover, was, as both Adam Smith and Hegel had asserted, private property. In the Paris manuscripts, Marx revealed that private property was the consequence of alienated labour, and, furthermore, that a system of private property necessarily gave rise to a money system and, within this, to credit and banking – with a concomitant increase in human alienation at each stage.

The means of perpetuating the alienation of labour, and therefore the separation of man from himself and his community, lay in private property, the very product of alienated labour, and in its alienation, i.e., in money. The relationship was reciprocal.

If the separation of the individual and his society (that is, politics itself or political domination which is the same thing, or for that matter all relations of subordination) were the product of a system of private property and such a system itself were the product of alienated labour, i.e., the relation of the *worker* to production, to labour, then, the overcoming of this separation, and 'all relations of servitude,' was to be found in the abolition of the relation of the *worker* to his labour, a change 'expressed in the *political* form of the emancipation of the workers.'

THE SECOND MANUSCRIPT: THE ANTITHESIS OF CAPITAL AND LABOUR

We surmised that the second set of questions which arose in Marx's writings prior to the *Manuscripts* concerned how the wage-worker was born of civil society, of the relations of private property, of industrial development, and why he was destined to confront capital and transform society based on private property. Aspects of these questions were examined in the first sections of the first manuscript where Marx set forth the concepts of wages, profit, and rent; but there was no systematic analysis of the contradiction between labour and capital.

Unfortunately, there are only four pages of this second manuscript extant, and since their pagination begins at forty, it is obvious that our surmise must remain largely a surmise. Yet not entirely, for an analysis of the existing part tends to bear out our supposition.

The few pages that remain contain a discussion of 'the relations of private property.' What Marx means by this phrase requires, in the absence of most of the manuscript, a short recapitulation. We have seen how Marx analysed private property as a consequence, a product, of alienated labour, and saw private property and alienated labour later develop a reciprocal relationship. This system of estrangement evolves in such a way that labour, the activity of production, becomes increasingly alienated, ever more a mere 'source of income' or means 'to earn a living.' In this development, analysed in the 'Comments on James Mill'[54] labour becomes less and less an activity confirming one's *social* nature and more and more an activity which is exchanged for wages. Hence, alienated labour as wage-labour becomes private property itself, i.e., a commodity exchanged for an equivalent. The earlier relationship of alienated labour and private property becomes the relationship of private property and private property, of *labour* as private property and private property as *capital*. Because wage-labour is a commodity, albeit not like the commodity proper, it may be seen as a form of capital, albeit a living form. It is 'private property as activity for itself.'[55] The extant portion of the second manuscript briefly deals with aspects of the relationship between these two elemental components of private property.

The manuscript begins with an incomplete sentence, viz., 'forms the interest on his capital,' or better, 'constitutes the return on his capital [Zinsen seines Kapitals bildet].' Since the discussion of capital in the first manuscript is based on Smith's analysis of industrial capital, whose profits derive from wage-labour, that is, from the difference between the price of labour, wages, and the exchange-value of the product of labour,[56] we may assume Marx is here examining the relationship between wage-labour and industrial capital.

Following the partial sentence, which implies that, inasmuch as capital is augmented through the efforts of labour, labour at best merely manages to reproduce itself while producing or augmenting capital, Marx remarks: 'The worker is the subjective manifestation of the fact that capital is man wholly lost to himself, just as capital is the objective manifestation of the fact that labour is man lost to himself.'[57] The phenomenon or existence of the workers, the human subject as mere wage-labour, as merely the source of capital, points to the fact that the *product* of wage-labour, capital, embodies estranged humanity. Similarly, the existence of capital, as the material expression of estranged labour, points to the fact that its source, wage-labour, is the essence of man estranged. This is Marx's first characterization of the relation between labour and capital.

This relationship, like the relation between alienated labour and private property, is reciprocal and self-reproducing. Marx writes: 'The worker produces capital, capital produces him – hence he produces himself; and man as *worker*, as a *commodity*, is the product of this entire cycle.'

Man as a commodity, as a wage-labourer, finds himself treated much as any commodity within this relationship. His value is nothing more than the price of his labour, which rises and falls 'according to supply and demand.' 'His human qualities only exist insofar as they exist for capital, *alien* to him.' His very existence, his life, as a human being is a matter of indifference to capital. Only his existence as wage-labour matters. In short, 'as soon as it occurs to capital (whether by necessity or caprice) no longer to be for the worker, he himself is no longer for himself: he has *no* work, hence *no* wages, and since he has no existence *as a human being* but only *as a worker*, he can go and bury himself, starve to death, etc.' If capital displaces the worker, he is no longer even a worker, and because that is all he is, once dismissed, once no longer a worker, he is nothing.

Marx depicts this predicament for the wage-labourer, that is, his existence as a mere commodity and his dependence on capital for this existence, as follows: 'The worker exists as a worker only when he exists for *himself* as capital; and he exists as capital only when some *capital* exists *for him*. The existence of capital is *his* existence, his *life*, for it determines the content of his life in a way synonymous with it [wie es den Inhalt seines Lebens auf eine ihm gleichgültige Weise bestimmt].'[58] As Marx earlier asserted, after Smith, capital is 'the *governing power* over labour and its products,' and because the interest of capital is solely the increase of capital, the entire aim of the production process – and thus, in effect, of human life – is the production of capital.

The human being, the free and socially conscious individual, then has no place in this system of production. Not only is man reproduced in the labour process as a commodity but also 'as a *mentally* and physically *de-humanized* being.' The process of producing 'the human commodity' is at the same time the process of creating a grotesque parody of the human being. Indeed, notes Marx, the 'great advance of Ricardo, Mill, etc. on Smith and Say' was 'to declare the *existence* of the human being ... to be *indifferent* and even *harmful* [als *gleichgültig* und sogar *schädlich*]' to the system of capitalist production.

In this vein, the political economist sees the human being only as a worker in the production process. 'Outside this labour relationship,' the worker is not recognized by political economy. Unemployed, old, or sick or as a beggar or criminal, the workingman becomes only a '*figure* who does not exist for political economy.' Instead, he exists 'for other eyes, those of the doctor, the judge, the grave-digger, bailiff, etc.'

Even though the worker is reproduced in the image of capital, as capital in himself, he is not at one with capital. It was a significant advance, writes Marx, that political economy should not only perceive *labour* to be the sole *source* of wealth but also the *contradiction* between labour and capital. Political economy, in his words, expounded 'the *inverse* relation between wages and interest on capital [das *umgekehrte* Verhältnis zwischen dem Arbeitslohn und den Zinsen des Kapitals], and the fact that the capitalist could normally *only* gain by pressing down wages, and vice versa. Not the defrauding of the customer, but the capitalist and the worker taking advantage of each other, is shown to be the *normal* relationship [das *normale* Verhältnis].'[59]

Political economy well understood the relation between labour and capital: the wages of labour and the return on investment were inversely related. The only way the return could be increased in principle [in der Regel], that is, ignoring fraud and windfall gains, was to depress wages; and conversely an increase in wages could only be won at the expense of the return on capital invested. This was 'the *normal* relationship'; that is to say, the inverse relation, the contradiction, between labour and capital was the principle of their reciprocal relationship.

With this point, Marx returns to the concept of private property and brings his analysis to a conclusion: 'The relations of private property contain latent within them the relation of private property as *labour*, the relation of private property as *capital*, and the *mutual relation* of these two to one another.' Here Marx is saying, if we may extrapolate, that the exchange of private property, historically and conceptually, contains the potential development of productive activity into wage-labour, into a commodity form; and it also contains the potential development of the product of man's activity into capital, i.e., private property for itself, private property for the increase of private property; and, furthermore, contains the potential development of the mutual relation of wage-labour and capital – because they are the opposite sides of the same coin, i.e., of private property.

Private property, it should be remembered, is the product of alienated labour and alienated labour manifests itself as private property. In the evolution of the exchange of private property, alienated labour and private property develop respectively into wage-labour and capital (money being the first form of capital). The mutual relation between the wages of labour and the return on capital is but the developed expression of the original relation between alienated labour and private property. They form a genuine contradiction in that one cannot exist without the other, yet each attempts to absorb the other. As Marx writes: 'The worker knows the capitalist as his own non-existence, and vice versa: each tries to rob the other of his existence.'[60]

The relationship is expressed more broadly in the following: 'labour, the subjective essence of private property as exclusion of property, and capital, objective labour as *exclusion* of labour, constitute *private property* as its developed state of contradiction – hence a dynamic relationship driving towards resolution.'[61] Thus, wage-labour and capital, because each owes its existence to the other, must express their existence in mutual opposition. This opposition can be *solved* in only one way, namely with the return of private property to its producer, with the transformation of the system of private property and the production of human property. In this regard, Marx concludes: 'This contradiction, driven to the limit, is of necessity the limit, the culmination, and the downfall of the whole private-property relationship.'[62]

In the course of development of the relations of private property, then, all forms of labour and property evolve respectively into wage-labour and capital. (Marx briefly examines in this manuscript how landed property succumbs to the advance of industrial capital.) When all the relations of private property have been resolved into the relation of wage-labour and capital, the development of the system of private property will have reached its zenith. This contradiction alone is the principle of modern society, and its solution comes only with the triumph of labour over capital, for the domination of capital over labour is the *status quo* and its persistence is the continuation of the contradiction.

THE THIRD MANUSCRIPT: THE TRANSCENDENCE OF SELF-ESTRANGEMENT

The reason for man's *separation* from himself and others and thus for the *political* nature of society has been examined. Likewise, the reason the proletariat must confront capital and transform society has been explored. But the third question that we suggest arises from Marx's earlier work, and which concerns the *nature* of transformed society, remains to be analysed. In the third manuscript, the central problem that Marx takes up is the nature of communism.

This is not the first place that he has considered this question. A concept of the unity of the general and particular, of society and its members, has been part of his method of critique throughout the writings considered so far. In the *Rheinische Zeitung* articles, he employs the concept of the 'true' or 'genuine' state; in the *Critique* of Hegel, he uses the notions of '*res publica*' and 'true democracy'; and in the *Deutsch-Französische Jahrbücher* articles, there appear the definitions of 'human community' and 'human emancipation.' All of these concepts are but different expressions of a unified relationship: they are the definition of the essence of man or of society, which is the same thing. The concept of communism is another such expression. Already in 1843, Marx equates the *definition* of society [die Gesellschaft] with man's 'communal essence [das kommunistisch Wesen].'[63] But it is only in the third manuscript that he explicitly takes up the meaning of communism.

It is only now that he can understand *how* 'the world becomes philosophical and philosophy becomes worldly,' as he wrote in 1841, because only after an analysis of the nature of private property and the contradiction between labour and capital was it possible to grasp how and why existing man throughout history evolved in the direction of his essence, of communism; and only after the *critique* of political economy by means of the concepts of labour and alienated labour was it possible to understand the complete nature of man (his social essence and its basis in productive activity) and why communism as the essence of man was the necessary consequence of man's history. It follows that it is only now he can give consideration to the meaning of communism.

The third manuscript is less of an integral whole than the first two. Its sections bear little obvious relation to each other. About one-third is a critique of Hegel's dialectic, which is not irrelevant to the question of communism but *directly* concerns Hegel's philosophy and not communism. There are a few pages in which Marx discusses 'money,' but most of the ideas raised here are the same as those already treated in the 'Comments on James Mill.' Another one-third, approximately, is concerned with the concept of communism and with the light that this definition throws on several hitherto unsolved questions concerning the development of man. It is this section which principally interests us.

This section begins with the sentence: 'The transcendence of self-estrangement follows the same course as self-estrangement [Die Aufhebung der Selbstentfremdung macht den selben Weg wie die Selbstentfremdung].'[64] We suggest this means that the development of the system of private property (of self-estrangement) is at the same time the development of the possibility of its transcendence. In other words, the relations of private property at any particular stage of its development would suggest a concomitant *meaning* of its transcendence. Each stage would give rise to its own theory of transformation, which necessarily would be incomplete or reformist because the stage of development would be incomplete. Only with the historical resolution of the relations of private property into the elemental relation between labour and capital does the possibility of comprehending the nature of self-estrangement and its supersession arise. Only then can communism be properly understood as the outcome of the development of private property, as the transcendence of self-estrangement.

Given that the development of self-estrangement leads to the transcendence of self-estrangement, Marx writes: 'communism is the *positive* expression of annulled private property [des aufgehobnen Privateigentums].' By the adjective 'positive,' he means that, with the culmination of the relations of private property, communism is no longer an implied or 'dogmatic abstraction' or a 'special,' particular, 'expression of the humanistic principle,'[65] as found in the theories of Proudhon, Fourier, and Saint-Simon. It is, rather, a state of existence which comes into being with the transformation of the system of private property. It is, in other words, the logical and necessary *corollary* of 'annulled private property.'

With the culmination of the system of private property – with the negation of private property as exclusive, individual private property – communism is first expressed 'as *universal* private property [das *allgemeine* Privateigentum].' This first form, writes Marx, is 'only a *generalisation* [*Verallgemeinerung*] and *consummation* [*Vollendung*],' of the relation between labour and capital. The development of capital has, in other words, through the medium of competition come to a close, producing a single monopoly capital on one side and making everyone a wage-labourer on the other side. As Marx writes: 'The community [die Gemeinschaft] is only a community of *labour*, and equality of *wages* paid out by communal capital – by the *community* as the universal capitalist. Both sides of the relationship are raised to an *imagined* universality – *labour* as the category in which every person is placed, and *capital* as the acknowledged universality and power of the community.'[66]

The first form of communism, then, is the final expression of capitalism. Because the relations of private property comprise the first form, 'crude [rohe] communism' as Marx calls it, epitomizes the character of private property. It is only a stage or phase of the development of the baseness of private property, 'of private property wanting to establish itself as the *positive community*'[67] [ist also nur eine *Erscheinungsform* von der Niedertracht des Privateigentums, das sich als das *positive Gemeinwesen* setzen will]. If many capitals are in themselves the material, summary, and alienated expression of man's productive relationships, then, they are also the implied alienated expression of community. When capital becomes a single monopoly capital and all the members of society mere wage-labourers, then capital asserts itself 'as the *positive community*,' as no longer merely the implied community but as the real, existing community by virtue of the fact that the essence of community, its human members, exist only as wage-labourers – as men estranged from the product of their labour, themselves and their community – or conversely, by virtue of the fact that, given the persistence of the relations of private property, capital *is* the expression of community, albeit in an alienated form.

In his discussion of this first form of communism, Marx employs an argument which, in today's context at least, appears somewhat peculiar. He writes that just as private property as exclusive, individual property passes into 'universal private property,' that is, all property owned by all, by the community, so too does the position of the woman, within 'crude communism,' pass from 'a form of exclusive private property' (marriage) to a form of 'communal and common property.' This 'idea of the community of women,' he asserts, 'gives away the secret' of this form of communism. In that women 'pass from marriage to general prostitution,' so does the relation of capital and labour pass from private, particular prostitution to 'a state of universal prostitution,' i.e., the relation between all as labourers and the community as capital. This revealed secret appears to be intended as criticism of Plato, or perhaps of medieval or Renaissance theories of communist utopias. But Marx extends this argument, concerning the relationship between men and women, making it a means of judging the state of humanity of any society. Here, at length, is the argument:

The direct, natural and necessary relation of person to person is the relation of *man to woman*. In this *natural* species-relationship man's relation to nature is immediately his relation to man, just as his relation to man is immediately his relation to nature – his own *natural* destination [Bestimmung]. In this relationship, therefore, is *sensuously manifested*, reduced to an observable *fact*, the extent to which the human essence has become nature to man, or to which nature to him has become the human essence of man. From this relationship one can therefore judge man's whole level of development. From the character of this relationship follows how much *man* as a *species-being* [als Gattungswesen], as *man*, has come to be himself and to comprehend himself; the relation of man to woman is the *most natural* relation of human being to human being [Menschen]. It therefore reveals the extent to which man's *natural* behaviour has become *human*, or the extent to which the *human* essence in him has become a *natural* essence – the extent to which his *human nature* has come to be *natural* to him. This relationship also reveals the extent to which man's *need* has become a *human* need; the extent to which, therefore, the *other* person as a person has become for him a need – the extent to which he in his individual existence is at the same time a social being [Gemeinwesen].[68]

The relationship between men and women in the first form of communism gave the lie to this form. But, according to Marx, the relationship can be employed to 'judge man's whole level of development [die ganze Bildungsstufe des Menschen beurteilen].' How is it that he can make such a claim as this, as argued above? First, it must be understood that he is here employing the method of critique, that he is saying that the level of organic organization of any particular society may be criticized (judged, discerned) by comparing its relations between men and women to the relation between man and woman 'in the manner in which the *direct* and *natural* species-relationship [Gattungsverhältnis] is conceived.' In an age of widespread sexual antagonism and ambiguity, the definition of the *essence* of *human* relations as that between man and woman is not easily accepted. But if we accept Aristotle on the notion of essence, as almost certainly Marx did, we find that the 'essential' refers to those attributes of a subject which are universal or necessary.[69] The whole of mankind is divided into male and female and their *union* is *necessary* for the creation and therefore definition of man. Just male or just female is inconceivable; male is defined in terms of female and vice versa; the one demands the other. The relation between male and female, then, is essential to the definition of man; it is *the* essential relationship, for neither can *exist* without the other. To be human is to stand in relation to another, but the 'most natural relation,' i.e., the relation *necessary* for the creation and definition of the human being, is that between man and woman. It follows, therefore, that in this relationship the degree of harmony and universality and desire for it lies the secret of the level of human development in any existing society.

The next stage of communism is still within the confines of the relations of private property. There are two possible forms it may take; the first is 'still political in nature – democratic or despotic.' By political Marx refers to the continuing separation of man from his community, politics being the consequence of the persistence of private property. That the separation takes a democratic or despotic form is beside the point. The second form of this stage of communism is characterized by 'the transcendence of the state [Aufhebung des Staats].' But even with this transcendence of formal politics, such a society is not freed of the effects of private property. In both cases, writes Marx, there is the awareness of the unity of man, of 'the supersession of man's self-estrangement.' But because 'the positive essence of private property' has 'not yet been grasped,' this stage of communism 'remains captive to it and infected by it.' In short, communism in this stage grasps its 'concept [Begriff] but not its essence [Wesen].' By this somewhat cryptic phrasing we suppose Marx to be saying that in this stage man understands what he is, i.e., he grasps the *form* of his alienation, he comprehends that God and the state, for example, represent or embody his social relations and he acts to return this estranged essence to himself. But what he has *not* grasped is his essence, 'the positive essence of private property,' that is, his essence as production for others: that in producing for others he produces himself. In not understanding this, man remains to some degree captive to the laws of the production of private property. The point is that man can now understand his alienation but not grasp the making of it; he has not comprehended the fact that he makes himself and therefore can determine his relation to others on the basis of the laws of beauty. He can grasp his social nature but cannot yet consciously realize it.

The transcendence of private property in both of these first forms of communism appears as the culmination of the relations of labour and capital. They are, then, forms of communism in which capital as the objective manifestation of man's estrangement still holds sway. The final form of communism, however, is that in which capital as universal capital and as man's estrangement is superseded.

Communism is the *positive* transcendence of private property as human self-estrangement, and therefore as the real *appropriation* of the *human* essence by and for man; communism therefore as the complete return of man to himself as a *social* (i.e., human) being – a return accomplished consciously and embracing the entire wealth of previous development. This communism, as fully developed naturalism, equals humanism, and as fully developed humanism equals naturalism; it is the *genuine* resolution of the conflict between man and nature and between man and man – the true resolution of the strife between existence and essence, between objectification and self-confirmation [zwischen Vergegenständlichung und Selbstbestätigung], between freedom and necessity, between the individual and the species. Communism is the riddle of history solved and it knows itself to be this solution.[70]

In this form of communism, then, the relations of private property no longer obtain. Man no longer produces himself in the shape of capital, but produces for himself and for others directly. He grasps 'the *human* nature of need,' that is, that each needs the other for existence as a human and fulfils this need directly, without mediation; and that all needs are social needs produced and satisfied in relation to others. Here, man comprehends his social nature and consciously exercises the means of realizing it. The idea of the 'return [Rückkehr] of man to himself' does not refer to a return to a golden age *or* to a notion of man who at one time existed; rather, it refers to man's union with himself, with the self (his social nature) which is the product of his own history, of his own making, but hitherto in an alienated form.

As for communism as 'fully developed naturalism,' Marx means simply that it would be governed by laws following from its own *nature* as a living *unity*. But this unity of the individual and his community is the very principle of humanism; hence the equation of communism as naturalism and humanism.

The conflict between man and nature and man and man would be resolved because this conflict is the consequence of the system of private property, of the exploitation of nature and man, of making use of both for turning a profit. With communism, furthermore, man's existence would conform to the principles of his essence; his 'objectification' would no longer be his alienation but the expression of his social being, his 'self-confirmation'; freedom would no longer be the liberty of one in opposition to the other but the recognition that one *is* the other; and the individual would no longer stand opposed to his community but find his community within himself, as himself.

Marx concludes with a flourish: communism 'is the riddle [Rätsel] of history solved.' First, what is the riddle of history? If history is taken simply as the course of man's development, then the riddle must be: whither man in his development? If the actual course of man's development is, as Marx has argued, the movement of private property, then, the direction of this movement is also the direction of history. The culmination of this movement is then also the culmination of man's history. And this is communism: the solved riddle. But how is it that communism 'knows itself to be the solution'? The end of history is the end of the movement of private property; communism is the culmination and transcendence of private property, and, in grasping this, it understands itself as the end of history.

At this point in the analysis of communism, there are two fundamental questions which arise; one concerns the nature of labour under communism. We have seen how alienated labour produces private property and how private property then becomes the means of labour's alienation. With the transcendence of this relationship, labour no longer is estranged, it becomes labour as *human* activity, i.e., the activity confirming one's social nature. Here is what Marx writes in the 'Comments on James Mill' regarding 'production as human beings,' that is, productive activity outside the realm of alienation. This passage, then, is *not* to be read as if Marx is beginning with the 'I' as a solitary ego; he is discussing the 'I and Thou' within a social relationship.

Each of us would have in *two ways affirmed* himself and the other person. 1) In my *production* I would have objectified my *individuality*, its *specific character*, and therefore enjoyed not only an individual *manifestation of my life* during the activity, but also when looking at the object I would have the individual pleasure of knowing my personality to be *objective, visible to the senses* and hence a power *beyond all doubt*.

2) In your enjoyment or use of my product I would have the *direct* enjoyment both of being conscious of having satisfied a *human* need by my work, that is, or having objectified *man's* essential nature, and of having thus created an object corresponding to the need of another *man's* essential nature.

3) I would have been for you the *mediator* between you and the species, and therefore would become recognized and felt by you yourself as a completion of your own essential nature and as a necessary part of yourself, and consequently would know myself to be confirmed both in your thought and your love.

4) In the individual expression of my life I would have directly created your expression of *your* life and therefore in my individual activity I would have directly *confirmed* and *realised* my true nature, my *human* nature, my *communal* nature.

Our products would be so many mirrors in which we saw reflected our essential nature.[71]

The point that Marx is making is succinctly put in the previous quotation on communism: labour as *human* production is 'the resolution of the conflict ... between objectification and self-confirmation.' The objectification of labour (as alienated labour) is no longer an *estranged* object which stands as a power *over* the producer; it is, instead, the *direct* material manifestation of the producer's social nature, and hence the expression of a power as *direct* fulfillment of the producer. The *act* of producing, moreover, is no longer estranged as wage-labour, no longer determined by the demands of capital, but now is an act performed as a *directly* social act, an act consciously performed as a confirmation of one's social essence. Labour as *human* production is here the direct, conscious, active, and necessary means of establishing what one is, a social being.

Instead of being 'an alienation of life,' as in a system of private property, work now becomes 'a free manifestation of life, hence an enjoyment of life.' Instead of being the alienation of one's individuality, work becomes the affirmation of individuality, i.e., not individuality as isolation as in a system of private property, but the truth of individuality, the relation to others.

The second question which arises concerns the meaning of society. Prior to communism, society comprises the institutions, customs, religion, laws, and, above all, the political state of a given social formation. All of these aspects of society are so many forms of estranged relations. With the arrival of communism, they are all resolved into *human* relations, that is, relations based on a conscious recognition of man's social essence. As Marx cautions in defining communism: 'Above all we must avoid postulating "society" again as an abstraction confronting [gegenüber] the individual. The individual *is* the *social being* [das *gesellschaftliche Wesen*]. His manifestation of life – even if they may not appear in the direct form of *communal* manifestations of life carried out in association with other men – is, therefore, a manifestation and affirmation of *social life*.'[72]

The point made here devolves on the fact that the individual and his relations comprise a unity of opposites. The individual is nothing outside of his social relations, and society is nothing but the interrelationships of its individual members. In a system of private property, the individuals who produce these relations produce them in an estranged manner. Society and all its aspects, then, appear in an estranged form. Under communism, however, the relations of private property, which give rise to estranged society, are transcended and a direct unity of these opposites, the individual and his relationship, is established. Here, then, 'society' no longer exists as an 'abstraction' in opposition to the individual, because only 'society' which is estranged society exists outside of man. It is not that 'society' disappears; only its estranged forms of existence do. Because the individual is the subject in this relation, the producer, the unity of opposites is embedded in him: he '*is* the *social being*.'

We have now seen how Marx perceives the stages of 'positively annulled property,' and how the final stage of communism is the end of the movement of private property, the end of history. It must not be assumed from this definition, however, that communism is the end of human development; it is *not* an ideal society which, having been achieved, signifies the conclusion of man's evolution. It is only the close of his unconsciously determined evolution. Communism signifies the dénouement of one period of man's becoming and the commencement of another. It is the end of political society and the beginning of human society. Marx writes: 'Communism is the position as the negation of the negation, and is hence the *actual* phase necessary for the next stage of historical development in the process of human emancipation and rehabilitation [der menschlichen Emanzipation und Wiedergewinnung]. *Communism* is the necessary form and the dynamic principle of the immediate future, but communism as such is not the goal of human development, the form of human society [das Ziel der menschlichen Entwicklung – die Gestalt der menschlichen Gesellschaft].'[73]

To grasp the meaning of communism as the negation of the negation, we must return to Marx's discussion of the development of private property. At first, private property takes the form of individual private property based on the labour of an individual owner.[74] Through its own development this mode of production is transformed into the capitalist mode, in which the goal of production is capital and not merely commodities. This mode is the 'negation' of the first. Capitalism itself evolves, in the direction of ever-increasing monopoly, such that the whole of society becomes dominated by a single capital and everyone becomes a wage-labourer. At this point capitalism as a system comes to a close; in this, it finds its 'negation.' Communism, which *is* initially the culmination of capitalist relations, then, is the negation of the negation.

Yet this negation of the negation is not the limit of man's advance. Marx asserts that, although communism is 'the necessary form [die notwendige Gestalt] and dynamic principle of the immediate future,' it 'as such is not the goal of human development.' The word for 'goal' is 'das Ziel' and is perhaps better translated as the limit or the extremity. What does Marx mean that communism is not the limit or boundary of human development, that it is not the form of human society? The answer is two-fold, lying first in the meaning of communism and second in the relation of communism to development.

The negation of the negation, in Hegel's philosophy, constitutes 'the absolute positive'; it is a unity which is 'self-mediating movement and activity.'[75] But one of Feuerbach's achievements, writes Marx, was to oppose the negation of the negation as 'the absolute positive' with 'the self-supporting positive, positively based on itself.'[76] Feuerbach did not regard the negation of the negation as the absolute positive; for him, rather, it was the necessary antecedent to the self-supporting, the absolute positive; it was not this positive because the negation of the negation was mediated with itself and this implicated its annulled or transcended premise.

Marx employs this distinction, arguing that communism is not the 'self-supporting positive.' 'Because of its character as negation of the negation,' he writes, communism 'as appropriation [Aneignung] of the human essence which is mediated with itself through the negation of private property, is not yet the *true* [*wahre*], self-generating position, but one generated by private property [von sich selbst, sondern vielmehr vom Privateigentum aus beginnende Position].'[77] Thus, the return of man to himself in communism is the return of man through the negation of private property; the return is therefore mediated by the negation. As Marx continues: 'Only through the supersession of this mediation [die Aufhebung dieser Vermittelung] – which is itself, however, a necessary premise – does positively self-deriving humanism, *positive* humanism, come into being.'[78] The state of affairs which comes after communism, after the negation of the negation, is 'the absolute positive' because it exists *not* by virtue of the absence or negation of private property but by virtue *solely* of the presence of self-mediating man. This is the first reason for saying that communism 'as such is not the goal of human development.'

The second reason lies in the relationship of communism, and its subsequent, self-generating position, to human development. Prior to communism, the course of human progress is the movement of private property. History, as this movement, is made by man, but in an estranged manner, not consciously. Nevertheless, it is made by man; indeed, history is man making himself. As Marx asserts, 'the entire so-called history of the world is nothing but the creation of man through human labour.'[79] When history ends, with the close of the movement of private property, it does not follow that man no longer makes himself; rather, it is that man no longer makes himself in an estranged manner, unconsciously. That man is social and creates this nature through his labour is the essence of man, and as the essence it is not variable. As man moves through time, therefore, it is not his essence but his existence which changes. As man moves from a system of private property to communism and beyond, he continues to make himself; only the mode of creation changes. In communism, man's existence no longer disaccords with his essence;[80] he makes himself consciously, that is, in agreement with his essence; his development hereafter is self-determined.

With the advent of self-mediating, *human* society, man's coming-to-be for himself is at an end. But as for human development, there is no end.

CONCLUSIONS

It will be evident to those familiar with the Paris manuscripts that there is much more in these writings than is captured here – and this is especially true of the third manuscript. The richness, depth, and breadth of the material must be read in the original to be appreciated.

Yet our intention was not to expound the whole of the *Manuscripts*; it was to discover the answers to the questions raised by Marx's prior work on the nature of politics. The first of these questions concerned the nature of private property, the reason why it was the presupposition of political society. The second concerned the rise of the working class out of the growth of industry, of the system of private property, and the nature of the contradiction between labour and capital. The third concerned the resolution of this contradiction, the nature of communism. The answers, while not as complete as they were to become by the end of his life, are certainly well-formed and by and large consistent with his later work.

The answers developed in all three manuscripts rest on Marx's critical review of the literature of political economy. Almost three-quarters of the first manuscript consists of such an analysis, which focuses on the meaning of the forms of private property: wages, profits, and rent. There is also a considerable amount of unpublished material by Marx on this literature, not to mention the published 'Comments on James Mill.' According to his method, as formulated in the D-FJ, this is precisely where Marx must begin. ('The critic can ... start out from any form of theoretical and practical consciousness and from the forms *peculiar* to existing reality develop the true reality as its obligation and its final goal.') On the basis of this analysis, he is able to draw several conclusions about the specific, internal logic of political economy, that is, the movement of the constituent parts of private property.

Although this movement can be grasped from the analysis of political economy, political economy will not reveal the reason for this movement for it does not understand, Marx argues, the nature of its principal element, private property. Greed and competition, conceived as inherent human characteristics, suffice as explanation for the political economist. To uncover the nature of private property is to comprehend the reason for its movement and to provide the basis for comprehending all the categories of political economy, their relations, and their logical outcome.

The last third of the first manuscript is concerned with the nature of private property, which Marx grasps through his analysis of alienated labour. As for his derivation of the concept of alienated labour, suffice to say here that he begins with an empirical fact, a paradox central to political economy, namely, that the worker becomes poorer the more he produces. By comparing *this* relation of the worker to the product of his labour with the intrinsic or essential relation, the *direct* relation, he is able to grasp labour, under modern economic conditions, as *estranged* productive activity.

The concept of productive activity is not a limited economic category; it is, as Marx argues, the means by which the individual establishes his link to society, it is the essence of man as a social being; it is man making himself.[81] From this fact Marx is able to draw out other aspects of alienation, the focus of so much attention in commentaries on the manuscripts.

By analysing the nature of labour as estranged activity, Marx is able to demonstrate, furthermore, the nature of private property. Alienated labour is the cause, the reason, for private property, argues Marx; and the relationship between alienated labour and private property, which later becomes reciprocal, is the basis for analysing the entire movement of private property. (For those who would doubt the significance for Marx of this relationship as stated here, it is very instructive to read section 2 of Chapter One in *Capital* I, entitled 'The Two-fold Character of the Labour Embodied in Commodities,' where Marx writes the following about the relationship of labour and property: 'As *this point* is *the pivot* on which a clear comprehension of Political Economy turns, we must go more into detail.' Emphasis added.) In so far as the relationship explains private property, it also explains the root of political relations, i.e., the separation of the individual from the collectivity.

The subject of the second manuscript is also a question which can be traced to the D-FJ articles, namely: why does the proletariat arise out of the development of industry, and why does it stand in contradiction to capital? Most of what little remains of this manuscript is a discussion of the contradiction between labour and capital, which is but the developed and concrete expression of the relation between alienated labour and private property. The movement spawned by this contradiction ultimately brings the system of private property to its culmination, at which point the system itself comes to a close. Thus, Marx is able to show, on the basis of the contradiction which is the essence of civil society, which in turn is the presupposition of political relations, why political relations arise and why they must be transformed.

If Marx is able to demonstrate the means and the preconditions for the transformation of the system of private property and, therefore, for the realization of the unity of the general and particular, the nature of this unity begs to be examined. The examination of its meaning is found in the third manuscript, although it is based on the discussion of the relationship between alienated labour and private property in the second.

Marx explores the meaning of this unity or 'the transcendence of self-estrangement' in a series of numbered discussions, not all of which are on the same level. The first three concern the nature of the stages of communism, of man's realized essence and they most directly concern our exposition because they comprise the question of this transcendence at the level of politics. The other discussions are not about politics *per se*. They concern several questions central to the nature of man, *which become clear once the realized essence* of man is comprehended. The fourth point, for example, is a discussion of the nature and development of the human senses and of the meaning of industry and science; the fifth is an examination of the nature of the genesis of man, i.e., his self-creation; and the seventh is a rambling exploration of the relation between needs, production, and the division of labour,[82] an analysis which Marx returns to in *The German Ideology*, with important results.

For our purposes, it is the sixth point which is the most significant, after the first three. It is here that Marx considers the Hegelian dialectic as found in the *Phenomenology of Mind* and the *Science of Logic*. There are two related aspects here directly relevant to this exposition, namely, the movement or stages of Hegel's dialectic and Feuerbach's revisions *and* the 'moving and generating principle' within the dialectic.

Both of these aspects are summarized by Marx in the following passage: 'The outstanding achievement of Hegel's *Phenomenology* and of its final outcome, the dialectic of negativity as the moving and generating principle, is thus first that Hegel conceives the self-creation of man as a process, conceives objectification as loss of the object, as alienation and as transcendence of this alienation; that he thus grasps the essence of *labour* and comprehends objective man – true, because real man – as the outcome of man's own labour.'[83] Here, expressed as Hegel's achievement in the realm of ideas, are the two summary ideas of the Paris manuscripts.

The first concerns the dialectic of human development. Hegel perceives it as a process which moves through stages: 'objectification as loss of the object,' 'alienation,' and then 'transcendence of this alienation.' From his analysis of political economy, Marx is able to discover a parallel movement in the development of private property. Private property begins in the form of the assertion of individual property; this form is negated as it is transformed into capitalism; and this negation is itself negated in the culmination of capitalist development, which is at the same time, the first stage of communism.

Although Hegel's dialectic concludes with the negation of the negation, Marx accepts Feuerbach's criticism and sees 'the self-supporting positive, positively based on itself' as the proper conclusion to the dialectic. This, for Marx, is beyond communism; it is 'positively self-deriving humanism, *positive* humanism, come into being.'

The second aspect brings the entire Paris manuscripts together. It concerns the underlying principle of this dialectical movement, the 'generating principle' of this process. It is to be found in labour, in productive activity. Human development, man himself, it is concluded, is the 'outcome of man's *own labour*.' In this one concept, which explains the essential unity of the individual and collectivity and which embodies the motive force of human evolution, is found all the potential that comprises the nature of man.

In the EPM, then, Marx answers most of the questions which arise in his previous analyses: the nature of private property, the principle of civil society, has been grasped; the reason for, and the nature of, the contradiction between labour and capital has been dissected; and the meaning of the transcendence of the system of private property has been set forth. There are, moreover, two developments in these writings which take them qualitatively beyond the earlier work. We refer to the contents of the passage cited above and their ensuing expansion in the text. One is to perceive human reality as dialectical movement and the other is to comprehend labour as the essence of man and, at the same time, the embodiment of the principle of motion giving rise to this dialectical movement.

With the discovery that man's essence as labour contains the 'moving and generating principle' of human development, that man's 'self-creation' is a process which is the 'outcome of man's own labour,' it might well be thought that the analytical pursuit of the essence of man would be at an end. Once the essence as motive cause or generating principle is grasped, it is self-explanatory and therefore requires no further analysis. It should provide, moreover, the explanation for all the characteristics and contradictions which appear in the subject matter. Indeed, the concrete manifestation of this contradiction in capitalist society, as that between labour and capital, is systematically analysed in the Paris manuscripts. The grasp of this principle, however, remains either very abstract, as a process of self-creation, or specific to the capitalist system, where it takes the form of the final or most explicit expression of the generating principle of human historical development. Marx has not yet grasped the nature of this contradiction in its form as a concrete universal.

5

The Critique of Politics:
writings from 1845 to 1847

By the time Marx began his analysis of political economy in 1844, his critique of political relations, at the level of politics, was by and large complete. The study of political economy and of Hegel's *Phenomenology of Mind* in 1844 appears to have been undertaken to fathom the premise of political relations, the means of transforming political society, and the resolution of this open contradiction or the meaning of communism. In the writings which follow the Paris manuscripts, therefore, there is little significant further development in the analysis of abstract political questions. There is, on the other hand, an expansion of the analysis of the nature of historical change and of the transformation of political society.

For the most part, the articles, books, and manuscripts written by Marx between 1845 and 1847 were intended as criticisms of existing socialist theories, of the adversaries of socialism, and of the critics of Marx. They were also written for purposes of self-clarification, and in order to propagate, to assert publicly, the results of his research. They were, then, works examining diverse questions and reiterating theories already by and large worked out.[1] The main exception to this generalization is found in *The German Ideology*, where the results of the Paris manuscripts are expanded.

There is insufficient material concerning politics in any of these works taken individually to merit separate examinations. The more or less straightforward exposition, employed in chapters 2, 3, and 4, can no longer be followed when none of the writings between 1845 and 1847 is principally concerned with subjects political. We shall, therefore, establish several rubrics, drawn from the earlier works and from Marx's 'Draft Plan for a Work on the State,'[2] and under these imposed, but not arbitrary, categories discuss the relevant political material extracted from the works written between the Paris manuscripts and *The Communist Manifesto*.

It may be objected that two of the key writings in this period (*The Holy Family* and *The German Ideology*) are the joint products of Marx and Engels. We defend the continued focus on Marx alone, however, for the following reasons. First, the evidence at first sight suggests these works *are* primarily the product of Marx. In *The Holy Family*, the table of contents indicates the author of each section and aside from three very short chapters and four even shorter sections of other chapters, the book is by Marx. *The German Ideology*, aside from the section in the second volume entitled 'The True Socialists,' bears Marx's style and the main ideas appear to follow logically from the questions pursued by Marx. Second, Engels' own modesty makes it clear that it is Marx's ideas that are the fundamental in these writings. Prior to their collaboration on *The German Ideology* Engels does say that Marx had already worked out the main principles that constitute the materialist conception of history. Engels admits, furthermore, in a preface to *The Communist Manifesto*, which is written after the period under consideration but which epitomizes the results of earlier work, that 'the basic thought running through the Manifesto belongs solely and exclusively to Marx.'[3] Third, all of the arguments regarding political relations, discussed below, can be traced to Marx's own earlier published or unpublished work. Despite these reasons, we do not suggest that Engels makes no contribution; we only point out that the central ideas in these works, especially those concerning political relations, are the product of Marx's systematic studies.

THE FRENCH REVOLUTION OR
THE HISTORY OF THE ORIGIN OF THE MODERN STATE

Marx's interest in the French Revolution was a lifetime preoccupation; from the earliest of his published writings to the latter years of his life, he showed an abiding concern with French history between 1789 and 1851. His knowledge of and interest in French history generally, and particularly in the Revolution, was well recognized during his life.[4]

In 1843 in Paris, Marx became engrossed in a study of the period of the Convention (1792–95) and, according to Arnold Ruge, he 'read enormously' and collected much material in preparation for a book on the Convention.[5] It is not clear that he intended to write a book only on the Convention, however; it is more likely, despite Ruge's references, that, in view of his analysis of Hegel's *Philosophy of Right* in 1843 and his extension of this anslysis of political relations in the *Deutsch-Französische Jahrbücher* articles, Marx was considering a book on the modern state.[6] A study of the Convention would comprise the opening section for such a work.

In late 1844, Marx drew up his 'Draft Plan,' which can only be understood as a plan for a critique of the state. The first point on it reads: 'The *history of the origin of the modern state* or the *French Revolution*.'[7] It is this juxtaposition which points to the significance that the French Revolution held for Marx – a significance he had recognized at least a year earlier.[8]

The first reference by Marx to the historical meaning of the French Revolution is found in his 1843 unpublished *Critique* of Hegel. He states: 'Only the French Revolution completed the transformation of the *political* into *social* estates, or changed the *differences of estate* of civil society into mere *social* differences, into differences of civil life which are without significance in political life. With that the separation of political life from civil society was completed. The estates of civil society likewise were transformed in the process: civil society was changed by its separation from political society. *Estate* in the medieval sense continued only within the bureaucracy itself, where civil and political position are directly identical. As against this stands civil society as *civil estate* ... [Here] *money* and *education* are the main criteria.'[9]

The French Revolution, then, resolved the components of the feudal estates, which were social classes invested with political rights, into two separate realms – the political and the civil, or into the spheres of public and private affairs. As a consequence, it produced the first society to become *as a whole* political; the first in which everyone, theoretically, stood in the *same relationship* to the collectivity as embodied in the political state. By the same token, it produced a civil society of social classes, which were strictly 'social' categories, resting on money and education; and it confined political relations to a periodic electoral event.

In making society as a whole a political society, a society whose fundamental division is between public and private realms, the French Revolution also produced the first clear-cut example of the limitations of the political viewpoint. Marx's next reference to the French Revolution comes in his 'Critical Marginal Notes on the Article by a Prussian' written in the summer of 1844, where he asserts: 'The *classic* period of political intellect is the *French Revolution*. Far from seeing the source of social shortcomings in the principle of the state, the heroes of the French Revolution instead saw in social defects the source of political evils. Thus, *Robespierre* saw in great poverty and great wealth only an obstacle to *pure democracy*.'[10] Pure democracy conceived as the constitutional representative state, it must be added. Robespierre and the Jacobins did not wish to do away with politics, rather to perfect it.[11]

Marx is arguing that the political perspective, which profoundly marked the 'heroes of the French Revolution,' is a perspective which *assumes* political society, divided society, that is, which accepts political society as the essence of society. From the political perspective, one can only see social ills as a question of private relations and as an assumed 'source of political evils'; whereas, according to Marx, it is political society itself, and its basis in the divisiveness of civil society, which is the source of social ills.

The notion that the French Revolution, as the first instance of modern political society, brought in its wake the idea that 'pure democracy' is a form of *representative* government reappears in *The Holy Family*. But here Marx argues that the bourgeoisie, after a time, disabuses itself of the idea. 'Finally in 1830, the bourgeoisie put into effect its wishes of the year 1789, with the only difference that its *political enlightenment* was now *completed*, that it no longer considered the constitutional representative state as a means for achieving the ideal of the state, the welfare of the world and universal human aims but, on the contrary, had acknowledged it as the *official* expression of its own *exclusive* power and the *political* recognition of its own *special* interests.'[12]

The significance of the date 1830 lies in the revolutionary overthrow of Louis XVIII and the establishment of a bourgeois monarchy under Louis Philippe, head of the House of Orleans. This form of constitutional monarchy was indeed the aim of the bourgeoisie in 1789, writes Marx; the difference in 1830 was the lack of illusion that such a political form was 'the ideal of the state,' an illusion displaced by the recognition that the constitutional monarchy was the formal expression of the rule of the bourgeoisie, that it was the political form corresponding to a society dominated by private interests.

The French Revolution was, then, a bourgeois revolution in which the old order of society dominated by the nobility and clergy was overthrown in favour of bourgeois interests. It would be to view the Revolution from a *political* point of view, however, to see it as the conflict of the bourgeois will to rule and the will of the old order.[13] It was the development of modern relations of exchange in the broadest sense, which gave rise to the necessity of revolution and its outcome, the modern state, the form of political rule of the bourgeoisie. As Marx wrote in 1847: 'the political rule of the bourgeois class arises from these modern relations of production,' i.e., 'the modern division of labour, the modern form of exchange, competition, concentration, etc.'[14]

The coming to power of the French bourgeoisie between 1789 and 1830 was a consequence of historical developments and not of political will. Indeed, even if the French proletariat had pursued their will to govern, their efforts could not have been sustained without further developments in the mode of production. As Marx puts it:

If ... the proletariat overthrows the political rule of the bourgeoisie, its victory will only be temporary, only an element in the service of the *bourgeois revolution* itself, as in the year 1794, as long as in the course of history, in its 'movement,' the material conditions have not yet been created which make necessary the abolition of the bourgeois mode of production and therefore also the definitive overthrow of the political rule of the bourgeoisie. The terror in France could thus by its mighty hammer-blows only serve to spirit away, as it were, the ruins of feudalism from French soil. The timidly considerate bourgeoisie would not have accomplished this task for decades. The bloody action of the people thus only prepared the way for it. In the same way, the overthrow of the absolute monarchy would be merely temporary if the economic conditions for the rule of the bourgeois class had not yet become ripe. Men build a new world for themselves, not from the 'treasures of this earth,' as grobian superstition imagines, but from the historical achievements of their declining world. In the course of their development they first have to *produce* the *material conditions* of a new society itself, and no exertion of mind or will can free them from this fate.[15]

The French Revolution was occasioned by the development of the bourgeois mode of production; as a consequence, it could only give rise to a form of rule corresponding to this mode. Attempts to supersede the relations of domination before the mode of production had outgrown them were destined to fail. In France in 1794, such was the case when history had set the conditions for a bourgeois, and not a proletarian, revolution.

In *The Communist Manifesto*, we read: 'The French Revolution ... abolished feudal property in favour of bourgeois property.'[16] In this simple sentence is summarized almost all of Marx's analysis of the Revolution.

There is very little else of any significance that Marx wrote concerning the French Revolution between 1845 and 1847. Despite these scattered references and the lack of any systematic analysis, it is possible to specify the importance of the Revolution in Marx's eyes. It is, for him, the historical event which ushers in the modern era. It is the revolution which, spawned by the development of trade and industry, is necessary to liberate these very forces which gave rise to it.[17] It is the destruction of feudal relations and their resolution into discrete realms of the civil and political. It produces a purely political form of rule, the modern representative state, which is but the relation of domination corresponding to the bourgeois mode of production, now liberated from the limitations imposed by feudal relations. In these ideas lie the significance of Marx's first point in his so-called 'Draft Plan'; namely, that the 'history of the origin of the modern state' *is* 'the French Revolution.' As such, it is the historical and logical starting point for 'a work on the modern state.'

What, however, did the study of the Revolution bring to the development of his theory? On the face of the evidence, it cannot be denied that his analysis of the Revolution allowed him to clarify many central questions concerning political relations.[18] Just which questions and the degree to which the analysis of 1789 clarified them are, however, matters which remain in the realm of speculation. This is not to say that such attempts have not been made, with respect to the questions of class struggle, the concept of class itself, the difference between political and human emancipation, the role of the masses, the class basis of absolutism, the 'rights of man,' and so on.[19] But it is to say that, although the argument appears to be well founded, it remains impossible to demonstrate. It cannot be determined *with certainty* how, or to what degree, the study of French history affected the development of Marx's critique of politics, or more broadly, his materialist conception of history.

THE RIGHTS OF MAN

Despite the above argument, it would be difficult to suggest that Marx's position with respect to the 'rights of man' did not derive from his study of the French Revolution. In his discussion of this question in 'On the Jewish Question,' he cites the Declaration of 1791, the constitutions of 1793 and 1795, and a book by Bouchez and Roux on the parliamentary history of the French Revolution. Nevertheless, for the reason above, our focus can only be on Marx's analysis of the 'rights of man' and the place of this analysis in his critique of politics and its development and *not* on the *effect* of his study of the Revolution on this development.

The brief comments by Marx on the 'rights of man' after 1844 are often accompanied by references to his article 'On the Jewish Question' where he analyses and sets forth with clarity most of the elements of the question. Nowhere does he go beyond this 1843 discussion and the following review can only serve to demonstrate this fact.

The 'rights of man,' claims Marx, in 1843, were 'discovered' by the North Americans and the French.[20] He is referring, of course, to the American and French revolutions in which privilege as inscribed in estate or appointment was overthrown and replaced by the privilege of private property. The essence of the rights of man is the privilege of private property.

This argument is made in some detail in 'On the Jewish Question.' Under feudalism, the power of the state was embodied in the person of the sovereign. State power in large measure was 'the *particular* affair of a ruler isolated from the people.'[21] The political revolution, which overturned this isolated sovereignty, 'necessarily smashed all estates, corporations, guilds and privileges' which comprised the preconditions of feudal absolutism. 'The political revolution thereby *abolished* the *political character of civil society.*' He continues: 'It gathered the dispersed parts of the political spirit, freed it from its intermixture with civil life, and established it as the sphere of the community, the *general* concern of the nation, ideally independent of those *particular* elements of civil life. A person's *distinct* activity and distinct situation in life were reduced to a merely individual existence. They no longer constituted the general relation of the individual to the state as a whole. Public affairs as such, on the other hand, became the general affairs of each individual, and the political function became the individual's general function.'[22]

Marx goes on to say that, as political relations are generalized, civil relations, now stripped of political character, become strictly individual relations. The political revolution liberates 'civil society from politics' thereby establishing politics as the 'general affairs of each individual,' but in so doing, it makes civil society as the arena of individualized man the very basis of modern political relations. In Marx's words: 'egoistic man,' that is, 'the member of civil society, is thus the basis, the precondition, of the *political* state.' As the precondition, the necessary antecedent and foundation, of the modern state, egoistic man 'is recognized as such by this state in the rights of man.'

This argument and others related to the rights of man (see chapter 3 above) were made by Marx in response to Bruno Bauer's *Die Judenfrage* in 1843. In July 1844, Bauer replied to Marx's criticism in the Young Hegelian journal, *Allgemeine Literatur-Zeitung.* In the autumn of 1844, in *The Holy Family*, Marx wrote a retort to Bauer's article, in which he found it necessary to make many of the same points again, albeit in an assertive rather than explicative manner. One passage which poignantly expresses the above argument is worth citing. Referring to his article in the *Deutsch-Französische Jahrbücher*, Marx explains:

It was shown that the *recognition of the rights of man* by the *modern state* has no other meaning than [that which] the *recognition of slavery* by the *state of antiquity had.* In other words, just as the ancient state had slavery as its *natural basis*, the *modern state* has as its *natural basis* civil society and the *man* of civil society, i.e., the independent man linked with other men only by the ties of private interest and *unconscious* natural necessity, the *slave* of labour for gain and of his own as well as other men's *selfish* need. The modern state has recognised this its natural basis as such in the *universal rights of man*. It did not create it. As it was the product of civil society driven beyond the old political bonds by its own development, the modern state, for its part, now recognised the womb from which it sprang and its basis by the *declaration* of the rights of man.[23]

Thus, the declaration of the rights of man is nothing more than the modern state acknowledging the force of private property which gave rise to it and which constitutes its foundation. The rights of man are the rights of the individual as the personification of private property.

The rights of man, then, are not to be mistaken for rights which are human, which reflect the unity of the individual and his collectivity. As Marx repeats: 'the *rights of man* do not ... free man from religion, but give him *freedom of religion*; ... they do not free him from property, but procure for him *freedom of property*; ... they do not free him from the filth of gain, but rather give him *freedom of gainful occupation*.'[24] For these rights to be *human* rights, in the sense Marx intends, they would have to be the recognition of man's freedom from religion, from property, and from wage-labour and profit. Quite consistent with the rights of man, however, indeed, *the very content of the rights of man*, is the estrangement of man's spiritual life in religion, the alienation of his activity in wage-labour and of the products of his activity in private property.

Chief among the rights of man recognized by the American and French revolutions are equality, liberty (freedom), security, and property. Marx does not say a great deal about any of these rights in his writings between 1845 and 1847, but scattered references are to be found. In *The German Ideology* there is a passage in which the right to freedom of labour is explicated in terms similar to the above discussion of the rights of man in general. In opposition to the statement by Max Stirner[25] that, 'The state rests on the *slavery of labour*. If *labour* were to become *free*, the state would be lost,' Marx asserts: 'The *modern* state, the rule of the bourgeoisie, is based on *freedom of labour* ... Freedom of labour is free competition of the workers among themselves ... Labour *is* free in all civilised countries; it is not a matter of freeing labour but of abolishing it.'[26]

As with the other rights of man, the freedom of labour is a right of individual man, a right to compete for labour, a freedom which is limited by the freedom of other competitors. Like the other rights, the freedom of labour is part of the very foundation of the modern state; that is, the state is able to stand over and be opposed to the people only because the people are comprised of competing individuals. The freedom of labour is already an existing fact and as such constitutes part of the very basis of the modern state. The state rests on free labour, which, in Marx's view, is wage-slavery. What must be transformed is free labour itself. Its abolition is the transformation of labour as estranged activity and, as a consequence, of the modern state which rests upon it.

The freedom to trade is another specific aspect of liberty as a right of man. It, too, is manifested in competing individuals and thereby constitutes part of the premise of the modern state. In the following passage, Marx demonstrates the illusory nature of the freedom to buy and sell. In reply to Proudhon's vision of the operation of 'free will' in the market place, Marx argues: 'The producer, the moment he produces in a society founded on the division of labour and on exchange ..., is forced to sell. M. Proudhon makes the producer master of the means of production; but he will agree with us that his means of production do not depend on *free will*. Moreover, many of these means of production are products which he gets from the outside, and in modern production he is not even free to produce the amount he wants. The actual degree of development of the productive forces compels him to produce on such or such a scale.'[27] The producer, then, is clearly not the personification of free will; his means of production, the object of his production, and how much of it he will produce are all by and large determined for him by the structure of the system the moment he begins to produce.

It is no more valid to think that the consumer is free than it is to imagine a free producer. As Marx goes on to point out: 'The consumer is no freer than the producer. His estimation depends on his means and his needs. Both of these are determined by his social position, which itself depends on the whole social organisation. True, the worker who buys potatoes and the kept woman who buys lace both follow their respective estimations. But the difference in their estimations is explained by the difference in the positions which they occupy in society, and which themselves are the product of social organisation.' Free choice, or liberty as a bourgeois right, is an illusion. The freedom to compete is to be a slave to competition and to confront the freedom of others in exercising your own. The freedom to choose is conditioned and limited by wealth and class position. True freedom – the critical, conscious unity of the individual and his collectivity – can only come with the transcendence of competition and of private property on which it is based.

Another of the fundamental rights of man is security. In his article 'On the Jewish Question,' Marx writes that security 'is the highest social concept of civil society, the concept of *police*, expressing the fact that the whole of society exists only in order to guarantee to each of its members the presentation of his person, his rights and his property.'[28] There are two points here: first, security is the most 'social' measure that civil society admits to or practises, and, second, it exists *as a consequence* of the very nature of bourgeois society, its competitive individualism. Security, then, although a right of man, is only so by virtue of the rights guaranteeing individual property. The modern state rests upon these latter and defends them through its security apparatus. It is inaccurate, therefore, to see the modern state as resting upon, or finding its basis in, the means of security.

Marx makes this point in *The German Ideology* in opposition to the 'true socialists' who assert that the modern state is founded on 'external compulsion.' 'We learn further ... that present-day society is based upon "external compulsion." By "external compulsion" the true socialists do not understand the restrictive material conditions of life of given individuals. They see it only as the compulsion exercised by the *state*, in the form of bayonets, police and cannons, which far from being the foundation of society, are only a consequence of its structure.'[29] The point is clear enough: security exists in order to protect the relations and interests of private property, which form the true basis of the state and the rationale for security. The state does not rest on police measures, even though it may appear to; rather, such measures must be employed to maintain the actual basis, the rights of man as a solitary individual, and – principal among these – the right of private property.

THE REPRESENTATIVE STATE: THE CONSTITUTIONAL AND DEMOCRATIC

Criticism in *The Holy Family* of Bauer's understanding of the rights of man leads Marx to raise the question of the representative state. The two issues are closely related: the degree to which the rights of man are realized is reflected in the *type* of representative state and in the *nature* of its inherent contradictions.

The criticism pertains to Bauer's understanding of the contradiction between privilege and freedom – more particularly, between religious privilege and freedom of religion – as the 'general contradiction' of the *political sphere* and to the idea that 'the abolition of *privilege*' is also the abolition of 'the *object* of privilege,' i.e., that the end of religious privilege brings with it the end of religion.[30] Marx argues that the contradiction Bauer refers to is not what Bauer suggests but is 'the contradiction of *constitutionalism*,' and, furthermore, that the abolition of this contradiction brings not the end of politics but its perfection.

The contradiction of constitutionalism is the persistence of political privilege in the face of the adoption of the rights of man, of individual freedoms. It is the contradiction that is found in the constitutional monarchy where certain powers remain in the hands of privilege, while other powers derive from individual rights which pertain to all. The resolution of this contradiction is the movement from the constitutional monarchy to the democratic representative state, 'the perfected modern state,' where all political powers originate in the equal rights of all. It would be to change 'from partial political emancipation to full political emancipation, from the constitutional state to the democratic representative state.'

Because Bauer perceives the contradiction between privilege and free rights, which is but the contradiction of *incomplete* political emancipation, as the 'general contradiction' of modern political relations, of the completed political state, he cannot grasp 'the absolute *imperfections*' of the modern state.[31] In other words, the resolution of this contradiction, which amounts to the completion of *political* emancipation, is thought by Bauer to be human emancipation. If, however, political emancipation is understood as human emancipation, then, the limitations and imperfections of the former, seen as the latter, are precluded from comprehension.

The point is, argues Marx in opposition to Bauer, that 'the developed modern state is not based ... on a society of privileges, but on a society in which *privileges* have been abolished and dissolved, on developed *civil society* in which the vital elements which were still politically bound under the privilege system have been set free.' Marx goes on to describe the abolition of privilege and the nature of civil society, the basis of the modern state. 'Free industry and free trade abolish privileged exclusivity [Bauer's term] and thereby the struggle between the privilege and exclusivities. They replace exclusivity with man freed from privilege – which isolates from the general totality but at the same time unites in a smaller exclusive totality – man no longer bound to other men even by the *semblance* of a common bond. Thus they produce the universal struggle of man against man, individual against individual. In the same way *civil society* as a whole is this war against one another of all individuals, who are no longer isolated from one another by anything but their *individuality*, and the universal unrestrained movement of the elementary forces of life freed from the fetters of privilege.' The point, that growth of trade and industry were responsible for the demise of feudal privilege, is not new with Marx, but it must be made in order to describe the nature of civil society and to grasp the *principle* of modern political relations, the contradiction in the modern state. Marx continues: 'The contradiction between the *democratic representative state* and *civil society* is the completion of the *classic* contradiction between public *commonweal* and *slavery*. In the modern world each person is *at the same time* a member of slave society and of the public commonweal. Precisely the *slavery of civil society* is *in appearance* the greatest *freedom* because it is in appearance the fully developed *independence* of the individual, who considers as his *own* freedom the uncurbed movement, no longer bound by a common bond or by man, of the estranged elements of his life, such as property, industry, religion, etc., whereas actually this is his fully developed slavery and inhumanity.'[32]

The principle of modern political relations is the contradiction between the democratic representative state and civil society. Far from being the completion of human emancipation, it is the perfection of man's estrangement, the separation of the individual from others, from his collectivity. This separation, which is the essence of all forms of political relations, is in its modern form simply the completion, the final expression, of the social duality which marks all of history, the contradiction between 'commonweal' and 'slavery.' Why slavery? Wherever man is cut off from a conscious relationship with his 'commonweal,' he has no control over 'public affairs,' which are in the final analysis 'his affairs'; and a person who lives under the control of another, or of the state, is by definition a slave. In modern society, characterized as it is by the contradiction between the democratic representative state and civil society, each member stands to the collectivity in both a human relation, which is temporary and formal, and a relation of bondage, which is continual and real. The slavery of civil society *appears* to be the epitome of freedom because for the first time in history the restraints on the movement of all the alienated aspects of life (the products of labour as private property, the practical side of knowledge as industry, the spiritual side of humanity as religion, and the political side as modern democracy, etc.) have been abolished, giving the appearance of freedom to individual life as estranged life formerly constrained by privilege. It is *only* an appearance because slavery is grounded in estrangement, and it matters not that the estrangement of modern society has been declared in the rights of man as unbounded. For this reason, what appears as freedom is in reality 'fully developed slavery and inhumanity.'

The modern democratic representative state, then, rests upon 'fully developed slavery and inhumanity,' in a word, civil society. The relationship of these two elements comprises the perfection of political relations. On the one hand, the modern democratic state, in theory and in form, is the government of all by all; in practice and in essence, it is the rule of all by private interests. On the other hand, the sphere of private interests, civil society, in theory and in form, is the realm of unbounded individual freedom; in practice and in essence, it is a world of slavery and inhumanity. In appearance, the relationship between free individuals and a democratic representative state comprise modern political relations. In essence, they are the relationship between unfree beings, slaves, and the rule of their products as private property – between the isolated members of civil society and the interests of private property expressed through the representative state.

LAW

The first published work by Marx which can properly be called political was concerned with the nature of existing laws – his critique of certain Prussian laws in the *Rheinische Zeitung*. To understand the scattered references to law between 1845 and 1846, it is necessary to reiterate briefly the argument in these articles.

The critique of existing laws in 1842-43 is carried out by comparing these laws to the definition of law. For Marx, this idea of law, or law in essence, is the expression of the unity of the individual and society; it is the legal face of universal norms. A particular law whose content conforms to the definition is rightfully considered a law in the true sense. A particular law whose content does not conform is by definition an imposition on society, a 'positive law' as Hegel would have it, an arbitrary measure. It is by means of this comparison that Marx makes his critique of existing Prussian laws.

There is a related critique in the *Rheinische Zeitung* articles, which concerns the concepts of right and privilege. Marx's criticism of the provincial assemblies which represent the estates, social classes which combined property and social and political privileges, takes the form of demonstrating how the estates employ the assemblies to make their own privilege into right, to abolish customary rights and create through legislation privileged rights, i.e., to sanctify in law the privilege of private property.[33]

This is precisely the point Marx makes in *The Holy Family* when, at the end of his discussion of the democratic representative state, he writes: '*Law* has here taken the place of privilege.'[34] Unlike the pre-capitalist state which rests upon privileged estates, the modern democratic state rests upon 'the practical abolition of privilege, *free* industry, *free* trade, etc.' As it comes into existence, the modern state makes its first *legislative act* the declaration of the rights of man, an act in defence of the 'freedoms' which constitute its premise. Law here in the most general sense comprises the rights of man. The essence of the rights of man is, however, private property. As Marx asserts in 'On the Jewish Question': 'The practical application' of these rights, of these freedoms, is 'man's right to *private property*.'[35] Central to the declaration of the rights of man, or, in other words, underlying 'the practical abolition of privilege,' then, is the right to private property. The declaration, as law in the broadest sense, takes the place of privilege. But law, as in the declaration or as in a more particular expression of these rights, is in essence the defence of private property. These rights, these laws, then, have a *practical* validity only for the possessor of private property, for the non-possessor, these rights are privileges outside his ken. Law in the modern state takes the place of privilege, but law is the expression of privilege in a new form: the privilege of private property.

It is not difficult to see how this conclusion leads to the consideration of another aspect of law in the modern state. If the possessors of private property find their rights based on possession and represented by the law, then non-possessors find themselves without rights and without representation by the law. Existing rights and laws cannot, therefore, be the expression of the will of the public, of the *general* will. The will which right and law do express and the nature of this will is a subject Marx examines in *The German Ideology* in response to Max Stirner, ironically called Saint Sancho. Marx begins by setting forth the two main historical views on the basis of right. 'In actual history, those theoreticians who regarded *might* [die *Macht*] as the basis of right were in direct contradiction to those who looked on *will* [den *Willen*] as the basis of right – a contradiction which Saint Sancho could have regarded also as that between realism [Realismus] ... and idealism [Idealismus].'[36]

It is not idealistic to view will as the basis of the definition of abstract right, but it is to understand it as the basis of existing right. From the viewpoint of realism, the basis of existing right is might or power. As Marx continues: 'If power [die Macht: better translated as might] is taken as the basis of right [des Rechts], as Hobbes, etc., do, then right, law, etc. [Recht, Gesetz] are merely the symptom, the expression of *other* relations upon which state power rests [die Staatsmacht beruht].' If general will were the basis of right, then, right and will would be synonymous, and thus no declaration of rights or defence of rights would be necessary. If power is taken as the basis, the view of realism, then *by implication* there is no *general* will and indeed right and law must be the expression of other relations, power relations, which presuppose the power of the state. Marx now explicates these relations:

The material life of individuals, which by no means depends merely on their 'will,' their mode of production and form of intercourse [ihre Produktionsweise und die Verkehrsform], which mutually determine each other – this is the real basis of the state and remains so at all the stages at which division of labour and private property are still necessary, quite independently of the *will* of individuals. These actual relations are in no way created by the state power; on the contrary they are the power [Machte] creating it. The individuals who rule in these conditions – leaving aside the fact that their power must assume the form of the *state* – have to give their will, which is determined by these definite conditions, a universal expression as the will of the state, as law, an expresion whose content is always determined by the relations of this class, as the civil and criminal law demonstrates in the clearest possible way. Just as the weight of their bodies does not depend on their idealistic will or on their arbitrary decision, so also the fact that they enforce their own will in the form of law, and at the same time make it independent of the personal arbitrariness of each individual among them, does not depend on their idealistic will. Their personal power [Ihre persönliche Herrschaft] must at the same time assume the form of average rule [eine Durchschnittsherrschaft]. Their personal rule [Ihre persönliche Macht] is based on conditions of life which as they develop are common to many individuals, and the continuance of which they, as ruling individuals [als Herrschende], have to maintain against others and, at the same time, to maintain that they hold good for everybody. The expression of this will, which is determined by their common interests, is the law [Der Ausdruck dieses durch ihre gemeinschaftlichen Interessen bedingten Willens ist das Gesetz.]

It is the 'material life of individuals,' the mode of production and form of intercourse, characterized by division of labour and private property, which is the basis of state power and also the basis of the 'will' of those individuals who are in a position of power. Their will, their power, is determined by this mode of production and through the state assumes the form of law. The power and will of the ruling class derives from the mode of production and form of intercourse. *Their* will is but the 'symptom' of these other relations. Marx argues further: 'The same applies to the classes which are ruled, whose will plays just as small a part in determining the existence of law and the state. For example, so long as the productive forces are still insufficiently developed to make competition superfluous, and therefore would give rise to competition over and over again, for so long the classes which are ruled would be wanting the impossible if they had the "will" to abolish competition and with it the state and the law.'[37]

The mode of production and form of intercourse determine not only the 'dominant will' but also the nature of the 'wills,' as it were, which are subordinate. Given this relationship, the desire on the part of subordinate 'wills' to overthrow the dominant 'will,' before such a time as the mode of production and form of intercourse determine the transformation, is destined to failure.

Rights and laws are not, then, the expression of an existing general will but the symbol of existing relations of power, of inequity and division – relations which comprise 'the material mode of life of individuals.' This same point is made by Marx in several subsequent works. For example, in criticizing Proudhon in *The Poverty of Philosophy*, Marx writes: 'it is the sovereigns who in all ages have been subject to economic conditions, but they have never dictated laws to them. Legislation, whether political or civil, never does more than proclaim, express in words, the will of economic relations. Was it the sovereign who took possession of gold and silver to make them the universal agents of exchange by affixing his seal to them? Or was it not, rather, these universal agents of exchange which took possession of the sovereign and forced him to affix his seal to them and thus give them a political consecration?'[38] In a similar vein, a passage in *The Communist Mani-*

festo, which is a retort to the critics of communism, reads as follows: 'your jurisprudence is but the will of your class made into a law for all, a will, whose essential character and direction are determined by the economic conditions of existence of your class.'[39] The point here is no different from that which Marx made more than a year earlier in *The German Ideology*.

The discussion so far has concerned only the question of civil law, that is, the law dealing with the private rights of the citizen. It is the law which, in the final analysis, reflects the *prevailing* relations of private property. But there is another area of law besides tort which has not yet been mentioned, and that is criminal law. Although Marx makes few remarks on criminal law, it is worthwhile examining some of his comments on crime and its punishment.

One of the few instances where Marx defines crime is found in *The German Ideology*. Here he writes: 'Like right, so crime, i.e., the struggle of the isolated individual against the predominant relations, is not the result of pure arbitrariness. On the contrary, it depends on the same conditions as that domination. The same visionaries who see in right and law the domination of some independently existing general will can see in crime the mere violation of right and law.'[40] The last point is clearly the general view that is held about the nature of crime, that is, that it is simply a violation of rights or laws founded on an existing general will. But, as Marx has argued, such a general will does not exist; existing right and law are the expression of relations of power founded on the mode of production and exchange. Just as right and law represent the relations and interests of the owners of private property, the violation of right and law, crime, represents the activity forced upon some by virtue of non-ownership of private property. The criminal and the criminal court are simply two sides of one aspect of the modern relations of private property.[41]

If crime and the criminal are products of a particular level of development of the state, which in turn reflects a stage in the development of relations of production and exchange, then the accompanying theory of punishment must also be a product of this level of development. Indeed, the very existence of penal theory is a statement pointing to the estranged nature of the social system, a particular level of development.

This point is made by Marx in criticism of Hegel's theory of punishment. 'According to Hegel,' he writes in *The Holy Family*, 'the criminal in his punishment passes sentence on himself.'[42] In other words, in so far as the individual and his society constitute a unity (Hegel admits this unity is only at the level of concepts), the criminal who is punished by society is punished by himself: his punishment, though meted out by society, is his own 'self-judgement' [Selbstrichtung]. It is not the notion of 'self-judgement' which Marx criticizes; rather, it is the meaning of the *existence* of a penal theory. He argues: 'A *penal* theory [Eine *Straf*theorie] which at the same time sees in the criminal the *man* [im Verbrecher den *Menschen*] can do so only in *abstraction* [in der *Abstraktion*], in imagination, precisely because *punishment* [die *Strafe*], *coercion* [der *Zwang*], is contrary to *human* conduct [dem *menschlichen* Verhalten widersprechen].'

It is not possible to construct a penal theory in which the criminal is also a human because penal theory can *only* be the product of estranged, divided society, and estranged society is not human society, i.e., society in which the individual and the collectivity constitute a *unity* of opposites. In *human* society it is precisely this *unity* which makes punishment an alien notion. For this reason, Hegel's *penal* theory would *only* be a theory in abstraction, but even in abstraction it is fraught with the contradiction between the notion of punishment and abstract man, man in essence.

A penal theory can exist only where laws stand outside of and opposed to the individual. Laws are the formal expression of the prevailing relations of power – relations which, as the prevailing relations, constitute the 'collectivity,' 'society' as estranged from the individual. Here lies the meaning of Marx's statement, still in relation to Hegel's theory of punishment, that 'Plato long ago realised that the law must be one-sided and take no account of the individual.' Law is the manifestation of 'society' separate from the individual and embodied in the state; as such, it takes no account of the individual. When the individual violates the law, of course, law takes account of him, but it is only a negative accounting, as punishment.

In human society, what becomes of punishment? As understood, punishment disappears; instead of the penalty exacted by the state, it becomes the 'self-judgement.' Marx writes: 'Under *human* conditions [Unter *menschlichen* Verhältnissen] punishment will *really* be nothing but the sentence passed by the culprit on himself. No one will want to convince him that *violence* from *without*, done to him by others, is violence which he had done to himself. On the contrary, he will see in *other* men his natural saviours from punishment which he has imposed on himself; in other words, the relation will be reversed [das Verhältnis wird sich geradezu umkehren].'

No longer will there be the judge, who embodies estranged society, to intone, as he passes sentence, that the guilty party has brought this on himself. Because 'society' has become embodied in each individual, the erring individual in recognizing his infraction against others will see it as against himself and will needs pass judgement upon himself. He will see in others not his punishers but his redeemers – for no longer do others constitute his negation, no longer is the freedom of others the limit of his freedom, now his relations to others constitute his very definition of himself and his freedom is his critical, conscious unity with others.

TAXES

Very little was written by Marx about taxes during the period 1842-47, but there are a few comments worth noting especially from the latter years of this period. The comments reveal how he understood the meaning of taxation and the place of taxes in the relationship between the state, the bourgeoisie, and the proletariat.

Just as Marx perceives laws as the expression of the state in legal terms, so he defines taxes as 'the existence of the state expressed in economic terms.' As he puts it in 1847 in an article entitled, 'Moralising Criticism and Critical Morality': 'The monarchy, like every other form of state, is a direct burden on the working class on the material side only in the form of *taxes*. Taxes are the existence of the state expressed in economic terms. Civil servants and priests, soldiers and ballet-dancers, schoolmasters and police constables, Greek museums and Gothic steeples, civil list and services list – the common seed within all these fabulous beings slumber in embryo is *taxation*.'[43] Marx's point is straightforward enough: the state and all its related aspects are 'a direct burden on the working class,' a burden which takes the form of taxes. As taxes increase, so do the direct and related functions of the state.

In a less general definition in *The German Ideology*, he draws out the relationship between taxes and the ruling class, the state and the working class: 'the bourgeois pay their state well and make the nation pay for it so that without risk they should be able to pay poorly; by good payment they ensure that the state servants are a force available for their protection – the police; they willingly pay, and force the nation to pay high taxes so as to be able without danger to shift the sums they pay on to the workers as a levy (as a deduction from wages).'[44] There are three separate points here. First, the bourgeoisie pays *its* state (its bureaucrats, police, etc.) well but obliges everyone (the nation) to pay so that its own contribution is disproportionately lower. Second, the good pay and, it might be added, the security of the civil servant ensures loyalty to the state and to the principles on which it is based. And third, by forcing the nation to pay, the bourgeoisie not only lessens its own share but also is able 'to shift' part of this share onto the workers 'as a deduction from wages,' as tax.

If this is the case, i.e, that taxes are a deduction from wages, as Marx argues, it does not follow, however, that low wages and the concomitant misery of the wage-earner are due to high taxes. He cautions against such reasoning and demonstrates its deficiencies by analysing the relationship between taxes and wages.

> The economic existence of the state is taxes.
> The economic existence of the worker is *wages*.
> To be ascertained: the *relationship* between taxes and wages.
> *Competition* necessarily reduces the average wage to the minimum, that is to say, to a wage which permits the workers penuriously to eke out their lives and the lives of their race. Taxes form a part of this minimum, for the political calling of the workers consists precisely in paying taxes. If all taxes which bear on the working class were abolished root and branch, the necessary consequence would be the reduction of wages by the whole amount of taxes which today goes into them. Either the employers' *profit* would rise as a direct consequence by the same quantity, or else no more than an alteration in the *form* of tax-collecting would have taken place. Instead of the present system, whereby the capitalist also advances, as part of the wage, the taxes which the worker has to pay, he [the capitalist] would no longer pay them in this roundabout way, but directly to the state.[45]

As Marx acknowledges, this argument is not his but one made by 'the *bourgeois* economists such as Ricardo, Senior, etc.' Indeed, it is very close to David Ricardo's reasoning and his criticism of Adam Smith.[46] Yet, with Marx the argument is directed at the 'speechifying saviours of mankind,' and their 'self-important demagogy,' who see in taxes the source of the people's misery. A rise or decline in taxes is accompanied by a rise or decline in wages; in neither case does the position of the worker change.

Taxes are a question of little interest to the working class, insists Marx. The level of wages, i.e., of *real* wages 'depends on the relationship between supply and demand [of workers]. An alteration in the mode of taxation may cause a momentary disturbance, but will not change anything in the long run.'[47] The argument would have remained consistent, had he added an alteration in the *level* of taxation.

On the other hand, taxes are an important question for the bourgeoisie. For them, 'the way in which taxes are distributed and levied, and the use to which they are put, are a vital question, both on account of its influence on trade and industry and because taxes are the golden cord with which to strangle the absolute monarchy.'[48] Marx does not continue with this point, but its expanded discussion in Smith and Ricardo does not appear to be inconsistent with what Marx might have written.

Taxes are, in short, the power of the state expressed in economic terms. The whole nation is expected to pay taxes, even though the state which taxes sustain defends the interests of only one class, the bourgeoisie. While the working class is obliged to pay taxes, taxes are not the cause of their condition. What produces the state, the relations of power and authority in society, in the first place is not taxes but the relations of production and exchange.

THE STATE AND CIVIL SOCIETY

In the 1843 *Critique* of Hegel, the existing relationship between civil society and the state (both the feudal and the modern representative state) was examined with fecund results. A discussion of the nature of civil society, though alluded to, was not attempted. In the articles and manuscripts which followed, to the end of 1844, Marx pursued the question of civil society, i.e., the nature of civil society as bourgeois society. He returned to the problem of the relation between civil society and the state in late 1845 and 1846 in the unpublished manuscript, *The German Ideology*, but the analysis here was much broader than before. Not only does he attempt to grasp the nature and genesis of this relationship and its evolution through history, but also he sets forth the contradiction arising between civil society and its premises as the very principle of movement in history, of the transformation of historical social systems. The conclusions spelled out in the 1846 manuscript comprise the 'general conclusion' Marx refers to in 1859 as 'the guiding principle of my studies.'[49] It is nothing less than a summary expression of the materialist conception of history, but here we are concerned only with those aspects of the theory which pertain to the relationship between civil society and the state and to the nature of their transformation.

The concept of civil society comes into being only when history has resolved human relations into two fundamental spheres, public and private. Here is what Marx writes: 'The term "civil society" emerged in the eighteenth century, when property relations had already extricated themselves from the ancient and medieval community. Civil society as such only develops with the bourgeoisie; the social organisation evolving directly out of production and intercourse, which in all ages forms the basis of the state and the rest of the idealistic superstructure, has, however, always been designated by the same name.'[50]

It is only with the rise of the bourgeoisie that civil society 'as such' develops; that is, it is only with the appearance of civil society in its essential form that the corresponding concept can emerge. Even so, the forms of social organization, which throughout history constitute 'the basis of the state' and which derive from relations of production and exchange, have been given 'the same name.' Civil society proper, then, comprises property relations in their own sphere separated from 'public affairs,' but the concept refers also to earlier forms of social organization in which this separation is not complete.

More specifically, Marx defines the concept as follows: 'Civil society embraces the whole material intercourse of individuals [Die bürgerliche Gesellschaft umfasst dem gesamten materiellen Verkehr der Individuen] within a definite stage of the development of productive forces [einer bestimmten Entwicklungsstufe der Productivkräfte]. It embraces the whole commercial and industrial life of a given stage and, insofar, transcends the state and nation [und geht insofern über den Staat und die Nation hinaus], though, on the other hand again, it must assert itself in its external relations as nationality and internally must organise itself as state [nach Innen als Staat sich gliedern muss].'[51] There are several points here. First, civil society is the 'material intercourse of individuals'; by this, he means the interchange or relations of property of any kind, the form of the exchange of the products of labour.[52] Second, these relations of property correspond to a 'definite stage of the development of productive forces.' About this relationship more will be said below. Third, inasmuch as civil society encompasses all the commercial and industrial relations in a society, it is a broader, more general category than the state or the nation. At the same time, it is precisely these commercial relations, which comprise civil society, which are expressed as the nation and as the state.

Returning to the second point, elsewhere in *The German Ideology* it is remarked that civil society is 'the form of intercourse determined by the existing productive forces at all previous historical stages and in its turn it determines these.'[53] The relation between civil society and the productive forces is defined by the verb 'bedingen,' meaning 'to stipulate' or 'to postulate.' The relations comprising civil society, then, are 'laid down' or 'specified' by the forces of production. Once established, the former in turn sets conditions on the latter. But this description has the form of a mere assertion, a conclusion without an argument. It is necessary to find the argument.

In viewing the genesis of this relationship and its historical development, Marx begins where man begins, with the first historical act. It is a composite of three aspects, the premises of human existence, which are delineated as follows. 'Life involves before everything else eating and drinking, housing, clothing,' et cetera. 'The first historical act,' therefore, is 'the production of the means to satisfy these needs, the production of material life itself.'[54] The 'means to satisfy these needs' refers to the instruments of production in the broadest sense; they constitute man's first separation from a direct relationship to nature. Implicit in this act is another, the second aspect of the first historical act: 'the satisfaction of the first need, the action of satisfying and the instrument of satisfaction which has been acquired, leads to new needs.' The creation of new needs takes man beyond the fundamental needs; the former is an extension and elaboration of the latter. New needs, in turn, demand new instruments of production. Implicit in this dynamic is the third aspect. In so far as men now begin to produce their life's needs, they also 'begin to make other men, to propagate their kind.' They produce social relations of an elementary but definite kind which correspond to or are conditioned by the mode of production. (At this stage, the mode of production is highly dependent on natural conditions.) 'These three aspects of social activity,' summarizes Marx, 'have existed simultaneously since the dawn of history and the first men, and ... still assert themselves in history today.'

The significance of the foregoing lies in the next step of the argument. The 'production of life' for man can now be seen as 'a twofold relation.' On the one hand, man must extract from nature the means of his existence and he does this by way of his instruments of production; on the other hand, the production of life is always within a social relation – 'social in the sense that it denotes the cooperation of several individuals [das Zusammenwirken mehrerer Individuen].' 'It follows from this,' concludes Marx, 'that a certain mode of production, or industrial stage, is always combined with a certain mode of cooperation, or social stage.' This mode of co-operation is conditioned by the mode of production; then, in turn, the latter becomes qualified by the former.

The elementary social relations, the mode of co-operation, which arise on the basis of the mode of production, contain at the same time an elementary or natural division of labour. This division of labour 'simultaneously implies the *distribution*, and indeed the *unequal* distribution, both quantitative and qualitative, of labour and its products, hence property.'[55] The mode of co-operation, in short, is always characterized by a form of division of labour and this form implies property. As Marx writes: 'Division of labour and private property are, after all, identical expressions: in the one the same thing is affirmed with reference to activity as is affirmed in the other with reference to the product of the activity.' He expresses the same point in a historical vein: 'The various stages of development in the division of labour are just so many different forms of property, i.e., the existing stage in the division of labour determines also the relations of individuals to one another with reference to the material, instrument and product of labour.'[56] The concept of civil society encompasses precisely these relations of property or, what amounts to the same thing, the form of division of labour. It is the system of social relations which rests upon a particular mode of production.

Still, the question remains: what is the relation between civil society and the state? How can Marx assert that civil society 'forms the basis of the state'?

We may begin the answer by making one further point concerning the relation between civil society and the forces of production, civil society being synonymous with the relations ensuing from the division of labour. The relationship is described as follows: 'Each new productive force, insofar as it is not merely a quantitative extension of productive forces already known ..., causes a further development of the division of labour.'[57] The point is that as the productive forces develop so too does the division of labour; in other words, the mode of co-operation, which implies from the beginning the division of labour, becomes less and less *directly* co-operative and more and more *indirectly* co-operative. With each new development of the productive forces, human relations become increasingly mediated relations: relations of private property for private property (barter), of private property for money (petty commodity production), of money for private property (capitalist production).

The development of the division of labour increasingly divides the elements of a social system *within* a mode of co-operation. Increasingly, individual interests correspond less with each other and therefore less with a general or societal interest. Yet, the latter cannot disappear because it comprises the framework, the *principle* of the relations between individuals within a given society. It becomes, in other words, the 'society' outside its members, a particular form of the division of labour, or relations of property, within which individuals indirectly co-operate.

This decline of direct forms of co-operation and the concomitant rise of social life resting on individual interests produces the need for the assertion of a general framework. Marx explains that: 'Just because individuals seek *only* their particular interest, which for them does not correspond with their common interest, the latter is asserted as an interest "alien" [fremd] to them, and "independent" of them, as in its turn a particular and distinctive "general" interest; or they themselves must remain within this discord, as in democracy. On the other hand, too, the *practical* struggle of these particular interests, which *actually* constantly run counter to the common and illusory common interests, necessitates *practical* intervention and restraint by the illusory "general" interest in the form of the state.'[58] The more the division of labour separates individual interests and creates the attendant conflicts between individuals and therefore between the individual and the 'community,' the greater the need for the 'community,' the general relations, to assert themselves in the form of the state, an estranged 'general' interest.

The community as community disintegrates with every new development in the division of labour. The common interest dissipates in the face of an increasingly antithetical individual interest. In the end, the community becomes nothing but the prevailing property relations within which its members exist as mutually antagonistic interests. There is an interdependence, to be sure, but it is an interdependence resting on the division of labour, reciprocity in estrangement. Antagonistic individual interests militate against any common interest *as* common interest and constantly seek advantages outside the prevailing property relations, the 'illusory common interest.' For these reasons, it is necessary that these property relations be established as the formal authority in the form of the state.[59]

Property relations, which arise out of the nature of the production process itself, are reproduced in daily productive activity. They are inherently relations of unequal distribution, and as such they imply class relations, relations of domination. The embodiment of property relations as the basis of authority in the form of the state, therefore, is *ipso facto* always the expression of class power.

The state is the 'illusory "general" interest' precisely because this 'general' interest is but the dominant form of property relations. And property relations are expressed as class relations, relations of power. In no society characterized by class relations, then, can there be a general interest which is truly general.

It is worth noting here that this view of the rise of the state out of civil society contains no sense of intent, design, or will. The state, as an estranged power, as the 'community' outside its members, arises because of the advance of the division of labour, because of the decline of the real community, of real common interests. The development of the division of labour is consonant with the development of private property which in turn is expressed as class relations. The state arises, therefore, as the expression of already existing and evolving class relations. The fact that the state is an instrument of the powers that be is a fact which derives from the nature of its genesis, not from design or will of the ruling class. As Marx puts it: 'The social structure and the state are continually evolving out of the life-process of definite individuals ... as they *actually* are, i.e., as they act, produce materially, and hence as they work under definite material limits, presuppositions and conditions independent of their will.'[60]

By way of conclusion we shall cite one further quotation from *The German Ideology*: 'the state is the form in which the individuals of a ruling class assert their common interests, and in which the whole civil society of an epoch is epitomized.'[61]

It is now possible to see how Marx began to examine the historical development of the state, in the first section of *The German Ideology*. The analysis of any epoch or society must begin with 'the instruments of production' and the social division of labour which arise as a consequence of the activity based on these 'instruments.' The level of the division of labour or the type of property relations which correspond to this division are directly related to the form of the state.[62]

SOCIAL TRANSFORMATION AND COMMUNISM

If Hegel were the first to perceive in history a rational process, he grasped it only as an evolution of ideas. This development of ideas does possess a rationality, which he articulates with compelling logic, but *only* because the *source* of ideas possesses a rationality. It is considered one of Marx's achievements to have uncovered the material basis of the rationality apparent in history.

Part of this 'law of development of human history,' as Engels refers to it, we have already examined very briefly above. We have outlined Marx's view of how man creates himself, that is his social relations, and the political system which epitomizes the relations of domination perpetuated by the mode of production. What we have yet to examine is the principle which underlies the transformation of these relations, of all social systems.

The principle of historical change is set forth several times by Marx in this period, not only in *The German Ideology* but also in letters and in *The Communist Manifesto*.[63] But nowhere is it put so well as in the 1859 preface to his first published economic work: 'At a certain stage of development, the material productive forces of society come into conflict with the existing relations of production or – this merely expresses the same thing in legal terms – with the property relations within the framework of which they have operated hitherto. From forms of development of the productive forces these relations turn into their fetters.'[64] The concept of relations of production is defined here as the relations of property; and as such it is no different from the earlier concept, in the period under consideration, namely, the 'form of intercourse' ('commerce' in French or 'Verkehr' in German). The concept of productive forces, on the other hand, is not so easily defined. It is only in *The Communist Manifesto* that some of the contents of this concept in reference to the capitalist mode of production are spelled out. They include: 'sub-jection of Nature's forces to man, machinery, application of chemistry to industry and agriculture, steam-navigation, railways, electric telegraphs, clear-ing of whole continents for cultivation, canalisation of rivers,' et cetera.[65] Clearly, he is referring to the instruments of production and exchange, in a broad sense.

The forces and relations of production do not always stand in open contra-diction. Indeed, the forces of production, as we have seen, give rise to corre-sponding relations, or 'mode of cooperation,' which in turn constitute the 'form of development of the productive forces.' These relations moreover are themselves a 'productive force,' writes Marx.[66] But it is not possible to be one thing and not that thing at the same time.

The difficulty lies in the fact that the forces and relations of production do constitute a contradiction, which is initially only implicit, and later, at a cer-tain stage of development, explicit. The argument is that, in the initial stages of development of a productive system, all the facets of the system are related as mutual conditions. At a certain point, this complementarity breaks down because the development of the instruments of production and exchange out-grows the relations of production. These relations, more specifically, the prop-erty relations, entail real material interests and class domination, both of which are maintained and defended by the state. This explains the relative stability of the relations of production and in part explains the incongruence which grows between the ever-developing instruments of production and exchange *and* the property relations, and which leads to the transformation of the latter. From a force of production, in a broad sense, the relations of production come to stand in open contradiction to the material forces of production.

This contradiction may find expression in a number of ways, including 'political struggles,' the 'battle of ideas,' 'conflicts of consciousness,'[67] and even the physical destruction of productive capacity. But when the forces of production can no longer be contained by the relations of property, the con-tradiction is expressed as class struggle. It is expressed in this manner because the relations and forces of production become represented by dif-ferent classes. The prevailing relations, which are relations of property, of domination, embody the interests of the ruling classes. At the same time, the ever-developing forces of production, which initially grew within the framework of these relations but now find these interests an impediment to further development, produce a new class whose interests are a consequence of the forces which produced it. This class, the productive class, is, within the framework of the old relations of production, also the dominated class;

but the more the instruments of production and exchange develop, the more this subordinate class is obliged to assert itself, as the product of new productive forces, against the class whose interests belong to the productive forces of an earlier period. Inasmuch as these latter interests are epitomized in and defended by the state, class struggle must be a struggle for political power.

Up to the present, the outcome of every political struggle has been a new political arrangement. Society remains political, that is, divided between civil and political life, between the individual and the collectivity; only the form changes. This has been the case because the productive forces have always been insufficiently developed to provide the basis for the abolition [Aufhebung] of private property. The *limited* development of instruments of production implies a division of labour, and with a division of labour there is always private property and therefore class relations based on the existing forms of property.[68] For this reason, all political revolutions prior to the development of 'large-scale industry and competition [der grossen Industrie und Konkurrenz]' result in new political forms and a new distribution of wealth, but not in the supersession of political society or of a mode of production giving rise to a division of labour.

The bourgeois revolutions were the political expression of developing productive forces which had outgrown the privilege of pre-capitalist property relations. In abolishing privilege, they established the conditions for the free development of the forces of production. Unhampered by privilege and encouraged by the sway of corresponding social and political relations, industry and commerce were able to expand at a historically unprecedented rate. The more the productive forces developed, so too did the division of labour and with it the accumulation of capital. All the different forms of private property, of division of labour, and social relations of past eras were resolved into their two elemental components. As Marx puts it: 'In large-scale industry and competition the whole mass of conditions of existence, limitations, biases of individuals, are fused together into the two simplest forms: private property and labour.'[69]

There are two consequences of this development of the productive forces into large-scale industry and commerce which Marx denotes. The first is that the productive forces are 'wrested away' from individuals who formerly stood in a direct relationship to them. The result is, on the one hand, that these forces are 'no longer the forces [Krafte] of the individuals but of private property.' On the other hand, the individuals now separated from the forces of production are also separated from 'all real life-content [alles wirklichen Lebensinhalts]'; that is, formerly, as masters of their instruments, the content of their lives, though limited and one-sided, reflected this mastery;

whereas, with large-scale industry, the productive forces are the masters of men, and man becomes an 'abstract individual,' with no direct relationship to the forces. 'By this very fact,' however, individuals are 'put into a position to enter into relation with one another *as individuals*.'[70] The advanced productive forces and corresponding division of labour have, by separating the producer from his instruments, resolved the differences between producers, formerly based on an elaborate division of labour, such that all producers now stand in the same relation to the instruments and thus no longer interrelate as producers of different products but as abstract producers. Their unity as human beings, though in the realm of estrangement, is now obvious.

The second consequence is that 'labour, the only connection which still links them with the productive forces and with their own existence, has lost all semblance of self-activity [der Selbstbetätigung] and only sustains their life by stunting it.' By self-activity, Marx means activity which is the positive expression of oneself, whether it be artistic or materially productive. Labour here is defined as the 'negative form of self-activity'; it is the 'alienated labour' of the Paris manuscripts. In the bourgeois era, labour loses any aspect of self-activity it may have had and becomes a mere means to existence.

Large-scale industry, therefore, gradually produces the means and the necessity for the transformation of the property relations within which it develops. It makes of the producers a single, large homogenous class by separating them from the means of production, thereby reducing them to 'abstract individuals,' the precondition of universality. It separates the members of this class from the product of their labour, thereby making them 'propertyless.' This condition, which is the denial of self-activity, makes their broad class interests the direct opposite of the owners of property. Large-scale industry also makes their labour, moreover, into simply a *means* to life, a fact which makes their very existence, as wages, stand in contradiction to the interests of profit. Marx concludes that: 'things have now come to such a pass that the individuals must appropriate the existing totality of productive forces, not only to achieve self-activity, but, also, merely to safeguard their very existence.'[71] The forces of production have produced a class which increasingly finds itself at odds with the prevailing relations of private property.

The necessity of appropriating the existing productive forces, *thereby* abolishing the old relations of production, rests on several preconditions. In other words, the possibility of transforming the social and political system as a consequence of the appropriation of the productive forces arises only on the basis of certain conditions. The first of these is that the productive forces themselves be 'developed to a totality [Totalität]' and 'exist within a universal intercourse [eines universellen Verkehrs].' By this we understand the comprehensive development of the forces in all spheres of production, within a world-wide system of exchange, that is, a development which is no longer a limited or one-sided mode of production, but a mode limited only by the prevailing relations of private property. 'From this aspect alone,' it may be seen that 'this appropriation must have a universal character corresponding to the productive forces and the intercourse.' To abolish private property, the revolution must be universal; otherwise an international division of labour persists and so too some form of private property. Given the *totality* of the productive forces, to take possession of them has this meaning: 'The appropriation of these forces is itself nothing more than the development of the individual capacities corresponding to the material instruments of production.' Earlier revolutions would have been nothing more than the development of new property relations which corresponded to new, but still limited, forces of production. With the development of the totality of productive forces, there is no longer a division of labour or property relations. There is only a mass of individuals whose capacities [Fähigkeiten] correspond 'to the material instruments of production.' With this revolution, instead of new property relations asserting themselves, there is now asserted a mass of individual capacities. Furthermore, 'the appropriation of a totality of instruments of production is, for this very reason, the development of a totality of capacities in the individuals themselves.' In other words, in appropriating the totality of instruments for *all*, the basis of any limited capacities is removed, and *all* may develop a totality of capacities.

The second precondition concerns 'the persons appropriating.' Unlike all earlier revolutionary classes, the modern proletariat alone is in a position to abolish private property. 'Only the proletarians of the present-day, who are completely shut off from all self-activity, are in a position to achieve a complete and no longer restricted self-activity, which consists in the appropriation of a totality of productive forces and in the development of a totality of capacities entailed by this.' All earlier revolutions were carried out by the classes based on restricted instruments of production and exchange; their revolutions could not but reflect the corresponding division of labour and relations of property. Only the modern proletariat, the product of the development of modern forces of production, is in a position to appropriate a totality of forces, to make this totality subject to all, and thereby eliminate the basis of division of labour and private property and make all property the property of all.

The third condition is 'the manner in which it [the appropriation] must be effected.'[72] Marx sets forth the argument very clearly: 'It can only be effected through a union [Vereinigung], which by the character of the proletariat itself can again only be a universal one, and through a revolution, in which, on the one hand, the power of the earlier mode of production and intercourse and social organisation is overthrown, and, on the other hand, there develops the universal character and the energy of the proletariat, which are required to accomplish the appropriation, and the proletariat moreover rids itself of everything that still clings to it from its previous position in society.' The passage does not require explication: it contains the last of the preconditions for the revolutionary appropriation of the developed totality of productive forces and the consequent supersession of private property.

We have now followed Marx in an outline of the principle he saw as the rationale for social transformation, for historical movement. We have seen that political relations or the state were but the 'epitome' of civil society or the prevailing property relations, and that each change in the nature of civil society was reflected in a concomitant change in the state. With the supersession of civil society itself, it would follow that the state, also, would be superseded having no longer any basis, need, or purpose. There is no discussion of this disappearance of the state in *The German Ideology* or the other works of this period, but there is a discussion of what happens with the supersession of private property.

When the preconditions above have been met, when the forces of production have developed to a totality, when all producers have been 'completely shut off from all self-activity,' and when the proletariat makes itself into a universal association, then historical society can be transformed, superseded. The meaning of this transformation is summarized as follows: 'Only at this stage does self-activity coincide with material life, which corresponds to the development of individuals into complete individuals and the casting-off of all natural limitations. The transformation of labour into self-activity [die Verwandlung der Arbeit in Selbstbetätigung] corresponds to the transformation of the previously limited intercourse into the intercourse of individuals as such. With the appropriation of the total productive forces by the united individuals, private property comes to an end.'[73]

Only now does labour, which is limited, one-sided, a denial of fulfilment, become self-activity, the positive, social expression of the individual. But it becomes so because the developed totality of productive forces no longer structures productive activity as labour, but provides the basis for productive activity to become self-activity by abolishing all former limitations. This developed totality of forces also transforms the basis of human interaction; whereas, previously, the basis of intercourse was money and intercourse was commerce or exchange, now it is based on self-activity, it becomes 'the intercourse of individuals as such.' Finally, the appropriation of the total productive forces means the end of private property because private property is the product of the limited development of these forces and the consequent naturally arising division of labour. With the total development, there is no longer a basis for the division of labour or private property.

The phenomenon Marx is describing here is communism. It is, he writes, 'the *real* movement which abolishes the present state of things.'[74] It is the movement, the negation of the negation, whereby all the contradictions, limitations, divisions, and estranged social forms and beliefs of past eras are resolved into a single relationship, that between individual and individual, or between the individual and his other. With the disappearance of the division of labour, social classes would no longer have any basis. The family would give way to communal organization of domestic needs. Religion and related doctrinal beliefs would dissipate in the face of the material reality of self-activity, of non-estranged activity. Occupationally related isolation, the separation of town and country, the divisions between localities and nationalities would all of necessity be transcended. The state, as well as all forms of political relations, which arise only by virtue of the existence of unfreedom, of relations of private property, would now no longer arise because property relations would no longer exist and man would be free, his social nature realized, on the foundation of the developed totality of productive forces.

Thus, it is 'only with large-scale industry that the abolition of private property becomes possible.'[75] And with this possibility, the transformation of the whole of social and political relations becomes possible. Only here does revolution mean the end of politics because it means the end of private property, the source of political relations.

Communism, the supersession of private property, is the natural outcome of the developed totality of the productive forces. The preconditions and, therefore, the necessity for communism, are a consequence of 'the now existing premise' – the development of the forces of production.

CONCLUSIONS

Because of the varied nature and purpose of the works written by Marx between 1845 and 1847, the political material in them has been extracted and examined under certain rubrics drawn mainly from his 'Draft Plan for a Work on the Modern State.' It was not my intention to attempt to fulfil the

'Draft Plan'; rather, by employing some of its subject headings, I was trying to provide a certain less-than-arbitrary rationale for the discussion of Marx's numerous comments on political questions which appear in these works without any systematic relation.

One could speculate on *how* Marx's studies up to 1844 might have fulfilled his 'Draft Plan.' His research on the history of the French Revolution (especially the period of the Convention) and of the American Revolution, for example, would have provided him with 'the history of the origin of the modern state,' and with a grasp of the nature of the rights of man and of the modern constitution. His work on political economy in 1843 and 1844, moreover, would have revealed the source of political relations in civil society and the nature of the relation between civil society and the state. And the manuscript study of Hegel's *Philosophy of Right* would have provided the basis for an analysis of the nature and relations of the divisions of power within the state. But the evidence suggests that Marx did not so much as begin to write the proposed work on the state, so there is little point in pursuing this speculation.

One might also conjecture about why Marx did not write up the 'Draft Plan': why, after all the practical criticism of the state in 1842-43, the analysis of Hegel's political treatise, the clarification of the meaning of political and human emancipation, and the critique of political economy had been worked out, did he not complete the projected book on the state? There are two related aspects to this question. First, it appears that Marx had answered most of the key questions about the nature of political relations in a broad, general sense. If one purpose in writing a book were to comprehend the subject matter, then, this had been done in manuscript form and some of it already was in print. Second, if another reason for writing it were to help *change* the state, on the assumption that the state represented an independent will, then, such a reason was undermined in his studies by the realization that the political will was a dependent factor, the mere expression of underlying power relations. The political point of view, he argued, wrongly assumed the independence of politics.

In this light, why write a book about a set of relations, which on the level of definition had been critically dissected, and which had been shown to be a consequence of another set of relations? His analysis revealed, furthermore, that the means of changing the state emerged from civil society, the very premise of the state. If part of the reason for writing about the state, therefore, were to change it, then, the point would be to write about the nature of the premise and *not* the state.

Marx's activities after 1847 are consistent with these conjectures. By the spring of 1848 he was fully engaged in writing and editing the *Neue Rhein-*

ische Zeitung in support of the worker and peasant uprisings throughout Europe, but particularly in Germany. With the close of the journal about a year later and the failure of the revolutionary upheavals, Marx retired to London in late 1849. Here, he took up his studies again, but he did not return to an analysis of the state; instead he undertook further analysis of its premise, civil society, or, more specifically, of political economy.

We have argued that by 1844 the analysis of political relations, at the level of politics, is by and large complete. After 1844, as we have seen above, there are few significant additions to the analysis at this level. But there is analytical development in this period in two directions: one concerns the nature of historical change, and the other concerns the relationship of the state to its premises. Both of these development, indeed all the important conclusions that Marx draws between 1845 and 1847, are founded on the making of the concept of the essence of man *more concrete*.

In the conclusion to the last chapter, it was argued that the concept of labour is seen by Marx as the root of the relation between man and fellow man. On the basis of this concept, he is able to argue that man makes himself – the first hint of the *basis* of man's *becoming* himself. But the definition of the essence of man as 'self-creation' through his own labour, the definition as generating principle at this level, is too abstract to provide an explanation of actual historical development. And the contradiction between labour and capital, as a concrete contradiction, is specific to capitalist society. The specific nature of labour, the elements which comprise the source or meaning of man's potential, therefore must be further analysed in order to provide Marx with the essence as a concrete universal containing the motive principle of human development.

Although the notebooks of Marx's research between 1844 and 1847 are not published, there is sufficient evidence from the research in 1844 to suggest how Marx might have made this next step in his analysis. We refer to sections of the 'Comments on James Mill' and point seven in the third manuscript, both of which, especially the latter, contain discussions of the relationship between need, production, and the division of labour. From these discussions one could derive the concept of what Marx calls in *The German Ideology*, 'the first historical act.'

The concept is the product of the analysis of the nature of human labour and it contains the contradiction which explains for Marx the basis of man's becoming man. The act, as discussed above, comprises three elemental and complementary aspects; namely, the production of the *means* to satisfy fundamental needs, the consequent development of new needs and therefore of new *means*, and the creation of *social relations* corresponding to the means of production. The interaction of these three elements is the source of man's self-creation in history. Because here is contained the explanation of historical movement and because here is specified the 'first cause,' as it were, this definition of the essence of man is more concrete than the earlier definitions.

The concept is the final step in Marx's broad analysis of the nature of man, hitherto grasped in political theory solely as a political nature. Here lies the explanation of the nature of the link between individual and species-life, of the manner in which man makes himself, of the transformation of social and political systems, of the rise of the state, of the nature of class struggle and of the preconditions for the end of history. Indeed, all of the concepts employed by Marx find their ultimate explanation in relation to this definition of man's nature, the 'first historical act.'

The derivation and use of this concept, we suggest, parallels that of the concept of labour in the Paris manuscripts. Just as the concept of labour as the essence of man was derived from the study of political economy and then employed in the critique of political economy, so now the concept of the 'production of life,' the 'first historical act,' as the essence of man is derived from the study of economic history, from the analysis of the concrete development of human society, and then employed in the critique of historiographers and historiography. Marx's materialist concept of history as set forth in *The German Ideology* is precisely this: a critique of existing historiography and the assertion of a new conception of history.

But what is the source of motion which underlies this conception of history? The first historical act contains, in embryo, the principle of human development, of human motion. The production of the means to satisfy fundamental needs, their satisfaction and the creation of new needs, form one side of a contradiction, the other side of which is the 'mode of cooperation,' the social relations, which arise from this initial productive activity. The means or forces of production constantly develop in concert with the satisfaction of existing needs and the creation of new needs; while, on the other hand, the relations of production remain relatively fixed. Hence, the greater the development of new productive forces, the more open becomes the contradiction between the forces and relations of production. This is the same contradiction which is expressed, in relation to more advanced stages of material production, as the conflict between the forces of production and the relations of production: the 'guiding principle' of Marx's studies hereafter.

The relationship between the mode of production and the rise of the state is also derived from the contents of this first historical act. Every mode of co-operation which corresponds to a mode of production implies a division of labour; indeed, every new development in the productive forces brings with it a concomitant increase in the division of labour. In turn, every division of labour brings the further disintegration of co-operative activity as real communal activity, the increasing separation of the individual from others, and the reformation of a mode of co-operation in the sphere of estrangement. The more the actual community dissipates in the face of increasing division of labour, the more need for it to re-establish itself in the sphere of estrangement. The rise of the state, therefore, reflects the growing mutual antagonism, based on the division of labour, between individual and class interests.

Just because the state is the embodiment of the prevailing property relations which correspond to the division of labour, it is also the embodiment of the principles and values which belong to the social class which owns property. The state, by virtue of its genesis, is always the representative of a ruling class. Similarly, the forces of production always find their representatives in a class of labourers; and in so far as new forces of production arise, so too does a new type of labouring class. The contradiction between the forces and relations of production, therefore, inasmuch as it becomes an open conflict, is always expressed as a conflict of classes and, moreover, as a contest for political power because the interests of the dominant class are embodied in the state.

From this point of view, we can now understand why human history has always been political history. Every class struggle in history, every revolution which succeeded, resulted in new political systems or a rearrangement of the old. The outcome was always political because the mode of production was always limited, and its limitations implied a division of labour, and hence relations of property, and founded on these relations individual and class antagonism. Only on the basis of the developed totality of the productive forces can the class struggle result in a non-political outcome, because only then can the division of labour be transcended and with it property and class relations.

The end of the division of labour is the end of political relations and the end of history. It is the end of history because the contradiction inherent in the nature of man will no longer be an open contradiction. The forces of production as a developed totality will no longer spawn a division of labour, but will allow the complete development of all the capacities of all individuals. As a developed totality, the mode of production, the basis of social relations, will transcend the expressions of social relations in estranged forms and provide the basis for relations between individuals as individuals. The end of history is the entelechy of man.

In these arguments as found in *The German Ideology*, Marx's critique of historical movement and political relations – his analysis of the growth of productive forces and concomitant changes in political forms – finds its completion in broad outline. He has uncovered the contradiction which lies at the heart of the essence of man; he refers to this contradiction as his 'guiding principle,' because it embodies the original or operative cause of man. It encompasses the definition of man as a concrete universal, meaning that the contradiction provides the means by which any aspect of human development may be comprehended.

Much of this discussion appears to deal with questions more related to the nature of man than to the nature of politics. It must be remembered, however, that political relations are but the expression of the open contradiction which comprises the abstract definition of man, the intrinsic relation between the individual and the collectivity.

Hereafter, Marx's theoretical work is intended to further the critique of political economy, the presupposition of political relations, and the basis of the modern proletariat. The practical work he engages in is intended to aid in the struggles of the emerging working class, that is, to help clarify the questions which confront the proletariat, the answer that history gave to its own final question.

6

Conclusions

THE DEVELOPMENT OF THE CRITIQUE OF POLITICS

The prevailing view of these early writings by Marx suggests that they comprise a set of disconnected works, sharing only the same author; that Marx was philosophically an idealist or Hegelian and politically a liberal or democrat throughout much of this period; and that he possessed no particular method of inquiry. Such judgements, made without due consideration of the content of these works, impair our ability to grasp the nature of his critique of politics and its development. The consequence can be seen when, by way of explanation of the writings and of the transition from one to another, commentators are preoccupied with the search for Marx's intellectual sources; with the description of his life history; with the discrete analysis of parts of the early work; and, to a lesser degree, with the description of the economic and political realities of the day. In the end, the prejudices remain intact and the comprehension of Marx's work from 1842 to 1847 is little advanced.

By analysing the content and method of the texts themselves, we can point to an unmistakable continuity in Marx's critique of politics, in which each step not only forms a logical link in its development but also in Marx's eyes remains valid in itself. The basis of this continuity lies in his method. Marx did possess and employ a method in a conscious manner; indeed, it was due to the possession of the way to proceed that these works have an underlying rationality, that they move in the direction of an ever-deepening grasp of the nature of politics, and that they end with a comprehension of the moving principle of human development. To discover the nature of this method and how it develops is to discover the implicit unity or rationality of Marx's early writings and to grasp fully their substance.

In the conclusions to each chapter, I attempted to define the method and trace its developments, to the degree that Marx revealed his manner of proceeding. Now, I shall attempt to analyse the development of Marx's method at a higher level of generalization in an effort to draw out more clearly the internal methodological dynamic underlying the writings between 1842 and 1847.

Marx's critique of politics begins in the *Rheinische Zeitung* articles. Here, we find a singularity of method and purpose: Marx is seeking to criticize the political state and also to solve the defects uncovered by the criticism. The act of criticizing takes the form of judgement, and judgement is always a form of syllogism. Critique, as Marx defines it here, is but the syllogistic, and the syllogistic is a part of the method of scientific inquiry, at least, as set forth by Aristotle and Hegel.

Whoever seeks to syllogize, however, must have a definition of the subject matter to be judged. Definition is the starting point of syllogistic or dialectical reasoning. It is against this definition or essence which the particular existence is measured; and it is this judgement which reveals the integrity of the particular.

In these articles, Marx employs a definition of the state as an organism, which he draws from 'recent philosophy,' an apparent reference to Hegel's *Philosophy of Right*. This definition as the essence of the state or society is, as we have argued, not a utopian ideal; rather, it is little more than a dictionary definition. Against this, he contrasts aspects of the existing state, with trenchant results.

His analysis of the political state in the *Rheinische Zeitung* is largely responsible for bringing the full weight of government censorship upon the journal. The restricted publishing rights and final closure of the journal oblige Marx to examine not only his method but also the nature of the subject matter. Even if the state had not acted as it did, however, the method itself would have begged revision. In the first place, as the means of effecting change, it could not have moved the entrenched material interests which the political state represented; and it was, in any case, easily silenced as the critical press. In the second place, as a method of inquiry, it was limited to drawing out the inconsistencies of the particular; so restricted, it would have soon exhausted its subject matter and have said nothing more than that it was contradictory or defective.

Neither the definition which comprised his starting point nor the method of inquiry as syllogistic was inconsistent with his later work. The same, however, cannot be said of his expectations of the syllogistic as a means of change. But this side of critique was likely a corollary of the restricted notion of the analytical method as *only* the syllogistic. That is, if inquiry, and therefore *comprehension*, were limited to demonstrations of inconsistencies, then, it would be easy to suppose that public exposure of these inconsistencies would effect their solution. The central difficulty with the concept of critique at this time, then, lay in its restricted use as the syllogistic: Marx could reveal the contradictions and inconsistencies but he could not explain them. A restricted method produced a restricted analysis and, therefore, false expectations of the possibility of change.

It is not clear whether it was his recognition of this limitation or the arbitrary action of the government in closing the journal, disproving the side of critique as practice, which forced a revision of his concept of critique. It is apparent, however, that Marx broadened the concept in his 1843 *Contribution to the Critique of Hegel's Philosophy of Right*. Here we find the positing of a method which sought an explanation in the analysis of the subject matter.

Instead of demonstrating the inconsistencies of reality by means of a comparison to essence, Marx now turned to analyse the existing nature of reality itself, and, from this empirical investigation, to define the subject matter. While the earlier method was solely deductive, the new procedure stressed the inductive side of analysis as the proper starting point and made deduction dependent on its results. As Marx observed in the *Critique*, this revised method allowed him not only to show the contradictions in existence but also to *explain* them by pursuing their genesis. Comprehension consisted now in understanding 'the specific logic of the specific subject.'

What the adoption of this new approach meant for Marx's studies must now be examined. How it provided the internal dynamic of scientific research, how it obliged him to revise his notion of the relationship between theory and practice, and how his research expanded until such time as an efficient and a final cause were uncovered: these are the questions we must try to answer.

The question of a methodological dynamic which propels the research in a certain direction must be examined first because the other questions are dependent on this dynamic. In the *Rheinische Zeitung* articles, critique contains no motive principle for expanding the analysis; as a method, it is static, seeking only to demonstrate existing contradictions, but unable to explain them. In beginning with an axiomatic definition of the state, Marx is able to prove the inconsistencies of the existing state, but is limited to this syllogistic demonstration. In the 1843 *Critique*, with the method revised, he undertakes an empirical investigation of the existing state itself; he pursues the nature of the contradiction between the political state and the people, which is one of his purposes in analysing Hegel's *Philosophy of Right*. It is in this shift of method, the move to a pursuit of the nature of the state, that the dynamic first makes its appearance.

Marx had demonstrated the existence of the contradiction between the state and the people in the *Zeitung* articles, and in the *Critique* he sought to comprehend it. To do this he had to ask what the nature of the connection or separation was; and to ask this, if we follow Aristotle's *Analytics*, was to ask what its 'middle' was. The middle here means 'proximate cause,' the immediate 'antecedent which necessitates a consequent,' the nearest reason for the nature of the thing. By examining the nature of the separation of the executive from civil society, the essence of politics, Marx discovered that the separation was a consequence of the particularistic nature of civil society. Hence, this nature of civil society was the 'cause,' the reason, for the separation of the state and its members.

The nature of the methodological dynamic may not be immediately recognizable, but it becomes apparent in the next step. The cause of the separation of political relations was found to rest in the nature of civil society, the chief characteristic of which Marx grasped in the *Critique* as private property: private property was the principle of civil society. But while this revelation explained political relations, it was not in any sense self-explanatory; in other words, private property or the nature of civil society itself required explanation. For precisely this reason, Marx's research moved in the direction of an analysis of the nature of civil society or private property. This began in the *Deutsch-Französische Jahrbücher* articles, particularly in the second part of 'On the Jewish Question,' and was completed in the Paris manuscripts. Here the 'proximate cause' of private property was revealed to be alienated labour. Labour, moreover, was grasped, through Hegel (and Smith and Ricardo), as containing the generating principle of human development, although the exact nature of this principle was not at this point comprehended. Marx had therefore explained the nature of politics through a series of proximate causes, but had not yet arrived at an end to the discovery of antecedent reasons.

The series comes to an end in *The German Ideology* where Marx, in analysing the nature of labour, i.e., of production, needs, and the division of labour, uncovers the elemental components of human production in the 'first historical act,' and from this derives the contradiction fundamental to the self-developing nature of man, namely, the contradiction between the forces and relations of production. Here the methodological dynamic comes to a rest because this contradiction is self-explanatory; it arises from first principles and, therefore, is elemental.

We see here the method by which science proceeds, as Marx appears to have practised it. The nature of a thing is comprehended by grasping its reason, its 'proximate cause'; and, in turn, the nature of this cause is sought in its 'proximate cause,' and so on. At each step, the analysis takes the form of an empirical investigation of the phenomenon in question. It is this dynamic which appears to contain the process which Marx understood as implicit in the scientific method and the expansion of knowledge.

Before going on to examine the meaning of this conclusion to the search for causes, we should examine one of the most important implications of this pursuit, at least with respect to Marx's critique of politics – namely, the relation between theory and practice. Marx's first formulation of critique subsumed both theory and practice: the role of the critic was not only to uncover the contradictions of reality but also to bring about their unity by means of the forum of the free press. The action of the government was undoubtedly sufficient to disabuse Marx of this notion of practice, if his recognition that material interests had a stake in the existence of these contradictions had not already done so. His new formulation of 'true criticism' in the 1843 *Critique* contained no reference to practice. But the use of this notion of critique was to bring in its wake the need for practice; as Marx remarked in the introduction to this work, the criticism of the theory of the state raised '*problems* which can only be solved by one means – *practice*.' In other words, to grasp the nature of the contradiction of the modern state was to understand that its solution lay in practice, and not in theory or appeals to reason. 'Material force must be overthrown by material force,' he wrote, meaning that if the contradiction rested on material force, then it would require a material force to solve it.

The actual link between theory and practice was argued in this introduction, and that argument remained Marx's fundamental position on the relation between theory and practice. Further comments by Marx on this relation can be found throughout this period after 1843, but they are not addressed so specifically to the problem of political relations as is this initial position.

There is another aspect to this question. If Marx's argument in the introduction concerning theory and practice meets with scepticism amongst latter-day commentators, his derivation of the proletariat as the emancipator of political society is often greeted with disbelief. To see how Marx concluded such a role for the proletariat, we must return to the method.

'True criticism,' as we have seen, seeks to explain contradictions by empirically analysing their nature. The nature of a contradiction is also its cause, its reason. By discovering the cause of a problem, one creates the possibility of perceiving its solution. In other words, to uncover the cause is to be able to perceive the requisites for a solution, that which is necessary for a resolution of the problem. This is precisely what Marx was attempting to do in the introduction, which he concluded by writing: 'When all inner requisites are fulfilled the day of German resurrection will be proclaimed by the ringing call of the Gallic cock.' The 'inner requisites' comprise his discussion of the proletariat and why it is destined to take on the role of emancipator. He has approached the question by determining first the reasons for a revolutionary transformation, then, the conditions for such an event and, finally, the class which met these conditions and why.

It should be noted that this same procedure was employed in the EPM and in *The German Ideology*. In the former, on the basis of the unveiled nature of private property – the contradiction between alienated labour and private property – he was able to set forth more concretely the reasons for revolution, the preconditions for revolution, and the preconditions for the transcendence of the system of private property. Similarly, in the latter, on the basis of the disclosed nature of human production, the contradiction between the forces and relations of production, he set forth the same albeit more concrete preconditions.

To return to the discussion of method, it might be well to restate the regression of causes which underlie these early writings. Marx began with an axiomatic definition, very likely drawn from Aristotle and Hegel. Employing a deductive method and a definition of the state as an organic unity in the *Rheinische Zeitung* articles, he was able to demonstrate that the existing state was defective, that it was characterized by a separation of the whole and its parts. He was able to pursue the reason, the 'proximate cause,' for this separation by revising his method to make it first inductive. In the 1843 *Critique*, he discovered through induction that the reason lay in the nature of civil society and that the principle of civil society, in turn, was private property. The nature of these causes was further explored in the D-FJ articles. It was in the Paris manuscripts, however, that the next major development took place; here, Marx pursued the nature of private property and uncovered its source in alienated labour. Labour, moreover, was grasped as containing the principle of generation of human society. The disclosure of the actual nature of this generating principle, however, came only in *The German Ideology* with Marx's analysis of 'the first historical act.' The contradiction arising in this act, in productive activity, was that between the forces and relations of production. Here the search for causes rests.

The most immediate reason why this regression ceases here has already been alluded to in characterizing this contradiction as self-explanatory. That is to say that it no longer gives rise to the quest for new reasons or causes because it is elemental and, as such, has no antecedents, except those which take the inquiry beyond the subject matter, i.e., to questions prior to man, prior to the 'first historical act.'

Marx attached considerable importance to this 'first cause,' this contradiction within the production process, calling it in 1859 'the guiding principle of my studies.' Some of the reasons, we surmise, were the following. First, it provided the ultimate reasons for the fundamental predicament of man, his political existence. It explained the rise of the division of labour and therefore of private property, which, in turn, was the reason for the separation of man from fellow man, which was the nature of civil society, the presupposition of political relations. Second, it constituted the starting point of movement in the development of man, indeed, it provided the principle of motion in human history. As such, it allowed Marx to grasp the nature of generation and degeneration of social systems. To grasp the principle of movement, moreover, was also to comprehend the 'end' or 'goal' of that movement: it was only by grasping this principle, in a specific form in the Paris manuscripts and in a general form in *The German Ideology*, that Marx was able to conceive communism as the goal of human development and to examine its meaning. Third, it explained the social nature of man, that man produced himself in the act of production, revealing the truth of the definition of man as a unity of the whole and its parts. Indeed, as the act of self-production, it embodied the definition of man and the goal of human development. And as this synthetic principle, it too was to be seen as the essence of man, but the essence as a concrete universal.

The universal that Marx began with in the *Zeitung* articles was abstract; that is, it contained no *differentia specifica*, no means of deducing the 'species' of the 'genus' man. In other words, although valid for all human societies, this abstract universal possessed no *differentia* which would permit an explanation of the specific forms taken by human societies. The writings up to *The German Ideology* revealed successive stages of the concretization of this abstraction. The principle of human history, of man making himself, as set forth in *The German Ideology*, the contradiction of forces and relations of production, is a concrete universal in that it contains the *differentia specifica* necessary to deduce or explain all 'species' of the human 'genus.' It is a synthetic definition which is self-explanatory.

There is a fourth point which follows from the above. Aristotle wrote in the *Posterior Analytics* (book II, 94a) that the scientific knowledge of a thing was the knowledge of its cause, and that there were four causes – namely: the definition or essential cause, the material cause, the efficient cause, and final cause. With the unveiling of the efficient cause in the 'first historical act,'

Marx succeeded in grasping the meaning of the four causes with respect to the nature of man. In these terms, then, he may be said to have scientific knowledge of the human predicament.

THE PRECONDITIONS OF MARX'S CRITIQUE

Our concern here is the preconditions of Marx's critique of politics. If, as has been argued, this critique completes the analysis of political relations, *at the level of politics*, and if the fundamentals of Marx's method predate his analysis of politics by several decades, if not more, then the question arises as to why this completion comes only in the mid-nineteenth century. If it is accepted that the method is adequate for this task long before Marx, one must look to the other variable here, namely, the adequacy of the subject matter. This we shall examine within the framework of Marx's argument.

At the centre of all political theories is the relationship of the individual to the collectivity. This has been recognized down through history; indeed, the definition of political theory rests on this relationship. As soon as man evolves to the stage at which the individual and the collectivity become separate entities – that is, as soon as the latter is embodied in the form of the state – political relations of a kind become manifest, and political theory, as the conceptualization of these relations, arises.

The nature of this relationship, however, can be comprehended only in the form in which it is actually manifest in history, or as it may be construed given the historical stage of development. Political theories always express either the chief characteristics of what exists as the essence or definition of political relations *or* what could exist given the existing mode of production. The latter is always expressed as a supposititious ideal or utopia, such as Plato's *Republic* and More's *Utopia*, or as a conscious experiment such as the efforts of Owen or Fourier. In neither case is political theory able to step beyond the conceptual powers of the day.

The science of man can grasp the nature of political relations only to the degree that this nature is revealed in the historical stages of the development of productive forces. Only as man appears at any particular stage in his development can he be understood.

The history of political theory, therefore, is a history of principal traits of the existing forms of political relations or of their possible forms, within a given stage in the development of productive forces. It is a history of the chief characteristics of actual or potential forms of the state corresponding to stages in the development of science and technology. To put it yet another way, the various forms in which the relationship between the individual and the collectivity appear or could appear, given the mode of production, constitute the history of political theory.

This history has always been a history of *political* forms because human society within recorded history has always been political, that is, characterized by a *division* between the individual and the collectivity. This division, according to Marx, arises from the *limited* development of the productive forces. And for him, it is precisely this limited development which produces a division of labour and relations of property, which, in turn, produce divisiveness or mutual antagonisms within a community, giving rise to the need for the 'community' to take the form of the state outside and above individual relations.

Prior to the modern era, political theory could not grasp the nature of politics as distinct from the nature of man because recorded history has been a history of limited developments in productive forces and therefore of political society. Political theory could do naught but assume man's nature to be political. A critique of political relations *per se*, therefore, was not possible as long as the existing forces of production were insufficiently developed to suggest a nature of man other than a political one.

To comprehend the nature of man as different from a political nature, i.e., to provide the basis for a critique of political relations *per se*, required the development of the productive forces to such a degree that political relations were perfected, that is, made into a single relation embracing all in the same manner: all individuals as individuals before the state. Only when human relations had been resolved into these elemental components, the individual and the community, as epitomized in the perfection, or completion, of political relations, could the nature of man as man, as opposed to the nature of man as a political animal, be grasped. Only by grasping the former can one comprehend the limitation of the latter.

This is the fundamental precondition of Marx's critique of politics. History had to perfect political relations before the nature of political relations itself became a question. The science of man had to wait until the development of the productive forces revealed the elementary components of human nature in the perfection of political relations before the nature of politics itself became a question. Only in this context could man perceive what he really was, his real nature as a unity of the universal and particular, but not before this context became real.

The context was, of course, the Industrial Revolution, spanning the latter half of the eighteenth century and the opening decades of the nineteenth century. This revolution in the productive forces brought a new division of labour in the process of production, a division of labour which was to destroy the old division with its modes of production and exchange, its concomitant political and social institutions and class structure. These changes were necessarily reflected in man's conception of his world; new theories were born, corresponding to the changes in the economic, political, and social spheres, which the new division of labour had wrought. These theories could but reflect the resolution of human relations in every sphere into their constituent parts, a product of the new division of labour.

New theories arose to explain the new mode of production, placing labour at the source of production, a fact which the new mode made manifest. New theories were cast to interpret the meaning of the French Revolution, the most momentous political event spawned by the new productive forces, which perfected actual political relations. And new theories arose to fathom the phenomenon of the modern working class – socialist theories which, despite their diversity, placed the proletariat at their centre. These were the conceptual counterparts of real phenomena, which were the theoretical prerequisites of Marx's critique of politics.

The rapid and dramatic changes in every sphere brought on by the industrial revolution also gave rise to a need to explain historical movement. Theory could no longer skirt the problem of change and development in the face of such revolutions in human affairs. It is in the dialectic of Hegel that an explanation for movement is best expressed, and whose implications for Marx will be discussed below.

The most immediate precondition is the French Revolution and the new political thories it engenders. The critique of politics required first of all the completion of political relations, and this the French Revolution did by resolving all former social, political, and economic relations, previously more or less integrated, into their respective spheres. By making the whole of society political, that is, by abolishing political privilege and placing all individuals in the same relation to the state, the political relation was perfected. The perfected system revealed the nature of politics as the separation of, and the consequent necessity for mediation between, the individual and the collectivity. But in revealing this separation it also raised the question of its opposite – namely, the unity of the individual and collectivity. This unity is the essence of human relations and the basis on which a critique of politics can begin.

The same contradiction, which when expressed as mutual antagonism comprises the definition of political relations, is, when expressed as a unity, the definition of man: it is the relation between the whole and the parts. This contradiction can be grasped only when it appears in reality as it does in the completion of real political relations. Prior to this completion, the completion itself was viewed as the goal or end of man's development, as, indeed, it was seen as the perfection of man's nature, his political nature. With the completion of the development of politics it was possible to see beyond politics to the essence of man within political relations. Hence, only with this completion is it possible to mount a critique of politics itself, to measure political relations by the essence of man.

It is noteworthy that following the French Revolution there is a period in which political theory attempts to grasp the revealed nature of man *within* a political point of view. We are referring to the organic theories of the state (for example, the theories of Burke, Fichte, Schelling, Hegel, etc.) which all include or are based on the notion of social contract but which attempt to accommodate the organic unity of the individual and collectivity, the essence of man, in the same theory. Despite their efforts, the accommodation is never achieved; in the first place, it is not possible for one theory to contain both the unity and disunity of the same two constituent elements; and in the second place, the unity they perceived was only implicit or essential; the reality was of disunity, of mutual antagonism between individuals and between the state and individuals.

Thus the French Revolution, in revealing the contradiction which in real life was expressed as conflict in the shape of politics, pointed also to the idea of its unity, and therefore to the essence of man. These theorists of the 'organic state' sought to incorporate in their theories the essential unity they could now perceive. They purported to find it in law, custom, tradition, primogeniture, monarchy, and so on, but in so doing they mistook the existing phenomena for an essential unity. The consequence was, first, that these phenomena, which in reality embodied political relations, and therefore relations of inequity, were perceived as the embodiment of the unity of the individual and the collectivity; and, second, that political relations were left uncriticized and still perceived as the nature of man. These theorists, then, attempted to couch politics in the framework of the essence of man *or* to find a place for the essence of man within political relations.

Even so, Marx remarked that it was an advance to conceive of the state as an organism because in this concept the essence of the state, of society, and of man, was expressed. And by conceiving the essence as an organism, the ground was laid for a critique of political relations.

Although the perfection of politics, a development of the subject matter, was a precondition of the critique of politics at the political level, a further development in the scientific appreciation of human development was required in order to go beyond this level. Although Aristotle had a theory of movement, it required a great deal of development before it could be employed to help explain human evolution. The development of a concept of the 'moving and generating principle' of man was required. Such a principle was discovered as a result of the massive and rapid economic changes of the eighteenth century and set forth in the economic theories of the day; labour was placed at the centre of human productive activity. It was Hegel who perceived its importance as the generating principle of man. For Marx to move beyond the analysis of political relations *per se*, the development of this concept of human productive activity, a product of the same forces which revolutionized his subject matter, was necessary.

If the concept of the organic state were a precondition for the critique of politics and if the concept of productive activity as the moving principle were the precondition for going beyond the political level, we still must explain why Marx began with a critique of politics and not, say, of economics to which ultimately he was to turn. Why this starting point to his early works? The explanation lies in the fact that it is the political state which appears to rule, to regulate, to judge, and to censor; in a word, it appears to determine, while other elements of society appear to be determined. Where else to begin but with the phenomenon which appears to decide the shape and nature of society? Where else to begin the analysis of reality but with the appearance of things?

By way of summary, we may say that the main precondition of Marx's critique of politics was the full development of the subject matter itself, the completion of politics. The historical evolution of political relations had to arrive at its end in order that its secret, i.e., the resolution of different forms of political relations into a single separation of the whole and its parts, could be discovered. So that this critique could be deepened to the extent that it grasped the nature of the 'first cause' of human evolution, the development of a theory of movement was necessary. The dialectic of Hegel was the second most important precondition of Marx's critique of politics, allowing him to explain the premise, the very nature of politics.

MARX AND THE END OF MODERN POLITICAL THEORY

By way of concluding remarks, let us speculate, generally but briefly, on the relationship of Marx's critique of politics to modern political theory.

The first point to be considered is the meaning of modern political theory, a theory whose principles arose with the advent of modern political relations, which began in rudimentary form in seventeenth-century England. The principles of political theory from this period still form the main foundation of all political theory pertaining to market societies down to the present day.

This definition gives rise to several questions. Why, for instance, do we say modern political relations begin in seventeenth-century England? The reason lies in the meaning of the revolutions of 1640 and 1688; they were *bourgeois* revolutions and the political outcome was the establishment of the rudiments of *liberal democracy*.[1] They are not the completion of liberal democratic relations, to be sure, but they are the beginning.

The principles referred to, following C.B. Macpherson's seminal essay, reflect the social characteristics of bourgeois society. Although liberal theory underwent revision, for example, by Locke with respect to sovereignty and later with respect to universal enfranchisement, the principles remain surprisingly stable. They are, in Macpherson's words: 'that man is free and human by virtue of his sole proprietorship of his own person, and that human society is essentially a series of market relations,'[2] and, we shall add, that the state exists for the protection and maintenance of these market relations.

The persistence of these principles requires explanation. They continually reappear in the foundation of all modern political theory because such theory, whatever the variant, pertains to the political systems of market societies; and these political systems by virtue of their nature, a product of market relations, must embody these liberal principles. They comprise the only valid foundation for political theory in a world of private property. It follows that a theory of these political systems which does not possess these principles must be either invention or theory severed from its foundation. In so far as the theory does possess them, how they are manifested in existing political relations provides the basis for the specific variation of the theory.

Let us now examine how Marx's critique of politics can shed light on the nature of liberal democratic *theory*, on its future, and on the various efforts mounted to revise it as a theory. Our argument proceeds from Marx's analysis of *political emancipation* in his article 'On the Jewish Question.' Here Marx asserts that political emancipation is the completion of man's political development. By this he means that political emancipation, because it arrives with the resolution of human life into public and private spheres and the secularization of the state, is the perfection of political relations. That is, the politically emancipated state cannot be extended as a system of purely political relations: it is the realization of man divided, of society separated into civil and political arenas. Here is the argument in his own words: '*Political emancipation is, of course, a big step forward. True, it is not the final form of*

human emancipation in general, but it is the final form of human emancipation *within* the hitherto existing world order ... One should be under no illusion about the limits of political emancipation. The division of the human
being into a *public man* and a *private man*, the *displacement* of religion from
the state into civil society, this is not a stage of political emancipation but its
completion.'[3]

If the process of political emancipation began in England in the seven-
teenth century, a concomitant of the rise to ascendancy of the bourgeoisie, it
was not completed until the twentieth century with the coming of universal
enfranchisement, a consequence of industrialization and the penetration of
capital into every sphere of production. The development of modern political
theory reflects this development of real political emancipation.

If the progress of political emancipation is a consequence of the development of the capitalist mode of production, then the transcendence of that
mode must also mean the transformation of its political corollary, perfected
political relations, which take the form of the modern liberal democratic
state. Since a theory of political relations can exist only where there is a basis
in reality for it, the transcendence of political relations is also the end of
political theory. Since the assumptions of modern political theory are the
principles of capitalist society, the demise of capitalism must be accompanied
by the close of modern political theory.[4]

To return to our definition of modern political theory, we have assumed
that all political theories pertaining to bourgeois societies possessed the basic
assumptions common to these societies. Yet it may be protested that since
Locke and his French counterparts modern theory has pursued an implicit, if
not at times explicit, counter-approach. A long line of theories beginning
perhaps with Rousseau, it may be argued, can be read as an evolving critique
of the tenets of liberalism. From Rousseau, one line proceeds through Kant
and Fichte and culminates in Hegel, to reappear later in England as a 'school'
of British idealism represented by T.H. Green, L.T. Hobhouse, and B.
Bosanquet. Another line owes much to Kant, namely utilitarianism, and
proceeds through J. Bentham and J.S. Mill, with Beccaria and Helvétius as
its European representatives. Whatever the tradition or school, the main
intent of modern political theory after Locke is not simply to grasp the nature
of the liberal democratic state but to rectify the logical inconsistencies of
classic liberalism.

This is not the place to review the content of these criticisms of liberalism;
suffice it to say that the central focus in each case is the nature of the social
contract, in a word, the nature of freedom. Nor is it the place to examine
their social bases; although we may suggest that the persistence of feudal

relations in Europe, long after their demise in England, may have provided one basis from which to criticize the notion of liberal freedom; and the French Revolution (not applicable to Rousseau), in so dramatically resolving man into his political elements, may have provided another basis on which to perceive the completion of man's political nature, the separation of the whole and its parts, and therefore also the opposite in theory – to wit, the *unity* of the whole and its parts. The rise of the working class also likely provided the basis for a variety of criticisms of liberal political theory. The great advance of all of these criticisms over liberalism proper was to pose the question of this unity.

Needless to say, the criticisms and their social basis are more complex. But the significant observation to be made is that each of these attempts to overcome the contradictions in liberalism is itself founded on liberal principles. It could not, of course, be otherwise as long as these theories purported to be explaining or describing the political relations of capitalist society. What these theories represent is the attempt to remedy the contradictions of liberal theory, perceived in the light of feudal remnants, the French Revolution, or the rise of the working class. But the attempts can be in theory only, for the contradictions of liberalism are the contradictions of real political relations in bourgeois society, the premises of which are retained by the critics.

To restate the point, the contradictions in liberal theory, in its principles and in any specific historical articulation, are nothing but the reflection of contradictions in existing liberal democratic political relations. The nature of liberal freedom, for example, the freedom of an individual as an individual, is in theory, because in fact, a contradiction; the freedom of one is delimited by the freedom of others. Similarly, the action of the state and the freedom of the individual constitute a contradiction in theory and in practice. There are many others which we can mention; namely, the contradiction between the power and authority of the legislature, between the constitution and the people, between private man and public man, and, in the case of the constitutional monarchy, between the privilege of the sovereign and the rights of the people. This does not exhaust the list, but it is sufficient to make the point: theory reflects reality and contradictions in reality, expressed in theory, cannot be overcome by revising the theory.

It is worthwhile noting that despite the criticism of liberalism which is found, implicitly, in these 'traditions' beginning with Rousseau – criticism, it should be noted, which at the level of theory leaves few of the contradictions of liberalism unexposed – it is still classic liberal democratic theory in one form or another, and not offspring from these traditions, which is the *touchstone* of political theory today in the West.

Attempts to remedy the 'logical' defects of liberal theory by the early nine-teenth century culminate with Hegel's *Philosophy of Right*. Here, he sets forth a description of the modern state, in the form of a constitutional monarchy, in which all the elements of bourgeois political relations, includ-ing the foundations, are laid out with a comprehensiveness and specificity which have, arguably, not been exceeded in political theory to this day.[5] Because it is an outline of a modern representative state, it necessarily reflects the nature of *that* state. Herein lies the central difficulty for Hegel. On the basis of the concept of the state as an organic unity, he is able to perceive the contradictions in liberalism and, indeed, his treatise contains implicitly a trenchant and devastating critique of these contradictions.[6] He grasps the contradictions of liberalism as a theory but sees its basis, the mod-ern representative state, as the completion of political development and therefore as the essence of the state. Seen as the essence, the proper subject matter of philosophy or science, it must possess the unity which Hegel knows characterizes the essence of man or the state *cum* society. Hence, the irony and central contradiction of his outline is the casting of the modern representative state, whose contradictions in liberal theory he incisively criti-cizes, in the mould of an organic unity.

Hegel's critique of liberalism or theories of natural right lays bare the logi-cal faults in the theory, and it is carried out on the basis of the *implied* unity he can perceive. The critique, then, is in the realm of theory; but the contra-dictions of liberal theory are the contradictions of liberal democratic reality and no amount of theoretical criticism can alter these real contradictions. This explains why liberalism is not displaced as the prevailing political theory by Hegel's insightful criticisms. Modern liberalism, with all its contradic-tions, in fact conforms to the real world, whereas Hegel's modern state depicted as an organism amounts to a theoretical statement out of step with the real world.

If liberal democratic theory adequately reflects the reality of the modern representative state, it may well be asked why Marx chose not to write a critique of some classic liberal treatise. The answer is found in the several reasons why he chose to analyse Hegel's political work. First, Hegel had already exposed implicitly and explicitly the major shortcomings of liberal theory, especially the central notion of freedom. This he had done on the basis of the assumed organic nature of the modern state, an erroneous assumption which nevertheless made possible his critique. Second, no liberal treatise had been as systematic or as complete as Hegel's work in depicting the modern representative state and its foundations in civil society and pri-vate property. All the elements of the liberal democratic state were present in his depiction, although Hegel sought to cast them in an organic mould as the essence of the state. As Marx remarked, in a frequently cited statement: 'Hegel is not to be blamed for depicting the nature of the modern state as it is, but for presenting that which is as the *nature of the state*.'[7] In a word, Hegel provided Marx with an accurate analysis of modern political relations, albeit depicted as an organism. Third, the critique of Hegel offered Marx the opportunity, as we have already mentioned, to criticize the speculative method. If Marx's first attempt at critique in the *Rheinische Zeitung* leaned heavily on Hegel's logic, then it could be assumed that by analysing Hegel's method some of the errors of this notion of critique might be uncovered.

The significance of the critique for Marx was two-fold: it demonstrated the logical inconsistencies of attempting to make that which in reality was contradictory into an organic unity; and it revealed the kind and nature of the contradictions which characterized the modern representative state. These two points underlay the two main conclusions of the critique; namely, that the contradictions in liberal theory were contradictions in the existing liberal state and could only be overcome by 'practical means' and not by theoretical revisions, and that the nature of the contradictions was to be explained by the nature of private property.

Herein lies the relation of Marx's critique of politics to modern political theory: for Marx a proper critique of liberal democratic theory could only be carried out by grasping the nature of property and the solution to the contradictions in liberalism was a question of practice. This relation rests on the respective treatment of private property.

The reason these traditions, from Rousseau to Kant and Hegel, could not overcome the contradictions so evident in liberalism lay in the retention of private property as essential to the nature of man; the possession of private property was perceived as the basis of the individual's humanity. But private property, as we see from Marx, was the basis of the fundamental contradictions of the liberal state. In retaining private property, therefore, these theorists retained the basis of the contradictions they sought to resolve.

This, of course, had to be because private property formed the foundation of the real state, and its contradictions. To ignore this fact or to attempt to eliminate private property from the theory would be tantamount to ignoring the central fact of modern political relations or to composing a theory with at best an oblique relation to reality. All of modern political theory must reflect the fact of private property or be condemned as invention.

The fundamental difference between Marx's critique of politics and modern political theory lies in their respective positions on private property. The latter, in which we include all shades of liberalism and 'conservatism,' makes private property a requisite of human nature, i.e., to be human is to possess private property, even if this property is only his own person, his own capacities. Marx, on the other hand, perceives private property as a *product* of human nature and as a *necessary* historical product, but *not* the essence of human nature. It is more than this; its appearance in history is also the *cause* of political relations, the separation of the state from its members.

The significance of this difference is that as long as private property is taken as the basic assumption about the nature of man, human nature must always be perceived as political; the completion of political development becomes the perfection of man; the search for the cause of political relations is not seen as necessary because the cause is human nature itself; the reason for criticizing or changing political relations does not arise, unless to perfect them, because this is to criticize or change what is natural. The liberal assumption about private property confines modern political theory, and its contemporary offspring, to a *political* perspective; and, therefore, it is condemned to confront unsolvable problems, problems intrinsic to the political itself.

The consequence of this state of affairs is that all modern political theory and its contemporary manifestations which go beyond sycophantic paeans to the system are confronted with the difficulty of solving real contradictions, but in the realm of theory. The proposals are varied and numerous and unsuccessful; they range from Rousseau's attempt to redefine the concept of property right, to Hegel's attempt to consign property rights to abstract realms, to Bentham's attempt to circumvent liberal assumptions on grounds of 'utility' while retaining the market society, to the contemporary efforts by C.B. Macpherson to redefine property and by J. Rawls to make private property, in the words of a critic, 'a contingent matter rather than an essential part of the doctrine.'[8] These by no means complete the list; they are intended only to be illustrative of the point. They are all unsuccessful because the various contradictions they seek to solve are real and can only be solved in the realm of practice.

The significance of Marx's critique of politics and his relation to modern political theory lies in his demonstration that the solution to the contradictions inherent in politics cannot be achieved in criticism which is solely *theoretical* or in the manipulation of the *concept* of private property, but that it is necessary to overcome the real existence of private property, the source of political relations, by real existing means.

Appendix
Alienated labour, division of labour, and private property

There is a passage in the Paris manuscripts, concerning the relation between estranged labour and private property, which has given rise to a certain amount of comment and criticism. It is of such central importance to Marx's entire life's work that it bears some review. The offending passage is as follows:

> *Private property* thus results by analysis from the *concept* of *alienated labour*, i.e., of *alienated man*, of estranged labour, of estranged life, of *estranged* man.
>
> True, it is as a result of the *movement of private property* that we have obtained the concept of *alienated labour* (*of alienated life*) in political economy. But analysis of this concept shows that though private property appears to be the reason, the cause of alienated labour, it is rather its consequence, just as the gods are *originally* not the cause but the effect of man's intellectual confusion. Later this relationship becomes reciprocal.
>
> Only at the culmination of the development of private property does this, its secret, appear again, namely, that on the one hand it is the *product* of alienated labour, and that on the other it is the *means* by which labour alienates itself, the *realisation of this alienation*.[1]

Let us consider the objections, by citing some of the critics and commentators themselves. David McLellan in his *Marx before Marxism*, immediately following citations from the first two of the above paragraphs, writes: 'This [i.e., the relationship between alienated labour and private property] has been called a *petitio principii*, and, strictly speaking this is correct: the idea of alienated labour presupposes private property just as much as it gives rise to it.'[2] McLellan characterizes Marx's discussion of the relationship as *petitio principii*; but to leave the matter at this is to say that the very point on which rests *all* of the analysis of the Paris manuscripts is a circular proposition which begs the question, which attempts to demonstrate a conclusion while presupposing it as the premise. Unfortunately, McLellan makes no further remarks on the subject; but, as we shall see below, Marx is arguing, on the contrary, that the *reciprocal* relation between alienated labour and private property is a later development; 'originally' alienated labour precedes private property, this latter being initially only *implied*. This argument is not a *petitio principii*.

Another but longer review of the question is found in John Plamenatz's *Karl Marx's Philosophy of Man*, where he introduces the problem with these words: 'If we consider what Marx says in the "Economic and Philosophical Manuscripts," we find him both unwilling to admit that alienation is an effect of private property in the means of production and unable to suggest another cause; we find him contradicting himself, or at least trying to have his cake and eat it.' Following an unhappy résumé of the argument as found in the above quotations from Marx, Plamenatz writes: 'In this early manuscript Marx claims to have done what there is no evidence that he even attempted. At the end of his "analysis of the movement of private property," he tells us that "private property appears to be the basis and the cause of alienated labour." But if, at this point of the argument, this is how it appears, it does so only because his own analysis suggests it. It is the impression that his account of the matter, so far as it is intelligible, creates; and yet, so he assures us at the end of the account the impression is false. What appears to be the basis and cause is really the effect. But Marx never explains how this is so; he nowhere in these early manuscripts (nor as far as I know anywhere else), makes a step towards showing that the private ownership of productive resources is an effect rather than a cause of labour's being alienated [sic].'[3]

It is unfortunate that Plamenatz sought to find the reason for his own mystification in Marx. In the manuscripts, Marx makes his case convincingly enough (see chapter 4 above); and, in his later work, despite Plamenatz's inability to find it, Marx spends considerable time examining the relationship, as we shall see below.

A prominent and orthodox Marxist also comments on this passage. Ernest Mandel in his *The Formation of the Economic Thought of Karl Marx* makes two remarks, the first in a footnote: 'It may be objected that there is a passage in the *Economic and Philosophic Manuscripts* in which Marx declares that alienated labour is the *cause*, and private property the *result*. But Jahn correctly observes that Marx is not dealing here with the problem of the *historical origin* of private property but rather with the problem of its nature, of how it reappears daily in a mode of production based on alienated labour.' (Jahn, W., 'Der ökonomische Inhalt des Begriffs der Entfremdung der Arbeit in den Frühschriften von Karl Marx,' in *Wirtschaftswissenschaft*, no. 6, 1957.)[4] And the second: 'In *The German Ideology*, the source of alienated labour is explained as being the division of labour and commodity production, an idea already present in the third of the *Economic and Philosophic Manuscripts*.'[5]

It must be said, contrary to what Mandel and Jahn assert, that Marx's discussion of the relationship between alienated labour and private property does indeed concern the 'historical origin of private property,' and we shall attempt to demonstrate this below. It is, moreover, not at all clear where in *The German Ideology* Marx points to the 'source of alienated labour' as located in 'the division of labour and commodity production.' The concept of estranged or alienated labour [die entfremdete, entäusserte Arbeit] does not actually appear in *The German Ideology*. The concept of estrangement [Entfremdung] does, but Marx's use of it is either within quotation marks or in a context indicating an irony directed at the Young Hegelians.[6] Mandel's assertions must be treated with circumspection.

There are two reasons why Marx eschews the use of the concept of alienated labour in *The German Ideology*. The first has to do with the widespread idealist employment of the concept of estrangement by the Young Hegelians: Marx was not going to risk having the notion of alienated labour, so central to his work, confused with the Hegelian notion of alienation or self-estrangement of ideas. The second has to do with the nature of the introductory section of Feuerbach: here Marx (and Engels) sought to spell out the materialist conception of history in terms of concrete, specific *economic* categories. Alienated labour is the abstract expression of a phenomenon which also has a real economic expression.

Let us cite what Marx does say about alienated labour and its 'economic expression' in the Paris manuscripts. 'The *division of labour* is the economic expression of the *social character of labour* within the estrangement. Or, since *labour* [Marx means wage-labour or alienated labour: all labour] is only an expression of human activity within alienation, of the manifestation of life as the alienation of life, the *division of labour* too, is therefore nothing else but the *estranged*, *alienated* positing of human activity *as a real activity of the species* or as *activity of man as a species-being*.'[7] On the same page, he also writes: 'As for the essence of the division of labour ... i.e., as for the estranged and alienated form of human activity as an activity of the species ...'

The division of labour, then, is *not* the source of alienated labour; rather, it is the real economic expression of the fact, first, that all labour is *alienated labour* and, second, that all labour is *social*. It refers to the real social nature of human productive activity which evolves historically, always within a system of estrangement. The division of labour refers to the interdependence of *particular* alienated activities; whereas, alienated labour refers to the estrangement of an abstract individual's activity. The division of labour is the actual social nature of man in the form of estrangement – the form it must take in history.[8]

It follows that Marx does not see the division of labour as the source of alienated labour, as Mandel would have it; and, furthermore, that the division of labour is merely the economic concept of the estranged social interaction of productive activity.

Before turning to examine the 'source' of alienated labour or the division of labour and their relation to private property, we must establish that Marx saw the relation of both of the first two concepts with private property in the same light. In the Paris manuscripts Marx writes: '*Private property*, as the material, summary expression of alienated labour, embraces both relations – the relation of the worker to labour and to the product of his labour and to the non-worker, and the relation of the non-worker to the worker and to the product of his labour.'[9] In *The German Ideology*, he asserts the following: 'Division of labour and private property are, after all, identical expressions: in the one the same thing is affirmed with reference to activity as is affirmed in the other with reference to the product of the activity.'[10] Because Marx perceives the division of labour as 'the social character' of real, existing labour in estrangement, he is able to make such strikingly similar statements about the relation of alienated labour and division of labour to private property.

To pose the question, what is the cause of alienated labour (Plamenatz) or what is the source of alienated labour (Mandel), is to mistake the nature of the question. All labour in *historical* society is to some degree and in some form estranged labour, and this remains the case until the supersession of communism, until 'self-deriving,' 'positive humanism comes into being.' It is through estranged labour, through the division of labour, that man evolves his social nature. Man's essence 'comes into existence as its opposite, in the form of estrangement,' as Marx put it.[11]

The division of labour arises spontaneously within the first historical act, the first act in which man begins to make himself. This act is a composite of three aspects which arise simultaneously: first, 'the production of the means to satisfy these [fundamental] needs'; second, 'the creation of new needs' from the 'action of satisfying and the instrument of satisfaction which has been acquired'; and third, in the process of 'daily re-creating their own life, [men] begin to make other men,' to establish social relationships the first of which is the family. 'These three aspects of social activity,' writes Marx in

The German Ideology, 'have existed simultaneously since the dawn of history and the first men, and ... still assert themselves in history today.'[12] Now the division of labour finds its first expression in this first historical act in the family. As Marx states it: 'the division of labour ... is based [beruht] on the natural division of labour in the family and the separation of society into individual families opposed to one another.'[13] Each of these aspects of social activity imply each other and therefore also the division of labour. In this sense, there is no 'source' or 'cause' of alienation; it is inherent in man's making of himself. Man's first historical act, then, is an act which implies estrangement, and thereafter man's entire history is a history of estrangement, ending with the end of history.

If the 'source' of alienated labour or the division of labour is accounted for by the very nature of human productive activity, the relationship between the division of labour and private property must now be examined. Implicit within this natural division of labour, says Marx, is 'the *distribution* [die Verteilung: apportionment, assessment], and indeed the *unequal* [ungleiche] distribution, both quantitative and qualitative, of labour and its products, hence property.' Thus, within the first natural division of labour lies latent the fact of property. The division of labour, distribution, and property imply each other; in this sense we cannot speak of the source or cause of property because it is inherent in the division of labour.

As the means of production develop, new needs are created, and so too are new social relationships; these new relations contain new divisions of labour. As expressed by Marx: 'Each new productive force, insofar as it is not merely a quantitative extension of productive forces already known ... causes a further development of the division of labour.' And each new development in the division of labour brings with it a corresponding new form of property. 'The various stages of development in the division of labour are just so many different forms of property, i.e., the existing stage in the division of labour determines also the relations of individuals to one another with reference to the material, instrument and product of labour.'[14]

As population increases, as needs grow, and as 'external intercourse' [äussern Verkehrs] expands in the shape of war and *barter*, so too do the productive forces expand and with them the division of labour. It follows that the form of property is also transformed. When the division of labour reaches a certain stage, which implies production for exchange and the expansion of internal and external intercourse (commerce, in the broadest sense),[15] property takes the form of private property.[16]

This same point as found in *The German Ideology*, i.e., that a certain stage in the development of the division of labour (of alienated labour), related to production for exchange, gives rise to private property, is repeated in Marx's later works. In the *Grundrisse*, for instance, there are several passages describing the development of forms of property and arguing that the appearance of private property depends on a certain attained level of division of labour and extended exchange or commerce.[17]

In *Capital* I, the concept of private property appears only very occasionally, mainly because it is subsumed in the concept of the commodity. The commodity is both use-value, as is all property, and exchange-value. The rise of private property is coterminous with the development of exchange-value. Here is part of Marx's exposition of the development of exchange-value (commodities) out of the 'direct barter of products': 'The articles A and B in this case [i.e., as mere use-values] are not as yet commodities, but become so only by the act of barter. The first step made by an object of utility towards acquiring exchange-value is when it forms a non-use-value for its owner, and that happens when it forms a superfluous portion of some article required for his immediate wants. Objects in themselves are external to man, and consequently alienable by him. In order that this alienation may be reciprocal, it is only necessary for men, by a tacit understanding, to treat each other as private owners of those alienable objects, and by implication as independent individuals.' Marx is describing the relation of two abstract producers who desire to exchange their mutual products. We can see in this passage the abstract relationship between the alienation of the product of one's labour and the implication of private property. This is an analysis of alienated labour, exchange, and private property which can also be found in the 1844 'Comments on James Mill.'[18] But this relation of two abstract producers is not how private property arises. Marx continues:

But such a state of reciprocal independence has no existence in a primitive society based on property in common, whether such a society takes the form of a patriarchial family, an ancient Indian community, or a Peruvian Inca State. The exchange of commodities, therefore, first begins on the boundaries of such communities, at their points of contact with other similar communities, or with members of the latter. So soon, however, as products once become commodities in the external relations of a community, they also, by reaction, become so in its internal intercourse. The proportions in which they are exchangeable are at first quite a matter of chance. What makes them exchangeable is the mutual desire of their owners to alienate them. Meantime the need for foreign objects of utility gradually establishes itself. The constant repetition of exchange makes it a normal social act. In the course of time, therefore, some portion at least of the products of labour must be produced with a special view to exchange. From that moment the distinction becomes firmly established between the utility of an object for the purpose of consumption, and its utility for the purposes of exchange-value. Its use-value becomes distinguished from its exchange-value.[19]

Here, then, is described the historical origin of exchange-value, the distinguishing characteristic of a commodity as opposed to the mere product of labour, the simple use-value. The rise of exchange-value is the genesis of private property; once it becomes part of a *system* of exchange or commerce, property must become private property; it must take the form of the commodity.

What is missing from the passage is the notion of division of labour. In *The German Ideology*, Marx argues that the division of labour must reach a certain stage before exchange leading to private property can occur, and indeed that private property is a direct consequence of the development of the division of labour. The reason it is omitted here is that Marx was specifically concerned with examining the relation between exchange and the rise of exchange-value, while *assuming* a certain stage in the division of labour. In an earlier section of *Capital*, however, he is quite clear about the relation between the division of labour and private property. 'To all the different varieties of values in use there correspond as many different kinds of useful labour, classified according to the order, genus, species, and variety to which they belong in the social division of labour. *This division of labour is a necessary condition for the production of commodities*, but it does not follow, conversely, that the production of commodities is a necessary condition for the division of labour.'[20] (emphasis added) Thus, in *Capital*, as in *The German Ideology*, the division of labour at a certain stage is a precondition for the production of private property.

It must be remembered, in summary, that each of these concepts – the division of labour, exchange, and private property – implies each other. The division of labour, however, is prior to the other two and is most directly dependent on the level of development of the forces of production in any given society.

To conclude, let us return to the Paris manuscripts where Marx writes: 'The examination of *division of labour* [der Teilung der Arbeit] and *exchange* [des Austausches] is of extreme interest, because these are *perceptibly alienated* expressions of human *activity* and *essential power* as a *species* activity and species power.'[21] Here again, he defines the division of labour as the expression of alienated social activity. And both the division of labour and exchange he defines as 'Wesenskraft' in the form of estrangement, i.e, the power, energy, vigour, substance, spirit, or capacities of the species, in alienated form. He continues: 'To assert that division of labour and exchange rest [beruhn] on private property is nothing but asserting that *labour* is the essence of private property.' In other words, in so far as the political economist sees division of labour and exchange as resting on private property, he is perceiving only the fact that labour (i.e., alienated labour) expresses itself as private property. In this fact, the facts of division of labour and exchange are subsumed.

In this short appendix, we have attempted to show that alienated labour and division of labour are related in that the latter is the real economic expression of 'the social character' of alienated productive activity in a system of limited productive forces. We have argued, also, that given the relation between alienated labour and division of labour, Marx expressed the relation of the two to private property in a very similar way, and that, in both cases, private property was a consequence; in the former, it was a product of estranged productive activity, and in the latter, it was a result of a stage in the development of the division of labour. Failure to understand this relationship precludes a comprehension of Marx's achievement in uncovering the 'law of motion' of human history in *The German Ideology* and how he arrived at this conclusion.

Notes

INTRODUCTION

1 E.g., I. Meszaros, *Marx's Theory of Alienation* (London 1970); E. Mandel, *The Formation of the Economic Thought of Karl Marx* (London 1977); L. Kolakowski, *Main Currents of Marxism*, 1 (Oxford 1978)
2 Auguste Cornu, *Karl Marx et Friedrich Engels*, I (Paris 1955), 202, 206
3 H. Draper, *Karl Marx's Theory of Revolution* (New York 1977), 89
4 E.g., L. Colletti, 'Marxism and the Dialectic,' *New Left Review*, 93, 1975; L. Althusser, *For Marx* (London 1977), 158
5 N. Lobkowicz, *Theory and Practice* (Notre Dame 19670; Meszaros, *Alienation*; Mandel, *Formation*
6 H.P. Adams, *Karl Marx in His Earliest Writings* (London 1965); Draper, *Theory of Revolution*; D. McLellan, *Marx before Marxism* (Harmondsworth 1970)
7 B. Nicolaievsky and O. Maenchen-Helfen, *Karl Marx* (1936; Pelican 1976), 34; F. Mehring, *Karl Marx* (1936; London 1951); M. Rubel, *Karl Marx: Essai de biographie intellectuelle* (Paris 1971); McLellan, *Marx before Marxism*, 66
8 'Letter from Marx to His Father,' *Marx-Engels Collected Works*, 1 (London 1975), 12 (hereafter MECW); in *Marx-Engels Werke*, Ergänzungsband (Berlin 1968), 4 (hereafter MEW)
9 Ibid
10 Ibid, MECW, 18; MEW, 8
11 G.W.F. Hegel, *The Phenomenology of Mind*, trans. J.B. Baillie (New York 1967), 86
12 L. Feuerbach, *Principles of the Philosophy of the Future*, trans. M.H. Vogel (New York 1966), 38
13 'Marx to His Father,' MECW, 1, 18; MEW, 8
14 Ibid, 17, 19
15 *Capital*, 1, 'Afterword' (New York 1967), 20

226 Notes

16 A. Koyré, 'Note sur la langue et la terminologie hégélienne,' in *Revue philosophiques de la France et l'étranger* (Paris 1931), 410-11, 414
17 'Economic and Philosophic Manuscripts of 1844,' MECW, 3, 343
18 Feuerbach, *Principles*, 35
19 'Difference between the Democritean and Epicurean Philosophy of Nature,' MECW, 1, 30 (hereafter 'Difference')
20 Ibid, 104
21 In what follows the terms 'idea' and 'concept' will be used interchangeably, as they are by Marx here, to signify the content of mind. Their content, in turn, is essence which will be defined as it appears below.
22 H. Ritter, *The History of Ancient Philosophy*, III (Oxford 1839), 429
23 'Difference,' 29
24 Ibid, 48
25 Ibid, 49
26 Ibid, 51-52. For the probable source of this argument, see G.W.F. Hegel, *Hegel's Logic*, trans. W. Wallace (Oxford 1975), 142.
27 Ibid, 52
28 Ibid, 53
29 Ibid, 50
30 Ibid, 54
31 Ibid, 60
32 A short discussion of essence as 'formless substratum' may be found in Aristotle, *Metaphysics*, ed. and trans. J. Warrington (London) 171.
33 'Difference,' 63
34 Ibid, 64
35 'Notebooks on Epicurean Philosophy,' MECW, 1, 423-4
36 For a discussion of such a view of philosophy, see F. Engels, 'Ludwig Feuerbach and the End of Classical German Philosophy,' in Marx-Engels, *Selected Works*, vol. II (Moscow 1949), 328. Engels writes: 'Truth, the cognition of which is the business of philosophy, was in the hands of Hegel no longer an aggregate of finished dogmatic statements, which, once discovered, had merely to be learned by heart. Truth lay now in the process of cognition itself, in the long historical development of science, which mounts from lower to ever high levels of knowledge without ever reaching, by discovering so-called absolute truth, a point at which it can proceed no further, where it would have nothing more to do than to fold its hands and gaze with wonder at the absolute truth to which it had attained.' See also Q. Lauer, 'The Marxist Conception of Science,' in R.S. Cohen and M.W. Wartofsky, eds., *Methodological and Historical Essays in the Natural and Social Sciences* (Dordrecht 1974), 378.
37 'Notebooks,' 491

38 'Difference,' 85
39 Ibid
40 Cf. N. Geras, 'Marx and the Critique of Political Economy,' in R. Blackburn, ed., *Ideology in Social Science* (Bungay 1972).
41 Regarding the analogy to Feuerbach, see S. Avineri, *The Social and Political Thought of Karl Marx* (Cambridge 1968), 9, 11, 13, 14; and D. Howard, 'On Marx's Critical Theory,' in *Telos*, 6 (fall 1970). Regarding the analogy to Kant, see D. Sayer, *Marx's Method* (Hassocks, 1979). There are many who would make this analogy, but Sayer's recent book has the advantage of spelling out the exact point on which his purported analogy between Kant and Marx is based. But how superficial it is. Kant was searching for *a priori* principles of *perception* and found only principles dependent, in the final analysis, on experience. Marx was searching for the principles of existing reality, the essential characteristics of reality, the nature and principle of motion of reality. There is not a hint of a search for the *a priori* in Marx's philosophy. The analogy is utterly inappropriate. See Max Horkheimer, 'Traditional and Critical Theory' in his *Critical Theory* (New York 1972), for a brief critical appraisal of Kant's methodology in relation to Marx.
42 Cf. Lobkowicz, *Theory and Practice* 374-81.
43 See MECW, 1, 738-9.
44 Not all accounts of Marx's method are quite so problematic. See, for example, B. Ollman, 'Marxism and Political Science: Prolegomenon to a Debate on Marx's Method,' in *Politics and Society*, 3, no. 4 (summer 1973). Nevertheless, Ollman *asserts*, without convincing evidence, that the method had five levels or stages. How Marx actually employed these levels in analysis is not made clear. How Marx came to adopt this multi-stage method is not discussed. The article is an assertion of what Ollman thinks Marx's method was from 1844 to the end of his life, and consequently, there is no exploration of the question of development of the method.

See also A.W. Gouldner, 'The Two Marxisms,' in *For Sociology* (London 1975), 427. Gouldner overshoots the mark with his definition. He writes: 'A critique takes a given belief system, a theory, ideology, or indeed science itself ... as problematic. It seeks to de-reify it, to de-mystify, to remove its objectivistic false consciousness, to offer an interpretation of it in terms of the everyday life of men living in and constrained by a specific society.' He is suggesting here that the critique is aimed at demystifying theory by comparing it to reality, thereby revealing the defects or inadequacies of the theory. But Marx's use of critique was to derive the *essence* or idea of a phenomenon and then to compare particular reality to that, thus showing the 'defects' of reality. It was not theory but reality that he wanted to change.

Even so, a theory was demystified by Marx by comparing it to the essence which went beyond the simple appearance of things. In so far as theory simply *reflected* the 'defects' of reality, the mere appearance, and did not penetrate to discover the essence, the 'inner connexions,' it was vulgar, bourgeois, or simply ideological.

45 See 'Afterword' to the Second German Edition, *Capital*, 1 (New York 1967), and the conclusions to chapter 4 below.
46 'Debates on Freedom of the Press and Publication of Proceedings of the Assembly of the Estates,' MECW, 1, 154
47 'The Leading Article in No. 179 of the *Kölnische Zeitung*,' MECW, 1, 200
48 'Difference,' 62
49 R. Pascal, *Karl Marx: His Apprenticeship to Politics* (London 1942?), 18; M. Rubel, *Karl Marx: essai de biographie intellectuelle* (Paris 1971), 32
50 R. Tucker, *Philosophy and Myth in Karl Marx* (Cambridge 1961), 15; Lobkowitz, *Theory and Practice*, 378. Marx's position on morality is profoundly different from the assertions of Tucker; see his 'Comments on the Latest Prussian Censorship Instruction,' MECW, 1, 118-19.
51 'Comments,' MECW, 1, 120; 'The Leading Article,' MECW, 1, 193
52 K. Popper, *The Open Society and Its Enemies*, 1 (Princeton 1962, 1966), 31; K. Popper, *Conjectures and Refutations* (New York 1963, 1965), 104-5. Popper argues this point on the level of analogy or name-calling. Modern essentialism, he writes, is 'very similar' to the arguments which 'led Plato to his doctrine of Forms or Ideas'; and he asserts a preference for his nominalism to the 'pretentious muddle' of the essentialists. He does not develop arguments beyond this level in support of his case.
53 'Marxism and Empiricism,' in B. Williams and A. Montefiore, eds., *British Analytical Philosophy* (London 1966), 231
54 Mezsaros, *Alienation*, 13. Despite the author's scathing tone in his comments about 'the artificial simplicity of commonplace-mongering neo-empiricism,' he does not develop his criticism of empiricism as does Taylor.
55 D.G. Charlton, *Positivist Thought in France* (Oxford 1959), 3; J. Joergensen, *The Development of Logical Empiricism* (Chicago 1951), 6
56 See, for example, the collection of critical essays: H. Morick, ed., *Challenges to Empiricism* (Belmont 1972).
57 Just such a broad use of the concept, as a 'common intellectual attitude,' is to be found in the book by L. Kolakowski, *Positivist Philosophy* (Harmondsworth 1972).
59 Charlton, *Positivist Thought*, 2
59 R. Harrison, 'E.S. Beesly and Karl Marx,' *International Review of Social History*, IV (1959), 234

60 (Ann Arbor 1961), 6
61 *Language, Truth and Logic* (New York 1946), 14
62 'Difference,' 58
63 See the numerous references in Geras, 'Marx and the Critique of Political Economy,' 284-6.
64 Ayer, *Language*, 134
65 Ibid, 90
66 'Difference,' 41; 'Comments,' 112-13
67 'Notebooks,' 425
68 Ayer, *Language*, 90
69 Ibid, 108
70 Kant, *Fundamental Principles of the Metaphysic of Morals*, second section, for his definition of the categorical imperative. Mill, *Utilitarianism*, chapter II, 'The creed which accepts as the foundation of morals "utility" or the "greatest happiness principle" holds that actions are right in proportion as they tend to promote happiness, wrong as they tend to produce the reverse of happiness.'
71 'The Leading Article,' MECW, 1, 200
72 'Debates on Freedom of the Press and Publication of the Proceedings of the Assembly of the Estates,' MECW, 1, 135
73 Marx, 'The Divorce Bill,' MECW, 1, 309. He writes: 'A *true* state, a *true* marriage, a *true* friendship are indissoluble, but no state, no marriage, no friendship, corresponds fully to its concept, and like real friendship, even in the family, like the real state in world history, so too real marriage in the state is *dissoluble*. No moral *existence* corresponds to its *essence* or, at least, it does not *have* to correspond to it.'
74 'Comments,' 110. He employs such words as 'Fehler' and 'Mangel' to convey this idea of defect.
75 Ayer, *Language*, 152-3
76 'The Leading Article,' MECW, 1, 191: 'Philosophy asks what is true, not what is held to be true. It asks what is true for all mankind, not what is true for some people. Its metaphysical truths do not recognize the boundaries of political geography; its political truths know too well where the "bounds" begin for it to confuse the illusory horizon of a particular world or national outlook with the true horizon of the human mind.'
77 Vol. 3 (New York 1967), 817
78 Marx to Kugelman, 11 July 1968, *Marx-Engels Selected Correspondence* (New York 1936), 247
79 'Difference,' 86
80 Marx to Engels, 20 March 1869, MEW, 32, 284

CHAPTER 1

1 The historical/biographical details of Marx in this period can be found in several works, for instance: A. Cornu, *Karl Marx et Frederick Engels*, I (Paris 1955); O.J. Hammen, *The Red 48'ers* (New York 1969); J. Lewis, *The Life and Teaching of Karl Marx* (London 1965); D. McLellan, *Marx before Marxism* (London 1970) and *Karl Marx* (London 1973); F. Mehring, *Karl Marx* (London 1936); B. Nicolaievski and O. Maenchen, *Karl Marx* (London 1973); and M. Rubel, *Karl Marx: essai de biographie intellectuelle* (Paris 1971).

2 See comments by G. Jung, manager of the *RhZ*, and by A. Ruge, editor of the *Deutsche Jahrbücher*, in *Karl Marx and Frederick Engels, Collected Works*, 1 (London 1975), 739 (herafter MECW).

3 MECW, 1, 738-9

4 These views are very prevalent and can be found in almost every commentary on these early writings, for example: H.P. Adams, *Karl Marx in His Early Writings* (London 1965). These articles demonstrate Marx's 'radical democratic idealism' (56). A. Cornu, *Karl Marx et Frederick Engels*, 1 (Paris 1955). Marx remains 'on the soil of bourgeois ideology' in so far as he accepted Hegel's model of 'universal reason' realized in the state. A. Cornu, *Moses Hess et la gauche hégélienne* (cited in Rubel, *Karl Marx*, 37). Cornu writes that the *RhZ* articles were 'tout imbu encore de la doctrine de Hegel.' H. Draper, in *Karl Marx's Theory of Revolution* (New York 1977), finds Marx in this period 'a democratic extremist' who is 'still imprisoned within the Hegelian conception of the "true state."' R.N. Hunt, *The Political Ideas of Marx and Engels* (Pittsburgh 1974), argues that 'Marx was a non-communist democratic republican.' M. Rubel, 'Notes on Marx's Conception of Democracy,' *New Politics*, 1, no. 2 (1962), writes: 'One can distinguish in the political career of Karl Marx two phases: first when he was a liberal and democratic writer, and second when he presents himself as a communist' (79). V.I. Lenin, 'Karl Marx,' cited in M. Löwy, *La théorie de la révolution chez le jeune Marx* (Paris 1970). He says of the *RhZ* articles: 'C'est ici que l'on voit Marx passer de l'idéalisme au matérialisme et du démocratisme révolutionnaire au communisme.' The Russian commentators tend to stay very close to Lenin's position. See, for example, O. Bakouradze, 'La formation des idées philosophiques de Karl Marx,' and N. Lapine, 'La première critique approfondée de la philosophie de Hegel par Marx,' where homage is carefully paid to Lenin's statement and Marx is labelled an 'idealist' prior to the 1843 *Critique* of Hegel. *Recherches internationales à la lumière du marxisme*, cahier 19 (1960). East German writers tend to follow the same position. See *Recherches*

internationales, cahier 19, and several writers cited by A.F. McGovern in 'The Young Marx on the State,' *Science and Society*, 34, no. 4 (1970), 430.

5 See, for example, Adams, *Karl Marx*; Bakouradze, 'La formation,' McLellan, *Marx before Marxism*, Rubel, *Karl Marx*. Attempts to systematize the *RhZ* articles can be found in H. Draper, *Marx's Theory*, chaps. 1 and 2; D. Howard, *The Development of the Marxian Dialectic* (Carbondale 1972), chap. 2; McGovern, 'The Young Marx'; Löwy, *La théorie de la révolution*. One notable exception is the two-volume work by A.Th. van Leeuwen, *Critique of Heaven* (London 1972) and *Critique of Earth* (London 1974).

6 See, for example, D. McLellan, *The Young Hegelians and Karl Marx* (London 1969); S. Hook, *From Hegel to Marx* (Ann Arbor 1962); L. Dupré, *The Philosophical Foundations of Marxism* (New York 1966).

7 'Notes,' MECW, 1, 85-6

8 'The Leading Article,' MECW, 1, 202

9 Ibid, 193

10 'Marginal Notes to the Accusations of the Ministerial Rescript,' MECW, 1, 363

11 Aristotle, *Politics*, 1253a, 25-29. The main difference to be noted is that between the concept of natural law as held by the ancient philosophers, the Roman lawyers, and Hegel, and those theories of natural rights as classically developed by Hobbes and Locke. Although the latter evolved out of the former, the essential elements of each stand in opposition. Natural law theories proceed from a notion of the whole; the relation of the individual to the community is natural, reflexive, and necessary; freedom is but the recognition of this necessity and law is the formal expression of freedom. Natural right theories proceed from a notion of the individual; the relation of the individual to others and to the ruling power is contractual; there is no community above and beyond the sum of the individuals; freedom is the absence of restraint; and laws are imposed restrictions on a theoretically unbounded freedom.

12 Bk. III, chap. 6, where he defines the state as 'an association of free men' characterized by equality and similarity and on which is based a 'political authority.'

13 In his *Philosophy of Right*, T.M. Knox trans. (Oxford 1975) 163, 176, 364

14 'Debates on Freedom of the Press and Publication of the Proceedings of the Assembly of the Estates,' MECW, 1, 145-6

15 Ibid

16 'Debates on the Law on Thefts of Wood,' MECW, 1, 232-5

17 'Debates on Freedom,' 146

18 This distinction is an important part of Hegel's argument in his essay, *Natural Law*, trans. T.M. Knox (Philadelphia 1975), 115. Ernest Barker has remarked

that in much of Europe, particularly Germany, 'law has been the basis of the theory of the state.' 'On the one hand, it [law] has provided the training of the *Staatsbeamtentum* [state functionaries]; on the other hand it has provided the concepts and the line of approach for *Staatswissenschaft*.' E. Barker, 'Translator's Introduction,' to O. Gierke, *Natural Law and the Theory of Society, 1500 to 1800* (Cambridge 1934), xx. Interestingly, this is the choice the faced Marx in 1837: to be a political functionary or to be a political scientist. See 'Letter ... to His Father,' MECW, 1, 20.

19 'Comments on the Latest Prussian Censorship Instruction,' MECW, 1, 109
20 Ibid, 111
21 Marx defines law as 'the positive, clear, universal norms in which freedom has acquired an impersonal, theoretical existence independent of the arbitrariness of the individual.' MECW, 1, 162. See Aristotle's *Politics*, Bk. X, chap. IX, 1180a, where he makes the distinction between 'rule of man' and 'rule of law': the former he calls 'positive law' which is arbitrary and the latter 'laws of morality' which are the embodiment of 'right,' 'a declaration emanating from Practical Wisdom and Intellect.'
22 'Comments,' 118. In his *Ethics*, Aristotle distinguished two kinds of 'Social Just,' the regulations between free and equal citizens, namely, 'natural and conventional.' The former is 'that which has everywhere the same force' and does not depend on enactment; whereas, the latter is strictly positive, its essence is its enactment. (Bk. V, 1134b)
23 'Comments,' 120. In the *Politics*, Aristotle made the distinction between lawful and lawless types of rule. They were based, as in Marx, on the nature of the law – the former on its naturalness, the latter on its positivity. (Bk. IV, chap. 4)
24 'Comments,' 120. Compare this definition of the state and others of Marx with Cicero, one of the most widely read writers of Roman jurisprudence, who argued, in the words of Sabine, that 'the state is a moral community, a group of persons who in common possess the state and its law. For this reason he calls the state, in a fine phrase, the *res populi* or *res publica*, "the affair of the people," which is practically equivalent in meaning to the older English use of the word "commonwealth."' G. Sabine, *A History of Political Theory* (London 1966), 166
25 See respectively 'Debates on Freedom,' 'The Divorce Bill' (two articles), 'Debates on the Law on Thefts of Wood,' and 'Communal Reform and the *Kölnische Zeitung*,' MECW, 1.
26 'Debates on Freedom,' 161
27 Ibid, 154
28 'Comments,' 130-1

29 'The Leading Article,' 199-200
30 'Comments,' 117
31 Ibid, 118
32 Ibid, 119. Hegel wrote that 'Jesus taught not an authoritarian but an autonomous ethics. The morality of the church, however, is founded on heteronomy.' 'True morality should be autonomous.' 'Hence, the church is unable to
bring forth "more than legal and routine virtue and piety."' Cited in J. Maier,
On Hegel's Critique of Kant (New York 1966), 19-20. Religion is to morality
as positive law is to natural law *as* heteronomy is to autonomy.
33 'The Leading Article,' 192
34 Because the estates [Stande] embodied both property and political rights,
Hegel sometimes referred to the Estates Assembly as 'Stande' or more
broadly as 'das standische Element,' the States General. Marx, however,
seemed always to make a distinction between 'der politische Staat,' 'Staat,'
and 'Stande.'
35 K. Marx, *A Contribution to the Critique of Political Economy* (Moscow 1970),
19: 'In the year 1842-43, as editor of the *RhZ*, I first found myself in the
embarrassing position of having to discuss what is known as material interests.
The deliberations of the Rhenish Landtag on forest thefts and the division of
landed property ... caused me in the first instance to turn my attention to economic questions.' Marx is saying that the laws on wood theft, etc., moved
him to turn to the study of political economy. But many commentators have
attempted to make much more of this statement. For example, R. Plant in
Hegel (London 1973) writes about Marx: 'His report for the *Rheinische
Zeitung* on the law concerning the stealing of wood from forests *led him to see
in the law not an expression of universal rationality*, but the undue influence of
one sectional group in civil society; the plight of the wine growers in the
Moselle region also constituted a concrete circumstance *which led Marx away
from his earlier Hegelian position*; the final breach occurred with the censorship
introduced by the government which involved the banning of the *Rheinische
Zeitung* ... The state appeared in reality very different from its transfigured
philosophical form, *being seen as the instrument of one sectional group and not
the guardian of the universal interest of society*' (195). The emphasis is added in
order to highlight three points. The first assumes that Marx made no distinction between the definition of law and existing laws; the second assumes
Marx was Hegelian; and the third misunderstands the nature of Marx's critique of the state.
36 'Debates on the Law on Thefts,' 245, 261
37 'On the Commissions of the Estates in Prussia,' MECW, 1, 305
38 'Debates on Freedom,' 150

39 'On the Commissions,' 297
40 Ibid, 306
41 'Communism and the Augsburg *Allgemeine Zeitung*,' MECW, 1, 220. In this period and in Hegel's writings, corporations were 'not the traditional, restrictive old guilds, but voluntary organizations into which persons organize themselves according to their professions, trades and interests.' S. Avineri, *Hegel's Theory of the Modern State* (Cambridge 1972), 164
42 N. Lobkowicz, *Theory and Practice* (Notre Dame 1967), 234-5
43 'Justification of the Correspondent from the Mosel,' MECW, 1, 348-49. This article on the Mosel region and the other on the law on wood theft formed, according to Heinz Lubasz, 'an essential part of Marx's initial problematic,' namely, 'the problem of poverty' (in *Political Studies*, XXIV, no. 1). The question of 'material interests' (to broaden Lubasz's point) was important in illuminating the inadequacies of Marx's approach, but it was only one of many issues analysed by Marx in this period.

The significance of the problem of poverty for Marx was the forceful evidence it provided of the enormous gulf between the interests of the state and the political state, the contradictory interests of the poor and the private interests represented by the government. Although Marx had perceived this dichotomy before he wrote these two articles, it was the analysis of these specific cases of 'material interests' which first highlighted the *contradictory* nature of these interests and which also pointed to the *inadequacy* of his proposal for a free press as a plausible solution and, more broadly, of his notion of 'theoretical practice.'

Interestingly enough, Marx himself makes much the same point as Lubasz. In *The Holy Family*, Marx writes concerning Proudhon: 'The first criticism of private property proceeds, of course, from the fact in which its contradictory essence appears in the form that is most perceptible and most glaring and most directly arouses man's indignation – from the fact of poverty, of misery.' MECW, 4, 34-5

44 'Justification,' 349
45 Hegel makes this same juxtaposition of 'society' and 'state' in his *Natural Law*, 65.
46 'Notes,' MECW 1, 85-86; letter to Ruge, 30 Nov. 1842, MECW, 1, 395; letter to Oppenheim, 25 Aug. 1842, MECW, 1, 392.

CHAPTER 2

1 'Preface,' *A Contribution to the Critique of Political Economy* (Moscow 1970), 20

2 There has been some debate over the period of composition of this manuscript. Rjazanov, the editor of the 1927 *Marx-Engels Historisch-Kritische Gesamtausgabe* (MEGA), suggested the period between March and August 1843.
Although others have suggested a date more than a year earlier, the evidence
tends to support the contention of Rjazanov; and the spring and summer of
1843 is now usually accepted as correct. For a fuller discussion of this question, see J. O'Malley, 'Editor's Introduction,' to K. Marx, *Critique of Hegel's
Philosophy of Right* (Cambridge 1970), xi, and A.F. McGovern, 'The Young
Marx on the State,' in *Science and Society*, 34, no. 4 (1970), 443. The manuscript remained unpublished in Marx's own day and was first published in
1927 in Rjazanov's MEGA. Its publication at this time produced different reac-
tions on the part of Western and 'Eastern' Marxists. For a discussion of the
differences, see L. Colletti, 'Introduction,' in Q. Hoare, ed., *Karl Marx: Early
Writings* (New York 1975).
  English quotations of Hegel are taken from T.M. Knox ed. and trans.,
Hegel's Philosophy of Right (Oxford 1975), hereafter *PR*. The German inter-
positions are taken from G.W.F. Hegel, *Grundlinien der Philosophie des Rechts*
in *Samtliche Werke* (Stuttgart 1964).
3 S. Avineri, 'Marx's critique of Hegel's "Philosophy of Right" in its systematic
setting,' *Cahiers de L'I.S.E.A.* (Aug. 1966), 47. Avineri writes: 'This study
[Marx's *Critique*] amounts to an application of Feuerbach's general critique of
Hegelian philosophy to the particular field of politics.' The same point is made
in his book (see below, note 5); and in his article, 'The Hegelian Origins of
Marx's Political Thought,' *Review of Metaphysics*, XXI, no. 1 (Sept. 1967). The
point is notable only for its superficiality and triteness. Similar views can be
found in, among others, L. Dupré, *The Philosophical Foundations of Marxism*
(New York 1966), 87.
  There are several exceptions to this view: for example, the work by A. Th.
van Leeuwen, *Critique of Heaven* (London 1972), and by J. Hyppolite, 'La
Conception Hégélienne de l'état et sa critique par Karl Marx,' in *Cahiers
internationaux de sociologie*, II (1947). For a rare sceptical view on Feuerbach's
influence on Marx, see the essay by I. Meszaros, 'The Controversy about
Marx,' in his *Marx's Theory of Alienation* (London 1970), 234-7.
4 L. Feuerbach, *The Essence of Christianity* (New York 1957), xxxv
5 'Marx's critique,' 46, and in his *The Social and Political Thought of Karl Marx*
(Cambridge 1968, 1975), 9
6 'Notebooks on Epicurean Philosophy,' MECW, 1, 458
7 But not in G. della Volpe, *Rousseau et Marx* (Paris 1974).
8 The examples are not difficult to find and they include some of the most
noted interpreters of Marx; see, for instance, G. Lukacs, 'Zur philosophischen

Entwicklung des jungen Marx,' in *Deutsche Zeitschrift für Philosophie*, 11, no. 2 (1954), 300, cited in J. Maguire, *Marx's Paris Writings* (Dublin 1972), 38.

9 See the Introduction above.

10 P.G. Stillman, 'Hegel's Critique of Liberal Theories of Right,' *American Political Science Review*, LXVIII, no. 3 (Sept. 1974)

11 *The Philosophy of History*, trans. J. Sibree (New York 1956), 456-7

12 Ibid, 449. Hegel writes: 'Plato in his *Republic* makes everything depend upon the Government, and makes Disposition the principle of the State.'

13 *PR*, 124. Hegel states: 'In Plato's state, subjective freedom does not count, because people have their occupations assigned to them by the Guardians' (280). For an excellent discussion of this 'failure of Greek ethics to achieve a notion of will,' see M.B. Foster, *The Political Philosophies of Plato and Hegel* (Oxford 1935), 131.

14 *PR*, 268

15 *The Philosophy of History*, 452. Hegel's political philosophy contains an incisive critique of liberalism. For an exposition of this critique in one section of his *Philosophy of Right*, see Stillman, 'Hegel's Critique of Liberal Theories of Right,' and J. Ritter, 'Personne et propriété selon Hegel,' *Archives de Philosophie*, XXXI, cahier 2 (avril-juin 1968).

16 *PR*, 156

17 5 March 1842, MECW, 1, 382-3. It is not likely Marx's intended criticism of Hegel was written at this time because of family difficulties and his increasing involvement with the *Rheinische Zeitung* later on.

18 G. Sabine, *A History of Political Theory* (London 1937, 1966), 166

19 These sections comprise paragraphs 257 to 320 of *PR*. As it was found, Marx's *Critique* began at paragraph 261 and ended at 313; but the first page was missing. Given the size of the pages, it was likely that Marx in fact began at paragraph 257.

20 *PR*, 160

21 *The Philosophy of Hegel* (New York 1924, 1955), 425

22 *PR*, 161

23 'Contribution to the Critique of Hegel's Philosophy of Law,' MECW, 3, 5 (hereafter 'Contribution'). Marx may well have criticized the initial paragraphs of the section on 'The State' in terms of these two points. For the German, see 'Kritik des Hegelschen Staatsrecht,' in *Marx/Engels Werke* (MEW), Band 1 (Berlin 1961), 203

24 'Contribution,' 6

25 See, for example, O'Malley, 'Editor's Introduction,' *Critique*, xxxviii.

26 'Contribution,' 7

27 Ibid, 8

28 Ibid, 9

29 Ibid, 11. Apparently Marx had written here 'organic,' although it is evident that 'inorganic' or 'mechanical' was intended.

30 Ibid, 12

31 Ibid, 13

32 Ibid, 14

33 Ibid, 18

34 *PR*, 179. The first two are 'the *general element* of the constitution and the laws, [and] consultation as the relation of the *particular* to the general.'

35 'Contribution,' 20

36 Ibid, 21

37 Ibid, 22

38 Ibid.

39 Ibid, 24. See also Stace, *The Philosophy of Hegel*, 431-3.

40 'Contribution,' 26

41 Ibid, 27

42 Ibid, 28

43 Ibid, 28

44 Ibid, 29. Marx's use of the concept of democracy clearly eludes R.N. Berki; see his 'Perspectives in the Marxian critique of Hegel's political philosophy,' in Z.A. Pelczynski, ed., *Hegel's Political Philosophy* (Cambridge 1971), 209.

45 'Contribution,' 37

46 Ibid, 38

47 Ibid, 41. For a worthwhile review of this section, see P. Naville, 'Critique de la bureaucratie,' in *Cahiers internationaux de sociologie*, XV (1953). For an unfortunately confusing review, see H. Lefebvre, *The Sociology of Marx* (New York 1968), 140-50.

48 'Contribution,' 48

49 *PR*, 154

50 Ibid, 360

51 'Contribution,' 48

52 Ibid, 49

53 Ibid, 50

54 Ibid. Hegel's attempt to construct an identity of civil society and state is also compared to 'the identity of *two hostile armies*, where every soldier has the "opportunity" to become, by "desertion," a member of the "hostile" army.' 'Indeed,' says Marx, 'Hegel herewith correctly describes the present empirical position.'

55 Ibid.
56 Ibid, 51. To this, Marx adds, 'The *examination* – this "link" between the "office of state" and the "individual," this objective bond between the knowledge of civil society and the knowledge of the state – is nothing but the *bureaucratic baptism of knowledge*, the official recognition of the transubstantiation of profane into sacred knowledge.'
57 Ibid, 52
58 Ibid, 53. Besides the 'hierarchical structure' there is 'the rights [Berechtigung] vested in local authorities and corporations.' But this 'protection' amounts to 'the unresolved conflict between bureaucracy and corporation.' '*Struggle*, the *possibility* of struggle, is the guarantee against defeat.' This is not exactly an identity. Furthermore, there is the civil servant himself: Hegel argues that his 'direct and moral education' should be a 'spiritual counterpoise' to the mechanical character of his knowledge and 'actual work.' As Marx clarifies it: 'The man within the official is supposed to secure the official against himself. But what unity!'
59 Ibid, 52
60 Ibid, 53
61 Ibid, 45
62 Ibid, 45
63 Note the similarity of this description to that in 'The Eighteenth Brumaire of Louis Bonaparte,' MECW, 11, 185-86.
64 'Contribution,' 46
65 Ibid, 48
66 Ibid, 54
67 Ibid, 55
68 There is irony in this criticism of Hegel for Hegel himself had harsh criticism for the advocates of gradualism. In his *Science of Logic* he writes: 'To explain appearance or destruction by the gradualness of the change means reducing the whole matter to absurd tautology and to imagining in an already complete state that which is in the course of appearing or being destroyed.' Cited in G.V. Plekhanov, *Fundamental Problems of Marxism* (London 1969), 46.
69 'Contribution,' 57
70 Ibid, 57
71 Ibid, 58
72 Ibid, 60
73 Ibid, 62
74 Ibid, 65
75 Ibid, 67-8
76 Ibid, 68

77 Ibid, 74

78 Ibid, 77

79 Ibid.

80 Ibid, 80

81 Ibid, 86

82 Ibid, 88. R.N. Berki does not understand Marx's position on mediation and as a result disavows the relation between Marx's discussion of 'extremes' and the critique of the state. See his 'Perspectives,' 206-7.

83 Ibid, 89

84 Ibid, 92-3

85 Ibid, 93

86 Ibid, 95

87 Ibid, 98

88 Ibid, 99

89 Ibid, 100

90 Ibid, 107

91 Ibid, 114

92 Ibid, 117

93 Ibid, 116

94 Ibid, 117

95 Ibid, 118

96 Ibid, 120-1. For just such a misinterpretation, see D. Howard, *The Development of the Marxian Dialectic* (Carbondale 1972), 77-8; and O'Malley, 'Editor's Introduction,' *Critique*, li.

97 'Contribution,' 121. In his 'Draft Plan for a Work on the Modern State,' Marx writes the following for the last part of his project: '*Suffrage*, the fight for the *abolition* of the state and of bourgeois society.' MECW, 4, 666

98 'Contribution,' 29

99 Ibid, 30

100 Ibid, 31

101 It is now possible to see the immense importance of this *Critique* in the development of Marx's thinking. Some commentators, however, have evaluated it less highly; for example, Meszaros, who writes in his *Marx's Theory of Alienation* that, with the grasping of the concept of alienated labour, 'the laboriously detailed analysis of particular fields of this philosophy – e.g., the earlier attempted "Critique of the Hegelian Philosophy of Right" – becomes superfluous' (19). Far from becoming superfluous, the *Critique* remains a trenchant critique of Hegel and of the modern constitutional system.

102 MECW, 3, 181

103 'Contribution,' 91

104 *Hegel's Logic*, W. Wallace trans. (Oxford 1975), 52
105 'Contribution,' 108

CHAPTER 3

1 There is, of course, an enormous range of issues and questions relating to particular states and to the relation of politics to other spheres of activity. But regarding political relations in themselves, Marx has made a thorough and profound analysis in the *Critique*. At least one commentator has recognized this point; L. Colletti writes: 'the *Critique* and the other shorter writings associated with it constitute a final, near-definitive step in the general theory of law and the state.' Introduction to *Karl Marx: Early Writings* (New York 1975), 48
2 Marx's own phrasing of this conclusion is found in his Preface to *A Contribution to the Critique of Political Economy* (Moscow 1970), 20.
3 'Letters from the *Deutsch-Französische Jahrbücher*,' MECW, 3, 134
4 D. Howard in *The Development of the Marxian Dialectic* (Carbondale 1972), accuses Marx of propounding in this letter 'the idealist theory that a revolution is a product of a change of consciousness,' and, furthermore, 'an idealist humanism whose "revolution" is a psychological phenomenon' (85). He is not alone in making such claims about this passage.
   Marx's use of the concept of shame may very well have derived from Hegel, who in *The Philosophy of Mind* wrote: 'In shame, one begins to be a little angry with oneself; for shame contains a reaction to the contradiction between what I appear to be and what I ought to and want to be, and is therefore a defence of my inner self against my incongruous appearance.' (Oxford 1976, 85) Shame in the Bible is the first reaction indicating man's 'fall' from innocence, shame is *in this myth* man's first step towards knowledge, self-consciousness; it is the initial mark of man's separation of subject and object. See *Hegel's Logic*, W. Wallace trans. (Oxford 1975), 42-3.
5 W.J. Brazill, *The Young Hegelians* (New Haven 1970), 90-1
6 'D-FJ Letters,' 134
7 Ibid, 138
8 Political relations disappear only under one condition, namely, under communism, where the separation of the universal and particular is resolved. Under despotism, political relations do not disappear but are completely one-sided: the embodiment of the whole, the state or dictator, imposes its will on the particular; the relationship is uni-directional.
9 'D-FJ Letters' 141
10 Ibid, 142

11 See Howard, *Development*, 89-90.

12 See D.J. Struik, Introduction to K. Marx, *Economic and Philosophic Manuscripts of 1844* (London 1973), 27-30, and K. Marx, *Economic and Philosophic Manuscripts of 1844*, MECW, 3, 295.

13 It is at this point that much of the letter reveals itself to be inspired by Hegel's Preface to *The Philosophy of Right*, a work Marx had just completed analysing, and by Hegel's Introduction to *The Philosophy of History*.

14 G.W.F. Hegel, *The Philosophy of History* (New York 1956), 19 and 49. Compare Marx's new formulation of his method to what Hegel wrote about his method: 'To consider a thing rationally means not to bring reason to bear on the object from the outside and so to tamper with it, but to find that the object is rational on its own account.' 'The sole task of philosophic science is to bring in to consciousness this proper work of the reason of the thing itself.' T.M. Knox trans., *Hegel's Philosophy of Right* (Oxford 1975), 35

15 See J. Macmurray, 'The Early Development of Marx's Thought,' in J. Lewis, K. Polyani, and D. Kitchin, eds., *Christianity and the Social Revolution* (London 1935).

16 Hegel, *The Philosophy of History*, 36

17 'D-FJ Letters,' 144

18 Ibid.

19 'On the Jewish Question,' MECW, 3, 147

20 Ibid, 149

21 Ibid, 151

22 Ibid, 152

23 Ibid, 153

24 Ibid, 154

25 Ibid, 155

26 Ibid, 159

27 Ibid, 160

28 Ibid, 161

29 Ibid, 162-3

30 Ibid, 164

31 Ibid.

32 Ibid, 165

33 Ibid, 167

34 Ibid, 168

35 Ibid, 170

36 Ibid, 171-3

37 Ibid, 174

38 Ibid.

39 K. Marx, 'The Question of Centralisation in Itself and with Regard to the Supplement to no. 137 of the *Rheinische Zeitung*,' MECW, 1, 182

40 See L. Feuerbach, *The Essence of Christianity*, trans. G. Eliot (New York 1957), and D. Strauss, *The Life of Jesus*, trans. G. Eliot (New York 1960).

41 'Contribution to the Critique of Hegel's Philosophy of Law, Introduction,' MECW, 3, 175-6

42 Ibid, 176

43 Ibid, 181

44 Ibid, 182

45 Ibid, 182. Compare to Feuerbach's 'categorical imperative': 'Hence, we have this categorical imperative: Do not wish to be a philosopher in contrast to being a Man; be nothing more than a thinking Man; do not think as a thinker, that is, with a faculty torn out of the totality of the real being of man and set up as something in and for itself! Think as a real, living being, as one exposed to the vivifying and refreshing surge of the sea of worldly experience; think in existence, in the world as a part of it, not in the vacuum of abstraction, like an isolated monad, an absolute monarch, an indifferent god! Then for a certainty thy thoughts will be unities of being and thought.' *The Philosophy of the Future* (New York 1966), 83

46 'Introduction,' 182. For the similarity of Marx's use of 'categorical imperative' to Hegel's use, see Hegel's definition of 'the judgement of necessity' which is 'the categorical judgement,' in Wallace trans., *Hegel's Logic*, 241. For the meaning of the concept in Kant, see J. Ebbinghaus, 'Interpretation and Misinterpretation of the Categorical Imperative,' in R.P. Wolff ed., *Kant* (Notre Dame 1967), 213. For a misinterpretation of Marx's use of the concept, see I. Meszaros, *Marx's Theory of Alienation* (London 1970), 75, where the author regards this 'categorical imperative' as an 'early' and problematic formulation by Marx.

47 'Introduction,' 183. Marx begins this argument with the sentence: 'For revolutions require a *passive* ['passiven'] element, a *material* basis.' The notion of a '*passive* element' has given rise to such interpretations as found in N. Lobkowicz's book, *Theory and Practice* (Notre Dame 1967); he wrote: 'Still he [Marx] seems to have looked at the proletariat just as any "planner" would look around for someone to carry out his ideas.' This suggestion would appear to be a misinterpretation in light of the fact that Marx clearly stated that the critic was to make real struggles the subject or starting point of his critique. Given this, he saw the critic as providing the proletariat with a coherent analysis of its own predicament and historic role; the critic was to be only the theoretical side of a struggle already in process or implicit in the social system.

The 'passive element' is the 'material basis.' Revolutions require a material basis because they cannot happen in a vacuum or in the realm of ideas. The 'material basis' in this case is the proletariat; it may be described as 'passive' in so far as initially it exists only 'in itself' but not 'for itself,' when it has come into being but as yet lacks consciousness of itself, when its essence is but a potentiality. The role of the critic is to discover through empirical analysis the implicit meaning of the proletariat and to articulate its nature. Marx's argument here points to the fact that while the critic may grasp the intrinsic meaning of the proletariat, he may find himself in a society *without* a material basis. The problem can be inverted: a system may produce a large proletariat and, at the same time, the material and ideological conditions which militate against the development of the theory necessary for it to become 'for itself.'

48 'Introduction,' 186
49 Ibid.
50 Ibid, 187
51 S. Avineri, 'The Hegelian Origins of Marx's Political Thought,' in *Review of Metaphysics*, XXI, no. 1 (Sept. 1967), 40; Lobkowicz, *Theory and Practice*, 288; C. Wackenheim, *La Faillite de la religion d'après Karl Marx* (Paris 1963), 200; D. McLellan, *Marx before Marxism* (Harmondsworth 1972), 203
52 'On the Commissions of the Estates in Prussia,' MECW, 1, 306
53 'Marginal Notes to the Accusations of the Ministerial Rescript,' ibid, 363
54 'Justification of the Correspondent from the Mosel,' ibid, 349
55 F. Engels, 'News from Prussia' and 'Further Particulars of the Silesian Riots,' MECW, 3, 531, 533
56 'Critical Marginal Notes on the Article "The King of Prussia and Social Reform,"' MECW, 3, 193
57 Ibid, 194
58 Ibid, 197
59 Ibid, 198
60 Ibid, 199
61 Ibid, 201
62 Ibid, 204
63 Ibid, 205
64 Ibid, 206

CHAPTER 4

1 'Contribution to the Critique of Hegel's Philosophy of Law,' in *Marx-Engels, Collected Works* (MECW), 3, 99-100

2 'Letters from *Deutsch-Französische Jahrbücher*,' ibid, 141; and K. Marx, 'Contribution to the Critique of Hegel's Philosophy of Law: Introduction,' ibid, 184-5

3 The first English translation was published in 1959. For a brief description of the contents of the unpublished notes see M. Rubel, 'Les Cahiers de lecture de Karl Marx, Part I, 1840-1853,' *International Review of Social History*, II (1957).

4 I. Meszaros, *Marx's Theory of Alienation* (London 1970), 11

5 Meszaros, like many others, is constrained by a preconception that the 1844 manuscripts represent a radical departure from the work prior to 1844; as a consequence, he does not look for continuity between works.

6 See, for example, J. Maguire, *Marx's Paris Writings: An Analysis* (Dublin 1972); B. Ollman, *Alienation* (Cambridge 1971).

7 The notion of a 'break' or a discontinuity between the Paris manuscripts and Marx's earlier work is widely accepted as beyond question; for example: N. Lobkowicz, *Theory and Practice* (Notre Dame 1967), 374: 'the Critique of Political Economy found in the *Manuscripts* is in no way a "logical consequence" of the ideas which Marx had developed in the *Deutsch-Französische Jahrbücher*.'

Meszaros, *Alienation*, 75: 'In the *Economic and Philosophic Manuscripts of 1844*, however, Marx makes a crucial step forward, radically superseding the "political partiality" of his own orientation and the limitations of a conceptual framework that characterized his development in its phase of "revolutionary democratism."' Meszaros also writes: 'Once in possession of this key [the concept of "labour's self-alienation"] that opens the doors of the Hegelian system as a whole, exposing to a comprehensive social criticism all its "secrets" and "mystifications," the laboriously [sic] detailed analysis of particular fields of this philosophy – e.g., the earlier attempted "Critique of the Hegelian Philosophy of Right" – becomes superfluous' (19). Such statements testify to Meszaros' mistaken comprehension of the continuity in Marx's work. He prefers to find an *unconscious* continuity rather than a conscious one.

E. Mandel, *The Formation of the Economic Thought of Karl Marx* (London 1977), 158: 'What we have here [in the manuscripts] is the *transition* of the young Marx from Hegelian and Feuerbachian philosophy to the working out of historical materialism.' L. Althusser, *For Marx* (London 1977), 156: 'the *Manuscripts* were the result of *Marx's discovery of political economy*.'

Discussions of this question of discontinuity may be found in: Mandel, *Formation*, chap. 10; Meszaros, *Alienation*, chap. VIII; I. Fetscher, 'The Young Marx and the Old Marx,' in N. Lobkowicz, ed., *Marx and the Western World* (Notre Dame 1967).

8 Although these questions remain to be demonstrated to be Marx's organizational rationale for the manuscripts, it can be seen that *if* they are the rationale such statements as the following by P. Naville indicate the limitations of his appreciation: the manuscripts 'terminate without coming to a conclusion, their writing having doubtless been stopped by external circumstances. Finally, the separate parts lack homogeneity.' *De l'aliénation à la jouissance* (Paris 1957, 1967), cited in E. Mandel, *The Formation*, 159. In light of our questions, it will be seen that the manuscripts do come to conclusions (i.e., the answers) and that the separate parts do reveal a homogeneity.

9 The first three titles were Marx's own; the title 'alienated labour' was added by the editors of the MEGA; in the original, there is no title preceding this section.

10 (New York 1937, 1965), chap. VIII, 64

11 Ibid, 51. Maguire sees this assertion by Marx as setting him apart from 'orthodox economics,' but it is, on the contrary, derived from 'orthodox economics.' See Maguire, *Marx's Paris Writings*, 43-4.

12 'Economic and Philosophic Manuscripts of 1844,' MECW, 3, 239 (hereafter EPM). This title is *not* Marx's title; if his plans to publish this work had materialized, the title he suggested was 'A Critique of Politics and of Political Economy.' By taking the 'Economic and Philosophic Manuscripts' as Marx's title, some writers have managed to compose a great many lines on Marx's intention and meaning. See, for example, J. van der Hoeven, *Karl Marx: The Roots of His Thought* (Assen 1976), 66-67.

13 EPM, 239-40

14 Ibid, 244

15 Ibid, 246-7

16 See note 21 in chap. 1.

17 Mandel appears to ignore Marx's reason for raising the difference between fixed and circulating capital and argues only that the use of these terms indicates Marx had not yet distinguished the concepts of constant and variable capital. *The Formation*, 32. Maguire misinterprets the reason Marx raises the distinction between fixed and circulating capital. *Marx's Paris Writings*, 47

18 EPM, 251

19 Ibid, 260

20 Ibid, 263. Smith writes: 'The interest of the first [landed property] ... is strictly and inseparably connected with the general interest of the society.' *Wealth of Nations*, 248

21 EPM, 264

22 Ibid, 269

23 Ibid, 270

24 Ibid, 271; K. Marx, F. Engels, *Werke*, Ergänzungband (Berlin 1968), 511

25 EPM, 272

26 Ibid.

27 Ibid, 273

28 Ibid, 274

29 G. Lukacs, *History and Class Consciousness* (London 1971), xxiv: 'Thus "alienation" when taken to its logical conclusion is identical with objectification. Therefore, when the identical subject-object transcends alienation it must also transcend objectification at the same time. But as, according to Hegel, the object, the thing exists only as an alienation from self-consciousness, to take it back into the subject would mean the end of objective reality and thus of any reality at all. *History and Class Consciousness* follows Hegel in that it too equates alienation with objectification (to use the term employed by Marx in the *Economic-Philosophic Manuscripts*).'

For Hegel, the identification means the end of reality; for Lukacs, it would seem to mean that socialist man would no longer produce, would no longer externalize himself in the real world. Lukacs also points out that this identification led some philosophers to see alienation as 'an eternal "*condition humaine*."' The 'philosophers of despair,' the existentialists, were transfixed by their failure to distinguish alienation and objectification.

Marx was fully aware of this problem in Hegel; in 1844 in a preserved note on *The Phenomenology of Mind*, Marx writes: 'Abolition of *estrangement* is identified with abolition of objectivity.' 'Hegel's Construction of the Phenomenology,' MECW, 4, 665

30 These implications, i.e., the consequent forms of alienation, which are discussed by Marx in the next several pages of the text, will be expounded here *very briefly* because the secondary literature on Marx has already lent an inordinate amount of space to their exposition.

31 EPM, 275. For a definition of 'species-being [Gattungswesen]' see the appended glossary.

32 Ibid, 276-7. In the same way, human knowledge accumulated throughout history, in the form of philosophy and science, becomes a means for the advancement of private property.

33 Ibid, 277

34 Ibid, 279. *Most translations change the word with the asterisk from men [Menschen] to powers [Machte].

35 Ibid.

36 Ibid, 280. This deduction by Marx (i.e., private property as a consequence of alienated labour) has given rise to much discussion in several commentaries on the manuscripts. The objections to Marx's formulation are varied and also

too long and complex to reproduce here. We can, however, identify the commentators/analysts and also defend Marx's argument by way of elaborating it.

See, for example, J. Plamenatz, *Karl Marx's Philosophy of Man* (Oxford 1975), 147-60; Lobkowicz, *Theory and Practice*, 310-12; and W. Jahn, 'Der ökonomische Inhalt des Begriffs der Entfremdung der Arbeit in den Frühschriften von Karl Marx,' *Wirtschaftswissenschaft*, no. 6, (1957), cited favourably in Mandel, *The Formation*, 161.

The origin of alienated labour, according to Marx, is found in the rudimentary exchange of the products of one's labour. In the *Grundrisse*, he writes that in simple exchange, property is posited 'only as the appropriation of the product of labour by labour, and of the product of alien labour by one's own labour, insofar as the product of one's own labour is bought by alien labour.' 'In the further development of exchange value this will be transformed, and it will ultimately be shown that private property in the product of one's own labour is identical with the separation of labour and property, so that labour will create alien property and property will command alien labour.' *Grundrisse* (Harmondsworth 1973), 238. In *Capital*, in the chapter on 'Exchange,' Marx makes a similar but more detailed analysis of exchange and private property. Rudimentary or primitive exchange, the exchange of the products of one's own labour, the estrangement of these products, *implies* a form of property. The development of a system of exchange, of a system of alienated products of one's own labour, gives rise to private property. See the Appendix.

37 EPM, 280. The translators/editors of the EPM in MECW, 3, find it necessary to footnote a comment on Marx's discussion of wages, alleging that by 'wages' and 'wage-labour' Marx means 'the capitalist system as such.' On the contrary, Marx's discussion of wages clearly suggests that the persistence of wages anywhere signifies the persistence of alienated labour and therefore a relationship of a capitalist nature between producers and society or producers and non-producers. This interpretation has obvious implications for the Soviet Union.

38 Ibid.

39 These notes were written about the same time as the EPM. They were first published in full only in 1932 in the *Gesamtausgabe*. In English, they were first published in full only in 1975, although portions of the notes were published in the late 1960s.

40 'Comments on James Mill, *Éléments d'économie politique*,' MECW, 3, 212. All subsequent quotations, unless otherwise indicated, are on this same page.

41 See *Grundrisse*, 145 and 157, and *Capital*, 1 (New York 1967), 73 and 94. In both works, private property has become the commodity; i.e., private property produced solely for exchange.

42 'Comments on James Mill,' 213

43 Ibid, 214

44 Ibid.

45 Ibid, 215

46 Ibid, 216

47 Ibid. Almost every aspect of the discussion of credit and banking in these 'Comments on James Mill' may be found in vol. 3 of *Capital*. A detailed examination of the ideas of those 'socialists' who saw in credit the demise of money (Saint Simon and Proudhon) is also in vol. 3, chap. XXXVI.

48 EPM, 281

49 'Comments on James Mill,' 217

50 Ibid, 218

51 Ibid, 219

52 EPM, 323

53 Ibid, 324. This quotation contains in German several puns on money, separation, and chemistry. (See *Marx-Engels Werke*, 565.)

54 'Comments on James Mill,' 220

55 EPM, 290

56 Ibid, 248. Adam Smith is cited as follows: 'He [the capitalist] would have no *interest* in employing the workers, unless he expected from the sale of their work something more than is necessary to replace the stock advanced by him as wages.' In classical theory, the rate of interest meant simply the rate of return on the capital invested.

57 Ibid, 283

58 Ibid, 284

59 Ibid, 285

60 Ibid, 289

61 Ibid, 294

62 Ibid, 285. L. Dupré, among others, remarks that in the manuscripts, 'Marx fails to show *how* the same necessity which causes man's estrangement will also cause his liberation.' *The Philosophical Foundations of Marxism* (New York 1966), 135

63 'Contribution to the Critique of Hegel's Philosophy of Law,' MECW, 3, 79; and 'Kritik des Hegelschen Staatsrecht,' in *Marx-Engels, Werke*, Band 1 (Berlin 1961), 275

64 EPM, 294

65 'Letters from the *Deutsch-Französische Jahrbücher*,' MECW, 3, 143

66 EPM, 295

67 Ibid, 296. The classic depiction of this 'positive community' in the ancient world is found in Plato's *Republic*. Aristotle makes the first critique of Plato's community of wives, children, and property in *The Politcs*, II.

68 EPM, 296
69 Aristotle, 'Posterior Analytics,' in *The Philosophy of Aristotle*, ed. R. Bambrough (New York 1963), 166-7; see also, Aristotle, *Metaphysics* ed. and trans. J. Warrington (London 1956), 9, on the concept of 'nature.'
70 EPM 296
71 'Comments on James Mill,' 227-8
72 EPM, 299
73 Ibid, 306
74 'Comments on James Mill,' 217-18. The argument presented here is clear but implicit in the manuscripts and the 'Comments on James Mill.' It is succinctly and explicitly stated in *Capital*, 1, 763.
75 EPM, 343
76 Ibid, 328
77 Ibid, 313
78 Ibid, 341-2
79 Ibid, 305
80 Ibid, 342. About atheism and communism, Marx says: 'They are but the first real emergence, the actual realisation for man of man's essence and of his essence as something real.'
81 The text makes it clear that Marx saw labour, defined broadly as productive activity, as the essence of man; that is, man's relations to others are established via his activity and man's relations are what man is.
82 EPM, 306ff. See also M. Lebowitz, 'Capital and the Production of Needs,' in *Science and Society* (1979); J.J. O'Malley, 'History and Man's "Nature" in Marx,' in *The Review of Policies*, 28 (Oct. 1966); and A. Heller, *The Theory of Need in Marx* (London 1976).
83 EPM, 332-3

CHAPTER 5

1 Marx and Engels themselves suggest that they are reiterations of theories already worked out. For example, in *The Holy Family*, they write: 'Critical Criticism makes it necessary to assert, in contrast to it, the already achieved results *as such*.' MECW, 4, 7. In *The German Ideology* and *The Poverty of Philosophy* there are many references to the arguments made in the articles published in the *Deutsch-Französische Jahrbücher* and asserted in *The Holy Family*. It must be noted that the presentation of political questions in these works, up to and including *The Communist Manifesto*, takes the form of *assertion* for the most part, and *not argumentation*. For this reason, the material is not nearly as interesting to follow as the earlier writings up to 1844.
2 MECW, 4, 666. This is presumed to have been written in November 1844.

3 *The Holy Family* was written in Paris in the autumn of 1844. 'In the spring of 1845,' writes Engels, 'we met again in Brussels, [and] Marx had already *fully developed his* materialist theory of history in its main features.' (emphasis added) F. Engels, 'On the History of the Communist League' (1885), in *Marx-Engels, Selected Works*, II (Moscow 1949), 312. See also Engels, 'Preface to the German Edition of 1883,' in *Marx-Engels, Selected Works*, 1 (Moscow 1962), 24.

4 See A. Ruge's letter to Feuerbach, 15 May 1844, where he writes: 'Marx veut ... écrire l'histoire de la Convention, il a accumulé à cet effet la documentation néccsaire et est arrivé à des conceptions nouvelles et très fécondes. [Il] veut utiliser son séjour à Paris pour ecrire ce livre sur la Convention.' See Ruge's letter to Fleischer to the same effect, cited in A. Cornu, *Karl Marx et Friedrich Engels*, 3 (Paris 1962), 11. See also Engels' reference to the numerous books on the French Revolution in Marx's library, cited in J. Bruhat, 'La Révolution française et la formation de la pensée de Marx,' *Société des études robespièrristes* (1964?), 141-2.

5 Cornu, *Marx et Engels*, 11

6 See also Marx's comments in the Preface to the Paris manuscripts. MECW, 3, 231.

7 'Draft Plan for a Work on the Modern State,' MECW, 4, 666.

8 The significance of the French Revolution that Marx drew out in 1843 was very likely at least implicit in the lectures on law and history taught by Edward Gans, a professor at Berlin and admirer of Hegel. Gans' enthusiasm for the French Revolution was well known. See Bruhat, 'La Révolution française,' 132. See also A. Stern, 'Hegel et les idées de 1789,' *Revue philosophiques*, no. 9-12 (1939); L.D. Rosca, 'Hegel sur la Révolution bourgeoise de France, 1789-1794,' *Nouvelles études d'histoires* (Bucharest 1965), 459-75; and J.F. Suter, 'Burke, Hegel and The French Revolution,' in Z.A. Pelczynski, ed., *Hegel's Political Philosophy* (Cambridge 1971).

9 'Contribution to the Critique of Hegel's Philosophy of Law,' MECW, 3, 80

10 'Critical Marginal Notes on the Article by a Prussian,' MECW, 3, 199

11 C. Brinton, *The Jacobins* (New York 1930, 1968), 219-20

12 *The Holy Family*, MECW, 4, 124

13 See Marx, 'Critical Marginal Notes,' 199, where Marx writes: 'The principle of politics is the *will*. The more one-sided and, therefore, the more perfected the *political* mind is, the more does it believe in the *omnipotence* of the will, and the more incapable it is therefore of discovering the source of social ills.'

14 'Moralising Criticism and Critical Morality,' MECW, 6, 319

15 Ibid, 319-20

16 MECW, 6, 498

17 In *The German Ideology*, Marx writes: 'Free competition inside the nation itself had everywhere to be won by a revolution – 1640 and 1688 in England, 1789 in France.' MECW, 5, 72-3

18 Bruhat writes: 'La révolution de 1789 avec son prolongement consulaire et impérial a permis à Marx d'éclairer le probleme de l'Etat et de se degager d'une conception toute hégélienne d'un Etat réalisation de l'Idée absolue.' 'La Révolution française,' 164. It is easy enough to agree with the first assertion by Bruhat, but the notion that Marx's study of the French Revolution allowed him 'to disengage himself' from a Hegelian concept of state requires first of all a demonstration that Marx held a Hegelian concept of the state. This is not an easy task.

19 See Bruhat, 'La Révolution française,' and A. Cornu, 'Karl Marx et la Révolution française,' *La Pensée*, no. 81 (Sept.-Oct. 1958).

20 'On the Jewish Question,' MECW, 3, 160

21 Ibid, 166

22 Ibid.

23 *The Holy Family*, 113

24 Ibid.

25 Max Stirner was the pseudonym of Johann Caspar Schmidt (1806-56), a Young Hegelian and author of *The Ego and His Own* [*Der Einzige und sein Eigenthum*] (1844). At least two-thirds of volume I of *The German Ideology* consists of Marx's critique of this book.

26 *The German Ideology*, 205

27 *The Poverty of Philosophy*, MECW, 6, 118

28 'On the Jewish Question,' 163

29 *The German Ideology*, 479

30 *The Holy Family*, 115

31 Ibid, 114. The point is very similar to that which Marx in 1843 made against Hegel who 'despised' certain theories which demanded 'the "separation" of the civil from the political estates.' The issue, says Marx, 'is the disputed question of a *representative* versus *estates* constitution. The representative constitution is a great advance, since it is the *frank, undistorted, consistent* expression of the *modern condition of the state*. It is an *unconcealed contradiction*.' 'Contribution,' 75. Whereas Bauer saw 'the modern condition' as the realization of human emancipation, Hegel saw it as contrary to the human definition, the concept of man.

32 *The Holy Family*, 116

33 See chap. 1 above.

34 *The Holy Family*, 116

35 'On the Jewish Question,' 163

36 *The German Ideology*, 329. See also *Die deutsche Ideologie*, in *Marx-Engels Werke*, Band 3 (Berlin 1962), 311.
37 *The German Ideology*, 330
38 *The Poverty of Philosophy*, 147
39 *The Communist Manifesto*, 501
40 *The German Ideology*, 330
41 For a very problematic exposition of Marx's position on the nature of crime, see P.Q. Hirst, 'Marx and Engels on Law, Crime and Morality,' in I. Taylor, P. Walton, and J. Young, eds., *Critical Criminology* (London 1975).
42 *The Holy Family*, 179. See also MEW, 2, 190. For a discussion of Hegel's theory of punishment, see D.E. Cooper, 'Hegel's Theory of Punishment,' in Z.A. Pelczynski, ed., *Hegel's Political Philosophy* (Cambridge 1971). See also G.W.F. Hegel, *Natural Law*, trans. T.M. Knox (Philadelphia 1975), 92ff.
43 'Moralising Criticism,' 328
44 *The German Ideology*, 201
45 'Moralising Criticism,' 329
46 *The Principles of Political Economy and Taxation* (London 1943), 145-7
47 'The Communism of the *Rheinischer Beobachter*,' MECW, 6, 225
48 'Moralising Criticism,' 329
49 Preface to *A Contribution to the Critique of Political Economy* (Moscow 1970), 20
50 *The German Ideology*, 89. The reference to the emergence of the concept of civil society was very likely derived from the book by A. Ferguson, *Essay on the History of Civil Society* (1789), which was well known to Marx.
51 *The German Ideology*, 89
52 As Marx wrote to Annenkov in 1846: 'I am using the [French] word *commerce* here in its widest sense, as we use *Verkehr* in German.' *Marx-Engels, Selected Correspondence* (New York 1934), 8
53 *The German Ideology*, 50
54 Ibid, 41ff
55 Ibid, 46
56 Ibid, 32
57 Ibid.
58 Ibid, 47
59 Because the relations between individuals appears to be the relations of atoms, it is easily concluded that the state holds civil life together. It is the other way around, in fact, argues Marx. Following a discussion of the nature of need under a system of private property, Marx writes: 'it is *natural necessity*, the *essential human properties* however estranged they may seem to be, and *interest* that hold the members of civil society together; *civil*, not *political* life is their

real tie. It is therefore not the *state* that holds the *atoms* of civil society together, but the fact that they are *atoms* only in imagination, in the *heaven* of their fancy, but in *reality* beings tremendously different from atoms, in other words, not *divine* egoists, but *egoistic human beings*. Only *political superstition* still imagines today that civil life must be held together by the state, whereas in reality, on the contrary, the state is held together by civil life.' *The Holy Family*, 120-1

60 *The German Ideology*, 35-6
61 Ibid, 90
62 See Marx's discussions of historical epochs, wherein the analytical tools are the instruments of production, the division of labour, and the relations of property. Ibid, 32-5, 41-3, 46-8, 63-74
63 See ibid, 52: 'In the development of productive forces there comes a stage, a development brought into existence out of the forces of production and means of intercourse, under which the existing relations cause only harm, in which they are no longer productive forces but destructive forces (machinery and money).' See also 'Letter to Annenkov,' 28 Dec. 1846, in *Selected Correspondence*, 8: 'Men never relinquish what they have won, but this does not mean that they never relinquish the social form in which they have acquired certain productive forces. On the contrary, in order that they may not be deprived of the result attained, and forfeit the fruits of civilisation, they are obliged, from the moment when the form of their intercourse (Fr. Commerce) no longer corresponds to the productive forces acquired, to change all their traditional social forms.' See also *The Communist Manifesto*, 489-90.
64 Preface to *Critique of Political Economy*, 21
65 *The Communist Manifesto*, 489
66 *The German Ideology*, 43
67 Ibid, 74
68 Ibid, 86: 'The division of labour implies from the outset the division of the *conditions* of labour [der Arbeitsbedingungen], of tools and materials, and thus the fragmentation of accumulated capital among different owners, and thus, also, the fragmentation between capital and labour, and the different forms of property itself.' MEW, 3, 66
69 *The German Ideology*, 85
70 Ibid, 86-7
71 Ibid, 87
72 Ibid, 88
73 Ibid.
74 Ibid, 49

75 Ibid, 64. There is a parallel here to the development of philosophy; just as the development of a totality of the productive forces obliges a transformation of the formerly corresponding relations of production, so the development of philosophy into a totality obliges philosophy to transform the reality on which it rests. See MECW, 1, 491.

CONCLUSIONS

1 For a discussion of how Marx and Engels viewed the English revolutions of 1640 and 1688, see C. Hill, 'The English Civil War Interpreted by Marx and Engels,' *Science and Society*, XII, no. 1 (winter 1948).
2 C.B. Macpherson, *The Political Theory of Possessive Individualism* (Oxford 1962), 270. There appears to be general agreement on these three principles: see G.H. Sabine, *A History of Political Theory* (1937, 1966), 546-47. If by modern political theory we mean theory founded on these principles of liberalism, we mean by classical political theory that which emphasizes the collectivity, the unity of the members of the state. Specifically, we are referring to the theories associated with Plato, Aristotle, Cicero, and Seneca, and medieval theories embodying a notion of divine harmony.
3 'On the Jewish Question,' MECW, 3, 155
4 In so far as some American political scientists boast about the American political system as the most highly developed and perfect form of liberal democracy, they are correct – in one sense but not in another. They are correct in so far as they point to their political system as the completion of political forms; that is to say, American republicanism is the highest development of political relations, the most complete separation of public and private spheres. But they are incorrect in so far as they assume that this political form as the perfection of political forms is the end of human development.

This culmination of political relations also gives rise to the notion of 'the end of ideology.' Ideology, as with political theory, does come to an end with the penetration of capital into every sphere of production, but not in the sense of its being over with, i.e., no longer necessary because man is perfected, which is, of course, the notion implicit in such claims; rather, in the sense that bourgeois ideology is the end, the last form of ideology, the only one which remains before all ideology is done away with, with the transcendence of political or class society.
5 Hegel has been seen in this light as representing the final criticism of liberal theory, in the realm of theory. His arguments against liberalism, it is suggested, have not been exceeded in depth and breadth by any critic to the present day, save Marx, whose criticism was not so much against liberal the-

ory as its reality, the modern state. The article by Z.A. Pelczynski, 'Hegel's Political Philosophy: Its Relevance Today,' in Pelczynski, ed., *Hegel's Political Philosophy* (Cambridge 1971), tacitly supports this view of Hegel, but unfortunately his appreciation of Marx's critique of Hegel is without much insight.

6 P.G. Stillman, 'Hegel's Critique of Liberal Theories of Right,' *American Political Science Review*, LXVIII, no. 3 (Sept. 1974); J. Ritter, 'Personne et propriété selon Hégel,' *Archives de Philosophie*, XXXI, cahier 2 (avril-juin 1968). These two articles make the case argued here very well, but their arguments are confined to the first part of the *Philosophy of Right*, namely, 'Abstract Right.' Hegel's critique of liberalism, however, can be found in every section of the work.

7 'Contribution to the Critique of Hegel's Philosophy of Right,' MECW, 3, 63. On page 91, Marx writes: 'Hegel's chief error is to conceive the *contradiction of appearances* as *unity in essence, in the idea*, while in fact it has something more profound for its essence, namely an *essential contradiction*.'

8 Jean-Jacques Rousseau, *The Social Contract*, chap. IX, 'Of Real Property.' J. Bentham, *Theory of Legislation*, as cited in W.T. Jones, ed., *Masters of Political Thought* (London 1947), 368ff. C.B. Macpherson, 'Liberalism and the Political Theory of Property,' in A. Kontos, ed., *Domination* (Toronto 1975). C.B. Macpherson, ed., *Property* (Toronto 1978). B. Barry, *The Liberal Theory of Justice* (Oxford 1975), 166. (This book is a critical review of John Rawls, *A Theory of Justice*, 1971.)

APPENDIX

1 *Economic and Philosophic Manuscripts of 1844*, MECW, 3, 279-80 (hereafter cited as EPM).

2 (Harmondsworth 1972), 224

3 (Oxford 1975), 148

4 (London 1977), 161

5 Ibid, 162. Plamenatz agrees with this point; see *Marx's Philosophy of Man*, 149.

6 MECW, 5, 48. How 'estrangement' was mistakenly employed by the Young Hegelians is explained by Marx on 88-9.

7 EPM, 317

8 K. Marx, 'Comments on James Mill, *Éléments d'économie politique*,' in MECW, 3, 220-1; see also, K. Marx, EPM,' 321.

9 EPM, 281

10 MECW, 5, 46

11 'Comments on James Mill,' 220-1. Given this, one can better understand Marx's affection for Aeschylus' play *Prometheus Bound*.

12 *The German Ideology*, MECW, 5, 42-3
13 Ibid, 46
14 Ibid, 32
15 Marx to Annenkov, 28 Dec. 1846, in Marx and Engels, *Selected Correspondence* (New York 1934), 8. 'Verkehr': traffic, movement to and fro (of persons), intercourse, connection, commerce, trade, communication.
16 *The German Ideology*, 72
17 *Grundrisse* (Harmondsworth 1973), 491-9 and 238
18 'Comments on James Mill,' 217-19
19 *Capital*, 1 (New York 1967), 87-8, see also 73.
20 Ibid, 42
21 EPM, 321

Glossary of Concepts

The comprehension of any philosophy or science requires an accurate grasp of the concepts employed: hence, this glossary of the main concepts found in Marx's early works.

There are other reasons for providing a glossary, which are specific to Marx's writings; that is, there are certain difficulties peculiar to his work. First, many of his concepts, because they derive from ancient Greek and classical German philosophy and from classical political economy, have passed out of contemporary use; they may thus give to his work the appearance of an archaic or abstruse philosophy, or they may render it incomprehensible to those not familiar with these traditions. Often a concept has persisted but the meaning has changed, producing inconsistencies of interpretation or, again, incomprehension. Second, Marx often clarified concepts in philosophy and political economy, giving them a rigour which they did not previously possess. Third, the misuse and popularization of some of Marx's concepts has made them considerably less rigorous than they ever were; certain concepts with precise meaning have become empty slogans. Fourth, the prevalence of certain philosophical/methodological tendencies in the West has made the comprehension of Aristotelian/Hegelian notions which are central to Marx very difficult. Fifth, a decidedly unscientific approach is commonly taken towards the analysis of the early works by Marxists and non-Marxists alike; often arguments are not substantiated with evidence from the texts; and rarely are key concepts carefully defined. As a consequence, opinion and accepted 'wisdom' often pass for knowledge.

We can *begin* to overcome these difficulties by defining the key concepts as we understand Marx to have used them with as much precision as possible.

ABOLITION [Aufhebung]
This concept is variously translated as sublation, supersession, transformation, transcendence, transubstantiation, overcoming, annulling, etc. It is suggested that

the immediate source of this concept in Marx is Hegel's work, where it integrates two seemingly contradictory notions: to abolish, i.e., to annul, to cancel, to do away with; and to preserve, i.e., to retain, to keep intact. The combination of these notions designates a dialectical transition in which the two sides of an open contradiction are merged or transformed to produce a result which takes a new form as the unity of the sides. In this result, this new form, the contradiction is annulled as a form of opposition but preserved as unity. See W. Wallace, trans., *Hegel's Logic*, 142.

ABSTRACT AND CONCRETE UNIVERSALS (Concepts)
This distinction derives from Hegel and is well expressed by one of his latter-day interpreters: 'An abstract universal is a genus which does not contain its species within itself. A wholly new conception of the nature of universals has to be evolved if deduction is to be possible, a conception according to which the universal, the genus, contains its differentiae (q.v.) and its species within itself, so that they can be extricated from it by a logical deduction. Such universals are called by Hegel *concrete* universals, and the discovery of their nature was the great advance which Hegel claimed to have made upon previous philosophers.' W.T. Stace, *The Philosophy of Hegel* (New York 1966), 84. For a discussion by Hegel, see W. Wallace, trans., *Hegel's Logic*, 229ff.

This description, while made of Hegel's distinction, is perfectly valid for Marx. By way of clarification we can draw examples of each from the early works. The concept of the state (society) or man as an organic unity of the whole and its parts is an abstract universal. It is perfectly valid in its own right *as an abstraction* relevant to all societies; but it does not contain the *differentiae* which would allow deductions from it to explain its 'species,' i.e., particular forms of society. The concept of man as the contradiction between the forces of production and relations of production, however, is a concrete universal, not only characteristic of all societies but also possessing the means for deducing the nature of *particular* societies. In this, the contradiction, lies its concrete validity, i.e., its *actual* relevance to existing societies throughout history.

From Marx's later work in political economy, we can point to *labour as such* as an abstract universal, with a concrete validity only in the modern bourgeois economy; and to the *commodity* as a concrete universal, valid as a concept throughout history and concrete because the 'synthesis of definitions' it possesses is a *real, existing* synthesis remaining the same throughout history. See K. Marx, Introduction to *A Contribution to the Critique of Political Economy* (Moscow 1970), 205ff.

ACTIVITY
Concepts embodying activity, motion, and process are central to Marx's materialism. His concept of man is expressed as a principle of motion; his concept of

knowledge is expressed as a process; indeed, all existence in Marx's view is infused with movement. The nature of this movement is dialectical. And the course movement takes is from potentiality to actuality. See K. Marx, 'Theses on Feuerbach,' MECW, 5, 3-6.

ACTUALITY, REALITY [Wirklichkeit]
In Hegelian philosophy, 'actuality is the unity, become immediate, of essence with existence.' (W. Wallace, trans., *Hegel's Logic*, 200) When essence as *subject* is realized, when it is at one with existence, it is actual. The meaning Marx attaches to the concept, however, is the *empirically* real. But this reality may be in the process of developing, and as such moving from potentiality to actuality, the latter being the culmination of development. A thing in process, then, may be viewed as *actual* in relation to its prior stages; but it is only truly real at the end of its development. A thing is actual in a relative sense at any stage but only absolutely real or actual at the culmination of its movement.

Marx's criticism of Hegel's use of 'actuality' in the 1843 *Critique* comprises, not the first, but his most detailed criticism to this date of Hegel's idealism. It greatly undermines the commonplace notion that Marx was an idealist or Hegelian in this period. See MECW, 3, 9.

ALIENATION and ESTRANGEMENT [Entäusserung and Entfremdung]
These concepts are employed interchangeably by Marx and by most translators. They are the summary expression of Marx's discussion of alienated labour [die entfremdete Arbeit, die entäusserte Arbeit], which he undertakes by way of the critique of political economy in the Paris manuscripts. Alienated labour is productive activity in which the producer and his product are separated, a separation characterizing all forms of production involving exchange. It can be said, therefore, that Marx saw human productive activity from very early times as alienated labour and latterly, in the capitalist mode of production, all labour as alienated labour.

It must be added that, in Marx's view, alienated labour implied private property; i.e., the cause of, or explanation for, private property was alienated labour. Once established, the relationship between alienated labour and private property became reciprocal: the production of private property implied alienated labour and production as alienated labour produced private property. The deduction of this relationship, in the manuscripts, marked a fundamental stage in the development of Marx's critique of politics.

From the analysis of alienated labour, Marx deduces three related aspects which, together with alienated labour, comprise the concept of alienation or estrangement. They are separation from the act of production, one's life-activity, from man's species-being, and from fellow man. (See chapter 4 above.)

APPEARANCE [Erscheinung]
In his *Logic*, Hegel writes: 'the existence is *Appearance*.' On the following page, he clarifies the point: 'Existence stated explicitly in its contradiction is Appearance.' (W. Wallace. trans., *Hegel's Logic*, 186-7) Allowing for the difference between idealism and materialism, the meaning of appearance in Marx's work is similar. Appearance is the manifestation of existence. If, as some assert, essence were appearance in Hegel and Marx, then, neither would see a need for philosophy as science because truth would be self-evident, the true nature of things would be manifest. Philosophy as science would be nothing because both see it as the pursuit of the essence in appearance.

BECOMING [Werden]
In the Paris manuscripts, Marx writes: 'Labour is man's *coming-to-be for himself* within *alienation*, or as *alienated* man.' (MECW, 3, 333) [Die Arbeit ist das Fürsichwerden des Menschen innerhalb der Entäusserung oder als entäusserter Mensch. MEW, Erganzungsband, 574] For Aristotle, as for Marx, the concept of becoming is the movement from potentiality to actuality, from potential being to actual being. In this quotation, he is arguing that it is through labour that man moves himself from his potential humanity to his actual humanity, but because labour is by definition alienated labour, this passage is made within the realm of alienation. Man becomes man first as alienated man.

CIVIL SOCIETY [bürgerliche Gesellschaft]
Marx employs this concept in reference to that 'sector of any social system which is concerned with production, and which has evolved sufficiently to manifest division of labour, private property, and classes, and which gives rise to different forms in the superstructure.' The concept is carefully defined by Marx in *The German Ideology*, MECW, 5, 89.

COMMERCE, INTERCOURSE [Verkehr]
This concept comprises the early formulation of that which was to become 'relations of production,' i.e., social relations in the broadest sense which arise on the basis of certain productive forces. See Marx's letter to P.V. Annenkov, 28 Dec. 1846, in *Marx-Engels, Correspondence* (New York 1934), 7-8.

CONCEPT [Begriff]
With Marx, concept is generally employed as an equivalent to definition.

CONCRETE
See Abstract.

261 Glossary

CONTRADICTION, CONTRARIETY [Widerspruch, Widersprechen]
See Opposition.

DEFINITION, DETERMINATION, DESIGNATION [Bestimmung]
Marx's use of this concept appears to correspond to that of Aristotle. In the *Posterior Analytics* (92b), he writes: definition is 'a set of words signifying precisely what a name signifies.' And in the *Topics* (101b), he states: 'a "definition" is a phrase signifying a thing's essence'; and in the *Metaphysics*: 'definition is the formula of the essence.' Definition, then, is a proposition which isolates the essential qualities of a thing.

The starting-point of the syllogistic is definition; and therefore all judgement rests on a definition, all deduction requires first a definition. But definition itself is a product of inductive analysis.

Inductive analysis is the pursuit of the 'middle term,' or 'proximate cause' of a phenomenon. The pursuit of 'proximate causes,' until the 'efficient' or 'final cause' is discovered, provides a definition which may be considered the true definition of the phenomenon. The whole of these early works of Marx, from 1842 to 1847, may be seen as the inductive pursuit of the essence of man.

Lenin appears to make a distinction between determination [Bestimmung] and definition [Definition]; the latter would correspond to an abstract universal, taking 'into account only the external features of the object'; and the former would correspond to a concrete universal, which embraces the internal logic, the *differentia* as efficient cause, of the object. The distinction has some merit, but I cannot find any such differentiation made systematically in Marx's works. V.I. Lenin, *Collected Works*, 38 (Moscow 1972), 253

DEVELOPMENT [Entwickelung]
This concept in Hegel refers to progression from the implicit [an sich, potentia] to the explicit [für sich].

DIALECTIC
There are two aspects to this concept; viz., the dialectic as *method* of research and of presentation, and the dialectic as the *principle* of generation or movement in nature. For the former, Marx owes most to Aristotle, and for the latter to Hegel; both mentors, however, discuss both aspects.

Regarding the dialectic as the motive principle in nature, we shall let Marx define the concept; in *The Poverty of Philosophy*, he writes: 'What constitutes dialectical movement is the co-existence of two contradictory sides, their conflict and their fusion into a new category.' (MECW, 6, 168) This movement has three aspects, sometimes referred to as the three 'laws' of the dialectic; namely, the transformation of quantity into quality, the unity of opposites, and the negation of the negation. Examples of all three can be found in *Capital*, 1.

The dialectic as a method of research has two aspects: inductive and deductive. The latter is the *syllogistic* and has been referred to as the form of *dialectical reasoning* since the time of Aristotle. It is the basis of all forms of judgement and requires a definition as its starting point. The *outcome* of Marx's early works may be viewed as the discovery of the 'true' starting point of the analysis of man. Because the contradiction between the forces and relations of production, the heart of so-called historical materialism, comprises the efficient cause of human development, of man, it is also the true definition of man; and therefore it forms the basis of a deductive method which can explain the existing particularities of all human societies throughout human development.

The inductive side of analysis is not so straightforwardly dialectical. Induction, or the empirical search for proximate causes, does have elements of the syllogistic, in an inverted sense, but is not *formally* syllogistical.

The method of presentation for Marx, in *A Contribution to The Critique of Political Economy* and *Capital*, appears to derive from Hegel's 'synthetic method.' See *Hegel's Logic*, 285-6. Presentation must commence with a concrete universal and unfold in the manner dictated by the dialectical contradiction as the motive principle contained in this universal.

DIFFERENTIA

'That which distinguishes one species from another of the same genus or an essential attribute, which when added to the name of the genus distinctly marks out the species; thus the attribute of rationality is the differentia of the species "man" from all other animals.' If rather than 'rationality' as the *differentia specifica* of man, as the above dictionary definition would have it, we follow Hegel and make labour, productive activity, the essence of man, and then follow Marx and find a contradiction within the act of production, and make this the essence of man, we arrive at the *differentia* which makes this last definition of man a *concrete universal*.

DIVISION OF LABOUR

The division of labour refers to the social nature of human productive activity, as it evolves within a system of estrangement. There is a relation between the concept of division of labour and alienated labour; namely, the former refers to the social interaction of *concrete* alienated productive activity, whereas the latter refers to the estrangement of an *abstract* individual's product and activity. (MECW, 3, 317) The division of labour stands first in a causal and then in a reciprocal relationship to private property. (MECW, 5, 46) The division of labour is the primary component in the concept of relations of production.

ESSENCE [Wesen]

Marx's notion of essence appears to be much closer to that of Aristotle than that of Hegel. And the former defined it much as it is defined in common usage today. Essence is 'that which constitutes the nature of a thing'; 'that which makes a thing what it is,' or 'that which differentiates a thing from all other things.' In the *Metaphysics*, Aristotle states: 'the essence of a thing is that which it is said to be *per se*.' The essence is the thing 'as such.'

The essence may be hypostasized as in Plato or Hegel; but for Marx it was always derived from the empirical examination of existence. For him, essence was present in the particular, as the foundation to the inessential; it did not exist 'as such.' The essence of a thing, therefore, comprised the content of the definition of the thing.

ESTATE [Stand]

This concept refers to a social class, based on a pre-capitalist mode of production, which is invested with political rights and social privileges.

EXISTENCE [*Dasein*]

For Marx, existence is the empirically real. And the manifestation of reality is its appearance. Existence is comprised of the inessential (the contingent) and the essential (the necessary), but they do not necessarily correspond. The object of scientific research is to abstract the essential from appearance.

FREEDOM

For Marx, freedom is the conscious, critical unity of the individual and his collectivity. For a discussion of the meaning of this definition of freedom as it is employed by Hegel, see G.W.F. Hegel, *Natural Law*, 89ff.

HUMANISM

A mode of thought, or intellectual system, whose central concern is the human condition. Whatever its variants as a philosophical tendency, a product of the Renaissance, it has always been a critical tendency. By its very nature, humanism is critical; Thomas More's *Utopia*, for example, contains an insightful critique of the English social and political order, taking the analysis far enough to grasp private property as the root of man's social and political predicament.

The Humanists of the Renaissance played a significant role in the re-introduction of ancient philosophy, especially that of Aristotle. From his work they developed methods of philological criticism, the foundation of all science. A worthwhile study on the relationship between humanism and Marx can be found in H.L. Parsons, *Humanism and Marx's Thought* (Springfield 1971).

HYPOSTASIZATION
The process of treating a concept or an essence as the subject itself and existence as the predicate.

IDEA [Idee]
For Hegel, the idea was the concept 'viewed concretely,' that is, 'in synthesis with the content which it gives itself.' For Marx, 'the ideal is nothing else than the material world reflected by the human mind, and translated into forms of thought.' *Capital*, 1, Afterword to the Second German Edition. Marx's early use of this concept is consistent with this later definition.

IDEALISM [Idealismus]
Idealism is most easily defined by contrasting it to materialism, the first such contrast being made by Aristotle in his 'Criticism of Plato's Idea Theory' in the *Metaphysics*. The difference is based on the perceived nature of the relations between essence and existence. The idealist makes the essence of things the real order of things; he gives an independent existence to the product of the mind – the idea or concept; he makes the real subject, existence, into a predicate, and the real predicate, the concept, into the subject. The materialist, on the other hand, grasps the concept as the product of inductive analysis; the essence is the predicate and reality the subject. The presence of the notion of essence, or idea, in itself, then, does not define idealism; it is how essence is understood and employed, how its relation to existence is conceived, that differentiates idealism from materialism.

IN AND FOR ITSELF, IMPLICIT AND EXPLICIT [an sich, für sich]
'Anything is "in and for itself" when it has become "*for itself*," i.e., consciously and explicitly, what it is "in itself," i.e., in its latent or potential nature.' From the English idealist, B. Bosanquet, *The Philosophical Theory of the State* (London 1920), 221n.

LAW [Gesetz]
In his 1842 article entitled, 'Debates on Freedom of the Press,' Marx defines law as follows: 'Laws are rather the positive, clear, universal norms in which freedom has acquired an impersonal, theoretical existence independent of the arbitrariness of the individual.' MECW, 1, 162. Such was his notion of 'true' law. Positive law, which was taken as the nature of most existing laws, however, was understood as the embodiment of privilege as legal right. See MECW, 1, 78.

MAN, HUMANITY
See Species-being.

MIGHT

Might is used in the sense of *power* based on strength or force.

MORALITY AND ETHICS [Moralität, Sittlichkeit]

In Hegel, these concepts refer to rationality in the social order, as abstract and concrete respectively. (See *Natural Law*, 112.) By contrast, in Marx, they are used interchangeably. In the *Rheinische Zeitung* articles Marx employs morality 'as such' as meaning 'the principle of a world that obeys its own laws.' (MECW, 1, 118) Morality, here, is the principle of a society which is self-regulating, self-determining.

The moral as commonly employed is understood as a *particular* morality, i.e., morality as Christian, Muslim, etc. The *general* sense of the word refers to behaviour which corresponds to the *social* nature of man; in this sense, the moral community, or morality, is but sociality in the abstract sense.

A discussion of Hegel's use of these terms in the *Philosophy of Right* may be found in the article by K.H. Ilting, 'The Structure of Hegel's Philosophy of Right,' in Z.A. Pelczynski, ed., *Hegel's Political Philosophy* (Cambridge 1971). It must be noted that Marx's use is not the same, but corresponds very closely to Aristotle's notion of 'natural' or 'social' justice. See Aristotle, *Ethics*, Bk. V, 1134b.

NATURE

In the *Metaphysics*, Aristotle defines several meanings of this concept, but concludes: 'the primary and proper meaning of "nature" is the essence of things which have in themselves (*qua* themselves) a principle of motion.'

OBJECTIFICATION [Vergegenstandlichung]

The act of objectifying, of making visible or tangible. All forms of human expression are forms of objectification. Objectification, so conceived, in the *direct* relationship between the subject and object, his expression. Alienation is the *mediated* relation between subject and object. It is this difference which is the centre of one of Marx's criticisms of Hegel: Hegel 'conceives objectification as loss of the object, as alienation.' (MECW, 3, 333)

ONTOLOGY

That science 'which investigates and explains the nature and essence of all things or existences, their qualities and attributes.'

OPPOSITION

In the 1843 *Critique* of Hegel (MECW, 3, 88-9), Marx identifies three types of opposition, all of which are relevant to Marx's critique of politics and philosophy. One we may call *contradiction*, a term not employed exclusively in the following sense but sometimes meaning inconsistency or contrariety. A contradiction is a reflexive relationship between extremes; that is, a relationship in which the extremes demand each other, in which the extremes can be defined *only* in relation to each other. In Marx's words, they comprise 'the differentiation of one essence.' He uses these examples: north pole and south pole are the differentiated extremes of one essence, pole; male and female sexes are the differentiated extremes of man; and to add another, the individual and his social relationships are the extremes of man/society. In each case, each side is defined in relation to the other; each *exists* only by virtue of the other.

Another form of opposition is *contrariety*. Here the extremes have 'nothing in common, they do not need each other, they do not supplement each other. The one does not have in its own bosom the longing for, the need for, the anticipation of the other.' This relationship is that 'between *two* essences,' i.e., unrelated essences; not as in contradiction, between the extremes of one differentiated essence. Contrary extremes differ in essence and have no necessary relationship. By way of example, Marx points to such extremes as 'pole and non-pole, human and non-human species (essences).'

PHILOSOPHY
Philosophy and science are synonymous in these early works. The object of both is to derive the essence from existence.

POWER
Power is the ability to act, and may be founded on might or right. *Authority* is power based on right.

PRINCIPLE or BEGINNING
Aristotle's definition of principle in the *Metaphysics* remains one of the most comprehensive. For our purposes, we shall limit the definition to the following. The principle of a thing is that from which it proceeds; it is its source or origin. In this sense, it may be seen as its original cause or its operative cause. Indeed, Aristotle writes that 'every cause is a principle.' 'Hence the common characteristic of all beginnings (principles),' he continues, 'is their being the original sources whence things either exist, or are produced, or are known. "Nature," "element," "thought," "free-will," "essence," are all beginnings or principles.' (*Aristotle's Metaphysics*, ed. and trans., J. Warrington, 3)

RELATIONSHIP [Verhältnisse]
Central to Hegel's criticism of empiricism (i.e., that empiricism understands reality to consist of unconnected units, of entities independent of one another) and to his own philosophy is the concept of *relation*. The concept refers to the *interdependence* of causes and effects. 'The terms of a "Verhältnisse," Hegel writes, 'only

have meaning in connection with one another' (cited by H.B. Acton, Introduction, to Hegel, *Natural Law*, 20).

The study of law or politics, then, is not concerned with 'pure qualities, but relations.' Most of the concepts employed by Marx demarcate a relationship, in which at least two elements stand in a necessary relation to each other.

RIGHT [Recht] and PRIVILEGE

In Hegel, 'natural law' [Naturrecht] comprised the fundamental rational principles of human behaviour, which were, conceptually, everywhere and always the same and which often constituted the basis of legislation.

In Marx, the concept of right is closely related (MECW, 1, 363). By rights, he means those *informal* claims, entitlements, and justifications which rest on 'natural law,' as defined above. Once formalized they comprise the content of true law. Privilege on the contrary, refers to special rights or, more commonly, 'positive rights,' which are specific to certain groups, stratas, classes, or individuals. They are not based on 'natural law' but depend for their existence on the sanction of *positive* law. Indeed, once formalized, privilege comprises the content of positive law.

The liberal notion of right comprises the privileges of private property; right here is bourgeois privilege. The doctrine of 'natural rights,' the principle of liberalism, is a reflection of the principle of bourgeois society, private property.

SOVEREIGNTY

The question of sovereignty is the question of the relations of power and authority in a given state. The problem is not where sovereignty resides in the state; this can be determined by empirical examination; rather, it is whence sovereignty derives. In his discussion of this concept in the 1843 *Critique*, Marx concludes that sovereignty, whoever or whatever appears to possess it, can be nothing but in essence the sovereignty of the people. In other words, all power and authority derive from the relations of individuals in a society. (See MECW, 3, 28-9.)

SPECIES-BEING [Gattungswesen]

This concept refers to the nature of man, a nature which *is* the *relationship* to the 'other.' Unlike other animals whose nature is simply the given characteristics of a genus or species *and* whose nature takes this form always in the same way regardless of contact with the genus, man, on the contrary, in order to be man, must interrelate with others; he can only be man as a part of whole; in this sense, man is a 'species-being' or 'genus-essence.'

The concept of man or humanity is the same: the individual *is* his relationship to others, and outside those relationships he is nothing; there is no such thing as the individual *qua* individual. The individual's relations to others comprise his community, the distinctiveness of which depends on how these relations evolve.

Man and his community are one and the same: man is not man outside of society and society is nothing without its members.

This abstract definition of man is made more concrete by Marx by specifying the nature of this relationship. Its definition requires the concept of labour or productive activity. It is not simply that man is social, i.e., that he must live in society to be human, but also that man himself *makes* his society, his social relations, and therefore himself. The relations which arise out of man's productive activity and exchange of products constitute the basis of his relations to others. These relations arise out of man's own activity, and therefore are the product of his activity. Hence, man makes his own social relations, albeit unconsciously, and, it follows, himself.

The misunderstanding of this concept, and of the nature of concepts *per se*, has given rise to many learned disquisitions on Marx's purported rejection of the concept of man. The evidence is usually confined to Marx's dismissive comment in the 'Notes on Wagner' about his analysis in *Capital* beginning with *Man* and to his criticism of Feuerbach's use of man in the 'Theses on Feuerbach.' The first has nothing to do with a rejection of the concept of man, but rather with a dismissal of the idea that his analysis began with this concept. The second is straightforwardly a criticism of the *hypostasization* of Feuerbach's concept of *man*. Pedantic lucubrations about Marx's supposed rejection shows, first, a failure to grasp the development of Marx's critique of politics, of the *existing* nature of man, and second, just how alienated Marxism itself is from its subject matter.

STATE [Staat]
The concept of the state is employed with two meanings in Marx's early works; they correspond to the contemporary dual meaning of the concept. In the *Rheinische Zeitung* articles and 1843 *Critique* of Hegel, it denotes the body politic, the self-governing community, the commonwealth, the totality of social relations in a community. The sense is conveyed in the modern concept of the *nation-state*. To distinguish the organs of government from the state so defined, the concept of 'the political state' [der politische Staat] is employed; the distinction is Hegel's. Later, Marx's use of state comes to mean principally the civil power, the seat of government and its organs, as separate from civil society, the sphere of individual, contractual relations.

To comprehend Hegel's *Philosophy of Right*, Marx's *RhZ* articles, and his *Critique* of Hegel, this distinction must be grasped. In this connection, we may cite T.M. Knox, the translator of Hegel's work on the state: 'Failure to realize this [i.e., the distinction] has been responsible for numerous misrepresentations of Hegel's position and his attitude to "the state."' See T.M. Knox, trans., *Hegel's Philosophy of Right* (Oxford 1975), 364-5. The same may easily be said about Marx's early works.

Selected and Annotated Bibliography

There are several English translations of the early works of Marx; but all of them in comprehensiveness and for the most part in quality of translation have been superseded by the new English *Marx-Engels Collected Works* (MECW). When complete, this edition will be more comprehensive than the existing collected works in German.

In German, the only completed edition of the collected works is the *Marx-Engels Werke* (MEW), begun in the 1950s with the last volume appearing in the late 1960s. An earlier more comprehensive edition was begun in 1927 under the editorships of Adoratski and Rjazanov, entitled *Marx-Engels Historisch-Kritische Gesamtausgabe* (MEGA); it comprised eight volumes of works and four of correspondence, published between 1927 and 1939; it was, however, never completed. A new *Gesamtausgabe* (MEGA) began to be published in 1975 and, although not yet complete, it now comprises almost one-half of its projected 100 volumes. In it the writings are printed in the languages in which they originally appeared. In French, the only relatively comprehensive edition is that which was edited and translated by J. Molitor; comprising nine volumes, *Oeuvres philosophiques* was published between 1927 and 1947.

The secondary literature on Marx and Engels would more than likely fill a small library. This selected bibliography is confined to those works pertaining to Marx's early writings, to related works which have been helpful in comprehending Marx, and to certain attempts by others to analyse the state or political relations.

The annotations are made only for those books directly relevant to our subject matter; and they often refer to specific aspects of the work, or specific problems pertaining to this exposition, rather than to the book as a whole.

Adams, H.P., *Karl Marx, In His Earlier Writings* (London 1940, 1965). Although the author perceives no inherent unity in the early works, this is still one of the better descriptive reviews of these writings.

Adelman, F.J., ed., *Demythologizing Marxism* (The Hague 1969)

Adler, M., 'L' "Utopisme" chez Marx et Engels,' in *Cahiers de l'I.S.E.A.*, (Etudes de Marxologie) IV, no. 11 (Nov. 1970). A French translation of the concluding chapter of Adler's book: *Die Staatsauflassung des Marxismus* (Wien 1922). The chapter is, first, a defence of the notion that the destruction of class society brings the destruction of the state, a product of class society, against the claims of Hans Kelsen that a harmonious society without a state is utopian. And second, it is an attempt to infer scientifically the probability of such a stateless society. Several passages from Adler's work are translated in Bottomore, T.B., and Goode, P., eds., *Austro-Marxism* (Oxford 1978).

Althusser, L., *For Marx* (London 1977)

– *Montesquieu, la politique et l'histoire* (Paris 1959)

– 'The Conditions of Scientific Discovery,' in *Theoretical Practice*, vol. 7/8 (1973)

Aris, R., *History of Political Thought in Germany* (London 1936, 1965)

Arthur, C.J., 'Editor's Introduction,' *The German Ideology* (London 1974)

– 'Towards a Materialist Theory of Law,' *Critique*, 7 (1977). An introduction to Pashukanis (Cf. K. Korsch).

Avineri, S., 'Marx and Jewish Emancipation,' *Journal of the History of Ideas*, 25, no. 3 (July-Sept. 1964). A salutary essay for those, and there are many, who would read Marx's article 'On the Jewish Question' as an example of Marx's anti-semitism. In his article, however, Avineri makes the Jewish question primary and the broader issues secondary; whereas, for Marx, the meaning of political emancipation is primary and the Jewish question simply his vehicle for discussing it.

– 'The Hegelian Origins of Marx's Political Thought,' *Review of Metaphysics*, XXI, no. 1 (Sept. 1967). The author calls his article a 'close look' at the 1843 *Critique*, but it is not close enough to avoid numerous misconceptions. First, he asserts that the method of Marx's commentary on Hegel is Feuerbach's 'transformative method'; since he nowhere substantiates this view, it stands as mere conjecture. Second, he draws a link between the idea of Hegel's bureaucracy as the 'universal class' and Marx's concept of the proletariat as embodying the 'general interest'; this is mere analogy, fraught with anomalies. Third, although he rightly emphasizes the importance of Marx's analysis of private property, he does not grasp its significance in the *Critique*. Fourth, he not only views Marx's analysis as being entirely 'within' the Hegelian framework, but also suggests 'that in a way Marx sought to actualize the ultimate postulates of Hegel's *Philosophy of Right*.' These are the opinions of one whose 'look' at the *Critique* is not so much 'close' as myopic.

– 'Marx's Critique of Hegel's "Philosophy of Right" in Its Systematic Setting,' *Cahiers de l'I.S.E.A.*, Etudes de Marxologie (août 1966). There are very few comprehensive expositions of Marx's *Critique*; this is one of them. Despite its comprehensiveness, it is open to all the criticisms made above of its shorter version. In one form or another, almost all the accepted interpretations of Marx's alleged Hegelianism, Feuerbachianism, etc., are to be found in this essay, side by side with several insightful but undeveloped observations.

- *The Social and Political Thought of Karl Marx* (Cambridge 1968). The problems with this book are legion; it should be read with great scepticism. For a criticism, see A. Gilbert, 'Salvaging Marx from Avineri,' *Political Theory*, 4, no. 1 (Feb. 1976).
- *Hegel's Theory of the Modern State* (Cambridge 1972)
- 'Consciousness and History: List der Vernunft in Hegel and Marx,' in W.E. Steinkraus, ed., *New Studies in Hegel's Philosophy* (New York 1971). The author strains to demonstrate the idea that Marx's notion of *praxis* is an attempt to bridge 'the gap left open by Hegel between action and consciousness in history,' the contradiction in his 'List der Vernunft.' Although Avineri has put his finger on a central question, namely, rationality in history, his treatment is unnecessarily awkward and therefore limited. Had he stated the question *in abstracto* and then examined its development in Hegel (its genesis in Aristotle) and its solution (may we be so bold?) in Marx, the essay would have drawn out a far profounder significance which lies in the question of 'List der Vernunft.'

Axelos, K., *Marx, penseur de la technique* (Paris 1961), translated into English: *Alienation, Praxis, and Techne in the Thought of Karl Marx* (Austin 1976)

Bailey, C., *The Greek Atomists and Epicurus* (Oxford 1928)
- 'Karl Marx on Greek Atomism,' *The Classical Quarterly*, XXII, no. 3 and 4 (1928). A complimentary but all too brief review of Marx's doctoral dissertation, which focuses on the interpretation of Epicurus but misses the broader implications, namely, Marx's attempt to establish a concrete basis for the nature of mind and to find the source of ideas in the sensuous world.

Bakouradze, O., 'La Formation des idées philosophiques de Karl Marx,' *Recherches internationales à la lumière du marxisme*, cahier 19, 1960. A descriptive and brief examination of the *Rheinische Zeitung* articles and the 1843 *Critique*, following Lenin's position that these early writings represented 'the passage of Marx from idealism to materialism and from democratic revolutionary to communism.' Like so many Russian and East German commentators on these works, the author is transfixed by the need to prove Marx's passage from idealism to communism.

Barbu, Z., *Le Développement de la pensée dialectique* (Paris 1947). A sweeping review of the dialectic from the philosophy of antiquity to the nineteenth century.

Barker, E., 'Translator's Introduction' to O. Gierke, *Natural Law and the Theory of Society, 1500 to 1800*, vol. 1 (Cambridge 1934). A discussion of the history of natural law prior to the period studied by Gierke. It contains interesting insights into the relation between the study of law and theories of the state in Europe.

Berki, R.N., 'Political Freedom and Hegelian Metaphysics,' *Political Studies*, XVI, no. 3 (Oct. 1968). The author tries to show that Hegel's notion of freedom is close to the concept of 'political freedom as *diversity*,' in contrast to the alleged Marxist conception of 'uniformity.' He does not appear to grasp the paradox of Hegel's notion of freedom: its basis in liberalism and its critique of the same; nor does he appear to understand the notion of freedom as unity of opposites. He is patently simplistic about Marxism, even confusing Marxism and 'Marxist societies.'

– 'Perspectives in the Marxian critique of Hegel's political philosophy,' in Z.A. Pelczynski, ed., *Hegel's Political Philosophy* (Cambridge 1971). This article is one of the few attempts to expound the main argument throughout Marx's 1843 *Critique*. While a genuine effort, its difficulties and omissions seriously detract from its value. The author does not, for example, discuss Marx's analytical method, except to intimate that Feuerbach's invertive method is employed. He also fails to see the importance of Marx's use of the concept of mediation to criticize Hegel's depiction of the legislature; he does not perceive the import of Marx's critique of primogeniture; he omits a discussion of the meaning of enfranchisement; and concludes by asserting that 'Marx's tone is here unmistakably that of the enraged nineteenth century liberal democrat.'

Berland, O., 'Radical Chains: The Marxian Concept of Proletarian Mission,' *Studies on the Left*, 6, no. 5 (1966). An attempt to examine the place of the proletariat in Marx's theory. The criticism of this article by R. Aronson in the same issue of the journal seizes upon all the weaknesses of Berland's effort – chief among them being that: 'he substitutes a biographical study of how the idea of proletarian revolution occurred to Marx for a study of what it means.'

Bigo, P., *Marxisme et humanisme* (Paris 1961)

Block, F., 'The Ruling Class Does Not Rule: Notes on the Marxist Theory of the State,' *Socialist Revolution*, no. 33 (May-June 1977)

Bloom, S.F., *The World of Nations* (New York 1941, 1967)

Bobbio, N., 'Is There a Marxist Theory of the State?,' and 'Are There Alternatives to Representative Democracy?,' in *Telos*, no. 35 (spring 1978). The first article is a well-written criticism of the methods of contemporary Marxists, but a poorly reasoned examination of Marx's critique of the state. The thrust of the author's position appears to be that a 'theory' of the state is not to be found in Marx and Engels. The second article is a discussion of the alternatives; it is characterized by a failure to appreciate the meaning of Marx's 'true democracy.'

Bosanquet, B., *The Philosophical Theory of the State* (London 1920)

Bottomore, T.B. and M. Rubel, eds., *Karl Marx: Selected Writings in Sociology and Social Philosophy* (Harmondsworth 1963)

– trans. and ed., *Karl Marx: Early Writings* (New York 1964)

– and P. Goode, *Austro-Marxism* (Oxford 1978)

Brazill, W.J., *The Young Hegelians* (New Haven 1970). A very good discussion of the different meanings of critique amongst the Young Hegelians.

Brewster, B., 'Fetishism in *Capital* and *Reading Capital*,' *Economy and Society*, 5, no. 3 (1976). An introduction to the fourth part of J. Ranciere's article on 'The Concept of Critique.'

Brown, B., 'The French Revolution and the Rise of Social Theory,' *Science and Society*, XXX, no. 4 (1966). A superficial examination, resting on quotations, of the French Revolution and its effect, principally in Germany. A large part of the article reviews Marx's comments on the Revolution but the significance of Marx's research is not drawn out.

Bruhat, J., 'La Révolution française et la formation de la pensée de Marx,' *Société des études robespièrristes* (1964?). In attenuated form the material in this essay appeared under a pseudonym, J. Montreau, 'La Révolution française et la pensée de Marx,' in *La Pensée*, no. 3 (1939). The principal object of the author was to gather together all Marx wrote on the subject of the French Revolution. The second was to attempt to evaluate how Marx's analysis of the Revolution affected the development of his 'concept of materialism and dialectic of history.' His second objective is necessarily a venture in speculation.

Calvez, *La Pensée de Karl Marx* (Paris 1956)

Caton, H., 'Marx's Sublation of Philosophy into Praxis,' *Review of Metaphysics*, XXVI, no. 2 (Dec. 1972). An attempt to examine the development of the relation between theory and practice in Marx's early work. The author makes a promising start, touching on many points which counter accepted wisdom, but because he fails to grasp that the concept of the unity of theory and practice cannot translate itself into reality, he fails to understand why the proletarian revolution has not yet been realized.

Carver, T., ed., *Karl Marx, Texts on Method* (Oxford 1975)

– 'Marx – and Hegel's *Logic*,' *Political Studies*, XXIV, no. 1 (1976)

– 'Marx's Commodity Fetishism,' *Inquiry*, 18 (1975)

Carlebach, J., *Karl Marx and the Critique of Judaism*, unpublished D. Phil. thesis, University of Sussex, 1973. When the author writes, Marx 'displayed ... such a complete lack of knowledge of Jews and Judaism, that his critique hardly warrants serious attention,' we can only wonder why such serious attention was paid. The answer seems to be to counter Marx's 'serious challenge to the "particularistic" attitude of Judaism which he rejected as narrow and alienating.'

The author's declared faith in the principles of Judaism above those of science raises serious questions about his intentions.

Chang, S.H.M., *The Marxian Theory of the State* (1931; New York 1965). A descriptive exposition of the theory, undertaken before the publication of the *RhZ* articles and the 1843 *Critique*, and leaning heavily on the work of Lenin and Engels.

Charlton, D.G., *Positivist Thought in France* (Oxford 1959)

Coker, F.W., *Organismic Theories of the State*, Columbia University, XXXVIII, no. 2 (1910; New York 1967)

Colletti, L., *From Rousseau to Lenin* (London 1972)

– *Marxism and Hegel* (London 1973)

– 'Marxism: Science or Revolution,' in R. Blackburn, ed., *Ideology in Social Science* (Bungay 1972)

– 'Marxism and the Dialectic,' *New Left Review*, 93 (Sept./Oct. 1975)

Cooper, R., *The Logical Influence of Hegel on Marx* (Seattle 1925). One of the early attempts to draw analogies between Hegel's concepts and those of Marx. The work is limited to this comparison/contrast, but it is illuminating on the question of the structure of *Capital* and its relation to Hegel's *Logic*.

Cornford, F.M., trans., *The Republic of Plato* (Oxford 1941)

Cornforth, M., *The Open Philosophy and the Open Society* (New York 1968)

Cornu, A., 'German Utopianism: "True" Socialism,' *Science and Society*, XII, no. 1 (winter 1948). A loosely argued review of the socialism of the 'Left Hegelians,' with an emphasis on Moses Hess.

– *The Origins of Marxian Thought* (Springfield 1957). This short book suffers from a rather strict reliance on a ready-made framework; e.g., Marx progresses from liberalism to communism. The Hegelian, Kantian, and Feuerbachian influences are briefly and unconvincingly treated.

– *Karl Marx et Frederick Engels, leur vie et leur oeuvre*, 1 (Paris 1955); 2 (Paris 1958); 3 (Paris 1962); 4 (Paris 1970). The author has dedicated a good deal of his life to expounding the work of Marx and Engels; the projected multi-volume series, the four above already published, is the culmination of his life's research. They comprise a detailed intellectual biography of Marx and Engels.

– 'Karl Marx et la Revolution française,' *La Pensée*, no. 81 (Sept./Oct. 1958)

Cottier, G.M.-M., *L'Athéisme du jeune Marx: ses origines hégeliennes* (Paris 1959)

Delfgaauw, B., *The Young Marx* (London 1967)

Doyon, J., *Le Concept d'aliénation religieuse dans Marx* (Sherbrooke 1962). An awkward and elementary attempt to interpret Marx's notion of alienation and religion.

Draper, H., 'Marx and the Dictatorship of the Proletariat,' *New Politics*, 1, no. 4 (1961)

– 'The Death of the State in Marx and Engels,' *The Socialist Register* (1970)

- 'Marx on Democratic Forms of Government,' *The Socialist Register*, 1974. More or less the first chapter of his book:
- *Karl Marx's Theory of Revolution*, Part I, 2 vols. (New York 1977). An extensively documented review of what Marx and Engels wrote on the state and bureaucracy. This vast project adds very little to existing knowledge about Marx's writing on political relations.

Droz, J., *L'Allemagne et la Révolution française* (Paris 1949)

Dupré, L., *The Philosophical Foundations of Marxism* (New York 1966)
- 'Idealism and Materialism in Marx's Dialectic,' *Review of Metaphysics*, XXX, no. 4 (June 1977)

Easton, L.D., 'Alienation and History in the Early Marx,' *Philosophy and Phenomenological Research*, XXII, no. 2 (Dec. 1961)
- and K.H. Guddat, eds., *Writings of the Young Marx on Philosophy and Society* (New York 1967)

d'Entrèves, A.P., *Natural Law* (London 1972)
- *The Notion of the State* (Oxford 1967)

Fetscher, I., *Marx and Marxism* (New York 1971). A set of his own essays, all revealing an ingenuous, though limited, appreciation of Marx's notion of critique and humanism.

Feuer, L.S., 'Dialectic and Economic Laws,' *Science and Society*, 5, no. 4 (1941). A genuine attempt to employ the laws of the dialectic as a means of criticizing the tenets of contemporary economic theory, as found in Marshall, Keynes, Shumpeter, etc.

Feuerbach, L., *The Essence of Faith According to Luther* (1844; New York 1967)
- *Principles of the Philosophy of the Future* (1843; New York 1966)
- *The Essence of Christianity* (1841; trans. G. Elliot, New York 1957)

Findlay, J.N., *Hegel: A Re-Examination* (London 1964)

Foster, M.B., *The Political Philosophies of Plato and Hegel* (Oxford 1935)

Friere, A. de Abreu, *La Révolution désaliénante* (Montreal 1972). A doctoral thesis which attempts to grasp the essence of Marx's early work by first comprehending the meaning of the critical method. The objective is logically sound, but the failure to dissect the meaning of critique makes for a superficial review of the early writings.

Fromm, E., *Marx's Concept of Man* (New York 1963)
- ed., *Socialist Humanism* (London 1967)

Gabaude, J.-M., *Le jeune Marx et le matérialisme antique* (Toulouse 1970). One of the earliest of a series of doctoral theses appearing in France critically analysing Marx's doctoral thesis.

Garaudy, R., *Karl Marx: The Evolution of His Thought* (New York 1967). Although Garaudy attempts to find the basis of Marx's thought in Feuerbach and Fichte, the book is crisply written and provides a good overview to Marx's life-work.

Gierke, O., *Natural Law and the Theory of Society, 1500 to 1800*, vol. 1 (Cambridge 1934). A classic study of the theories of natural law, their transcendence in the rise of social contract theories, and, in turn, the revision of the social contract by Rousseau, Fichte, and Kant.

– *Political Theories of the Middle Ages* (1900; Cambridge 1958)

Gilbert, A., 'Salvaging Marx from Avineri,' *Political Theory*, 4 (Feb. 1976)

– *Marx's Politics* (New Brunswick, NJ 1981)

Girardin, J.-C., 'On the Marxist Theory of the State,' *Politics and Society* vol. 1, no. 1 (1974)

Gold, D.A., C.Y.H. Lo and E.O. Wright, 'Recent Developments in Marxist Theories of the Capitalist State,' *Monthly Review* (Oct. 1975; Nov. 1975)

Goldstein, L.J., 'The Meaning of "State" in Hegel's Philosophy of History,' *Philosophical Quarterly*, XII (1962). An ingenuous discussion in which the author draws on anthropological literature to illuminate his case, with positive effect.

Gooch, G.P., 'German Views of the State,' in Gooch *et al.*, *The German Mind and Outlook* (London 1945)

Gough, J.W., *The Social Contract* (1936; Oxford 1963)

Gouldner, A.W., 'The Two Marxisms,' *For Sociology* (London 1975). The author wants 'to begin a Marxist critique of Marxism itself,' by grasping Marxism as 'an historical and social product' and then by making a 'critique' of Marxism. The attempt is hindered by a lack of historical knowledge and a misconception of the meaning of critique.

Gregoire, F., *Aux sources de la pensée de Marx* (Louvain 1947). These pages were designed as the first part of a course on Marxist philosophy. They consist of a simplified resumé of Hegel and Feuerbach, but very little on Marx.

Gurvitch, G., 'La Sociologie du jeune Marx,' *Cahiers Internationaux de Sociologie*, IV (1948). A lengthy ramble through the 1843 *Critique*, the Paris manuscripts, and *The German Ideology*. The article has little coherence.

Hammen, O.J., 'Economic and Social Factors in the Prussian Rhineland in 1848,' *American Historical Review*, LIV (1949)

– 'The Spectre of Communism in the 1840's,' *Journal of the History of Ideas,'* XIV (1953)

– *The Red '48ers: Karl Marx and Frederich Engels* (New York 1969). A useful and vivid intellectual biography, despite the openly antagonistic attitude of the author.

– 'Marx and the Agrarian Question,' *American Historical Review*, 77 (1972)

Harrison, R., 'E.S. Beesly and Karl Marx,' *International Review of Social History*, IV (1959)

– *Before the Socialists* (Toronto 1965)

Hegedus, A., 'Marx's Analysis of Bureaucracy and the Socialist Reality,' in *Marx and Contemporary Scientific Thought* (The Hague 1969)

– *Socialism and Bureaucracy* (London 1976)

Hegel, G.W.F., *The Phenomenology of Mind*, trans. J.B. Baillie (New York 1967)

– *Hegel's Philosophy of Mind*, trans. W. Wallace (Oxford 1971)

– *Hegel's Philosophy of Right* trans. T.M. Knox (Oxford 1976)

– *Hegel's Logic*, trans. W. Wallace (Oxford 1975)

– *The Philosophy of History*, trans. J. Sibree (New York 1956)

– *Natural Law: the Scientific Ways of Treating Natural Law, Its Place in Moral Philosophy, and Its Relation to the Positive Sciences of Law*, trans. T.M. Knox (Philadelphia 1975)

Heller, A., *The Theory of Need in Marx* (London 1976)

Hill, C., 'The English Civil War Interpreted by Marx and Engels,' *Science and Society*, no. 1 (winter 1948). As the title suggests, the article illustrates the fact that Marx interpreted the English Revolution in the same general way as he perceived the French Revolution; i.e., as a consequence of the contradiction between the forces and relations of production.

Hirst, P.Q., 'Marx and Engels on Law, Crime and Morality,' *Economy and Society*, 1, no. 1 (Feb. 1972). On the assumption that there is no continuity throughout Marx's works the author tries to demonstrate three periods in which Marx takes decidedly different views on the questions of law, crime, and morality: the 'Kantian,' represented by the *Rheinische Zeitung* articles; the 'Feuerbachian,' of which the Paris manuscripts is the centrepiece; and the 'Historical Materialist,' the period after 1845. This structure, as well as the author's argument, depends mightily on presumptive assertions.

Hodges, D.,C. 'The Dual Character of Marxian Social Science,' *Philosophy of Science*, 29 (1962)

– 'The Young Marx – A Reappraisal,' *Philosophy and Phenomenological Research*, 27 (1968)

– 'The Unity of Marx's Thought,' *Science and Society*, XXVIII, no. 3 (summer 1964)

– 'Marx's Contribution to Marxism,' *Science and Society*, XXIX, no. 1 (winter 1965)

Hoeppner, J., 'A propos de quelques conceptions erronées du passage de Hegel à Marx,' *Recherches internationales à la lumière du Marxisme*, cahier 19, wherein the author takes to task arguments by Kuczynski and Fetscher. The article contains many sweeping statements and loose arguments.

van der Hoeven, J., *Karl Marx, The Roots of His Thought* (Assen 1976). This book could have been a valuable contribution to the interpretation of Marx's early works. The author begins by searching out Marx's starting point and attempts to expound the central theme of the writings up to the 1844 manuscripts. Despite the fact that the book contains numerous insights throughout, its shortcomings outweigh its positive value. First, while the author does grasp Marx's starting point, as set forth in his dissertation, he comprehends it as the position of an idealist or Hegelian; this is to miss the major point of the thesis, i.e., a *materialist* explanation of self-conscious nature. Second, the author's account of the transition between works is contrived; there is no real attempt to demonstrate *why* Marx moved from one subject to another. Third, his understanding of Marx's notion and practice of critique is inadequate for providing a real basis for grasping these transitions. Fourth, the discussion of the concept of labour is plainly out of line with Marx's use of it. Fifth, the book concludes with a consideration of the EPM; to conclude here precludes a complete grasp of the purpose of these early writings.

Holloway, J. and S. Picciotto, 'A Note on the Theory of the State,' *Bulletin of the Conference of Socialist Economists*, V, no. 2 (Oct. 1972)

– *State and Capital* (London 1978)

Hook, S., *From Hegel to Marx* (Ann Arbor 1962)

Horkheimer, M., 'Traditional and Critical Theory,' in M. Horkheimer, ed., *Critical Theory* (New York 1972)

Howard, D., 'On Marx's Critical Theory,' *Telos*, no. 6 (fall 1970). The author reduces Marx's notion of critique to Feuerbach's invertive method and then attempts to relate it to the notion of fetishism.

– *The Development of the Marxian Dialectic* (Carbondale 1972). A review of Marx's work from 1841 to 1844. By and large, the import of these early writings escapes the author; there are significant misconceptions and omissions throughout.

Hunt, R.N., *The Political Ideas of Marx and Engels* (Pittsburgh 1974). A detailed exposition of the development of Marx and Engels' critique of politics. Despite the close examination, the author grasps the early works *only* within the framework of the change from purported liberalism to communism; he asserts with confident aplomb: 'Marx was a noncommunist democratic republican for about two years. He had rejected monarchism ... and by the end of 1843 he would embrace communism.' For all its detail, the analytical appreciation goes no deeper than this.

Hyppolite, J., *Studies on Marx and Hegel* (London 1969)

Iggers, G.G., *The German Conception of History* (Connecticut 1968). An analysis of the development of 'historicism' in Germany in the nineteenth century, with a discussion of natural law theories of the state and history.

Jaeger, H., 'Savigny et Marx,' *Archives de Philosophie du droit (et de sociologie juridique)*, XII (1967). A singular essay on one of the chief early influences on

Marx. Unfortunately, the author makes too much of what he considers an underlying similarity between Savigny, one of the principal representatives of the 'Historical School,' and Marx. Had Jaeger examined more closely Marx's critique of the 'School' and the nature of his definition of law, the relationship between this scholar of Roman Law and his critic would have appeared less paradoxical.

Jackson, J.H., *Marx, Proudhon and European Socialism* (New York 1958)

Jakubowitz, F., *Ideology and Superstructure in Historical Materialism* (London 1976)

Joergensen, J., *The Development of Logical Empiricism* (Chicago 1951)

Kahn, P., 'Société et Etat dans les oeuvres de jeunesse de Marx,' in *Cahiers Internationaux de Sociologie*, no. 5 (Paris 1948). The author makes useful, if now well-known, distinctions between civil society and bourgeois society and between the state and the bourgeois state.

Kamenka, E., *The Ethical Foundations of Marxism* (London 1962)

- *The Philosophy of Ludwig Feuerbach* (New York 1970)

- *Marxism and Ethics* (London 1969)

- 'The Primitive Ethic of Karl Marx,' *Australian Journal of Philosophy*, 35 (1967)

- and A. Tay, 'Karl Marx and the Law of Marriage and Divorce,' *Quadrant*, 15 (winter 1960)

- 'Karl Marx, Analysis of Law,' *Indian Journal of Philosophy*, I (1959)

Kauder, E., 'The Intellectual Sources of Karl Marx,' *Kyklos*, XXI (1968). A superficial review of the commonly accepted 'sources' of Marx's theories, but useful as a bibliography for commentaries on Marx.

Kaufman, W.A., 'The Hegel Myth and Its Method,' *Philosophical Review*, LX (1951), reprinted in A. MacIntyre, *Hegel* (Notre Dame 1976). A thorough criticism of the intellectual dishonesty of Karl Popper by one of America's respected academics.

Kolakowski, L., *Marxism and Beyond* (London 1971)

- 'The Myth of Human Self-Identity: Unity of Civil and Political Society in Socialist Thought,' in L. Kolakowski and S. Hampshire, eds., *The Socialist Idea: A Reappraisal* (London 1974)

- *Main Currents of Marxism*, 1 (Oxford 1978). A combined biography and review of Marx's work. The interpretation is made with confidence, probably because it is so close to accepted opinions. The doctoral dissertation, for example, is described as 'almost wholly within the limits of Young Hegelian thought' (104). The book reaffirms existing descriptions of the content of Marx's work but contributes little to our knowledge.

- *Positivist Philosophy*, Harmondsworth, 1972

Koren, H.J., *Marx and Authentic Man* (Pittsburgh 1968)

Korner, S., *Kant* (Harmondsworth 1955)

Korsch, K., *Karl Marx* (1938; New York 1963)
- *Marxism and Philosophy* (London 1970)
- *Three Essays on Marxism* (London 1971)
- 'En guise d'introduction,' (1930) in E.B. Pashukanis, *La Théorie générale du droit et le marxisme* (Paris 1969)
Koyré, A., 'Note sur la langue et la terminologie hégélienne,' *Revue philosophiques de la France et l'étranger* (Paris 1931)
Krader, L., ed., *Anthropology and Early Law* (New York 1966)
- *Dialectic of Civil Society* (Assen 1976)
Krieger, L., 'Marx and Engels as Historians,' *Journal of the History of Ideas*, XIV, no. 3 (1953). A sympathetic review of the historical writings of Marx and Engels. The article is not pertinent to the early works.
- *The German Idea of Freedom* (Boston 1957). Very useful in comprehending the broad intellectual context of the political ideas of Hegel and his epigones.
Lapine, N., 'La Première Critique approfondie de la philosophie de Hegel par Marx,' *Recherches internationales à la lumière du marxisme*, cahier 19. An analysis of the 1843 *Critique*. The author argues that the *Critique* marked Marx's passage from idealism to materialism; that previously, in his dissertation, Marx embraced a Hegelian and idealist position; and that political and social events in Germany and, more importantly, Feuerbach's work awakened Marx to the problems of 'speculative philosophy.'
Lauer, Q., 'The Marxist Conception of Science,' in R.S. Cohen and M.W. Wartofsky, eds., *Methodological and Historical Essays in the Natural and Social Sciences* (Dordrecht 1974)
Lawrence, C., 'Roots of the Marxist Concept of Practice,' *Science and Society*, 13, no. 3 (1949). A good, albeit brief, review of the development of the notion of practice and its place in the materialism of Marx, i.e., its primacy in relation to theoretical development.
Lefebvre, H., *La Pensée de Karl Marx* (Bordas 1956)
- *The Sociology of Marx* (New York 1968)
- *Dialectical Materialism* (1940; London 1968)
- 'Les Rapports de la philosophie et de la politique dans les premières oeuvres de Marx (1842-1843),' *Revue de metaphysique et de morale*, no. 2-3 (Paris 1959)
van Leeuwen, A.Th., *Critique of Heaven* (London 1972)
- *Critique of Earth* (London 1975). Two of the better analytical studies of Marx's early works. The author, however, relies heavily upon long quotations from Marx.
Levin, M., 'Marxism and Romanticism: Marx's Debt to German Conservatism,' *Political Studies*, XXII, no. 4 (Dec. 1974). The modesty of the author's conclu-

sions cannot save his efforts from the judgement that they are baseless specula-
tions resting on the thinnest of arguments by analogy.

Lewis, J., *The Marxism of Marx* (London 1972)

– *The Life and Teaching of Karl Marx* (London 1965)

Lichtheim, G., *Marxism* (London 1965)

– *From Marx to Hegel* (New York 1971)

Linebaugh, P., 'Karl Marx, the Theft of Wood, and Working Class Composition:
A Contribution to the Current Debate,' in *Crime and Social Justice*, 6 (fall-
winter 1976). The author misunderstands the nature of Marx's critique of law,
i.e., the use of essence of law to measure or judge the nature of existing laws,
and sees the 'idea' of law as an indication of Marx's alleged idealism. He
writes, for example: 'His [Marx's] criticism of the law rested upon an *a priori*,
idealist conception of both the law and the state.' Fortunately, the misconception mars only his discussion of Marx but does not affect his longer examination of the changing nature of law in early nineteenth-century Germany.

Livergood, N.D., *Activity in Marx's Philosophy* (The Hague 1967). An English
translation of Marx's doctoral dissertation, prefaced by a suggestive essay on
the concept of activity in Marx.

Lobkowicz, N., *Theory and Practice* (Notre Dame 1967). Certainly one of the
more serious examinations of the early works. The book has several shortcomings, however. The author has cast his treatment of Marx in the general mould
of a search for 'salvation'; such a working assumption necessarily prejudices the
appreciation of Marx: it goes far in usurping a rational explanation for the
development of these writings. Despite the author's evidently serious contem-
plation, the comprehension of the periods of Marx's development does not
often go beyond accepted wisdom; thus, for example, the *RhZ* articles are
described as containing 'little more than brilliantly written and extremely sarcas-
tic criticisms of the policies of the Prussian government'; and about the method
in the 1843 *Critique*, the author writes: Marx 'simply took over Feuerbach's
scheme for criticising Hegelianism.' There is in the book one of the better discussions of the concept of critique, in which the problems of 'is/ought,' tele-
ology, and potential, among others, are raised. But in the end, Lobkowicz's
failure to grasp the meaning of critique is blamed on Marx's alleged confusion,
and no coherent analysis of Marx's method emerges.

– Karl Marx and Max Stirner,' in F.J. Adelman, ed., *Demythologizing Marxism*
(The Hague 1969). An attempt to account for the detail and length of Marx's
critique of Stirner in *The German Ideology*.

– 'Karl Marx's Attitude toward Religion,' *Review of Politics*, 26, no. 3 (July
1964). Despite minor inaccuracies and a belief that Marx's work was 'messi-

anic' and 'salvific,' the article manages to capture the meaning of Marx's critique of religion; it also contains a review of Hegel's position on Christianity and of Feuerbach's critique of Hegel.

Löwith, K., 'L'Achèvement de la philosophie classique par Hegel et sa dissolution chez Marx et Kierkegaard,' *Recherches Philosophiques*, 4 (1934-35). The article is an attempt to spell out the significance of Hegel's philosophical system, i.e., Hegel's work as the culmination of the world's philosophy, and to suggest how it was 'resolved/destroyed' by those who came after. Amongst these he singles out Marx and Kierkegaard as the principals in the 'attack' on Hegel's system, the former in his 'revolutionary philosophy of practice' and the latter in his 'experimental psychology.' The article is necessarily speculative since the argument to be demonstrated is somewhat obtuse and the possibility of proving it, even if it were less vague, very uncertain.

- 'Mediation and Immediacy in Hegel, Marx and Feuerbach,' in W.E. Steinkraus, ed., *New Studies in Hegel's Philosophy* (New York 1971)
- 'Man's Self-Alienation in the Early Writings of Marx,' *Social Research*, 21, no. 2 (1954)
- *From Hegel to Nietzsche* (London 1965)

Löwy, M., *La Théorie de la révolution chez le jeune Marx* (Paris 1970). An attempt to trace the development of Marx's political theory. The work is not critical of accepted notions about this development; i.e., Marx's passage from idealist to materialist, from liberal democrat to communist; it wastes no time analysing the 1843 *Critique* (2½ pages); and it treats most changes in the development as they are conventionally understood. The book adds very little to existing knowledge.

de Lubac, H., *The Un-Marxian Socialist: A Study of Proudhon* (London 1948)

Lubasz, H., ed., *The Development of the Modern State* (New York (1964) 1966)
- 'Marx's Initial Problematic: The Problem of Poverty,' *Political Studies*, vol. XXIV, no. 1 (1976). A sophisticated attempt to make the question of Marx's concern for the poor the underlying rationale of the *Rheinische Zeitung* articles.

Lukacs, G., 'Moses Hess and the Problems of the Idealist Dialectic,' *Telos*, 10 (winter 1971)
- *The Young Hegel* (London 1975)
- *History and Class Consciousness* (London 1971)
- *Hegel's False and His Genuine Ontology* (London 1978)
- *Marx's Basic Ontological Principles* (London 1978)
- 'Les Manuscrits de 1844 et la formation du marxisme,' in *La Nouvelle Critique* (Paris, June 1955). With little apparent appreciation of the manuscripts as an integral whole, Lukacs searches for statements which herald Marx's 'dialectical

materialism' and revolutionary socialist point of view. There are many *assertions* about what Marx is doing in these writings but little argumentation.

McCoy, C.N.R., 'The Logical and the Real in Political Theory: Plato, Aristotle, and Marx,' *American Political Science Review*, 48 (1954). A suggestive essay on the relation between essence and existence in these three philosophers. The antipathy of Catholicism to Marxism unfortunately here skews the content of this otherwise central question and of the question of Marx's relation to Aristotle.

– 'Ludwig Feuerbach and the Formation of the Marxian Revolutionary Idea,' *Laval Theologique et Philosophique* (Quebec 1951)

McGovern, A.F., 'Karl Marx's First Political Writings: The Rheinische Zeitung, 1842-1843,' in F.J. Adelman, ed., *Demythologizing Marxism* (The Hague 1969). A thorough review of the *RhZ* articles. This is one of the better treatments of the early Marx, relatively free from the hackneyed assertion that Marx here was a liberal democrat. McGovern examines the articles one by one in chronological order, treating each as a unit, thereby obliging himself to explain the broad context in each case, limiting the generalizations he might have otherwise drawn.

– 'The Young Marx on the State,' *Science and Society*, 34, no. 4 (1970). One of the best, albeit brief, reviews of Marx's critique of politics between 1842 and 1846. A remarkably sympathetic understanding of Marx – for a Jesuit.

McLellan, D., *The Young Hegelians and Karl Marx* (London 1968). A descriptive review of the ideas of the Young Hegelians and their influence on Marx.

– *Marx before Marxism* (Harmondsworth 1970). One of the better reviews of Marx's early works up to the Paris manuscripts.

– *Karl Marx, His Life and Thought* (Bungay 1973)

– Marx's View of the Unalienated Society,' *Review of Politics*, 31, no. 4 (Oct. 1969). A short essay, drawing together some of the numerous passages in which Marx spoke of the nature of communist society.

McMurtry, J., *The Structure of Marx's World-View* (Princeton 1978). The author's objective is to 'reconstruct Marx's 'categorical framework, and its determining relationships, and, at bottom, its concept of human nature.' His case for the need for such 'reconstruction' is weak indeed, resting on the unsubstantiated statements of a narrow and peculiar grouping of commentators on Marx; while almost none of the serious recent analyses and expositions of Marx's conceptual structure is examined or even mentioned.

Macmurray, J., 'The Early Development of Marx's Thought,' in J. Lewis, K. Polanyi and D.K. Kitchin, eds., *Christianity and the Social Revolution* (London 1935). Despite all that has been written about Marx's early works since 1935, this article is amongst the very few which grasps the nature of Marx's early development. It is somewhat discursive but nonetheless a genuine and sympathetic comprehension of these works.

Macpherson, C.B., 'Edmund Burke,' *Transactions of the Royal Society of Canada*, LIII, series III (June 1959)

– *The Political Theory of Possessive Individualism* (Oxford 1962)

– 'Politics: Post-Liberal-Democracy?' in R. Blackburn, ed., *Ideology in Social Science* (Bungay 1972)

– 'Democratic Theory: Ontology and Technology,' *Democratic Theory: Essays in Retrieval* (Oxford 1973)

– 'Liberalism and the Political Theory of Property,' in A. Kontos, ed., *Domination* (Toronto 1975). An attempt to circumvent the 'central problem of liberal-democratic theory,' which is the contradiction of private property rights and the 'ethical principle of liberal democracy.' The argument is a laboured effort to redefine property, in an attempt to eliminate the exclusiveness of private property.

Maguire, J.M., *Marx's Paris Writings: An Analysis* (Dublin 1972). As the introduction states, this book is the 'first full-length study of Marx's Paris writings to appear in English.' Unfortunately, because the author does not grasp the underlying rationale of these works, he writes an exposition in which the reasons Marx undertakes this research are not discussed. As a consequence, Maguire falls back upon several standard interpretations of Marx's Hegelianism, Feuerbachianism, etc., and can provide no sense of where Marx is coming from or where he is going in the Paris writings.

– *Marx's Theory of Politics* (Cambridge 1978). In chapter 1 of this book the author attempts to grasp the nature of Marx's early position on politics. There is little coherence in this attempt; it is a contrived discussion which randomly draws on texts from different stages within the early period, which gives no sense of what Marx was trying to do in these stages, and which reveals no apparent grasp of Marx's notion of politics in this period.

Maier, J., *On Hegel's Critique of Kant* (New York 1939, 1966)

Mandel, E., *The Formation of the Economic Thought of Karl Marx* (New York 1971). Replete with misconceptions about the writings up to 1846. The author, for example, paints Marx as a 'sentimental humanist,' whose writing is 'essentially philosophical.' Humanism and philosophy are, of course, understood as pejoratives but nowhere are they defined. Rather than trace how Marx's critique of political economy developed, Mandel measures the early work against the accomplishment of the later analysis of capital; the conclusion is straightforward: the early work does not possess the refinement, the precision, or all the concepts which are to be found in the later; i.e., had Marx *begun* in 1841 with the theories he developed by 1867, he would not be guilty of the shortcomings Mandel apparently perceives.

Mannheim, K., 'The History of the Concept of the State as an Organism: A Sociological Analysis,' in K. Mannheim, *Essays on Sociology and Social Psychology* (Oxford 1953)

Marcuse, H., *Reason and Revolution* (London 1968)

– *Negations* (London 1968)

Markovits, F., *Marx dans le jardin d'Epicure* (Paris 1974). A rambling attempt to come to grips with the notebooks to Marx's dissertation. She asserts that the dissertation was not considered by Marx to be 'scientific,' and that underlying it is a polemic against Hegel. But neither the meaning of science nor the nature of the polemic is made clear.

Mehring, F., *Karl Marx* (1918; London 1936). The earliest biography of Marx. It is far from superseded by latter-day biographies.

– 'La Thèse de Karl Marx sur Democrite et Epicure,' *La Nouvelle Critique*, 61 (1955). A valuable study which situates the thesis by Marx in the then current debates on the relation of antique philosophy to Christianity and to the Enlightenment. The essay is suggestive of a much broader significance for the thesis than is usually perceived.

Meszaros, I., *Marx's Theory of Alienation* (London 1970). There is no other interpretative work on Marx's Paris manuscripts which matches the depth of Meszaros' appreciation. Even so, the work is not without its faults. The most obvious, perhaps, is the principle of organization employed; the author has not sought to discover Marx's own rationale but, instead, has imposed academic categories as the structure for his discussion. While not incorrect in itself, such organization militates against a comprehensive grasp of the material, not to mention the repetition of key arguments that it demands. There is, moreover, no analysis of the reason for writing the manuscripts; the questions which moved Marx to develop such a concept as alienation are not discussed, except in the form of external influences. This is no small shortcoming if one is concerned to explain the development of Marx's ideas. The author also misconceives the nature of Marx's earlier writing, referring to it as the 'phase of "revolutionary democratism,"' and asserting that the 'labouriously detailed analysis' found in the 1843 *Critique* 'becomes superfluous' in light of the concept of alienated labour. There is a misconception of the dichotomy of the 'is' and 'ought' as employed by the early Marx, which is not a small problem if the meaning of Marx's critical method is to be comprehended. Despite these difficulties, Meszaros' work stands as one of the best appreciations of the 1844 manuscripts.

Mins, H.F., 'Marx's Doctoral Dissertation,' *Science and Society*, XII, no. 1 (winter 1948). A genuine attempt to grasp the import of Marx's dissertation. It is marred by the following completely unsubstantiated conclusion: 'Its weakness lies in the fact that it is "still entirely on idealistic ground," still deep in the

philosophy of concepts and far from the natural sciences.' Such orthodoxy of
opinion profoundly hinders the proper comprehension of Marx's thesis.

Miliband, R., 'Lenin's "The State and Revolution,"' *The Socialist Register* (1970)

- *The State in Capitalist Society* (London 1968, 1973)
- *Marxism and Politics* (Oxford 1977)

Moore, S., *The Critique of Capitalist Democracy* (New York 1957)

- *Three Tactics: The Background in Marx* (New York 1963)
- 'Marx and the Origin of Dialectical Materialism,' *Inquiry*, 14 (1971)

Morris, G.S., *Hegel's Philosophy of the State and of History* (Chicago 1887)

Naville, P., 'Critique de la bureaucratie,' *Cahiers Internationaux de Sociologie*, XV
(1953). One of the very few attempts to expound the section on bureaucracy in
Marx's 1843 *Critique* and quite an accurate exposition.

- *De l'Aliénation à la jouissance* (Paris 1957)

Nicolaievsky, B. and O. Maenchen-Helfen, *Karl Marx: Man and Fighter* (1936;
Harmondsworth 1976)

Nova, F., *Friedrich Engels: His Contributions to Political Theory* (New York 1967)

Oestereicher, E., 'Praxis: The Dialectical Source of Knowledge,' *Dialectical Anthropology*, 1, no. 3 (May 1976). A review of theories which argue for the primacy
of practice in the acquisition of knowledge.

Offe, C. and V. Ronge, 'Theses on the Theory of the State,' *New German
Critique*, no. 6 (fall 1975)

Oizerman, T., 'Le Problème de l'aliénation dans les travaux de jeunesse de
Marx,' *Recherches internationales à la lumière du Marxisme*, no. 33-34 (1962).
An attempt to make the case that alienation is a scientific concept.

- 'The Social Meaning of the Philosophy of Hegel,' *Soviet Studies in Philosophy*,
IX, no. 4 (spring 1971)

Ollman, B., 'Marxism and Political Science: Prolegomenon to a Debate on Marx's
Method,' *Politics and Society*, 3, no. 4 (summer 1973). Ollman asserts that the
method has five levels or stages but does not explain how he arrives at this
conclusion. How Marx employed these levels in analysis is not clear; how Marx
came to adopt this multi-stage method is not discussed; how Marx decided on
the order of material in presenting his theory is not raised; how this method is
scientific in nature is not described; how this method is related to the problem
of theory and practice is not apparently an issue. These and other difficulties in
the article make it profoundly prolegomenary.

- *Alienation: Marx's Conception of Man in Capitalist Society* (Cambridge 1971)
- 'Marx's Vision of Communism: A Reconstruction,' *Critique*, no. 8 (summer
1977)

Olsen, R.E., *Karl Marx* (Boston 1978). An attempted overview of selected issues/
problems in Marxism. The work is superficial and highly derivative.

O'Malley, J., Editor's Introduction to Karl Marx, *Critique of Hegel's Philosophy of Right* (Cambridge 1970). A fulsome introduction, which grasps many of the specific points in the *Critique*, but misses its general nature. Much of the problem lies in the author's unsubstantiated vision of Marx: 'But even while criticizing Hegel's institutional conclusions, Marx remains within the general framework of Hegel's doctrine.' Such an assertion requires first clarification as to its meaning, and second demonstration; O'Malley provides neither. The apparent inability to grasp Marx's method allows the author to assert further, again without any regard for demonstration: 'In fact, he [Marx] formulates the basic features of his own social and political theory through a systematic rejection of the agencies for social-political unity offered by Hegel. For Hegel's bureaucracy he eventually substitutes the proletariat as universal class; in place of landed property under primogeniture he advocates the abolition of private property; and he demands in place of the Assembly of estates [Stande] the institution of universal suffrage as the medium *par excellence* for the abolition [*Aufhebung*] of the state-civil society duality' (p. 11). Well before O'Malley, these three points were part of the commonly accepted interpretation of the *Critique*; like all such 'knowledge,' they derive their authority from repetition and not demonstration.
- 'History and Man's "Nature" in Marx,' *Review of Politics*, 28 (Oct. 1966). A good discussion of the question of 'needs' and its relation to production. The article is limited by the failure to introduce the questions of private property and division of labour.
- 'Marx's "Economics" and Hegel's Philosophy of Right: An Essay on Marx's Hegelianism,' *Political Studies*, XXIV, no. 1 (1976)
O'Neil, J., 'On Theory and Criticism in Marx,' in P. Walton and S. Hall, eds., *Situating Marx* (London, n.d.). An attempted defence of Marx's method against the criticisms of Althusser and Habermas. The method has to be understood before it can be defended.
- 'The Concept of Estrangement in the Early and Later Writings of Karl Marx,' *Philosophy and Phenomenological Research*, XXV (Sept. 1964)
Pajitnov, L., 'Les Manuscrits Economico-Philosophiques de 1844,' *Recherches internationale à la lumière du marxisme*, cahier 19. Part I is a superficial review of many of the early commentators on the Paris manuscripts. Part II is an attempt to situate the manuscripts in Marx's work and to isolate the principal concepts.
Parsons, H.L., *Humanism and Marx's Thought* (Springfield 1971). A genuine attempt to grasp the meaning of Marx's humanism. The author fails to come to grips with the nature of 'ought' in Marx and ignores the question of private property, thereby limiting what can be said about the humanism of Marx.
Pascal, R., *Karl Marx: His Apprenticeship to Politics* (London 1942?). Published by *Labour Monthly*, a very good review of Marx's *Rheinische Zeitung* articles. But

it is unfortunately very difficult to obtain. The review grasps the issues and
Marx's arguments very well, but paradoxically and gratuitously repeats the
common wisdom that here Marx was an 'idealist,' 'Hegelian,' 'liberal,' etc.

Pashukanis, E.B., *Law and Marxism: A General Theory* (1929; London 1978)

Pelczynski, Z.A., 'An Introductory Essay,' in T.M. Knox, ed., *Hegel's Political Writings* (Oxford 1964)

- 'The Hegelian Conception of the State,' in Z.A. Pelczynski, ed., *Hegel's Political Philosophy* (Cambridge 1971)

Plamenatz, J., *Karl Marx's Philosophy of Man* (Oxford 1975). The best of the serious critics of Marx.

Plant, R., 'Hegel and Political Economy, Part I,' *New Left Review*, 103 (May-June 1977)

- 'Hegel and Political Economy, Part II,' *New Left Review*, 104 (July-August 1977)

- *Hegel* (London 1973)

Plekhanov, G.V., *In Defence of Materialism* (1895; London 1947)

- *Fundamental Problems of Marxism* (1908; London 1969)

Pranger, R.J., 'Marx and Political Theory,' *Review of Politics*, 30, no. 2 (April 1968)

Ranciere, J., 'The Concept of "Critique" and the "Critique of Political Economy."' This article was first published in French in the first edition of L. Althusser, *et al.*, *Lire le Capital* (Paris 1965), but was withdrawn in subsequent editions. In English, it was published in four parts, three of which appeared in 1971-72 in an obscure journal, now defunct, *Theoretical Practice*, and the fourth in *Economy and Society*, 5, no. 3 (1976). The article is extremely laboured and pedantic, is fraught with inconsistencies, and sheds little light on the meaning of critique.

Reyburn, H.A., *Hegel's Ethical Theory* (Oxford 1921). The first five chapters expound the presuppositions of the *Philosophy of Right*.

Ritter, J., 'Person und Eigentum,' *Marxismus Studien IV* (1960); reprinted in French as 'Personne et propriété selon Hegel,' *Archives de Philosophie* (avril-juin 1968), XXXI, cahier 2. An explanation/exposition of the first section of Hegel's *Philosophy of Right*, 'Abstract right.'

Rosdolsky, R., 'La Neue Rheinische Zeitung et les juifs,' *Etudes de Marxologie* (August 1963)

Rotenstreich, N., *From Substance to Subject: Studies in Hegel* (The Hague 1974). There is some discussion of Marx here on the question of abstraction and concreteness.

- *Basic Problems of Marx's Philosophy* (Indianapolis 1965)

Rothman, S., 'Marxism and the Paradox of Contemporary Political Thought,' *Review of Politics*, 24, no. 2 (April 1962)

Rubel, M., 'Les Cahiers de lecture de Karl Marx, I: 1840-1853,' *International Review of Social History*, II (1957). A descriptive review of the contents of Marx's unpublished notebooks up to 1853.

- 'Les Cahiers de lecture de Karl Marx, II,' *International Review of Social History*, 5 (1960)

- 'Notes on Marx's Conception of Democracy,' *New Politics*, 1, no. 2 (1962). A review of published and unpublished material by Marx on democracy. Rubel is not altogether clear about the distinction between the essence of democracy and the concept of existing democracy.

- 'Fragments sociologique dans les inedits de Marx,' *Cahiers internationaux de sociologie* XXII (1957). Long quotations from the *Grundrisse*, joined by an analytical commentary.

- *Karl Marx: essai de biographie intellectuelle* (Paris, 1971). A descriptive examination of Marx's work. As with most of these overviews, the author assumes but nowhere demonstrates a framework in which Marx passes from idealism to materialism and communism.

- and M. Manale, *Marx without Myth* (Oxford 1975)

Ruhle, O., *Karl Marx: His Life and Work* (London 1929)

Sanderson, J.B., 'Marx and Engels on the State,' *Western Political Quarterly*, XVI, no. 4 (Dec. 1963)

- *An Interpretation of the Political Ideas of Marx and Engels* (London 1969)

Sayer, D., *Marx's Method* (Hassocks 1979)

Shaw, M., 'The Theory of the State and Politics: A Central Paradox of Marxism,' *Economy and Society*, 3, no. 4 (1974)

Schacht, R., *Hegel and After* (Pittsburgh 1975). A brief but genuine though not very systematic analysis of selected questions in several of the early works.

- *Alienation* (New York 1971)

Schaff, A., 'Le vrai visage du jeune Marx,' *Recherches internationales à la lumière du marxisme*, cahier 19 (1960). Schaff's main object is a criticism of an article by L. Kolakowski. 'Karl Marx and the Classical Definition of Truth.'

- 'Marxist Dialectics and the Principle of Contradiction,' *Journal of Philosophy*, LVII (Jan.-Dec. 1960). An attempt to explain the inconsistency between dialectical contradiction and the principle of contradiction in formal logic.

- 'Studies of the Young Marx: A Rejoinder [to L. Kolakowski],' in L. Labedz, ed., *Revisionism: Essays on the History of Marxist Ideas* (New York 1962)

Schonfeld, W.R., 'The Classical Marxist Conception of Liberal Democracy,' *Review of Politics*, 38 (1971)

Schmidt, A., *The Concept of Nature in Marx* (London 1971). A careful and valuable consideration of the subject in the title. The author, however, unconvincingly asserts a dichotomy between the young and mature Marx. Perhaps related to this assumption is the author's neglect to discuss Marx's doctoral dissertation, where Marx presents his first appreciation of the concept of nature.

Seigel, J., *Marx's Fate: The Shape of a Life* (Princeton 1978)

Sowell, T., 'Karl Marx and the Freedom of the Individual,' *Ethics*, 73 (1963). While the author ably points out questions about freedom and democracy which have not been examined in Marx, his article contributes very little towards answering them.

Speir, H., 'From Hegel to Marx: The Left Hegelians, Feuerbach and "True Socialism,"' in H. Speir, *Social Order and the Risks of War* (New York 1952). A competent but brief review of the political theories of, and relations between, Hegel, Ruge, Stein, Cieszkowski, and Feuerbach.

Stace, W.T., *A Critical History of Greek Philosophy* (London 1920)

– *The Philosophy of Hegel* (1924; New York 1955)

Stillman, P.G., 'Hegel's Critique of Liberal Theories of Right,' *American Political Science Review*, LXVIII no. 3 (Sept. 1974). A tightly argued review of the first part of Hegel's *Philosophy of Right*. Stillman shows well how Hegel makes an incisive criticism on logical grounds of the major tenets of liberalism, but he does not explain why liberalism persists while Hegelian political theory is consigned to the history of theories.

– 'Hegel's Idea of Punishment,' *Journal of the History of Philosophy*, 14, no. 2 (1975)

Struik, D.J., Introduction to *Economic and Philosophic Manuscripts of 1844* (London 1973). The author does not discuss the nature of the relation of the manuscripts to Marx's work before and after: the significance of the concept of labour is not grasped in relation to the development of Marx's early writings.

Sumner, C., *Reading Ideologies: An Investigation into the Marxist Theory of Ideology and Law* (London 1979)

Swingewood, A., *Marx and Modern Social Theory* (London 1975). There is very little about Marx in this book which is precise and accurate.

Taylor, C., 'Marxism and Empiricism,' in B. Williams and A. Montefiore, eds., *British Analytical Philosophy* (London 1967). A discussion of how the British empiricist tradition made the comprehension of Marxist concepts difficult in Britain, which is limited by an awkward appreciation of Marx.

– *Hegel* (Cambridge 1975). An exposition of Hegel in the Canadian idiom. The book is a comprehensive, straightforward description of the Hegelian system, marred by a speculative conclusion which asserts but does not argue a case for a 'rift' in Marx's thought between 'scienticism' and 'expressivism.'

Therborn, G., *Science, Class and Society* (London 1976)
- 'What Does the Ruling Class Do When It Rules,' *Insurgent Sociologist*, 6, no. 3 (1976)
Thomas, P., 'Karl Marx and Max Stirner,' *Political Theory*, 3, no. 2 (May 1975)
- 'Marx and Science,' *Political Studies*, XXIV, no. 1 (March 1976)
Tönnies, F., *Community and Society* (1887; New York 1963)
- *Karl Marx: His Life and Teachings* (1919; Michigan 1974)
Togliatti, P., 'De Hegel au Marxisme,' *Recherches internationales à la lumière du marxisme*, cahier 19 (1960). A description of the commonly accepted view of Marx's relation to Hegel. It is organized on the basis of three periods, as first set forth by Plekhanov: the first ending with the completion of the dissertation (Marx as a reluctant Hegelian); the second ending with *The Holy Family* (the 'decisive battle with traditional Hegelianism'); the third beginning with *The German Ideology* (the 'arrival of the full elaboration of scientific socialism'). The analysis is descriptive and the arguments gratuitous.
Troeltsch, E., 'The Ideas of Natural Law and Humanity in World Politics,' Appendix I, to O. Gierke, *Natural Law and The Theory of Society, 1500 to 1800*, 1 (Cambridge 1934). An attempt to take Gierke's study into the nineteenth century. Among other traditions or schools, the author discusses the Romantic 'counter-revolution' in political and social theory.
Tucker, R.C., *The Marxian Revolutionary Idea* (London 1956). One of the better expositions of the views of Marx and Engels on the state. The material is drawn from their work after 1845.
- *Philosophy and Myth in Karl Marx* (Cambridge 1961). One of the earliest reviews in English of the pre-1845 writings of Marx. The author makes much of Marx's alleged Hegelianism and Feuerbachianism and baldly asserts that Marx was a moralist, but the book does contain several insights into the relation between the early writings and the later works.
- 'The Cunning of Reason in Hegel and Marx,' *Review of Politics* 18, no. 3 (July 1956)
Turner, D., *On the Philosophy of Karl Marx* (Dublin 1968). Short, definitional, essays on various 'topics,' for example, 'individualism,' 'work,' 'revolution,' 'critique.'
Vasquez, A.S., *The Philosophy of Praxis* (London 1977)
Venable, V., *Human Nature: The Marxian View* (New York 1945). A very good attempt to reconstruct Marx's notion of human nature, given that Marx's work before 1845 was not considered in the analysis.
Voegelin, E., 'The Formation of the Marxian Revolutionary Idea,' *Review of Politics*, 12, no. 3 (July 1950). An attempt to comprehend the formation of Marx's critique of politics. One drawback, the author himself admits, is that the review

is descriptive rather than analytical. Another is his misconception of Marx's analysis of socialist man and the means of realizing socialism. And yet another is the lack of an organizing principle for the essay itself.

Volpe, G. della, *Rousseau et Marx* (Paris 1974)

Wallace, W., 'Relations of Fichte and Hegel to Socialism,' in W. Wallace, *Lectures and Essays* (Oxford 1898). An attempt to demonstrate the validity of the proposition that 'Hegelianism is the true parent of Socialism.' The thesis is put succinctly: 'Hegel laid the egg, if the Socialists hatched it.' The argument, however, is confined to an examination of the organic or corporatist views of Fichte and Hegel – very weak reasoning in light of the French socialist literature appearing about the same time.

Zelený, J., 'Kant, Marx and the Modern Rationality,' *Boston Studies in the Philosophy of Science*, XIV (Dordrecht 1974)

– *The Logic of Marx*, trans. and ed. T. Carver (Oxford 1980)

Index

212; limits of political freedom 103-6; and natural law and natural right 231n; of the press 33-6; as solution to defects of modern state 42, 113; and punishment 178-9; and representative state 171-3; and slavery in civil society 172-3; of trade 169-70

French Revolution: and establishment of modern state 105-6, 163-7; and German patriotism 93; and Jewish question 100; and political theory 207-8; and rights of man 104-6

God: and analysis of money 135-6; and the idea 7; and philosophy 9

Hegel, G.W.F.: and the dialectic 207-9; and the critique of liberalism 213-14; and man's self-creation through labour 159-61; and Marx 7-10, 45, 109, 186; his concept of mind 13; and natural law 231n; and history of philosophy 17; on shame 240n; notion of the state 30, 199-200; mentioned 41, 47, 142, 147-8, 162, 174, 177-8, 193, 203

Historical materialism: see Materialism

History: and communism as end of 153-7, 191-2, 196; and division of labour 220-4; first historical act 182-3; Hegel's view of 49; materialist conception of 181-92; Marx and Hegel on 186; principle of 181; as history of private property 140, 142, 153; and social emancipation 108

Human being: and alienated labour 131; bourgeois man as 105-6; as commodity 144-7; communism as realization of 152-7; and contradiction 207-8; and crime and punish-

ment 177-9; and critique 110; and critique of early notions of communism 97; and democracy 82; and despotism, freedom 95-6; and division into spheres 73; essence of, and Marx's critique of politics 194-7; first historical act 182-3; and human activity 153-4, 191-2; human emancipation 100-8, 111-12, 155-7, 172; human life versus political life 117; human nature 116-17, 147-8, 154-5; human property and private property 128; human rights 104-8; and labour and capital 144; meaning of 12, 91, 141; and meaning of money 134-40; as member of civil society 168-70; private property as requisite of human nature 214-15; as property owner 141-2; and relation between male and female 149-51; religion and human essence 109; social nature explained 204; see also Essence, Labour

Human self-consciousness: origin of 12-13

Humanity: communism as realized humanism 152-3; definition of 24; inhumanity and civil society 172-3; relation to freedom 94-5; see also Human being

Idea, the: and critique 18-19, 86-7; in Hegel 49-50, 55; and Hegel's organic state 58-61; in reality 7, 8, 16; and sovereignty 59-61

Idealism: definition of 6, 48; and empiricism 23-4; and Hegel 8, 54; of Hegel contrasted with Marx 98; and Marx 48, 88; Marx's critique of Hegel's 54-8

www.ingramcontent.com/pod-product-compliance
Lightning Source LLC
Chambersburg PA
LVHW032101040426
936CB00040B/635